Obscure Locks, Simple Keys
The Annotated *Watt*

C. J. Ackerley

Edinburgh University Press

© C. J. Ackerley, 2005, 2010

Transferred to Digital Print 2011

First published by the Journal of Beckett Studies Books, 2005.

Edinburgh University Press Ltd
22 George Square, Edinburgh
Printed and bound in Great Britain by
CPI Antony Rowe, Chippenham and Eastbourne

www.euppublishing.com

Book design: Jack Clifford

A CIP record for this book is available from the British Library

ISBN 978 0 7486 4151 2 (paperback)

The right of C. J. Ackerley
to be identified as author of this work
has been asserted in accordance with
the Copyright, Designs and Patents Act 1988.

For Mia Rose,

born December 25, 2004,

who lepped in the wom

when the duck was served

"An artist should ruthlessly destroy his manuscripts after publication lest they mislead academic mediocrities into thinking that it is possible to unravel the mysteries of genius by studying cancelled readings."

—Vladimir Nabokov, commentary on *Eugene Onegin* I.15.

Table of Contents

Acknowledgements	6
Preface	8
Prefatory Statement	11
Introduction	
a. *Watt*'s Place in the Series	12
b. The Publication of *Watt*	14
c. The *Watt* Manuscripts: An Overview	21
d. The Geology of the Imagination	24
A Note on Methodology	27
Annotations	
Part I	28
Part II	87
Part III	146
Part IV	186
Addenda	205
Addendum 1	
Textual Changes and Errata in the Major Editions of *Watt*	219
Addendum 2	
The Evolution of *Watt*	232
Bibliography	
a. Works by Beckett	261
b. Critical studies relevant to *Watt*	264
c. General studies used in this work	269
Index	273

Acknowledgements

As ever, to Stan Gontarski, for his constant encouragement of my work and his generosity in offering the *Journal of Beckett Studies* as an outlet for it. We not only survived eight years of collaboration working on the *Grove Companion to Samuel Beckett* (2004), but our friendship is the stronger for it. This study has benefited from consultation with and contributions from scholars all over the world, but also from the indefinable support from many others, who have largely negated what Beckett in *Proust* calls that irremediable solitude to which every human being (or academic) is condemned.

In New Zealand: to my colleagues, for holding the fort as I fled the barricades, and especially to Lisa Marr, for reading my drafts and appreciating some of the more oblique asides; to Ken Laloge, for help with the logical paradigms; to George and Hilary Troup, for distracting me in Mexico; to John and Katherine Dolan, *pod Moskovaya vechera*; and to Wyn Jones for listening as I waxed enthusiastic about what must have seemed a pointless project.

In the USA: to the staff of the HRHRC (Austin) for their unfailing professionalism and courtesy; to Elva Griffith of the Special Collections at Ohio State University, and to the late Holly Hall of the Special Collections at Washington University, St. Louis, both of whom went out of their way to make me welcome; to Lois Overbeck and Catherine du Toit, for their friendship in Austin; to David Hayman (Wisconsin), for details of the manuscripts; to Ruby Cohn, for her support and appreciation; to Laura Lindgren (New York) for her precise proofreading; to Pat and Yolanda McCarthy (Miami) for their hospitality, and to Pat for interminable discussions on *Watt* and *Ulysses* that seemed to improve as the Jamesons sank lower. Most of all, the staff of JOBS in Tallahassee: in particular, Dustin Anderson, Jack Clifford, Amber Coady, Lauren Gibaldi, Zachary Hanson, and Paul Shields, for their hospitality and help with the editing. The final section of my Introduction, "The Geology of the Imagination," reworks an article that recently appeared in the *Journal of Beckett Studies*.

In the UK: to the staff of the BIF, Reading, and particularly Mike Bott, Brian Ryder, and Julian Garforth for welcoming me yet again; and to Julian for inviting me to present a paper on "The Geology of the Imagination" at the BIF series (2004); to Dirk van Hulle, for offering to publish it; to Sean Lawlor, whom I met there for the first time; to Damian Love, for reading my drafts and allowing me to pillage his ideas and dissertation; to Matthew Feldman, for generously offering me his transcription of Beckett's notes; and to Mark Nixon, for allowing me access to various obscure materials in his possession. I must express my gratitude to Edward Beckett, not only for his gracious permission for me to use unpublished manuscript materials but for his kind words, at the Sydney conference, as to my deployment of them in *Demented Particulars*. The *Watt* annotations, much more so than the *Murphy* ones, rely heavily on archival materials. I am grateful to the Harry Ransom Center (Austin), Ohio State University (Columbus), Washington University (St. Louis), Trinity College (Dublin), and the BIF (Reading) for permission to cite the many and varied manuscripts, typescripts, notebooks, and bibliographical ephemera without which this study would have been impossible; and to Stan Gontarski for showing me the Beckett-Rosset correspondence.

In Tasmania: to Ralph and Joy Crane (and Callum and Rhiannon) for their hospitality; and to Ralph and the School of English, Journalism and European Languages, University of Tasmania at Hobart, for offering facilities and making me feel so welcome during the final stages of this project.

Finally, a True Story: I have dedicated these annotations to my first grandchild, Mia Rose Vachon, not simply because she came into the world on Murphy's birthday (see *Demented Particulars* #32.7), 25 December 2004, but because her decision to do so manifested itself during a dinner party on the eve, at which a duck was served and my daughter's labor pains began, beneath the groaning board. I cannot say that no trace of this dollar appeared upon her face, nor did she go up the stairs wringing the carpetrods to come down leading the infant by the hand; yet there was a feeling of relief when the guests departed, and somewhat more than three minutes later she was a mother. Like Watt (**80.6**), I sometimes wonder what became of the duck.

An Art of Incompletion:
A Preface

S. E. Gontarski

On his death in 1851, J. M. W. Turner bequeathed a studio-full of his paintings to the people of Britain. Most would finally hang in the national gallery of British art, the legacy of Henry Tate now called Tate Britain, but Turner's executors and various museum curators puzzled over which of those stored paintings to exhibit, that is, which were completed enough to hang and which were not. Many were never exhibited during Turner's lifetime and had less the look of a painted image than its afterimage or the ghost of a painting. The more closely the paintings were examined, the more difficult it was to distinguish those finished from those abandoned or rejected in some state short of completion. Some, like *Norham Castle, Sunrise* (1845), were clearly signed, but to the curators they still possessed that ghostly, hazy, unfinished quality that marks much of Turner's late work. Many were, moreover, if not monochromatic, at least used color sparingly, producing studies in grays and blacks like *Disaster at Sea* (1835). That is, as Turner developed, his work grew less and less detailed, distinctions among objects grew less clearly defined, the works less conventionally colored, and so the whole gave the appearance of incompletion. The process might even be described as a vaguening, the scene somehow ill seen if not ill stated. Even *Goring Mill and Church* (1806-7) (or *Cleave Mill* as it is called on the attached plaque) retains raw, exposed canvas. Recently Tate Britain folded the issue into its Turner exhibit with a feature called "Finished or Unfinished?" As the exhibit points out, the question is complicated by the fact that Turner often exhibited work in various states of completion, regularly submitting apparently "unfinished" work to Royal Academy exhibitions, at least for the opening days, "completing" (which often meant simply signing) the paintings just before full public viewings. For many contemporary critics Turner thus anticipated at least Impressionism, if not the rebellious spirit of Modernism itself as he moved the subversion of expectations and particularly issues of completion to center stage. To twenty-first century eyes the indistinctions of Turner's late style, however, make him our contemporary.

Such resistance to what we might call the studio finish has characterized Samuel Beckett's entire creative career, the unfinished look itself become the textual (or textural) finish. His first novel *Dream of Fair to middling Women*, was (perhaps) never completed, even as he tried assiduously to have it published. His third (but second published) novel, *Watt*, is, to all appearances, such an incomplete, unfinished project as well. In a sense, it perhaps has to be. One need only thumb through its pages to notice gaps in the text and what look to be omissions, absences, authorial queries, or compositional notes, all of which suggest that the work was halted (temporarily or permanently) rather than completed. The 37 item "Addenda" with which the novel "ends" (if that is the word), for example, seems to confirm that suspicion as a footnote informs readers that "Only fatigue and disgust prevent its incorporation" into the body of the text. Had it been found in a trunk at his death, Beckett's manuscript might easily have gone unpublished by his executors who might have deemed the project incomplete and abandoned. Incompletion, however, grew to become the principal rhetorical trope of the novel, an acknowledgement of the irresolution that dominates both physical and metaphysical worlds, life and art. What is clear with *Watt* is that Beckett was determined to exhibit *this state* of the work to a public and struggled to find a willing publisher.

Despite such authorial subversions of the text, the exposure of so much raw canvas, say, both the lacunae and the excesses, the unincorporated fragments, remain, as we see now, crucial to the narrative, extending it forward and backwards. In this current, exhaustive study, *Obscure Locks, Simple Keys: The Annotated* Watt, C. J. Ackerley details the art and craft of such incompletion. Reconstructing the novel and its context is something of an archeological project, residua and ur-versions of scenes buried in the "Addenda" and compositional notebooks. His genetic analyses lead, however, less to a reconstruction of what Beckett himself has deconstructed than to the re-emphasis on the irremediable persistence, the necessity, of its gaps, a demonstration of how the novel eludes fulfillment. Such textual anomalies and the signals of incompletion that characterize this text emphasize finally its openness, its failure to achieve completion or closure, either in rational thought or its textual echo. They suggest irresolution and negation, textual and aesthetic, and so anticipate the epistemological crises that dominate Beckett's subsequent work, particularly *Molloy*, *Malone Dies*, and *The Unnamable*, as well as much of the late drama. *Watt* thus remains enthymemetic (as well as anti-mimetic), is, in fact, about those lacunae and so it anticipates a body of work that will help define the post-War literary era. Among the authorially disparaged "Addenda" sits an emblematic poem that Beckett thought good enough to published separately as "Tailpiece" to conclude (if that is the word) the 1984 *Collected Poems, 1930-1978* (London: John Calder):

> who may tell the tale
> of the old man?
> weigh absence in a scale?
> mete want in a span?
> the sum assess
> of the world's woes?
> nothingness
> in words enclose?

While the poem's tone and its parallel interrogatories seem rhetorically inconclusive, the questions evasive, suggesting the epistemological uncertainties of late-modernism and postmodernism, its metaphysical enigmas are situated among biblical mysteries. In a manuscript notebook for the novel, as Ackerley demonstrates, Beckett noted their source in Isaiah 40:12, "Who hath measured the waters in the hollow of his hand, and meted out heaven with a span, and comprehended the dust of the earth in a measure, and weighed the mountains in scales, and the hills in a balance?" Words like "meted" and "span" overtly echo the King James tone, and the last two lines of the poem respond to Isaiah 40:17: "All nations before him are as nothing, and they are counted to him less than nothing, and vanity." In Isaiah the interrogatories develop into greater interrogatories: Who can claim to have God's privileged perspective? Conclusions about the nature of existence from a limited number of examples (or accidents), the amount of water one can contain in the hollow of one's hand, say, are thus inevitably inconclusive, mere vanity and so nothing. Beckett was fascinated by such perspectivism as outlined in Diderot's "Le Rêve de d'Alembert" (1769), which intimates the relativity of immortality (the mortal whisky's grudge against the immortal decanter is the trope Beckett used in *Proust* [21]). A version of "Le Rêve" appears in *Dream*, that within the memory of the rose no gardener has been known to die (175). This is echoed in "Draff": "No gardener has died, comma, within rosaceous memory"(175), the trope repeated, commaless, in "Echo's Bones" (19). Such perspectivism dominates the modernist ethos, of course; as Turner's late work suggests, and as a whole school will subsequently celebrate, one can at best record impressions, even as they are ill seen, ill heard, and thus inevitably ill recorded.

As both artists developed, their imagery vaguened. The result is imagery hazened, a studied, a crafted indistinction. Beckett thus situates himself (and his art) in the midst of such a late-modernist or early postmodernist ethos, exploring the issues of perspective and so consciousness, of perception much celebrated but doomed to distortion and incompletion, for the remainder of his career. Ackerley does the spadework to unearth the foundations and connections of what appear isolated fragments, recondite references, and mathematical serialism to expose an ur-narrative, a pre-history. The result is a look at the novel as both events (diachronic) and as system (synchronic). The signature unfinished state of Beckett's work (later overtly tagged as fragments or pieces) results in an art of perpetual becoming, liminality as the condition of post-War art. As he did with his *Demented Particulars* (Journal of Beckett Studies Books, 1998, second edition, 2004), Ackerley's neo-genetic criticism (or the new textual studies, what the French call *critique génétique*) charts the crafted details of Beckett's art of incompletion and thus lays a foundation for future study of Beckett impossible to ignore. It is the most comprehensive study available of Beckett's most enigmatic novel and details the "how" not only of (the still critically-underrated) *Watt* but also of Beckett's entire post-War explorations of voice and consciousness. Ackerley's "Annotated *Watt*" is thus a tour de force that lays bare much of the novel's pre-history and so exposes the architectonics of incompletion; it enriches the novel that Beckett wrote even as it details the novel that he did not.

Prefatory Statement

Obscure Locks, Simple Keys first appeared as a Journal of Beckett Studies Book in 2005, and, excellent as the editing was, a few gremlins wrought their worst. Hence the mangled mathematics of Note **#183.4**, where 438,976 should have included 'neuf cent soixante-seize' and the nonsensical 'on a verso inplication' deleted. I am grateful to both Mark Nixon and Matthew Feldman for various kindnesses, but in Note **#74.8** the credit should have gone to Mark. But for the frigid machinery of the time-space relation, I might have added more details: the likeness of the great white throne of Revelation 20:11 to Mr Knott's great big white chamber pot (Note **#212.1**), for instance. Major changes in the evolutionary history of *Watt* since 2005 concern two recent corrected texts: that edited by Laura Lindgren for the Grove Press Centenary Edition (2006), and that by me for the new Faber series (2009). 'Addendum 1', textual changes and errata in the major editions of *Watt*, is now less a blueprint for a better edition of *Watt* than an historical record of horrendous error and carnage. However, my anecdote of the duck and, indeed, my granddaughter whose birth occasioned it, remain as delightful as ever.

Chris Ackerley, February 2010

Introduction

a. Watt's *Place in the Series*:

Watt, an improbable novel, was written under impossible conditions. Or vice versa. Begun in Paris 11 February 1941 and continued while Beckett was on the run from the Gestapo, it took shape from 1943 to 1945 while he was sitting out the war in Roussillon, in the Vaucluse some forty miles north of Avignon: "*Le prince d'Aquitaine à la tour abolie.*" After the war, writing to George Reavey (14 May 1947), Beckett said of his ugly duckling: "It is an unsatisfactory book, written in dribs and drabs, but it has its place in the series, as will perhaps appear in time." He added that he had composed the book "first on the run, then of an evening after the clod-hopping." He told Lawrence Harvey that it was "only a game, a means of staying sane, a way to keep my hand in" (Harvey 222; Bair 327). To Ruby Cohn, he dismissed it as "An exercise" (*Canon* 112), to reflect and to counter the long hours of ennui as he waited for nothing to happen, a critique of rationality to help retain his sanity. This is disingenuous, if only because Beckett had taken the notebooks with him when he fled Paris, and kept them with him until he returned. Knowlson tells the tale (310; Beckett to George Reavey, 5 August 1964), which others have elaborated, of how the manuscript was confiscated by the War Office in England as Beckett was en route to Ireland (1945), the officials having their deep suspicions about the cryptic nonsense they had intercepted.

Beckett recalled to Gottfried Büttner (12 April 1978): "*Watt* was begun in Paris 1942 [*sic*], then continued evenings mostly in Roussillon and finished 1945 in Dublin & Paris." He added: "It was written as it came, without pre-established plan" (Büttner 5-6). Again, this is both misleading and truthful: misleading, as it fails to acknowledge the extent of rewriting, revision, and careful resetting of the text over several years; truthful, because it intimates that the novel was not written to a blue-print, that its only unity, as Belacqua hoped for his novel (*Dream* 132), is an involuntary one. While the novel reflects the care and love directed toward its demented particulars (the straws, the flotsam of existence) and the shaping of these into absurd but often beautiful paragraphs, the overall structure is fragmented. *Watt* is not a well-wrought pot, but rather a text in perpetual evolution (even after its first publication).

Despite its Roussillon provenance, *Watt* was written in English and evokes the environs of Foxrock, Dublin, and the landscape south of that city of the plains. Mr. Knott's house is based on Cooldrinagh, Beckett's family home; Watt's journey to it can be traced from Harcourt Street Station to the Leopardstown racecourse; and many characters and details have their originals in the world of Beckett's childhood. As Michael Robinson has noted (101), whatever Watt's personal vagaries and indistinctness, the background of decaying country houses, local trams, trains, and verdurous ditches is unmistakably Irish; the details are documented in Eoin O'Brien's stunning account of "the Beckett country." Hugh Kenner's early summary (1961), indebted to Vivian Mercier, notes the Dublin setting and acknowledges that the novel was written as a pensum, with thousands of meaningless words; and he sums up the effect (23): "the subsumption of distant memories into a style, the withdrawal of candlestickmaker's reality from a time and place now unattainable: Ireland, where old men sit on benches and strange men in lonely houses employ servants, and words are incessantly agitated and the mind is never still. This Ireland, at Roussillon between 1942 and 1944, Beckett delivered over from the remembered realm of irreducible being to the mental world where logic mimes the possibility of order and sentences linked less certainly to fact than to one another move unimpeded through the dark." My critical approach by and large aligns itself with this earlier orientation, rather than with those that have dominated *Watt* studies more recently.

As Knowlson indicates, the important feature of *Watt* is its "comic attack on rationality" (303). The first influential study of *Watt*, Jacqueline Hoefer's "*Watt*" (*Perspective* 1959), drew attention to the impasse of rationalism. Hoefer argued that the irrational cannot be reached with rational tools; but rather than seeing this in terms of the Cartesian debate that had informed *Murphy* (and would continue into the *Three Novels*), she discussed it in terms of logical positivism and with specific reference to Wittgenstein, notably his figure in the *Tractatus* of the ladder that must be cast away as soon as it is climbed. Although Beckett indicated that he had not read Wittgenstein at this time (Fritz Mauthner would have been a better bet), Hoefer's argument, in many ways excellent, left a lasting trace on the critical tradition, in much the way that Samuel Mintz's perspective (in the same volume) did for *Murphy*, ensuring, and rightly so, that the philosophical preoccupations of each novel would be prominent.

The Cartesian dimension of *Watt* should not be ignored. Watt's recollection, added late to the final draft, about "dying in London" **(212.1)** affirms its radical continuity with *Murphy*, where Beckett had explored the dualism of mind and body and the Cartesian catastrophe that ensues when these cannot be reconciled. *Watt* takes the form of a frustrated mystical quest, but one sustained by a different Cartesian framework. In the *Meditations* Descartes argued that the one certainty that can be established is the fact of one's consciousness and so of one's existence: *cogito ergo sum*. In the *Three Novels* Beckett would interrogate the cogito, and challenge this certainty, but for Descartes it formed the foundation upon which the understanding of God could be established (for Beckett, however, the limits of what can be known). *Watt* places itself within this Cartesian series by its application of the *Méthode*, Descartes's attempt to rationalize and sustain his philosophy of doubt; in Arsene's words, to eff the ineffable. The essence of Knott being inaccessible to Watt's rational understanding of his attributes, this attempt leads to disaster, and finally to madness.

Adrien Baillet's *La Vie de Monsieur Des-Cartes* outlines (12ff) Descartes's four rules, from which arose "un méthode," the bedrock beneath my excavation of *Watt*:

1. De ne rien recevoir pour vrai qu'il ne connût être tel évidemment
2. De deviser les choses le plus qu'il serait possible pour les mieux résoudre
3. De conduire ses pensées par ordre en commencant par les objets les plus simples pour monter par dégré jusqu'à la connaissance des plus composées
4. De rien omettre dans le dénombrement des choses dont it devait examiner les partes.

Watt acknowledges, implicitly, each of these principles: he accepts as true only that which is presented so clearly and distinctly as to exclude all ground of doubt (**26.1**); he divides difficulties into as many parts as possible, the better to understand them (**26.6**); he orders his thoughts, beginning with the most simple and rising by degrees to the understanding of the more complex (**27.4**); and he makes enumerations so complete that he might be assured that nothing is omitted (**29.3**). The result is disastrous, and so, like Murphy, he participates in a Cartesian catastrophe that is equally the outcome of a failure to reconcile the inner self to the contingencies of a contingent world.

In the 1980s two monographs appeared, both unsatisfactory. John Di Pierro's *Structures in Beckett's* Watt (1981) is a waste of trees (fortunately, very few); and if Gottfried Büttner's *Samuel Beckett's Novel* Watt (1984) is little better it at least offers scattered insights based on his acquaintance with Beckett. Yet Büttner fails to acknowledge, let alone reconcile, the great gulf between Beckett's emphatic rejection of the anthropomorphic tradition in Western culture and the anthroposophy of Rudolf Steiner that forms his own red nucleus of faith. No good independent study of *Watt* (there are several excellent shorter ones) has appeared since. Personally, I blame George ["Bando"] Bush, but there may be another reason.

The recent fashion for *post-modern* theory (my solitary dactylic ejaculation) has had the unfortunate consequence that valuable insights into the fascinating particulars (the *ideal real*) of Beckett's creative imagination have been largely obnubilated; yet *Watt* is a text that insists upon its particulars (Beckett noted of Democritus [TCD 1067/75] his "capital idea" that "the only fruitful basis of investigation is the <u>sensible discreet [sic] particular</u>"). As the "tumulus" begins to roll away, however, interpretation seems to be regaining some of its kick, with respect to the way that Beckett's early work (and so his later) makes allegiance to a long cultural tradition and to what Stan Gontarski has called "the agency of authorship" (introduction to *Demented Particulars* 9). If it is true, as Gontarski asserts, that *Murphy* represents the peak of Beckett's early grafting technique, *Watt* is obliquely instructive in this respect, for its "place in the series" is largely determined by the curious conditions under which it was written, without easy access to the literary, philosophical, and theological works to which it [in]constantly makes allusion. In this sense, *Watt* (like the fiction that follows it) is dislocated from the very traditions that most inform it; the novel testifies eloquently to a world in ruins, and Watt's fragile mind, like the ruins of St. Lô, is a poignant emblem of recent trauma. In this sense, *Watt* is not unlike T. S. Eliot's *The Waste Land* of the generation before, cultural chaos as an image of inner disintegration, and vice versa, fragments shored up against the ruin. *Obscure Locks* places *Watt* against its background, both personal and cultural, to offer a reading, or "helps" toward one, in empathy with the many and various strands of experience that went into both its making and Watt's undoing.

b. The Publication of Watt.

If the genesis of *Watt* was fraught, its journey to the light of day was even more so. Once the typescript was released from the War Office, Beckett took it to T. M. Ragg at Routledge, Ragg having been instrumental in getting

Murphy published. As Knowlson records (310-11), Ragg and Herbert Read were friendly but emphatic in their rejection of *Watt*, finding it "too wild and unintelligible" for post-war publication, given their limited supply of paper. Nor did Denis Devlin have any success in trying to interest an American publisher when he took a copy to Washington. Beckett left the typescript with Curtis Brown, who sent it to Nicholson and Watson (the Unnamable's "whore-sons" [Knowlson 685]). He then placed it with Richard Watt of the London agency, A. P. Watt and Son, but the sympathetic magic failed. The manuscript was sent out to numerous houses, including Chatto & Windus, Methuen, and Secker & Warburg; reports ranged from hostility to bafflement. One reader (Harold Raymond, for Chatto & Windus, 8 April 1946) commented: "I fancy that he has read James Joyce excessively and tried to model his writing on that of Joyce at his more obscure and bestial moments, but has not succeeded in capturing anything of Joyce's tremendous vitality and power, in his own way, to create characters." Raymond added in his own hand: "If S.B. had been going to get there he would have got nearer there by now . . . Let's down this." Knowlson cites (311) Frederick Warburg's response to Richard Watt (October 1946): "Puns would be too easy but the book itself is too difficult. It shows an immense mental vitality, an outrageous metaphysical skill, and a very fine talent for writing. It may be that in turning this book down we are turning down a potential James Joyce. What is it that this Dublin air does to these writers?" Beckett then asked George Reavey to act as his agent, but Reavey had no success, despite an encouraging nibble from Hamish Hamilton (Bair 366).

Watt was thus effectively put into the bottom drawer, "the leaves turning yellow" (Knowlson 355), as Beckett began the "frenzy of writing" in French that would produce, in short time, his most important critical articles, the four novellas, *Mercier et Camier*, *Molloy*, *Malone meurt*, *L'Innommable*, and *En attendant Godot*. *Watt* did not fade entirely as four extracts, each varying slightly from the final text, appeared in small magazines: *Envoy* 1.2 (January 1950): 11-19 [pp. 16-24 of the first edition]; *Irish Writing* 17 (December 1951): 11-16 [the beginning and the final paragraph of part III]; *Merlin* 1.3 (winter 1952-53): 118-26 [the end of Watt's stay in the house of Mr. Knott]; and *Irish Writing* (March 1953): 16-24 [the Galls father and son], with a note stating that an "unexpurgated edition" of *Watt* would appear in the late spring from *Collection Merlin*.

The *Merlin* connection mattered most. Richard Seaver, a young American in Paris, had read Beckett's first French novels (*Molloy*, *Malone meurt*), and attended (17 February 1952) a studio radio broadcast of excerpts from *Godot*. He was one of a group termed by Beckett, in affection and exasperation, the "Merlin Juveniles." *Merlin* was a Paris-based English-language "revue trimestrielle," also distributed from Limerick, Maine, published by a small group of expatriates led by Seaver and Alexander Trocchi (Editors) and Alice Jane Lougee (Publisher), who sought to re-establish in the 1950s the intellectual climate of the 1920s. They wanted to revive the "little magazines" and were "deeply engaged" by the thought of Sartre and Camus (Knowlson 355-56). The group included Christopher Logue and Austryn Wainhouse, whose dubious connections with the Olympia Press would prove important, and the South Africa writer, Patrick Bowles, whom Beckett later engaged to translate *Molloy* into English.

Excited by what he had read, Seaver published an essay about Beckett's novels in the autumn 1952 issue of *Merlin*. Hearing rumors about an unpublished novel in English, he asked if he might publish an extract. He tells how he wrote to Beckett, but heard nothing until one rainy afternoon when a tall gaunt figure knocked on the door and handed over, almost without a word, a manuscript in black imitation-leather binding; the *Merlin* group sat up to all hours that night, reading it aloud (Seaver, preface to *I Can't Go On, I'll Go On*, xv; Knowlson 357). Beckett gave Seaver and Trocchi permission to publish an extract, but stipulated the inventory of Mr. Knott's attire and the stations of the furniture in his room (Seaver, "Beckett and *Merlin*" 23-24); Seaver later asked if this intractable piece had been chosen as a sign of good faith, and says that Beckett did not disagree (**199.2**). The extract appeared in *Merlin* 1.3 (winter 1952-53): 118-26; *Merlin* later published a piece from *Molloy* (2.2 [autumn 1953]: 88-103); and "The End" (2.3 [summer-autumn 1954]: 144-59). Their emblem, a blackbird, features on the pen Mr. Saposcat sells to himself (*Malone Dies* 210).

The *Merlin* pre-publication "Extract from *Watt*" led circuitously to the Olympia Press *Watt* under the imprint of "Editions Merlin." In Seaver's words (24): "when, in the autumn of 1953, having lost relatively little money on the magazine, we determined we would expand and see if we could lose more money more quickly by publishing books, the first book we chose to publish was, of course, *Watt*." This they could not do, under French law, without a French publishing house acting as *gérant*, or manager (Knowlson 357). Maurice Girodias (son of Jack Kahane who fifteen years earlier had invited Beckett to translate de Sade) agreed to be the associate (some of the *Merlin* group were already writing and translating "erotic fiction" for his new Olympia press). An agreement was reached with Beckett, if not a formal contract, and an advance of 50,000 old francs ($100) was duly paid. Seaver says that the manuscript was in impeccable condition, so there were few queries, let alone any changes. A full-page advertisement for *Watt* appeared on the back cover of *Merlin*'s spring-summer issue of 1953, in a list of "unusual books" from the Olympia Press: John Cleland's *Fanny Hill*, Henry Miller's *Plexus*, de Sade's *Justine* and *The Bedroom Philosophers*, Apollinaire's *Amorous Exploits of a Young Rakehell*, and an anonymous *The Debauched Hospodar* ("The erratic and explosive loves of a Roumanian prince in Paris and the voluptuous Orient"). A further promotion in the fall issue gave details of the forthcoming printing:

> *Watt* (a novel) by SAMUEL BECKETT
> Ordinary Edition (*1100 numbered copies*) 850 fr.
> Special Edition (*25 signed copies of a deluxe paper*) 2,500 fr.

Prices were also given in dollars ($2.50 or $6.50) and sterling (17/6 or £2.10.0).

Writing to George Reavey (12 May 1953; Bair 431), Beckett expressed his relief that "our old misery, *Watt*" was about to come out at last. The novel gives its publication date as "LE 31 AOUT 1953," under the imprint of the Collection Merlin and in association with the Olympia Press. The print run was detailed at the outset of the novel:

>THERE HAVE BEEN PRINTED OF THIS WORK ONE THOUSAND ONE HUNDRED TWENTY-FIVE COPIES, OF WHICH TWENTY-FIVE ARE ON FINE PAPER, LETTERED A TO Y AND SIGNED BY THE AUTHOR, AND ELEVEN HUNDRED, INTENDED FOR GENERAL CIRCULATION, NUMBERED FROM 1 TO 1000.

The twenty-five copies on fine paper, signed by Beckett, have wrappers of whitish beige, rather than the "magenta cover with its somewhat lurid frame of asterisks" (Knowlson 694) that so horrified Beckett when he saw the first edition. Beckett's copies of the fine edition (#Y, pages mostly uncut) and of the first edition (#85, lightly annotated) are both held at the BIF.

Although Beckett said on 1 September 1953 that he had not seen a copy, on 4 August 1953 (on the basis of the galleys?) he had complained to Barney Rosset about the Olympia text, with its mis-spellings, and inverted letters: "To find one word deliberately distorted and the next botched by the type-setter can spoil the tone so easily. Also it is a shame that the type-face used is so scrubby and ugly." He repeated to George Reavey (29 September 1953) his dismay at the "awful magenta cover" and the number of errors. Richard Seaver commented (25): "As for the awful color of the cover page, I can only assume there was a special on magenta. The book was typeset and printed at the Imprimerie Richard in Paris, and despite all the author's care in typescript, the 'Printer Richard,' who was touted to us as especially good because of his knowledge of English, managed to infiltrate so many typos that no matter how carefully we tried, we could never eliminate them all. . . . [Beckett's] only consolation, perhaps, was the memory that Joyce, too, had suffered the same indignity at the hands of French printers with *Ulysses*, and survived."

This is not entirely fair. The *Imprimerie Richard* ("24, Rue Stevenson, Paris XVIII") has been much abused for the errors, and rightly; but to a greater extent than either would admit Beckett and Seaver were responsible for many mistakes, as they passed without comment many errors that had entered the galleys, these continuing into the Olympia text and often the Grove. There is little evidence to suggest that Seaver tried "carefully" to improve matters, but Beckett made many changes to and corrections on the galleys, and these by and large were respected. The Frog Song and Addenda posed particular problems, and Beckett spent considerable time (and money) insisting that Olympia get them right.

Watt shares with Nabokov's *Lolita* the dubious distinction of having been first published by the Olympia Press, a quag from which both authors extricated themselves with considerable difficulty. Beckett's major reason for agreeing to the Merlin-Olympia deal was to get the book into print to attract English and American publishers. Ireland was a different problem as *Watt*, like *More Pricks than Kicks* before it, was banned (22 October 1954; Bair 434, 697) shortly after it appeared. As events transpired, Beckett not only had difficulty extracting any royalties (Knowlson 358), but Girodias created trouble when Beckett entered into negotiations with Barney Rosset of Grove Press with respect to an American edition; this effectively delayed that publication until 1959.

Rosset had bought a small reprint house in New York, in 1951, and was building it into the "most aggressive, innovative, audacious, politically active, and often reckless publishing concern in the United States" (*Grove Companion* 237). He contacted Beckett (18 June 1953), promising to make his work known in America; and Beckett, with *Watt* about to come out in France, responded positively. From the outset, both expressed interest in seeing *Watt* appear under the Grove imprint, Rosset writing (4 August 1953):

> My suggestion on *Watt* is that part of the edition bear the imprint of Grove Press on the title page, that the reverse of the title page say Copyright 1953 (or by Samuel Beckett, and we will undertake to copyright it for you in this country). The Grove part of the edition, at least, should be printed on good paper and put in a binding up to American standards. The book should be sold to us at cost by Merlin and the profit to you and them (whatever your arrangement with them is) will come out of royalties on which we will make a small advance. This will keep the price of the book at the lowest possible figure and give it a fighting chance to get sold.

Beckett replied (1 September 1953):

> Watt, I believe, is out, but I have not yet seen it. Standards of book presentation are not the same here as with you and the resources of Merlin are very limited. What matters to me is that this work refused by a score of London publishers in the years following the war is at last between boards. A handsomer edition in America would of course give me great pleasure. I am so hopelessly incompetent in these matters that it is better I should not intervene with Merlin. I am in advance agreement with whatever arrangement you come to with them.

That arrangement took time, as the fragmentary correspondence between Rosset and Beckett over the next few years reveals. Beckett noted (15 March 1956): "We are trying to recover same rights from Girodias who has behaved badly over both *Watt* and *Molloy*" ("same" refers to the Merlin rights having been transferred to Olympia, and the problems that ensued when Jérôme Lindon wanted to buy them). He suggested, however (30 August 1956), that Rosset's proposed Evergreen selection should include the beginning of part III of *Watt*; for whatever reason, this did not eventuate. The wider issue was revisited in 1957, as Rosset determined to publish not only *Murphy* but also *Watt*. He asked Beckett (13 March 1957): "If we wish to do an edition of *Watt*, would we have to get permission from Girodias or someone else, or would you be able to give us permission to proceed—and would the idea ever interest you anyway?" Beckett's reply (20 March 1957) indicated that chances seemed brighter: "Re *Watt*. Lindon is your man. More trouble with Girodias. I should be happy for you to take it on, and I don't think there should be any difficulty about rights. Lindon knows the situation." Rosset responded positively (23 March 1957): "*Watt* - happy to know about that and I will write to Lindon and make arrangements with him." Suitable arrangements were made, as Judith Schmidt of Grove Press wrote to Beckett (24 June 1957), enclosing a check for $100 as an advance for *Watt* and asking him to let "M. Lindon" know it had been sent.

The American first edition appeared in 1959, offset from the original Olympia plates, which had survived a vice squad raid, the plates seized as evidence for the prosecution (Bair 434). There were four "editions": a specially bound and signed edition of 26 copies lettered "A" through "Z" (plus four copies *hors commerce*, numbered "1" through "4"; a limited edition of 100 numbered copies; a cloth-bound edition, selling at $3.50; and a trade paperback (Evergreen Books, E-152), selling at $1.75, or 13/- in the UK. The Evergreen cover, designed by Richard Brodney, featured the circle and dot used for all the early reprints, the blue dot misplaced, the circle cut rather than breached, and the background not white but greenish-beige (**128.6**). Beckett acknowledged its safe arrival (10 April 1959): "Thanks for copy of *Watt* (excellent cover)." Judith Schmidt responded (23 April 1959): "Under separate cover, we're sending you No. 1 of the 'hors commerce' limited edition of *Watt*. Barney is keeping No. 2. To whom would you like us to send 3 and 4?" No reply is recorded.

Beckett's copy of the Olympia printing, now at the BIF, records changes apparently intended for the Grove Press edition. Some changes were made, including the restoration of a missing sentence (**19.3**), but a mystery surrounds the precise use intended of Beckett's corrections, as the marked copy was apparently not sent to Grove and many of the errors noted remain unchanged. For all its delightful idiosyncrasies (**45.6**), the Grove text is faulty. Beckett took greater care with a further set of corrections, this time on his copy of the first Grove Press printing, when preparing his text for John Calder's Jupiter edition (1963). Beckett's copy of the Grove is also at the BIF, missing pages 137-38 and 161-92, which were presumably marked up in the same manner as the rest.

A British edition was long in coming, but *Watt* had been available in the UK. Interest in it, or in its author, had led to the reading of an extract on BBC 3 (7 September 1955). John Calder obtained distributional rights, and when the Olympia text was reprinted in January 1958 (anticipating Grove by eighteen months) in their *Traveller's Companion* series it was advertised in both francs (Fr. 1,200) and sterling (15/-). This edition reset the original, using a different printer ("S.I.P., Monteuil"), but it followed the Olympia text in most essentials, offering a more compact volume, but with more pages (280), minor corrections (but a few new errors), and green cloth boards and red endpapers to replace the notorious magenta. Calder was also the designated "Foreign Distributor" of the Grove Press edition of *Watt* in the UK, after its 1959 publication, such copies marked "John Calder Ltd. / London" in small type at the bottom of the title page.

Calder's edition, Jupiter Books #2 (*Murphy* his first), appeared in October 1963, by arrangement with Olympia Press. The cloth-bound edition (18.5 x 12 cm, 255 pages) sold at 15/- and the trade paperback (issued simultaneously) at 8/6, the latter in a design by John Sewell and with a portrait of Beckett on the front cover. This text has been the unchanged template of subsequent reprintings, including the Picador edition (1988), Calder's authority lasting in Britain until 2005, when the Estate qualified its support. The Calder edition, as the last in a sequence, is technically more "correct," Beckett having taken some care with his recommended changes (for instance, the use of hyphens in compounds such as "ground-floor" and "first-floor") as well as correcting the proofs; but questions arise less from the correction of obvious errors than the later changes of the text. Beckett in his dealings with Calder was deferential, but he had cause for concern as the edition is careless with detail. Calder introduced many new errors (see **#36**, omission of the threne), and he used his own initiative to regularize the spellings and punctuation. His intuition was not always right, and *Watt* remains, in any edition, a deeply flawed text. Beckett told several scholars that the question of error was a vexed one, some intentional and others not (**104.7**). The entry for "error" is the longest in my Index, and although other varieties of sin are recorded the record of textual aberration is scary. These matters are discussed in detail in my individual annotations, keyed to the Index; and further addressed in my two Addenda.

Beckett was long insistent that he did not wish *Watt* to be translated into any other language. He wrote to Loly Rosset, Barney's then wife, noting that "*Watt* in French is something horrible" (20 January 1954). He reiterated to Judith Schmidt (7 August 1959): "The position re *Watt* is simple: I do not want it translated into any language. I have said so to Girodias." Curiously, the endpapers of his Olympia text are covered with notes identifying potential difficulties ("hard words") in a possible French translation: *sun go down* (23); *hureburs* (28); *stands* (29); *equipendency* (31); *sudarium* ("unchanged") (33); *screw yourself up* (40); *dental wedge porch potique* (44); *half-hunter gunmetal demi-chronomètre* (46); *standard* (48); *excoriations* (49); *celery bank* (68); and *ravanastron* (71). Although their date is uncertain, they are not obviously related to the 1968 translation (Beckett also notes changes for Grove) and may indicate an earlier intention to translate *Watt*. A fragment in French of Arsene's Runner Duck poem has survived from a very early time (**45.6**). Admussen notes (92) that Beckett "abandoned an attempt to translate the novel in 1960"; but there may have been earlier tries.

Beckett seems to have reconsidered after a letter from Judith Schmidt (25 January 1965): "Dear Sam, / Several years ago you wrote to tell me that you did not want *Watt* totbe [*sic*] translated. Have you possibly changed your mind about this? We've just had a letter from Aschehoug & Co. (Norway). They say they have acquired the Norwegian translation rights to some of your works, and want to know if these rights are available for *Watt*. Please let me know." The answer was presumably yes, as the Norwegian translation ("oversatt av Olav Angell, Kjell Askildsen og Solveig Schult Ulriksen") appeared in 1969; it is apparently the only translation to have used the Grove text as its template, all others preferring Calder. Other foreign publishers showed a similar interest, so, reluctantly or otherwise, Beckett enlisted Ludovic and Agnès Janvier to help with the onerous task of rendering *Watt* into French. As the Janviers later recalled (Janvier 57), "notre traduction ne lui a pas plu de tout," yet they were crucial elements in a process of triangulation. Beckett felt reluctant to revisit his previous "moi," but having worked assiduously with his translators he took their French text over and made it very much his own, ensuring that the rhythms and cadences were right. Ludovic recorded (58) his particular pleasure when Beckett accepted "ma trice" for "My wom" (**13.5**): "C'était la victoire de la journée." Beckett's role in this "collaboration" was thus considerable, as it had been when Patrick Bowles translated *Molloy* into English, so the French translation (Minuit 1968) can be considered one of his works, in a way that the

German translation of *Watt*, with which he assisted Elmar Tophoven (also in the late 1960s, and working substantially from the French), is not.

The evidence for this assertion is also to be found in the Samuel Beckett Special Collection at Ohio State University, Columbus, which holds the notebooks, typescripts, and galley proofs used in the preparation of the French translation (I prefix "Ohio" to my citation of these). The collection includes Beckett's personal copy of the Jupiter text, in which he noted significant problems and suggested cuts; this notes on the title page: "*Samuel Beckett / Copy from which / French translation / made / Paris 1967-68.*" There are six notebooks, dated from "Paris 25.3.67" to "Paris 24.2.68," but with other times and places (Ussy, Berlin) frequently specified (details in Admussen 92-94). A final typescript (195 pages) includes the signed statement: "Typed and / corrected by the / author. No other / copy in existence. / *Samuel Beckett* Paris April 69." The collection includes other loose items, such as the translation of the madrigal, "To Nelly" (**11.2**), which Beckett reserved to himself, and which gave him a lot of trouble but equally much pleasure. The French translation, then, must be if not included in at least appended to the "series" as it gave Beckett a final opportunity to correct and reshape the text in certain crucial ways.

c. *The* Watt *Manuscripts: An Overview.*

Richard Admussen comments (7): "The first holograph version of *Watt*, chaotically written and filled with multiple and elaborate doodles and drawings is certainly the most fascinating single Beckett item to be found anywhere." Agreeing with this, Carlton Lake, past curator of manuscripts at the Harry Ransom Center, has called the *Watt* notebooks the "white whale" of Beckett studies, glowing among the thousands of modern manuscripts at the HRHRC "like a luminous secular relic." He describes them with joy (76): "magnificently ornate, a worthy scion of the Book of Kells, with the colors reduced to more somber hues. The doodles, cartoons, caricatures, portraits *en cartouche* include reminiscences of African and Oceanic art, the gargoyles of Notre Dame, heraldry, and more." The cover of Lake's catalog reproduces two of the more flamboyant pages of the drafts, but his summary of the notebooks (*No Symbols* 75-76, Item #157) is more restrained (further details in Admussen 90-92, and Coetzee 252-54):

> "Watt." Autograph manuscript, signed, 1940-1945, 945 pp. Written in ink and colored crayons, in six notebooks, folio, 4to, and small 4to, and on loose sheets, some laid in notebooks, some separate.
> With many changes, deletions, and additions, and numerous doodles, sketches, mathematical calculations, rhyming schemes, and drawings. The first notebook is signed and marked "Watt I," with the following note: "*Watt* was written in France during the war 1940-45 and published in 1953 by the Olympia Press." On an inserted sheet, Beckett has written, "Begun evening of Tuesday 11/2/41." The first page of the second notebook is dated "3/12/41." Notebook 3 shows

the date "5.5.42" on the first page of text. The cover of the fourth notebook is marked "Poor Johnny / Watt / Roussillon," and page 1 is headed, "Roussillon, October 4th, 1943." On the cover of Notebook 5 Beckett has written, in variously colored inks, "Watt V / Suite et fin / 18.2.45 / Paris / Et début de L'Absent / Novembre-Janvier 47/48." He has indicated that L'Absent is *Malone Meurt*. Page 99 has the note, "End of the continuation of *Watt*. Conclusion in Notebook VI." Although in Notebook I, Beckett placed the completion of *Watt* in 1945, he concludes the sixth notebook with "Dec 28th 1944 / End."

His next entry (76, Item #158) describes the typescript (Admussen 92):

"Watt." Typed manuscript [some carbon copy], signed, 297 pp., 4to and folio.

Marked at the beginning, "Original typescript of / *Watt* Incomplete / Samuel Beckett." With numerous autograph revisions and deletions, in ink, colored crayons, and pencil. Some doodles and mathematical calculations. With substantial differences from the published text.

The relationship between the notebooks and typescript is spelled out by neither Lake nor Admussen, the logical (but misleading) implication being that the former preceded the latter. My Annotations, Index, and Addenda distinguish between "early drafts," "typescript," "late drafts," "galleys," and "final text" as if these, too, were simple categories, with the typescript neatly positioned between the early drafts and later additions or revisions. This is imprecise. The categories are neither clear nor distinct; nor does the [early] typescript constitute or correspond with any one period of creation. Further, the final typescript is missing. By making these distinctions I could recast a confused manuscript history in a convenient paradigm, but the more complex tale should be told, if only to ensure that references to the drafts can be related to a plausible process of composition.

I am not alone in thus simplifying the problem. Ruby Cohn discusses an "Ur-*Watt*," but this is a useful abstraction rather than a tangible text, streamlining a complex evolutionary process. She follows Richard Admussen in designating the HRHRC notebooks as A1 to A6; I have preferred "NB1" to "NB6," partly to distinguish my denominations from theirs, but also to avoid confusion with J. M. Coetzee, whose detailed study of the drafts offers a schema complementary to but different from mine.

Coetzee's Ph. D. dissertation (Austin 1965) on the *Watt* materials defines three different "levels" of the drafts (96): **A**, a first holograph draft, 282 pages, itself a compendium of four stages (A1 to A4), testifying to a complex (and at times inchoate) evolution of plot, structure, and style; **B**, a typescript recension with holograph corrections, incomplete (but coherent); and **C**, a conflation of part of B with a new holograph draft of 163 pages (mostly Notebooks 5 and 6, but not in one tidy form). Cohn's comment that the published novel was extracted from the holograph (the six notebooks) "via an incomplete typescript" (*Canon* 113) does not reflect the complexity of this process. Coetzee assumes that since C is close to the published text (which he refers to as **W**) there are missing only the printer's copy and the proofs. This must be qualified: the fate of the printer's fair copy is unknown but the galley proofs, which Coetzee did not access, are held at Washington University, St. Louis (with a photocopy now at the BIF). These must correspond closely to that missing final typescript, although (a) errors appeared on the galleys, and (b) Beckett introduced new material. These qualifications apart, Coetzee's schema is valid. However, a practical problem arises in that (a) his distinctions are subtle; (b) they require a tolerable familiarity with the drafts; and (c) they do not settle into a convenient paradigm. A definitive study and/or facsimile publication is needed (David Hayman is currently working toward these); but in their absence I have preferred a distinction of convenience between "early" and "late" drafts, and, bridging the two, what I have designated "TS," or [early] *typescript*.

This latter also needs to be qualified. This typescript (Coetzee's level B) is largely a revision (1944) of the early drafts (his level A; NB1 to NB4), and preliminary to the text as revised and continued (mostly NB5 and NB6; his level C). However, some of the materials in it, although typed, belong to Coetzee's level "A"; notably the first few loose pages. Though numbered as part of the HRHRC typescript, conceptually and chronologically many of the first pages do not entirely belong to the later recension (Coetzee's level "B"). Yet they cannot be called "early," as the act of typing implies a later rehearsal; their retention implies an acceptance of early material into a later rescension; and some handwritten corrections and insertions indicate an even later perspective (Coetzee's level "C"). Problems often arise when hierarchical distinctions are imposed upon discrete and/or continuous evolutionary processes, but for the sake of simplicity (and to locate references more easily) I use "TS" as if the typescript were a unity, in accordance with the HRHRC numeration (Admussen 90-92), to avoid Coetzee's more complex differentiations. This should not affect the annotations, as my "TS" references will normally imply his level "B," and an accompanying "NB1" through "NB6" should prevent confusion; in ambiguous instances I have added "early" or "very early" (or "late" and "very late") as further clarification.

This Introduction offers merely an overview of the textual changes of *Watt*; the evidence for any assertions may be considered in my Addendum 2, "The Evolution of *Watt*," which delineates major differences of detail and structure from one level to another. There I look at *Watt* at nine levels of textual stratification. My "level 1" ("early drafts") and "level 3" ("late drafts") embrace, respectively, NB1 to NB4 and NB4 to NB6; between them is "level 2," the typescript ("TS"). My "level 4" is the (missing) final typescript, a hypothetical entity constructed from the late drafts before it and the galley proofs ("level 5") set from it. My other four levels are the published *Watt*, differences between the editions complicating any definition of the so-called "text"; for the Olympia ("level 6"), Grove ("level 7"), and Calder ("level 8") versions each incorporate and make significant textual changes, with new errors entering even as others are corrected. The French translation is noted as a further speciation. A final consideration is the need for a further recension ("level 10"), an "ideal" edition of *Watt*.

I do not mean a perfect one (perfection is not of this world), but rather one derived from a careful consideration of its evolutionary history (the textual *ideal real*, as it were) and an editing rationale applied accordingly. As matters currently stand, there is no definitive, let alone any accurate "text" of *Watt* (a comment arising out of hard bibliographical evidence rather than a fashionable assertion). This study might be considered a prolegomena to such an edition.

d. *The Geology of the Imagination.*

James Knowlson has testified (46-47) to Beckett's love of stones, noting that as a child he might bring them home to protect them from the waves (compare Watt's solicitude for the key [145]). Beckett later rationalized this impulse as an early fascination with the mineral, with petrification, and with Freud's pre-birth nostalgia for a return to the mineral or inorganic state (*Grove Companion* 220). In *transition* 21 (March 1932), following the surrealist manifesto, "Poetry is Vertical" (which Beckett signed), Gottfried Benn's "The Structure of the Personality" defined a geology of the "I," reviewing advances in neuro-psychology. To Thomas MacGreevy (14 August 1937), Beckett likened the painting of Jack B. Yeats to that of Watteau, praising its inorganism, the way that its figures are finally mineral. The Whoroscope Notebook includes (62v) a geological table, copied from an encyclopedic source unknown, listing the geological eras from the Pre-Cambrian to the present; and preceded by another note (62r): "The geology of conscience—Cambrian experience, cainozoic [*sic*] judgments—." The French "conscience" better conveys than the English "imagination" the stratification of guilt and repression, as in the poem "ainsi a-t-on beau" (1938), where the mind is conceived as a landscape where great saurians abound and where the transitory nature of human consciousness and memory (first kisses, a father recently dead) is as nothing against the past, the ages of the mammoth and the dinotherium.

In the early typescript of *Watt* (146-49), Arsene outlines to "Johnny" Watt: "the unconscious mind! What a subject for a short story"; and the attempt to go "deep down in those palaeozoic profounds, midst mammoth Old Red Sandstone phalli and Carboniferous pudenda . . . the Cambrian! the uterine! the pre-uterine . . . the agar-agar . . . close eyes, all close, great improvement, pronounced improvement" (**#7**). This was defined as "auto-speliology" [*sic*]. The impulse continues into *Molloy*, whose protagonist (with his sucking-stones) lives deep down: "oh not deepest down, somewhere between the mud and the scum" (14); and *How It Is*, where the mud is an amorphous plane between the rock below and the light above (compare Quin's early sense of the waste and the sky, **#22**). The impulse was not new, as these mindscapes constitute a return to the mineral as in the poems of *Echo's Bones* (and the short story of that title), centered about the conceit of the bones that are turned to stone. A like sentiment appears in the epigraph to *Proust*, Leopardi's "E fango è il mondo" ["The world is mud"], with its distant anticipation of *How It Is* and the struggle of incipient form to emerge from formlessness, as in Dante's *Inferno* VII.121-26, in Cary's translation: "Fixed in the slime . . . But word distinct can utter none." Consider, too, Malone's intention to tell a story about a stone (*Malone Dies* 182); the Unnamable's "stupid obsession" about "depths" (293) and his sense that he must "utter" lest he "peter out" (307); he feels trapped in the skull like a fossil in a rock (393). Lucky's short statement recalls the labors lost of Steinweg and Peterman, the skull of Golgotha and stones of Connemara, existence reduced to bare bone and stone. "Cascando" depicts Woburn crashing to the sea, his face in the stones, the sand, the mud; *Eh Joe* recounts the suicide of a woman, her lips, breasts, and hands clutching the stones; and in "Rough for Radio II" Fox returns to the inner depths, "all stones all sides," and the voice of his fetal twin yelling, "let me out. Peter in the stones."

The geology of the imagination in *Watt* arises from the sense of the self as trapped between the light and the rock, the tragedy of a consciousness denied the metamorphosis it seeks and so condemned to return to the mineral from which it somehow arose. Diderot's "Le Rêve de d'Alembert" articulates precisely this paradox of life generated from the plane of inert sediment, and returning to it, his literal reading of *momento quia pulvis es, et in pulverem reverteris*, of Genesis 3:19: "for dust thou art, and unto dust shalt thou return"; one of Beckett's obsessive texts. In his *Méthode* (pt. III), Descartes had determined to find the ground of assurance, casting aside loose earth and sand, that he might reach rock or clay. In *Proust*, Beckett had contended that the only fertile research is "excavatory." Murphy's attempts to go into the dark and ancient parts of his mind, pictured as a place and as stratified, afford such pleasure that pleasure is not the word. Yet *Watt*'s consciousness, like that of the protagonist of *How It Is*, is denied the transcendence it craves; his use of the Cartesian *Méthode* fails to reach the bedrock of assurance; and Arsene's successive excoriations of the understanding (*Watt* 48) lead to less the intrauterine pleasures of the re-integrated matrix than to the "mirthless" laughter at that which is unhappy. *Watt*'s "place in the series" may be defined as a prelude to the later, powerful writings that move ever deeper within the self, but finally dismiss the impulse to move to a higher synthesis, the apotheosis of mud in the life in the light, as "All balls" (*How It Is* 158).

Watt defines the physical and metaphysical position of Beckett's later protagonists, one on the "ground floor" who seeks a higher understanding, but for whom this is denied. This binary opposition is complicated by the tripartite nature of the world in which he occupies a purgatorial position, in the mud, between the rock (the mineral, the *Inferno*) and the light (transcendence, the *Paradiso*). On the one hand there is the world as defined by the Platonic Idea, where mathematical laws and logical paradigms accessible to reason intimate that higher understanding; on the other there is nature, inorganic, mineral, irrational; and between these is the human predicament, with the need to come and go, with a consciousness of the light yet unable to grasp more than the occasional particular, the straws of understanding. This is the world, not of mathematics (the Idea) nor biology (unaccommodated man), but of physics, in the Greek sense of that word ("*physis*") as defined by Windelband (73) in terms of the relationship between the unchanging order of things and the world of change; and subject to the laws of motion, because, as Malone concludes, in order not to die you must come and go, come and go (*Malone Dies* 232). Mr. Knott abides; his servants come and go.

Beckett accepted Windelband's thesis that the main divide in Greek thought was not that between Aristotle and Plato (materialism versus Ideas), but rather between these and the Atomists (Democritus, Epicurus, Lucretius). The triumph of Christianity and its doctrine of the survival of the soul after death led to the acceptance of the one and eclipse of the other. For Beckett, Windelband's importance lay in his rejection of the dogma, attributed to Protagoras, that man is the measure of all things, an "anthropomorphic insolence" **(202.1)** that has shaped a sense of the natural world so intricately that most of Western philosophy has simply taken it for granted. *Watt*, in a passage added late, notes (77): "For the only way one can speak of nothing is to speak of it as though it were something, just as the only way one can speak of God is to speak of him as though he were a man, which to be sure he was, in a sense, for a time, and as the only way one can speak of man, even our anthropologists have realised this, is to speak of him as though he were a termite." The cynicism, perhaps Sam's as it is expressed at Watt's expense, aligns the central metaphysical issues of the novel with Beckett's distrust of reason (particularly Cartesian rationalism) and his rejection of the impulse towards anthropomorphism for a sense of nature as indifferent to mankind, as *atomistic*, *mineral*, and *inorganic*.

For all that *Watt* is critically placed in the Beckett canon, the text is incongruous; it is in English even as Beckett had committed himself to writing in French; its logical paradigms offer a challenge unlike that posed by any other text; and its "fossil remains" demand a special reading if anything is to be made of them. The Addenda constitute the most curious set of incongruities in an incongruous text; and they testify to a textual pre-history that makes the narrative assume a different shape when its evolution is considered. In my "Fatigue and Disgust" (1993), I argued that the Addenda of *Watt* preclude any possibility of a finished or determinate quality to the text; and that they constitute an enigma of the deepest kind: "fossil records that bear witness to earlier stages of creation, and which, like all the records of the rocks, pose insoluble problems for creationists"; a testament to a rich textual world that once was but no longer is. Several lustra later, I have no reason to change that opinion.

Like a landscape, a "text" is an uncertain entity, and the "reading" of it varies with those wandering over it. Yet reading is not an innocent activity, and textual experience (loss of the innocent eye) is a complex matter. A geologist will see in the surrounding rocks the eloquent testimony of the past, the layering and stratification that indicates the survival of different stages and eras of composition; an historian will sense the invisible presence of the past, the ghosts and fluxions that leave "traces" upon the present; and a writer will be aware that each and every phrase "calls" to other writers "in this long chain of consistence, a chain stretching from the long dead to the far unborn" (*Watt* 134). Christina Rossetti's "Remember me," for example, cannot escape the resonance of the final words of the ghost of Hamlet's father. Beckett "escaped" from English partly to avoid entrapment in the mesh of words and phrases woven by Shakespeare and Joyce; *Watt*, written in France but in English, is perhaps his farewell to the tradition he loved, but felt that he must forsake.

The cumulative effect of this argument is to suggest that a "reading" of *Watt* requires something more than other texts demand (or, perhaps, that this text exposes hermeneutical processes that in other works remain decently buried). I call such a reading, hesitantly, a "dianoetic" approach to the text, one that laughs at itself, to be sure, as it seeks the impossible, but one that asserts the pertinence of historical, geological, linguistic, literary, and evolutionary elements, inaccessible as these may be. Beckett could not have expected his readers to be aware of anything more than hints and intimations of earlier textual worlds and lost chords, but his inclusion of the Addenda testifies to an intention, one construed at risk. That a complete reading is impossible is beside the point (or, perhaps, is the point): the phenomena obnubilate the noumena; and even if Arsene's mystical experience is not an illusion he is "suggered" (as the galleys of *Watt* would have it) if he can understand how it could have been anything else (45). The scholarly consolation is that there is much to do in service of the text, and however futile that activity there are nevertheless occasional moments that make us feel, as when Watt hears Mr. Graves pronouncing "third " and "fourth" as "turd" and "fart" (143), that we are perhaps prostituting ourselves to some purpose. For is there not finally something of that sense of joy that Moran experiences on returning from his quest (*Molloy* 169), when he considers the language of bees, with rapture in the thought that here is something he can study all his life and never understand?

A Note on Methodology

My title is taken from *Watt*, and intimates the sentiment that "Obscure keys may open simple locks, but simple keys obscure locks never" (124); more prosaically, that the text will remain an enigma no matter how much explanatory context is advanced. The unstated hope is that the obscure keys may open the simple locks, and even some of the obscure ones. References to *Watt* are, by default, to the first Grove Press printing; but the nature of this exercise requires the frequent citation of other editions, notably the Olympia and Calder texts. My annotations are keyed to the Grove, but also [in square brackets] to the Calder, in turn the matrix of the Picador. Translations, if not otherwise specified, are my own. Cross-references are mostly in the form of **bold** numbers; references to *Watt* are often given as a bare, unbolded number; other texts (listed in the Bibliography) are cited by author's name or short title as seems most convenient. These measures are simply a matter of economy, as the process of reference is intensive. Round brackets are used for (normal) parentheses, but square brackets for authorial intrusions [mine], some cross-references (where ambiguity is a danger), and in my discussion of the drafts to distinguish something that is occurring at a different "level" of the evolutionary process. I use strikethroughs to indicate items crossed out on (as opposed to deleted from) the text; a double strike indicates a greater opacity. Quotations retain their original spelling and punctuation, which occasionally leads to the apparent incongruity of British and American usage in the one paragraph. I am reminded of John Cleese, at the height of the Clinton-Lewinsky affair, noting three matters of protocol that distinguish the British from the Americans: a common language, so that neither can understand the other; that when the British have a World Series they invite other nations; and that when greeting their head of state they go down on one knee only. As Watt observes (216), "It was an inferior cigar."

TITLE

Watt: earlier Quin, the *reductio* ("qui ne") of the interrogatives "who, what, where, by what means, why, in what way, when" (*quis, quid, ubi, quibis auxiliis, cur, quomodo, quando* [*qualis*]) listed on the first page of the first draft of what became *Watt* (before Quin/Knott assumed their later lineaments). First name unknown, the early "Johnny" long gone. The second, a monosyllable, invites reflection: the archaic verb, to *wat* (or *wot*), "to know"? Speculative. A wattman? Good point (**16.5**). A what-knot? Who knows? Swift's servant, Watt, who botched his master's wardrobe (Smith 38)? Ingrate. An anaglyph from Beckett's great matrix of "M"s ("W" an inverted "M")? Wow. Henry J. Watt (1879-1925), disciple of Oswald Külpe, who studied the associative reaction to report more experience from the period of preparation than that of actual reaction? Introspective. A measure of electrical current? Ample (**12.10**, **69.4**). The etymology, as Walter, Watkins, Watson, of "by the water" (Di Pierro 31), whence it follows that Watt's sign is Aquarius and he is attached to the fishwoman? Crrritic (but she was a Mrs. Piscoe). Arsene inquires: "I beg your pardon. Like Tyler? Haw!" (**48.2**); but has the grace not to say, "What?" (**18.2**). James Watt's steam-engine, ever near, was avoided until the French translation. The obvious, said Beckett, is always right: a basic morpheme articulates an elementary question: "What?"; to meet an impassible, inevitable answer: "[K]not." Out of such fundamental sounds Watt's frustrated quest to understand the mystery of his master, a center seeking its circle, assumes its ineluctable shape.

I

7.1 [5]: I: Beckett was concerned that the text be suitably indented, as the Olympia Press had given no indication of its proposed settings, and parts II, III, and IV in their galleys ran on without a break. He noted at the top of the first plate (G1): "Ch. 1: Commencer p. 7 avec 20 lignes - 38 lignes sur les autres pages." The numbers indicate the lines of type on the first (20) and subsequent (38) pages. Beckett did not insist on the change from Arabic to Roman numerals here, but noted on the inside back cover of his Olympia copy, "uniformly 'Haus!' (I)"; Roman figures throughout. The Olympia text is inconsistent: parts II, III, and IV have Roman figures, but part I retains an Arabic 1. The first Grove Press edition uses Roman throughout, but an anomaly appears in some reprints (e.g., the tenth), where part I is unnumbered.

7.2 [5]: Mr Hackett: in earlier drafts (NB1, 39ff; TS, 23ff), Hunchy Hackett, a "strange man," turns up during the night at the house of Mr. Quin (forerunner of Mr. Knott). His role was reduced until almost incidental, finally frustrating the reader's expectation that the prelude should bear some distinct relationship to the ensuing plot. The opening foreshadows what follows, in terms of what can be known, which is not much; but Mr. Hackett does not reappear, to the reader. The name suggests Francis Hackett (1883-1962), a minor Dublin writer of historical fiction (*Grove Companion* 242); perhaps the "Mr Hackett" of Joyce's *Portrait* (199). Büttner notes (117) that it echoes "Beckett."

7.3 [5]: It seemed to be occupied: the late draft (NB4, 177), a radical rewriting of the opening, reads: "It was occupied." Beckett's final writing embraced hundreds of similar small changes (such as the "of course" added in the next sentence and the multiple commas), often designed to provoke a tension between what *is* and what *seems*.

7.4 [5]: He knew they were not his: the Olympia text omitted "they," an error continuing into Grove but silently corrected on reprinting; however, the error persists into Calder. Either way, the challenge to logic in the following conditional clause is disconcerting.

7.5 [5]: Yes, it was not vacant: a deliberate contradiction, as in the popular song: "Yes, We Have No Bananas" (1923).

7.6 [5]: the dilemma: the "extreme simplicity" (compare Buridan's ass) is belied by Beckett's poem "Dieppe" (1937), which dramatizes a like moment of choice and was later incorporated into *Watt* (**40.5**). This, the first such dilemma in the novel, offers the fundamental paradigm of logical, almost dehumanized choice (but not all possible choices) that characterizes the others.

8.1 [6]: he could have touched it with his stick: as Stephen Dedalus in the "Proteus" chapter of *Ulysses*, to verify its existence. The stick for Malone exemplifies the problem of self-extension, as at the outset of Schopenhauer's *World as Will and Idea*, of the body in immediate or intermediate relationship to the self and with respect to the space through which it moves (*Grove Companion* 542). See **32.2**, **82.1**, **144.3**, and **158.4**.

8.2 [6]: for the tram, for a tram: the grammatical and existential distinction between the definite and indefinite articles reflects that between the particular and the type (**96.2**).

8.3 [6]: the plethoric reflexive pronoun after *say*: the excessive or unnecessary addition of "to himself," as in the French construction, "se dit"; implying, Ruby Cohn suggests (*Canon* 121) that "some of the avalanche of *said*s in the novel may be mental rather than vocal." Yet, as David Hesla has noted (188), the reflexive structure of consciousness constitutes the "self" as "the reflecting-reflected dyad," and to that extent the omission of the pronoun entails an absence of that quality, or process. Here, as frequently in the final text, the manuscript "thought" (NB4, 179) or another verb has given way to an impassible "said." Compare *Watt* (134, 158). As Kenner notes (37), such details urge on us "the physical book, a typographical artifact which is somehow 'about' its own existence." Indeed; but such reasoning can be excessive, as witness Mathew Winston's contention, on the dubious evidence of this first footnote, that the entire text is Sam's creation, and that Watt (hence, *a fortiori*, Knott) is pure invention.

8.4 [6]: What a shame: as in *Candide*'s "Che sciagura d'essere senza coglioni" ["Oh what a shame, to be without balls"], uttered by the eunuch confronted by the impenetrable beauty of Counégard. See **85.7** and **#35** for like echoes, and for the words originally sung by Erskine and Watt when making Quin's poss. The French "Quel dommage" (8) loses this innuendo. The abrupt break first entered the late draft (NB4, 181) (**238.1**).

9.1 [6]: as God is my witness: Romans 1:9: "For God is my witness." God as a witness that [not "who"] cannot be sworn is not in the drafts, but finally becomes a refrain. Compare John 5:31, the words of Christ: "If I bear witness of myself, my witness is not true." Beckett marked in his copy of Proust: "Dieu m'est témoin que j'ai sincèrement voulu" (*Swann* II.103); Madame Verdurin wishes to bring Odette up "dans un atmosphère plus noble et plus pure," but admits, "la patience humaine a des bournes."

9.2 [6-7]: The policeman replied briefly to this: not in the early drafts; but improving on his "Community how are you . . . a fat lot the likes of you cares for the community" (NB4, 181); Mr. Hackett threatens to have him up before the Commissioner. In *Murphy* (42), the dogberry is a Civic Guard; here, like Flann O'Brien's third policeman, he is more of a British bobby, a detail that helps place the text in the mythological present (**56.3**).

9.3 [7]: from the loving: in the late draft (NB4, 181), "from the recent encounter." For the act itself, compare the couple in silhouette (*Malone Dies* 238): "they must be loving each other, that must be how it is done."

9.4 [7]: his hunch protruded: the first mention of the deformity. Mr. Hackett's pose is that of Punch, who has curious encounters with a policeman; but in the middle distance is the twisted figure, small and acerbic, of Giacomo Leopardi.

9.5 [7]: the last trams pass. oh not the last: Grove Press corrected Olympia's "past," overlooked in the galleys (G1), but introduced an erroneous period. This remained in all Grove printings but was corrected by Beckett for the Calder edition. The error was a consequence of "oh not the last, but almost," which is not in the late draft (NB4, 183).

9.6 [7]: the still canal: Dublin's Grand Canal: the setting of "Enueg I," the landscape ugly, the stillborn evening filthy green; the backdrop of the finale of *Mercier and Camier*.

9.7 [7]: greens and yellows: emblematic of the decay of nature, the emerald in its sere, as in *Mercier and Camier* (109): "the pretty colours, expiring greens and yellows vaguely speaking: they grow paler and paler but only the better to pierce you, will they die, yes they will" (*Grove Companion* 236). Compare the "green tulips" of "Enueg II," the "aerugo" sky of "Ding-Dong" (38), insistent greens and yellows in *Murphy*, and the "unpleasant yellow colour" of Watt's moon (**30.3**). The common source is the "green and yellow melancholy" of *Twelfth Night* (II.iv.116). Watt's greatcoat (218) was once green and his hat yellow; now the coat is yellow and the hat green.

9.8 [7]: a gentleman . . . a lady: a curious decorum, in that "gentleman" and "lady" are used until the lady reveals (13) that they are respectively "Goff" and "Tetty"; after which these Christian names are used invariably, until Goff insists that his name is Nixon (18); whereafter "Mr Nixon" and "Mrs Nixon" are used consistently. Mary Bryden suggests (*Idea of God* 165) the conjunction of Ger. *nichts* ("nothing") and Gk. *on* ("being"). The late draft (NB4, 191ff) attests to Beckett's intention ("~~gentleman~~" and "~~lady~~" crossed out; "Goff" and "Tetty" written in). The shabby gentility is not unlike that reported by Miss Reynolds in Birkbeck Hill's *Johnson Miscellanies* (II.288-89), a conversation between Samuel Johnson, a Gentleman, and a Lady.

10.1 [7]: not having the force: in the late draft (NB4, 183) "strength"; the change accentuating the French expression, as in the opening of Flaubert's *Bouvard et Pécuchet*, whose eponymous heroes cannot rise (from a bench), "n'en ayant pas la force." *Watt*'s narrator (141-42) laments the unconsummated amours of Watt and the fishwoman: "That he who has the time should lack the force, that she who has the force should lack the time." In the French text (10), the word lacks the resistance of its English equivalent.

10.2 [8]: stroke his hunch: a token of good luck added after the late draft (NB4, 184). If Malone needed a hunchback one would come running, "proud as punch" (*Malone Dies* 180) (**9.4**); but he will soon be abandoned, in the dark, without anyone to play with.

10.3 [8] the outer world: the action to follow, like that of *Murphy*, intimates a retreat from the Big World of contingency to the little world of the mind, which may not prove sustenant (for Watt it does not). Compare Paul Valéry's M. Teste (*Grove Companion* 602); Mr. Hackett and Watt share a literary ancestry with this denizen of the mind, but Watt is finally incapable of minimizing outward circumstances and accepting life as a process that is merely *facultative* (**19.5, 32.7**). In comparison, then, Mr. Hackett has accommodated himself more successfully to the outer world.

11.1 [8]: the primeur: in French, *avoir la primeur de*, "to be the first to hear of"; "les primeurs" are the first fruits of the season. Added to the late draft (NB4, 185).

11.2 [9]: TO NELLY: the opening line reads in the early drafts (NB1, 14, 16; TS, 7) "sweet Nymph." The lovesick writer, Grehan, earlier Green, is a piano tuner (**72.1**), in the wars a lance-corporal and later simple private (NB1, 15); also a fiddler when the Palestinian Retriever is bred with the Irish Setter (**111.1**). He addresses his (unfinished) lines to "Anthea" [*sic*]; compare Richard Lovelace (1618-57), Cavalier poet and lover of Honour More. Beckett has conflated "To Lucasta, Going to the Wars" with "To Althea, from Prison"; both are mentioned in his English literature notes (TCD 10970, 18r). Lovelace is a model for Grehan's first stanza, the poem thereafter becoming more demented. In a draft for the French translation (Ohio, NBI), Beckett called it a "madrigal"; on the typescript (Ohio TS, 3) "Grehan" reverts to "Green." This difficult rendition appears at the end of the drafts (Ohio, NBVI), the final version dated

"Ussy 6.2.68." A tangential note: the Irish actor, James Quin (**20.3**), claimed that his mother was Nell Gwynne.

11.3 [9]: *Jug-jug! Jug-jug!*: the nightingale; not Keats's immortal bird, pouring forth its soul in ecstasy, but rather (via Eliot's *The Waste Land*) an Elizabethan emblem of adulterous betrayal ("nightingale" a metaphor for streetwalker). Eliot echoes Trico's song from John Lyly's *Campaspe* V.i.32-36, the "prick song" of Philomela:

> *What Bird so sings, yet so dos wayle?*
> *O 'tis the rauish'd Nightingale.*
> *Iug, Iug, Iug, Iug, tereu, shee cryes,*
> *And still her woes at Midnight rise.*
> *Brave prick song.*

"Jug Jug" was added to the early drafts (NB1, 16); "Towhit! Towhoo" the first refrain. The bird songs disappear from the French translation (11-12), which instead repeats the last phrase of each first line.

11.4 [9]: My wanton thoughts: compare Lovelace, "To Althea, from Prison" (lines 5-8): "When I lie tangled in her hair / And fettered to her eye, / The Gods that wanton in the air / Know no such liberty." The thoughts were originally "loving" (NB1, 14).

11.5 [9]: Byrne: after Deputy J. J. Byrne, the well-named Chairman of the Censorship of Publications Board in Ireland during the 1930s, "five fit and proper persons" responsible for the Register of Prohibited Publications on which Beckett's name had duly appeared (#465). Beckett's vitriolic (then unpublished) essay, "Censorship in the Saorstat" (1934), took aim at the attitude to sexuality and contraception. Byrne is described as having "burst his buttons" in defense of the common-sense man, arguing it was unnecessary to read the whole of a book (*Ulysses*) before passing judgment on it (*Grove Companion* 78). In the French translation (11), he becomes "Dunn" (echoing "donne").

11.6 [9]: Hyde: as in Douglas Hyde (1860-1949), scholar and politician; founder of the Young Ireland Society (1891) and Gaelic League (1893; a possible pun on "erst"); author of *Love Songs of Connacht* (1893); first Professor of Irish at UCD (1905); Free State Senator (1923-26); and first President of Ireland (1938-45). To Grehan, more Jekyll than Hyde. An early rough draft read: "palpates Hyde's hand amid her skirts" (NB1, 14). In the French translation (11) he becomes "Denis" (echoing "dénie").

11.7 [9]: Echo: intimating the Elizabethan echo-song, in which the love-sick swain pours out his passion to the surrounding hills and vales, which return his last words ("tomorrow . . . sorrow"). Spenser's "Epithalamium" (**12.8**) has some features of the echo song.

12.1 [9]: *Pu-we! Pu-we!*: cry of the piteous peewit, or lapwing (*Vanellus vanellus*).

12.2 [9]: *Cuckoo! Cuckoo!*: intimations of cuckoldry (laying its eggs in another's nest).

12.3 [10]: *Cupid's flow'r*: from *A Midsummer Night's Dream* IV.i.72-75, Oberon releasing Titania from the spell: "Be as thou wast wont to be; / See as thou wast wont to see; / Dian's bud o'er Cupid's flower / Hath such force and blessed power." Note the ambiguity of Grehan's "Upon discharge."

12.4 [10]: *hey nonny O*: Shakespeare's carefree lover and his lass: "With a hey, with a ho, with a hey-nonny-no" (*As You Like It* V.iii.16). Alternatively, the "hey nonny nonny" of *Much Ado about Nothing* (II.iii.32), Balthazar's song: "Sigh no more ladies, sigh no more / Men were deceivers ever."

12.5 [10]: Diana's blushing bud: Diana, or Artemis, goddess of the chase and chastity ("*in statu quo*"), foe to Cupid (**12.3**). The French text (12) lacks the Shakespearean ring: "Tu vas revoir sous la fleur d'Aphrodite / Le bouton d'Artémis fidèle au statu quo."

12.6 [10]: kindle: in the dual Elizabethan sense of igniting and giving birth.

12.7 [10]: *Tuwhit! Tuwhoo!*: the cry of the owl, companion in his misery to Job (30:29). Compare Robert Graves, "The Voice of Beauty Drowned": "How say the others all around? / Piercing and harsh, a maddened sound. / With *Pretty Poll, Tuwit - tuwoo / Peewit, Caw-caw, Cuckoo-cuckoo.*"

12.8 [10]: *Epithalamium*: a song "before the bridal door"; a wedding song. Edmund Spenser's instance (1595), the best-known, offered Beckett a part-model in its alternation of long and short rhyming lines. Beckett noted of Spenser's *Amoretti* and *Epithalamium*: "For his future wife Elizabeth Boyle. 'Maidenly' Spenser" (TCD 10970, 8r).

12.9 [10]: *Hymen*: son of Apollo and the muse, Clio; God of marriage and guardian of the marriage bed, on which his blessings he bestows. In his notes on English literature (TCD 10970, 8v), Beckett drew attention to Samuel Daniels's pastoral tragedy, "Hymen's Triumph" (1614), the lyrical interludes of which celebrate the joys of love.

12.10 [10]: Ample, said the lady: thus in the galleys, refining a witticism present from NB1 (16): "Enough" said McEvoy; and the typescript (7): "Enough" said Quin; to the late draft (NB4, 188): "More than enough" said the lady. A following line, "The spirit is exhausted, said the gentleman," was excised in the galleys (G2).

12.11 [10]: the night that Larry was born: echoing the 18th-century Irish ballad, "The Night before Larry was Stretched" (in the "Cyclops" chapter of *Ulysses*). The night before Larry dies, "the boys they all paid him a visit," to drink and play cards. In the late rewriting (NB4, 189), Larry was perhaps ~~Arthur~~ [crossed out, obscure] and the phrasing innocent: "the evening before

~~Arthur~~ was born." Larry, for Beckett, is short for Lazarus, either the beggar received into Abraham's bosom (Luke 16:22-26) or the dead man raised by Christ, one who compounds the crime of having been born by returning to life.

13.1 [10]: How old is Larry now: that Larry's forty years is roughly Beckett's age at the time of writing is obvious; yet what follows reflects Beckett's insistence that he could recollect the experience of his own birth (**13.5**, **101.3**).

13.2 [10]: D.V.: *Deo volante*, "God willing." Mr. Hackett's "Dee always vees" improves on his earlier "God always permits" (NB4, 189).

13.3 [11]: Tetty: Samuel Johnson's endearment to his much older wife, Elizabeth.

13.4 [11]: Cream and Berry: a pseudo-couple, complementary characters, as Neary and Wylie, Mercier and Camier (to whom the Unnamable [409] applies the term), Molloy and Moran [perhaps], or Vladimir and Estragon. And, maybe, Knott and Watt. See **101.7**, **102.4**, and **103.2**. "Berry" was earlier (NB1, 37; TS, 25) "Sparrow" and the duck a goose, which does not explain "what had become of the duck" (*Watt* 80). One Cream, "father of the judge," appears in *The Old Tune* (177), Beckett's 1963 adaptation of Robert Pinget's *La Manivelle*; Cream's companion, Gorman, mentions a Molly Berry (187). Knowlson identifies his original (333) as "a heavily built old man" who lived at Killiney.

13.5 [11]: leaped in my wom: in Luke 1:41, when Elisabeth heard Mary's salutation, "the babe leaped in her womb." Early drafts (NB1, 37; TS, 27) read "womb,"; the change ("wom~~b~~") occurs in the late draft (NB4, 191). Beckett told Peggy Guggenheim that he retained a terrible memory of his mother's womb; Bair comments (328), echoing a letter to Arland Ussher (26 March 1937), that Beckett's memories began with a dinner party given by his father, at which his mother presided. The episode shapes Quin's first memories of his "journey towards the light of day" (**#20**). The French text reads (13): "trice," as in "matrice" ["umbilical cord"]; this was Ludovic Janvier's suggestion (Janvier 58).

13.6 [11]: to leap, like a salmon: compare "lepping" in "Dante and the Lobster" (18); and the protagonist's reaction in *First Love* (44) to Anna's pregnancy: "if it's lepping . . . it's not mine." Leixlip ("Salmon-leap") on the upper Liffey near Lucan is the scene of Nemo's suicide-leap in *Dream* (182). The simile was a final addition; the late draft (NB4, 195) reads "bound."

13.7 [11]: dollar: imitating the French *doleur* (Beer 53); in earlier drafts (NB1, 37; TS, 27), "unspeakable anguish"; the change was made on the late draft (NB4, 191), the crass rendered crasser. The French text (13) says simply, "ces labours."

14.1 [11]: osy: in early drafts (NB1, 37), *osé*, "daring"; the change made on the typescript (29). A "roly-poly" is a sponge cake spread with jam, rolled into a log, and sprinkled with icing sugar. The French text reads (14): "Pas trop gallois" [Welsh].

14.2 [11]: not only in the mouth: compare Groucho Marx's reply to the lady who said she had ten children because she loved her husband: "Madame, I love my cigar. But I do not keep it in my mouth all the time."

14.3 [12]: liquors: you know, *liqueurs*.

14.4 [12]: the groaning board: the table; an epithet magnificently transferred.

14.5 [12]: slosh: in *Murphy* (168) snooker, a hypomanic teaching a Korsakow's syndrome. The pool table, an image of the Newtonian universe, of mechanical worlds in collision, here intimates an incongruous fiasco. Although the French text (14) reads "snooker," billiards is implied (**15.3**, **15.4**). Ruby Cohn's deep *Canon* off the cush (121): "where, resembling copulation, balls are potted," invokes the nervous professional on his wedding night, who, reassured by his best man that it was just like snooker, chalked his cue but hesitated too long, torn between the pink and the brown.

14.6 [12]: a scissors: Mr. Knott's discarded garments include a knickerbockers and a pant (**100.2**); Beckett is perhaps disputing with Joyce (*Portrait* 231) that "a ballocks" is the only surviving instance of the English dual.

15.1 [12]: found under a cabbage: how children come into the world, the French "dans un chou" equivalent to the English "under a gooseberry bush." Compare Mr. Hackett's earlier: "I know what it feels like for the child" (NB4, 195).

15.2 [13]: Professor Cooper: a cooper is a barrel-maker, one who puts bands around them. The name suggests the Reverend William M. Cooper, otherwise James Glass Bertram, compiler of *Flagellation and the Flagellants* (1869), "a true History of the Rod as an instrument for correctional purposes in the Church, the State and the Family" (*Grove Companion* 111), as drawn on by Beckett in "Sanies II" and *Dream*. This was a final change, the late draft (NB4, 195) replacing "~~Lyster~~" with "White."

15.3 [13]: a long thin jenny: in billiards, a losing hazard in which the object ball lies near the cushion and inside a line joining the cue ball to the adjacent pocket. It is a long jenny when played into a corner pocket from the other end of the table; a short jenny when played into a middle pocket. In "What a Misfortune" (118), Belacqua's pursuit of Thelma bboggs is like "a long losing jenny down the whirlpool of a pocket."

15.4 [13]: the black of all balls: billiards is played with three balls: a white cue ball; a white object ball with a black dot; and a black ball. Cream is attempting not to sink the black (which would then be out of play, whereas the white dot if sunk may be replaced) but to go in off the black, a trickier shot. His "queue" was earlier a "cue" (NB4, 195).

15.5 [13]: augmented radiance: compare "Rough for Theatre II" (84), where A looks at the sky: "And to think all that is nuclear combustion. All that faerie."

15.6 [13]: protuberances: compare Garrick on Tetty Johnson (Boswell, *Life* I 99): "very fat, with a bosom of more than ordinary protuberance." Tetty Nixon offers the kind of sentiment that Beckett defined in the Whoroscope Notebook (22) as: "The giveaway of excessive affability to the hideous and infirm." Mr. Hackett's "Yes" is thus a subtle corrective, not a further bizarre self-indulgence.

15.7 [13]: the Glencullen Hacketts: Glencullen is in the Dublin hills, close to Foxrock. The first draft (NB1, 41) reads "Rathcullen," the change to "Glen" appears in the typescript (31). To the inquiry of Barry McGovern, whose mother was a Hackett, Beckett replied that the Glencullen Hacketts were fictive (Barry McGovern to CA).

15.8 [13]: I fell off the ladder: Mr. Hackett's physical "accident" anticipates Arsene's metaphysical sense of "existence off the ladder" (**44.7**, **44.8**), and translates into mundane terms (his deformity) the mystical conceit of falling from the *scala perfectionis* by which the soul ascends to God.

16.1 [14]: Prince William's Seat: the highest point between Glencullen and Glencree in the Wicklow hills, a bleak, furze-covered summit crowned by large flat rocks (*Grove Companion* 456). O'Brien (353) derives the name from the "Coronation Plantation" of William IV. Mr. Hackett's father is breaking stones in one of the many quarries there at Queen Victoria's command. Quin's house is "made of granite, wrest from the neighbouring mountains" (TS, 81). The distant clink of stonecutters' hammers is heard in *Malone Dies* (206, 286) and *First Love* (44).

16.2 [14]: the goat: image of the preterite, of those passed over by the Good Shepherd. Added to the late rewriting (NB4, 196v) to match the goat that appears at the end of the novel (**223.3**), as Watt passes by for the last time.

16.3 [14]: The pub, or the chapel, or both: in the early drafts (NB1, 43; TS, 32), it being his birthday, Mr. Hackett's mother had slipped out to say a prayer (or light a candle) for him in the chapel, and to drink a glass to his health in Johnny Fox's pub.

16.4 [14]: Night is now falling fast: compare the evening hymn, "Now the Day is Over" (**57.1**). A pre-publication "Extract from *Watt*," in *Envoy* 1.2 (January 1950): 16-24, begins with this scene and ends as darkness closes in (*Watt* 24). *Envoy* was a short-lived (1949-50) Dublin monthly; in a letter to its editor, John Ryan (15 December 1949), Beckett restored his punctuation which (he said) he still preferred "to that of your compositor"; adding that it was "important (for me) that this text should not be inflicted with inverted commas." See **18.2**, **20.1**, and **21.1**.

16.5 [14]: a tram: motion combined with inevitability, as Watt's passage through the novel. Compare one of Beckett's favorite limericks, by Maurice E. Hare (Harvey 242):

> *There was a young man who said, "Damn!*
> *I suddenly see what I am,*
> *A creature that moves*
> *In predestined grooves—*
> *In fact, not a bus but a tram."*

A "wattman" (as "Puncher and Wattman" of Lucky's speech in *Waiting for Godot*) is one who changes the points, to allow trams and trains to change direction. As Ruby Cohn notes (*Canon* 113), a journey is an old metaphor for life, and both the novel and Watt's significant life within it are bounded by terminals.

16.6 [14]: a man or a woman: echoing Eliot's *The Waste Land* (lines 364-66): "I do not know / If it is a man or a woman / But who is that who passes by." See **225.2**. The "solitary figure" in the drafts (NB4, 199) was scarcely distinguished from the dim wall behind "him" (rather than "it"). Compare Watt's coming to his going (245).

16.7 [14]: a roll of tarpaulin: a heavy waterproofed material, typically tarred canvas, used for roofing and weather-proofing; compare Mrs. Rooney in "All That Fall" (25). For Watt's greatcoat, see **217.4**.

17.1 [14]: Watt: unlike the Nixons (**9.8**), Watt is named immediately, which raises questions about narrative perspective; Mr. Hackett asks for and is told the name (18), but Beckett chooses not to play the same game.

17.2 [15]: an expression that we shall not record: in the late draft (NB4, 201), Mr. Hackett wishes to know whether it is "A male or a female one."

17.3 [15]: five shillings, that is to say, six and ninepence: Watt offers four shillings and fourpence; Mr. Hackett deduces that he owes "only two and threepence." The figures do not add up, and so challenge the reader's sense of logic. The French text (17) retains the British currency. The situation can be "explained": over seven years, simple interest at 5 percent would improve 5/- to precisely 6/9; were Watt to repay 4/4 he would have paid off the accumulated interest of 1/9, and reduced the principal by 2/7, leaving a debt of 2/5 (Mr. Hackett's "only two and threepence" teases). During those seven years the only item that the text acknowledges Watt having bought, from a one-legged man, is a boot. Watt requires only one, since he has found, on the seashore, a shoe, stiff with brine but otherwise shipshape. The boot cost eightpence (219), the precise deficiency of the original loan. The logic is impeccable ("Summo, ergo sum"), but the absurdity remains.

17.4 [15]: he is setting out on a journey: with the overtones of a spiritual quest, but one doomed to failure, for Watt learns nothing by his experience. His subsequent report to Sam, its sentences inverted, in the asylum that becomes his refuge, his journey's end, mocks that of the hero who brings enlightenment to those to whom he returns (**166.1**). More literally, Goff says that if he takes the money Watt could not buy his train ticket.

17.5 [15]: the best thing for him: echoing the sentiment, that it were better never to have been born. Beckett copied the tag: "Optimum non nasci, aut cito mori" ["best is not to be born, or to die quickly"] into the Whoroscope Notebook (85v, the final entry), and deployed it frequently (*Grove Companion* 62).

18.1 [16]: the bridge: the Charlemont Street Bridge that crosses the Grand Canal south of Harcourt Street Station. Watt is traveling not from the center of Dublin but from the south, since he gets off before the bridge, which he must cross to reach the station. He gets off opposite Mr. Hackett and the Nixons. As this must be the left side of the street (for this is Ireland), it follows that the three observers, said to be "on the far side of the street" (16), are sitting on the east side of Charlemont Street, looking west. Hence Goff's comment (15) about the northwestern skies, the silhouette of Watt against the last wisps of day (18), and Mr. Hackett's final view of the sky (24). Mr. Hackett's seat, then, can be precisely located on Charlemont Street, just south of the Canal and east of the bridge.

18.2 [16]: You haven't told us his name: in the pre-publication "Extract from *Watt*" (13) in *Envoy* (**16.4**), when Mr. Hackett asks this, Mr. Nixon says, "Watt" ["What?"]; in a handwritten insert on the manuscript of *Envoy* (3), question and answer are repeated. Here, the jest is that the obvious joke is not made.

18.3 [16]: a period when I did not: anticipating Arsene (**57.4**, **57.5**) about the coming and abiding of Mr. Knott.

19.1 [16]: He is gone: Mrs. Nixon elects the French *passé composé*.

19.2 [17]: I think of him: a narrative suggestion (a) of the affinity between Mr. Hackett and Watt, implying (b) that the reader's understanding, or failure to understand, Mr. Hackett will anticipate a like understanding, or failure to understand, Watt.

19.3 [17]: That depends where he got on, said Mr Nixon: a line inadvertently omitted from the Olympia edition, though present in the galleys (G5); added by hand to Beckett's personal copy and to one given to Aidan Higgins; restored in the first Grove printing.

19.4 [17]: the terminus: the central terminus of the Dublin United Tramways was near Nelson's Pillar, O'Connell Street; but Watt is coming from the other direction, on a line from one of the south-central suburbs such as Clonskea, Rathgar, Upper Rathmines, or Harold's Cross. This unwarranted speculation is provoked by the textual insistence as to where he could have got on (we will never know). The curious contract Beckett makes with his reader often rewards but sometimes frustrates such inquiry.

19.5 [17]: a merely facultative stop: Fr. *arrêt facultatif*, a stop by request only. The detail was added as an insert to the late draft (NB4, 204), and is retained in the French translation (19). Beckett used the word in a letter to

Thomas MacGreevy (18 October, 1932) of two poems ("Serena I" and "Serena II") that "did not represent a necessity." Mr. Nixon's impeccable demonstration that the request must have come from Watt does not explain why Watt has chosen to get off here nor why the conductor's voice is raised in anger; if such simple matters are inexplicable, what chance, then, of understanding the greater mystery of Watt's relation with Knott?

19.6 [17]: the station: Harcourt Street Station, the city terminus [the round end] of the Dublin and South Eastern Railway (the "Slow and Easy") to Bray [the square end]; Beckett's regular mode of travel between his Foxrock home and the city. Its "pretty neo-Doric colonnade" is recalled in "Text 7"; but the old man in *That Time*, returning (as Beckett did in 1950) to the folly of his youth, finds the terminus "all closed down and boarded up" (231), the colonnade crumbling. The last train departed 31 December 1958, after which the line was closed and the tracks torn out (O'Brien 220, 371).

20.1 [18]: the driver: the French translation cannot resist (20): "le wattman" (**16.5**); in the *Envoy* manuscript (5), "wattman" replaces "~~driver~~" (**16.4**).

20.2 [18]: turn the other cheek: the words of Christ (Matthew 5:39): "whosoever shall smite thee on thy right cheek, turn to him the other also." Consider George Frederic Watts's equestrian statue, *Physical Energy*, mentioned in *Murphy* (152); the unit of energy is, of course, the *watt*.

20.3 [18]: fast asleep in Quin's Hotel: the rhythm intimates, "fast asleep in Abraham's bosom"; the rhyme, Wynn's Hotel (Lower Abbey Street). Quin was the early protagonist of *Watt*, the name implying "quin" or "qui ne," negative intentionality, with a suggestion of the Irish actor, James Quin (1693-1766). Quin appears in several texts: "Echo's Bone's" (21), his "happy expressions"; *Mercier and Camier* (119), "someone who does not exist"; and *Malone Dies* (251), having passed on to Malone his "flannel" (woolen singlet). The Saxon tells Lemuel that he has "Dreamt all night of that bloody man Quin again" (*Malone Dies* 282); in *Malone meurt* this appears in English, as it does (152) in the Spanish original of Augusto Roa Bastos, *Yo el Supremo* (1974).

21.1 [19]: the accoutrement: the outfit; awkward in English, but more natural in French (21). The galleys (G5) had "accowtrement" [*sic*], which Beckett left; the correct spelling in the late draft (NB4, 209) suggests an error, not an affectation, but the use of the "w" form in the *Envoy* extract (**16.4**) was sanctioned by Beckett who wrote to the editor, John Ryan (15 December 1949): "'Accowterment' [*sic*] is intentionally misspelt." Neither Olympia nor Grove (nor *Envoy*) took note; the Calder text reads: "his accoutrement." Moran and Macmann use the word (*Molloy* 124; *Malone Dies* 258). Johnson's Dictionary has it as a synonym for "equipment," in the entry following "equidependency" (**31.1**).

21.2 [19]: the frigid machinery of a time-space relation: that is, he leaves it to chance. The phrasing echoes, distantly, Stephen Dedalus's description of the "spiritual-heroic refrigerating apparatus" of Dante (*Portrait* 252).

21.3 [19]: a native of the rocks: the late draft (NB4, 211) crossed out "island" for "place"; the galleys (G6) read "rocks." The French translation (22) adds: "Monsieur Hackett n'avait pas lu ses *Eglogues* pour rien." The source is identical, a letter to Lord Chesterfield (7 February 1755), in which Johnson's rejection of Chesterfield's belated offer of patronage finds curious phrasing: "The shepherd in Virgil grew at last acquainted with Love, and found him a native of the rocks"; the image, rather than the words, is from Virgil's first *Eclogue*. Before his 1936 visit to Germany, Beckett translated this letter into German, the phrase reading: "ein Felsenkind zu finden" (BIF 5003, 47).

22.1 [20]: the last flowers: "Enueg II" and *Dream* (28) depict the green tulips of evening as an incongruous, even unnatural beauty (**9.7**).

22.2 [21]: he touched you: that is, he borrowed money; yet one of several (truthful, gentle, strange) intimations of Christ.

23.1 [21]: who . . . what . . . how . . . where: Mrs. Nixon is unaware that her rhetorical despair echoes the classical categories ("quis, quid, ubi, quibis auxiliis, cur, quomodo, quando [qualis]") from which her very world arose (see my Addendum 2), the elements of *memoria technica* by which any subject can be divided into all possible parts for analysis, or by the application of which disputation can be indefinitely extended.

23.2 [21]: a boot: the galleys (G6) record the change of "shoe" to "boot," in accordance with the later "explanation" (**219.1**) as to why only one is needed. The boot cost 8d, which is perhaps why Watt retains 4/4 (**17.3**).

23.3 [21]: the sun to go down on the least hint of an estrangement: Ephesians 4:26: "let not the sun go down on your wrath."

23.4 [22]: milk: Watt's galactophilia reflects Robert Burton's contention (*Anatomy* 1.2.2.i, 142), that "Milk increaseth melancholy." In the *Dream Notebook* (#539), Beckett recorded from Giles, *Civilisation of China* (173-74): "A bottlenosed man may be a teetotaller." Consider, fleetingly, the anagram of JOHN MILK, otherwise H_2O.

24.1 [22]: Now it was quite dark: compare the ending of *Mercier and Camier* (122), where, alone, Mercier watches the sky go out, its last throes engulfed, with a Miltonic sense of "Dark at its full" (123). As Cohn comments (*Canon* 120), Mr. Hackett's last word is "What?"—the question that Watt never asks.

24.2 [22]: Watt bumped into a porter: the text from here until "there were no crusts in Watt's nose, tonight" (*Watt* 39) was included in John Calder's 1967 *A Samuel Beckett Reader* (41-53). Lucky was once conceived by Beckett as a station porter.

24.3 [22]: The devil raise a hump on you: one thinks (D.V.) of Mr. Hackett (**19.2**); but there is an echo of the "Hades" chapter of *Ulysses*, Reuben J. Dodd's "The devil break the hasp of your back" (Pat McCarthy to CA).

25.1 [23]: Watt's smile: see **27.5**.

25.2 [23]: Mr Lowry: not mentioned in the later draft (NB4, 219), nor elsewhere; any significance in the name (the painter, L. S. Lowry?) remains uncertain.

25.3 [23]: his warm nest: Harvey notes (358) the embryonic overtones of this image. O'Brien describes (350) the newspaper stall as the focal point of the Harcourt Street Station, papers delivered from it to the first-class carriages. The newsagent's moustache anticipates that of Moran (*Molloy* 119), another of unusual acerbity.

26.1 [24]: Watt's hat: the late draft, "Yes, it was his" (NB4, 221) became "Was it possible that this was his hat," the question mark deleted (until Calder "restored" it). Unlike Murphy, who never wears a hat as it awakes poignant memories of the caul (*Murphy* 73), or Molloy, who is attached to his (*Molloy* 11), Watt seems indifferent to such insignia (**56.2**). The incident intimates Descartes's first precept in the *Méthode* (**26.6**, **27.4**, **29.13**): "De ne rien recevoir pour vrai qu'il ne connût être tel évidemment" ["To accept as true nothing that he did not know to be so clearly and distinctly"] (Baillet 12). The German Diaries record (II.53): "Hard hat = <u>steifer Hut</u>, <u>melon</u> or <u>Hartmann</u>"; Watt's hat is later called a "block hat" (**218.5**), but the French translation prefers "melon."

26.2 [24]: his bicycle: as Kenner notes (117), bicycles pass before Watt at the beginning and end of his transit (one is discharged, 245, for a Miss Walker). Like the Cartesian centaur of Beckett's early works, the image of the man carrying the bicycle up and down the stairs has a distinct irony. The bicycle intimates (like the tram) an essential dualism of man and machine.

26.3 [24]: Mr Staunton's handbook: the *Chess Player's Handbook* (1847), by Howard Staunton (1810-74), went through twenty-two editions and taught thousands the basics of the game. Staunton was the leading player of his day, though his avoiding Paul Morphy compromised that claim. Beckett inherited from his father a set of Staunton chessmen, later stolen from Ussy.

26.4 [24]: Evans: not in the late drafts (NB4, 221); but compare Boswell (*Life* II, 209), Goldsmith's apology for beating one Evans, a bookseller. See also **28.1**.

26.5 [24]: Watt . . . got into the train: no indication has been given of its presence (being at the round end [**244.2**], it need not "arrive"), just as no indication will be given of Watt's departure (**245.2**).

26.6 [24]: He is sorting the cans, said Watt: in accordance with Descartes's second precept in the *Méthode* (**26.1**, **27.4**, **29.13**): "De deviser les choses le plus qu'il serait possible pour les mieux résoudre" ["To divide difficulties into as many parts as possible, the better to understand them"] (Baillet 12). Cohn notes (*Canon* 115) the oddity of Watt's deduction, given that the porter has just knocked him down.

26.7 [24]: a punishment for disobedience: as Sisyphus, once King of Corinth, who had attacked travelers with a large stone and defied the gods, and whose punishment in Hades was to roll uphill a large marble block that always rolled back. Beckett tells his story in the Whoroscope Notebook (32), and his early notes from Otto Rank, *The Trauma of Birth* (TCD 10971/8, 36), include: "Punishments representing primal situations, with stress on painful aspects. Ixion his 4-spoked wheel; Tantalos [*sic*] on wheel, threatened with stone, eternally tortured by hunger & thirst; Sisyphus, for ever rolling back the stone; Christ, the spokes of the wheel bearing the cross." This is the immediate source of the references to Ixion and Tantalus in *Murphy* (21). The detail was present in the drafts of *Watt* before Beckett read Camus's "Le Mythe de Sisyphe" (1942), to which Moran alludes (*Molloy* 133): "But I do not think even Sisyphus is required to scratch himself, or to groan, or to rejoice, as the fashion is now" (*Grove Companion* 529).

26.8 [25]: his back to his destination: Hesla suggests (62) an echo of Dante's *Inferno* (XX), where the sorcerers and diviners have their heads twisted round so that they cannot see where they are going, but only where they have been. A better (more bizarre) reason is suggested by Beckett's notes from Rank's *The Trauma of Birth* (TCD 10971/8, 35): "Dream of travelling: such details as missing the train, packing & not being ready, losing luggage, etc, so painfully realised in the dream, can be understood only when one interprets the departure as meaning <u>separation from the mother</u>, & the luggage as symbolising the womb, which as we know is replaced by all kinds of vehicles. Forward movement in the dream is to be interpreted as regressive. Cp. disinclination of many persons to travel with their backs to the engine, & <u>sortir les pieds en devant</u>." To be taken with a large grain of salt (Watt has little luggage), but the point is made, twice, that Watt has his back to the engine, and the large gentleman sitting diagonally opposite indeed rests his feet on the wooden seat "before" him. The detail is taken up, with mockery, in *Mercier and Camier*, in the train with Madden (40), where Mercier sits with his back to the engine; and by the Unnamable (406), who queries "the meaning of your back to the engine" (Matthew Feldman to CA).

27.1 [25]: The compartment then was not so empty: the apparition of Mr. Spiro is uncannily like that of Herr Silbermann in a novel that Beckett was unlikely to have read, Vladimir Nabokov's *The Real Life of Sebastian Knight* (1941). The coincidence, while striking (*Murphy* 26), is presumably accidental, as is the oddity of the note from Rank's *The Trauma of Birth* immediately after the "Dream of travelling" (**26.8**): "Spermatozoa dream (Silberer), regression to spermarium" (TCD 10971/8, 35). The serial world plays curious tricks on occasion.

27.2 [25]: Mr Spiro: a name deriving from the classical tag, *dum spiro spero* ["while I breathe I hope"]; indeed, a "dumb" sentiment, given Genesis 3:19: "for dust thou art, and unto dust shalt thou return," as implicit in "anagram of mud." This bright and cheerful sentiment was added as a later inset (NB4, 222v). The French text (28) adds an awkward footnote: "Mot anglais signifant à peu près boue." Beer cites this (60) as evidence of how one frame of reference (French) can create ambiguity in another (English, or Latin). Pilling suggests a sentiment cited in the *Dream Notebook* (#721) from the Preface to the *Anatomy of Melancholy*: "parvus sum nullus sum altum nec spiro nec spero"; in Burton's paraphrase: "I am insignificant, a nobody, with little ambition and small prospects."

27.3 [25]: he began with the essential: that is, the name, by which the mind can classify phenomena (Robinson 116). Beckett used "the essential and the incidental" to review Sean O'Casey's *Windfalls* (1934) in *The Bookman* 87 (Christmas 1934): 111; the phrase hints at the Nominalist/Realist controversy, the Nominalist "essence" being the name and "less important matters" the incidentals. Beckett cites O'Casey's point that the essential and the incidental are not inimical to each other, since the latter facilitates "a definition of the former" (*Grove Companion* 183); but this reconciliation he did not often admit. He believed, rather, that the mind at best might grasp the straws and flotsam of existence (incidentals), but that the rationalist attempt to derive from these any sense of allegory (the essential) was the "last form of animism" (German Diaries 4, 15 January 1937).

27.4 [25]: one after the other, in an orderly way: not only will Watt try to understand Mr. Knott's essence from his accidents (**27.3**), but, worse, he will observe the third precept of Descartes's *Méthode* (**26.1**, **26.6**, **29.13**): "De conduire ses pensées par ordre en commencant par les objets les plus simples pour monter par dégré jusqu'à la connaissance des plus composées" ["To order his thoughts beginning with the most simple and rising step by step to the knowledge of the more complex"] (Baillett 12).

27.5 [25]: Watt's smile: compare Belacqua's smile as "a mere question of muscular control" ("Dante and the Lobster" 18). On the last page of his third Johnson notebook Beckett wrote in large letters: "Johnson's 'ghastly smile' Hill's <u>B</u> V. 48 N. 1." This refers to George Birkbeck Hill's annotations to Boswell's *Life* (vol. 5, 48, n1): "the sneer of Johnson's ghastly smile," which, Hill adds, is "borrowed from *Paradise Lost*" (II.845-46): "And Death / Grinned horrible a ghastly smile." Watt is not unlike Samuel Johnson, who inherited a "vile melancholy" from his father (**30.4**). Unlike Dante, who smiles thrice, Watt will not smile again unless something upsets him; this anticipates Arsene's mirthless laugh (**48.3**). However, if he does not smile, Watt appreciates Mr. Graves's way of saying "turd" and "fart" (**143.2**).

27.6 [25]: *Crux*: on the analogy of *La Croix*, a Catholic daily founded by Vincent de Paul Bailly (1832-1912) in 1883, and still active; designed as a popular defense of the Church, it was quickly accepted as an orthodox voice, despite going beyond the sanction of Rome.

27.7 [25]: tonsure: changed on the galleys (G8) from "~~ringworm~~."

27.8 [26]: *has J. Jurms a po? Yes*: the drafts (TS, 116; NB4, 224) record the effort Beckett spent trying to create an anagram from the names of Jesus, Mary, and Joseph. His first tried to use the name "Murphy," but to little avail ("as Murphy sees . . . J. Murphy S.J. . . ."); later efforts, more eclectic, were equally unavailing. Indeed, the "winning entry" is imperfect, with an extra "a" and lacking a second "e." My best effort is less holy dove than poor pidgin: "Murphy see Joss? Ja!" The French text disappoints: "*Recomposez les seize lettres de la Sainte Famille sous forme de question avec réponse*. Solution gagnante: *Me réjouis-je? Pssah!*" (29). The prize offered in another early competition (NB1, 95; TS, 75) was a "self-propelling wheel-chair" from Lourdes (**106.3**).

28.1 [26]: the eels of Como: Beckett's source, as Mary Bryden discovered (*Idea of God* 78), is E. P. Evans, *The Criminal Prosecution and Capital Punishment of Animals* (1906), a remarkable account of medieval to post-Reformation trials of animals for crimes against humanity and the promotion of faith by denouncing devils inherent in delinquent animal forms. Evans tells of Bartholomew Chassenée (b. 1480), who made his reputation as counsel for some rats on trial for having feloniously eaten and wantonly destroyed the barley-crop; Beckett notes "the egregious jurisconsult Barthélemy de Chassanée, in the fifth part of his first consultation, Lyon, in-folie, 1531" (TS, 105). His treatise originated "in an application of the inhabitants of Beaune to the ecclesiastical tribune of Autun for a decree of excommunication against certain noxious insects called huberes or hurebers, a kind of locust or harvest-fly. The request was granted, and the pernicious creatures were duly accursed" (Evans 22). Of the pestilent creatures in *Watt*, only the hurebers of Beaune exactly echo Evans, though the "bloodsuckers" of Lausanne (25) are kin to the leeches. An earlier list (NB2, 25; TS, 105) is closer to Evans, suggesting that Beckett later added his own variations; these informed McGilligan's meditations in the Doria Gallery (**28.9**). Among the horrors anathematized in Evans are the hideous worms of Lake Constance (29-30); the slugs of Autun and Beaujeu (36-37); the locusts of Valence and caterpillars of Laon (276); the snails of Lyons and weevils of Mâcon (277).

The galleys (G8) further confused this paragraph by scrambling the order of the lines, Beckett indicating the required sequence as if correcting a sestina:

What do	1
you know of he abjuration, excommunication, mal-	2
slugs of Mâcon, the worms of Como, the leeches of	5
Como, the hurebers of Beaune, the rats of Lyon, the	4
ediction and fulminating anathematisation of the eels of	3
Lausanne and the caterpillars of Valence.	6

28.2 [26]: Mâcon: in the *département* of Saône-et-Loire, near the Vaucluse where *Watt* was mostly written. In *Waiting for Godot* (39.b), Estragon rails against the "Cackon country"; in *En attendant Godot* (86), "Vaucluse" is followed by "Dans la Merdecluse!"

28.3 [26]: a neo-John-Thomist: D. H. Lawrence and Saint Thomas Aquinas unhappily met? Better Ferdinand in *The Duchess of Malfi* (I.ii), of a woman's fondness for the part which, like the lamprey, hath never a bone in't: "Nay, I mean the tongue." In the French text (29), Monsieur Spiro is a more orthodox "néo-tomiste."

28.4 [26]: promiscuities: in the etymological sense of "indiscriminations," as in the example from Milton's *Paradise Lost* cited in Johnson's *Dictionary*: "Glory he requires, and glory he receives, / Promiscuous from all nations." In the French text (29), Monsieur Spiro is explicitly interested in the "histoires du cul."

28.5 [26]: *Podex non destra sed sinistra*: "the arse not with the right but the left" (*destra* a medieval form of "dextra"); the question of which hand to use to wipe ("absterge") the bum. Moran considers this (*Molloy* 166).

28.6 [26]: freethinkers: in the late draft (NB4, 227), "even Anglicans."

28.7 [26]: *A Spiritual Syringe for the Costive in Devotion*: that is, for the constipated faithful; compare St. John of the Cross, his Dark Night of the Soul, as recorded from Dean Inge (*Christian Mysticism* 224), "consonantally adjusted" to "Dark Shite of the Hole" to facilitate the hypostatical enema, cause of St. Teresa's post-evacuative depression (*Dream* 185).

28.8 [26]: *Lourdes*: in the typescript (73, 115), the address was simply "Poste Restante, Lourdes," and did not mention the "Basses-Pyrénées," a *département* in south-west France, in the Basque region. Lourdes, a site of pilgrimage celebrated for its miracle cures, is in the Hautes Pyrénées, further east; the writer, penniless and decrepit, has ended up there, in a room lit feebly by "a snippet of his last underpants floating in rancid dripping" (Coetzee 99-100). To a query from John Fletcher (24 May 1964), Beckett wrote: "I can't remember whether Basses P is a slip or deliberate" (HRHRC, Carlton Lake Collection 2.8). The error is retained in the French translation (30).

28.9 [26]: A rat . . . eats of a consecrated wafer: Evans notes (33): "We laugh at the subtleties and quiddities of mediaeval theologians, who seriously discussed such silly questions as the digestibility of the consecrated elements in the eucharist." The drafts (NB2, 15ff) recount the tale of the *Mus eventratus mcgilligani*, and Matthew David McGilligan, Master of the Leopardstown Halflengths. How the Master got to Rome is worth the telling, his theological thesis considering the following question (TS, 99-103):

> If a rat gnaws or nibbles a consecrated host, does he gnaw or nibble the Real Body? If he do not, what has become of the Body? If he do, what is to shall be done with the rat?
> To the first of these questions McGilligan replied that the rat did indeed gnaw or nibble the Real Body, and this conclusion he supported with quotations from the works of Saint Thomas

Aquinas, Saint Bonaventura, Peter Lombard, Alexander of Hales, the Four Great Doctors of the West, the Four Great Doctors of the ~~East~~ Middle-West, Sanchez, Suarez, Henno, Soto, Diana, Concina, Dens, O'Dea and others.

To the second question McGilligan contented himself with simply replying that the Body being consubstantial with the Host, as much of the former was in the rat as he had gnawed or nibbled of the latter, and as much still in the latter as he had not gnawed or nibbled thereof.

To the third question McGilligan replied that the rat, when caught, should be pursued with all the rigour of the canon laws and pontifical decrees, adding that in this connexion a number of difficulties arose, which delicacy forbade him to formulate, and whose elucidation required a scholarship not possessed by him, & only to be obtained, in his humble opinion, by a long period of tranquil study in the Eternal City.

Pressed by a deputation composed of four lay coadjutors and a professed of the three vows to overcome his scruples and reveal the difficulties that rose up in his mind in connexion with the chastisement of the rat, McGilligan replied that he craved leave to withdraw to his cell and there consider the matter with prayer and fasting. This being readily granted, McGilligan disappeared into his cell with a stale turnover and a jug of fresh water, and there considered of the matter with such despatch that two hours later he was able to gratify the deputation with the following statement:

"Gintlmin, afther havin considthered the matter from ivery angle, Oi foind its me jewity tew lay befower yis dem pints what rus up in me moind aprfops de conclewision of me pore little taysis, doantcha know, swaypin tew wan soide aich an ivery considtheration owenly de wan, viz., obayjence tew me higherarsical sewpayriers, an thrustin yis'll kape me in moind, doantcha know, varbey saypiens, viddylikeit:

"Pint wan: Wance yis'v cotta howlt on de rat, howwa yis ter know wuddit be de roight rat yis've cotta howlt on, ower wuddent it.

"Pint tew: Sewposin tis de roight wan, wud it be me jewity tew adower de bitta d'host what he's afther swallyin up.

"Pint thray: Sewposin tis me jewity so tew dew, what are yis tew dew wid d'ould rat? Are yis tew burren him? Thin yis burren de Rale Body. Are yis t'open him up an levvy it owit de bist way yis can? For tew putt it back in de kiebowerium, ower fer tew et it yerself, seeance teenent?

"Pint fower: Sewposin yis doant ketch a howlt on d'ould rat unthil afther what he's bane an - afther what he's bane - bane an done his doolies, purissimavirgoemendacormuemetcarnemmeam,* thin whire are yis? Wuddit be me jewity-"

"McGilligan" said the 3-Vow-Man, "not another word, not a word more. Join the Roman Holiday under the conduct of Brother Carameluelis, departure Monday, Westland Row, 8 a.m."
* *virgin most pure chastise my heart and flesh*

For the continuation and conclusion of this story, see Addendum **#3**.

28.10 [27]: *Martin Ignatius MacKenzie*: "Ignatius" reflects the name of Saint Ignatius Loyola, crippled founder of the Jesuit order; hence, perhaps, the Lourdes connection. The song is drafted in NB1 (60, 62-65; there said to be that of the "unhappy" accountant); the final words are given as in the typescript (51). Its effect, on Quin, was to affirm the sensation of being nothing in an unbroken waste, beneath a cloudless sky (**#22**):

The Chartered Accountant's Saturday Night, or, Two Voices Are There
by
Martin Ignatius MacKenzie (nothing to Sir George)

As home I staggered late last Saturday,
Oer the herbaceous waste of Salisbury,
Harshly I heard a voice within me say:
Mackenzie, in this world where all is merry
Why is't that thou alone art far from gay,
Far, far from gay, extremely far from gay?

Thou ailest not, as far as one can see,
Thine appetite is good, thy nights are sound,
Neer missest thou thy morning W.-C.,
Thy sexual life is normal, smooth and round.
Whence then this misery, this misery,
This extra-ordinary misery?

No power can hurt the National Two Percents,
Thy bank-account, if small, is still enough,
Thy wages rise by annual increments,
And every other Saturday thou art off.
Shall then thy heart be wrapt in cerements,
Veins, valves and ventricles, in cerements?

Shall be? It is. And why? I know not. Whence?
I care not. All I know and all I care
Is sorrow without ground, and indigence
In plenty's midst, and hope-begot despair.
What change remains? Six shillings and eight pence.
Six silver shillings and eight copper pence.

Then stole my breaking brain assuaging oer
Softly a voice: Mackenzie, well I wis,

> Oft leaden is the ledger, and long the score,
> And bitter the compute. Think then on this:
> Two twos - oh miracle of love - make four,
> Sweetly sweet two and two make sweetest four.
>
> Be this thy pendulum, thy speculum,
> Thy postulatum, measure, image, haven,
> Thy laudanum and opobalsamum,
> To lull the soul, and heal, the soul engraven
> With this of goodness, beauty, truth, the sum,
> The end, the upshot: Summo, ergo sum.
>
> Pant, pant no more, Mckenzie, after what
> Can never, never slake th'accountant's thirst.
> Swab, swab those sobs, Mackenzie, it is not
> Becoming in an auditor's heart to burst.
> Tot on, tot on, Mckenzie, onward tot,
> Fear God, smoke less, honour the king—and tot!

29.1 [27]: question one . . . question three: logically, this implies that the answer to question one is "Yes." Yet question two cannot be dismissed so easily, in the light of Augustine's query (*Confessions* VII.1), as to whether there is "More God in an elephant than in a sparrow (Sophistry of spatial divinity)." Beckett noted (*Confessions* III.7): "God's being not bulk; for the infinite bulk contains parts lesser than its infinitude; so not wholly everywhere" (DN #87). Belacqua raised the question in "Echo's Bones," of an elephant and an oyster, Lord Gall of Wormwood impatiently replying: "Exactly the same amount." Had McGilligan's answer to question two (**28.9**) been disputed, the consequences of question three might have been avoided.

29.2 [27]: He did so at length: the list was originally shorter (NB2, 19): "St Thomas Aquinas, Saint Bonaventura, Peter Lombard, Alexander of Hales, the 4 great doctors of the West, the 4 great doctors of the East (TS, 101: the "Middle-West"), St Stanislaus Kostka, etc etc." Other names appeared at the bottom of the page (NB2, 19): "Sanchez, Suarez, Henno, Soto, Diana. Concina, Dens, O'Dea and others" (TS, 101). Three further points: (1) "O'Dea and others" are neither in NB2 nor the final text; (2) St. Stanislaus Kostka is not a theologian nor a Doctor of the Church, but the patron saint of youth; Beckett took the name (Joyce's saint's name) from *Portrait* (56) or the "Cyclops" chapter of *Ulysses*; and (3): "for he was a man of leisure" is a very late addition.

29.3 [27]: Saint Bonaventura (1221-74): John of Fidanza, Franciscan theologian, who studied in Paris under Alexander of Hales. Beckett noted his work on mysticism with reference to the *Reductio Articum ad Theologiam* (TCD 10967, 161r). Known as the "Doctor Seraphicus," he was canonized in 1482 by Sixtus IV, and ranked sixth among the Doctors of the Church by Sixtus V in 1587. His was a hylomorphic view of the soul, holding that man has a plurality of forms corresponding to the grades of perfection in him, the lower forms subordinated to the highest, the rational soul, in the process of becoming. His *apex mentis*, or mystical sense of the mind consubstantial with the uncreated ground of the deity, is invoked in *Dream* (17).

29.4 [27]: Peter Lombard (1100-64): Bishop of Paris and *Magister sententiarum*, whose celebrated *Sententiae* were written 1145-50. These four books are a collection of opinions of the Church Fathers on the doctrine of the Sacraments, defined as not simply the sign of a sacred thing but capable of conveying the grace of which it is a sign.

29.5 [27]: Alexander of Hales (c. 1175-1245): *Doctor Irrefragibilis*, English scholar and theologian who made his mark on Paris as a teacher, with John of Rochelle, Bonaventura, and Roger Bacon among his pupils. His *Summa Universae Theologiae* correlated the Augustinianism of his day with the philosophy of Aristotle and the Arabs; Beckett noted that this work introduces scholastic method "far more cogently" than the earlier summits (TCD 10967, 161r).

29.6 [27]: Sanchez: François Sanchez (1562-1632), a Portuguese teaching at Toulouse, each chapter of his *Tractatus de multum nobili et prima universali scientia quod nihil scitur* (Lyons 1581) concluding with a resounding "Quid?" (Windelband 362).

29.7 [27]: Suarez: Francisco Suarez (1548-1617), Spanish theologian and Jesuit, the last eminent exponent of scholasticism, who sought a middle way between Nominalism and Realism and tried to reconcile the quietism of Luis Molina with more orthodox doctrines of grace and election. His influential treatise refuting the divine right of kings and directed against the oath of allegiance that James I demanded was burnt by the hangman and its perusal forbidden under severe penalty. Mentioned in Joyce's *Portrait* (242).

29.8 [27]: Henno: Francisco Henno, O.F.M. (1662-1714), author of the *Theologia dogmatica ac scholastica de Deo uno et trino* (1712-13), a study of the *principia* of Thomas Aquinas and Duns Scotus.

29.9 [27]: Soto: Dominic Soto (1494-1560), Dominican theologian whose *Summulae* (1529) secured a triumph of moderate Realism over the errors of Nominalism. Called to the Chair of Theology at Salamanca, he was later chosen as imperial theologian to the Council of Trent and Confessor to Charles V.

29.10 [27]: Diana: Antonino Diana (1586-1663), moral theologian of Palermo and celebrated as a causist. His *Resolutiones Morales* met wide approbation; its frontispiece was a figure of the Cross with the legend, *non ferro sed ligno* ["not iron but wood"]. He was made consultor of the Holy Office of the Kingdom of Sicily, and an examiner of bishops.

29.11 [27]: Concina: Daniello Concina (1657-1756), Dominican preacher and theologian at Venice, whose *Theologia Christiana* (12 vols., 1749-51) was directed against the Jesuits. He was an authority on the Lenten fast.

29.12 [27]: Dens: Peter Dens (1690-1775), theologian of Louvain and the seminary of Mechlin, and part-author of a 14-volume work, *Theologia ad usum seminariorum* (1777).

29.13 [27]: other voices: the first of many permutations in the novel. Watt hears voices "singing, crying, stating, murmuring" in his ear. This he deals with in accordance with Descartes's fourth precept in the *Méthode* (**26.1**, **26.6**, **27.4**): "De rien omettre dans le dénombrement des choses dont il devait examiner les partes" ["To make enumerations so complete that he might be assured that nothing was missing"] (Baillet 12). But something is missing: the sequence appears to exhaust the possible combinations: {A, B, C, D}; {AB, AC, AD, BC, BD, CD}; {ABC, ABD, BCD}; {ABCD}; but errs in offering only fourteen of the possible fifteen [sixteen] combinations, that omitted being {ACD}: "sometimes they sang and stated and murmured," as John Mood (259) first noted. This is also omitted from the French translation (30), despite the full paradigm being written out in the manuscript (Ohio NBI). Further complications arise from the comment that "there were others," and that Watt understood all, much, some or none (conditions affecting the potential combinations); but the sequence is largely satisfying, a model for those following. The Calder text introduces an erroneous "murmurmured" into the penultimate variation. The variations may be displayed as a truth-table:

Singing	Crying	Stating	Murmuring
t	f	f	f
f	t	f	f
f	f	t	f
f	f	f	t
t	t	f	f
t	f	t	f
t	f	f	t
f	t	t	f
f	t	f	t
f	f	t	t
t	t	t	f
t	t	f	t
f	t	t	t
t	t	t	t

This reveals that two of the permissible sixteen propositions are absent, those being the one noted above, {t f t t}, and the case when all voices are silent: {f f f f}.

29.14 [27]: The racecourse: in Beckett's world, the Leopardstown racecourse, visible from the Foxrock railway station, and, according to Addendum #3, scene of the demise of the Master of the Leopardstown Halflengths. The white rails and red stands feature in *All That Fall* (25) and *How It Is* (29).

29.15 [27]: so   ?   when empty: the late draft reads (NB4, 228): "so (Indian artist)ish when empty." Either the Indian artist could not be recalled, or Beckett preferred to retain the gap (**32.4**), because on the galleys (G9) he instructed the typesetter in large marginal letters: "Respecter la disposition du manuscrit: un point d'interrogation au milieu d'un espace." He also specified " so   ? " and " plus d'écarf / espace de six signes. " On the galleys of the French translation (Ohio G25), he likewise instructed: "élongir espaces" (this was repeated for like instances).

30.1 [28]: anhelating: Fr. *anhéler*, to gasp or pant; the breathing less heavy in the French translation (31).

30.2 [28]: canon laws . . . pontifical decrees: canonical laws are those regulating the activity of the Church, but issued by Council or Synod; pontifical decrees those issued by the Pope, or Pontifex, ex cathedra.

30.3 [28]: an unpleasant yellow colour: Murphy in the moonlight forces back his lids so that the yellow oozes into his skull (*Murphy* 106). This is a reaction to what Beckett had called in *Proust* (80) the "incurable gangrene of Romanticism." Yet Watt leaves Mr. Knott's house (222) on a night of "incomparable splendour," the moon not far from full.

30.4 [28]: Watt's way of advancing: like that of many of Beckett's protagonists, Watt's movement reflects an Occasionalist dyspraxia, a lack of synchronization between the clock of the body and that of the mind. Kenner (87) defines it as: "a congeries of gestures owing no intelligible relationship, united apparently by happenstance." There is a model for Watt's walk in Miss Hawkins's description of Samuel Johnson in George Birkbeck Hill's *Johnson Miscellanies* (II, 139): "His walk was heavy, but he got on at a great rate, his left arm always fixed across his breast, so as to bring the hand under the chin; and he walked wide, as if to support his weight . . . He made his way up Bolt Court in the zig-zag direction of a flash of lightning; submitting his course only to the deflections imposed by the impossibility of going further to right or left." Boswell had recorded (*Life* 425; pt. IV): "When he walked, it was like struggling gait of one in fetters." The suggestion is supported by the use of Johnsonian "hard words" in the passage following. The paradigm goes through one complete sequence, for movement east; it invites a like description, the points of the compass rotated by 90 or 180 degrees, for movement north, west, and south. The unnamed narrator of *How It Is* gresses through the mud in a not dissimilar manner (11): "right leg right arm push pull."

30.5 [28]: tardigrade: "slow-moving," as *tardigradous* in Dr. Johnson's *Dictionary*. The pattern is sigmoidal, as that of a reptile, fish, or amphibian; or an arthropod of the class *Tardigrada* (Pat McCarthy to CA). More simply, "sloth-like"; for the *Tardigrada* are also a sub-order of the edentates ["without teeth"], comprising the sloths; Beckett had recorded in the Whoroscope Notebook (25): "tardigrade & edentates."

31.1 [29]: perfect equipendency: culled from Johnson's *Dictionary*, where "equipendency" is defined as "The act of hanging in equipoise" and illustrated thus: "The will of man, in the state of innocence, had an entire freedom, a perfect equi-pendency and indifference to either part of the contradiction, to stand or not to stand."

31.2 [29]: Lady McCann: Knowlson records (625) that during Beckett's boyhood there was in Foxrock a taxi-driver named McCann. The name appears in Joyce's *Portrait* (195): "MacCann marched briskly towards them."

31.3 [29]: a funambulistic stagger: that of a tightrope walker, the French *funambulesque* (32) having more of the sense of "eccentric" or "outlandish."

31.4 [29]: the gentlemen: an error introduced in the galleys (G9) and not corrected in the Olympia edition. Beckett noted the correction ("gentleman") for Grove, but as it remained unchanged he marked it again for Calder, who made the change.

31.5 [29]: Mr Walpole: Hugh Walpole (1884-1941), English novelist whose *Judith Paris* (1931) Beckett borrowed from Yvonne Lob in Roussillon, and in which he found a moving description of how bears turn their heads when baited (Knowlson 297-98). The passage continues: "He was a very old bear, who had been travelling for an infinity of years; he was very weary and did not understand why things were as they were" (*Judith Paris* 71). Watt, too, understands nothing, and becomes an object of pity. The bear represents dignity in suffering and, lifting its head, becomes finer than its tormentors, like the protagonist of "Catastrophe" (1982), baited and humiliated (*Grove Companion* 625).

31.6 [29]: because of old habit: one explanation of why Lady McCann leaves by the first train in the morning, if not of the innuendo of her remaining in bed on Sundays, receiving there the mass, and other meals and visitors (*Watt* 240). Coetzee, more directly, calls her "an angry whore" (139).

32.1 [30]: cavalier ascendents: Lady McCann's ancestors who had fought for Charles I against the Roundheads during the English civil war (1642-48); but (despite her catholic traditions) the word implies "Ascendency," the privilege assumed by the protestant English squirearchy in Ireland. The MacCanns [sic], the name in popular mythology derived from Gaelic *cana*, "wolfhound," hail from Co. Armargh, on the southern shore of Lough Neagh. "Mc" (instead of "Mac") indicates Scots ancestry rather than Irish, whatever the gap and question mark might imply. The late draft (NB4, 234) has the same hiatus, Beckett then probably intending to fill it.

32.2 [30]: a stone: related to the stick (**8.1**, **144.3**) by the problem of self-extension: when a stick becomes a stone, or missile, how does it relate in an inter-mediate way to either self or body, and how does the self occupy the space through which it moves? Such matters are not, one assumes, the concern of Lady McCann, but through the agency of the stone her extended self intrudes upon the body and space of Watt.

32.3 [30]: providential: in "Dante . . . Bruno . Vico .. Joyce" (4-5), Providence is defined (from Croce's Italian) as a mind both diverse and with all contraries but always superior to the humanity whose ends it thereby serves more fully, Beckett adding: "What could be more definitely utilitarianism?" A like irony infiltrates Watt's escape. Compare Bill's boy Sam (101): "paralysed by a merciful providence from no higher than the knees down."

32.4 [30]: deficient in ? : not in *haemoglobin*, which does not act as a coagulant; but rather in *fibrinogen*, which does (Marcel Fernandes to CA); the hiatus may indicate Beckett's sense that "haemoglobin" is not precisely the right word. See the footnote on haemophilia (**102.7**). The gap and question-mark are present in the late draft (NB4, 234) and needed no adjustment in the galleys.

32.5 [30]: ischium: a posterior bone of the pelvic girdle, as in the Whoroscope Notebook (35): "Ischial tuberosities." The late draft (NB4, 235) reads: "on the right section of his bosom"; the French text (34), "à la hanche droite."

32.6 [30]: setting himself . . . in motion: in a manner soon to be adopted by Lucky, similarly laden, in *Waiting for Godot*; many details and gestures of the drama are thus anticipated in Beckett's prose.

32.7 [30]: faithful to his rule: the mode of secular quietism deriving (however unaware Watt may be of this) from the *De Imitatio Christi* of Thomas à Kempis, which had moved Beckett considerably by its quiet intensity, its modesty, and its unflinching acceptance of pain (see the entries for "quietism" and "Thomas à Kempis" in the *Grove Companion*). Murphy has a similar ethos, an indifference to the contingencies of a contingent world. A common ancestor of Murphy and Watt is Valéry's "Monsieur Teste": one who minimizes external circumstances, a "mystique sans Dieu" who is "hors de ce monde," and whose sense of life is as something *facultatif* (**19.5**) that passes from one zero to another, a *via purgativa* that does not lead to a *via unitiva* (Bryden 26).

32.8 [30]: sudarium: literally, a cloth for wiping sweat, but specifically the veronica, the cloth with which St. Veronica wiped Christ's brow, and which retained miraculously the imprint of His face. The Whoroscope Notebook records (24): "Sudarium (Veronica's cloth)." The final addition of "sudarium" (not in NB4, 237) developed the latent potential of "station"; it remains a moot point whether Watt's journey to Knott's house exemplifies a *via dolorosa*, but he makes several stops along the way. Hesla (62) makes an elaborate comparison with the Stations of the Cross, redeeming himself from absurdity by the comment that the pattern is not sustained but disappears almost immediately. The French text (34) states simply: "le petit linge rouge." Yet Beckett was attracted to the motif: the "true icon" appears in "Enueg II," "What a Misfortune," *Endgame* (Hamm's "Old stancher!"), and "Nacht und Träume." See **117.4**.

32.9 [31]: or a bomb fallen on his bum: the change from "head" (NB4, 237) to "bum" was made on the galleys (G10).

33.1 [31]: the feeling of weakness: compare Watt's similar feeling on his departure, this experience perhaps that "already mentioned" (see **223.4**), despite the space of 190 pages and the indefinite passage of time.

33.2 [31]: his knees drawn up: Watt has adopted the embryonic posture, favored by many of Beckett's characters. The ditch, like that at the end of Molloy's journey, intimates a process of birth, Watt "reborn" into Knott's service. A similar process of birth unfolds at the end of the novel, where Watt is covered by bloody slops (**241.2**).

33.3 [31]: the parts of the body are really very friendly: in accordance with the Italian proverb, "una mano lava l'altra, e tutte e due lavano il viso" ["one hand washes the other, and they both wash the face"], as recorded in the Whoroscope Notebook (24). Celia in *Murphy* (12) makes a similar acknowledgement: "The friendship of a pair of hands." The sentence does not appear in the late draft (NB4, 237). The phrasing, "upon the neck" and "under the distant palms" (the latter with an unattended tropical irony), imitates the Italian (or French) construction, and (in English) distances Watt's self from his body.

33.4 [31]: the breath that is never quiet: Keats's "Take into the air my quiet breath" ("To a Nightingale"), a motif used in "Dante and the Lobster" (22), *Dream* (107), "Malacoda," and *Murphy* (229). The movement of the leaves shares Arsene's sense of the seasons (*Watt* 57).

33.5 [31]: two things that Watt disliked: for Watt's dislike of the moon (its unpleasant yellow color), see **30.3**; his dislike of the (equally yellow) sun curiously changes when he is in the asylum (**153.3**).

33.6 [32]: hyssop . . . hemlock: associated respectively with the death of Christ, given to drink of a sponge dipped in hyssop (John 19:29); and Socrates, who drained the poisoned cup. Calder erroneously describes the hemlock as "pounting." In the early drafts (NB3, 22; TS, 162-63, 201), "we" encountered in a ditch a mysterious sign, which (anticipating Watt's later aphasia) he reads, or fails to read, from the bottom, backwards:

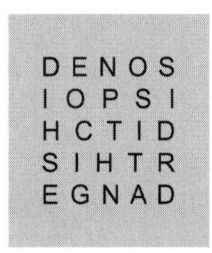

```
D E N O S
I O P S I
H C T I D
S I H T R
E G N A D
```

33.7 [32]: from without: compare the later difficulty experienced by the Unnamable and by the protagonist of *How It Is* in determining whether the voice within is identical to that without; this is the first intimation in Beckett's writing of a major enigmatic theme. Here, the uncertainty of whether the voice is within or without heralds Watt's forthcoming psychic disintegration. See also **91.1**, for a consideration of Watt's "little voice."

33.8 [32]: a mixed choir: in Goethe's *Faust* I.784 (see **#24**, "Die Merde hat mich wieder"), Faust, about to take poison, hears the Easter bells and affirms his allegiance to the Earth. The early typescript heralds a "Distant Mixed Fifth-rate Choir" (115); a later note (NB5, 182) states: "call the choir a descant." Mixed choirs are heard, fleetingly, in *Mercier and Camier* (25), *Molloy* (21), *Malone Dies* (208), and *How It Is* (107). In each, a distant prospect of salvation is combined with a distrust or rejection thereof. At the end of "Play," Beckett outlines instructions for the Chorus, and sets out the words of the two women, W1 and W2, and the man, M, in precisely the pattern used for the threne in *Watt*, but lacking the bass (although M hiccups) and the music. In the late draft (NB4, 238-40), Watt, "an indifferent musician," hears it as "A flat major, but it was most probably in C sharp major, for Watt was inclined to hear a note [*sic*] flat" (but see **34.1** and **#36**).

34.1 [32]: Fifty two point two: in the revision of the early typescript (221), this song replaced the earlier threne (NB2, 34-37; TS, 115), "With all our heart" (**#34**). In this revision the music sung by the "Angel voices as before" is more detailed, in C major as heard by Watt (who hears a tone [*sic*] flat), the conductor still only a principality, four beats to the bar, and the tempo defined as: Mesto quasi arrabbiato. Marcatissima la misura ["sadly, as if enraged/rabid. Mark extremely the regularity of the tempo"]. The song is for four voices, including the bass, who cannot sustain the notes ("Hem! . . . Christ . . . phew! . . . Jesus!"). It was omitted from the galleys (10), Beckett noting: "Musique et note. Réserver 1 page entière—cliché à fournir" ["Music and note. Save one whole page—inset to be supplied"]. The music, or at least the part for the soprano, is given at the end of *Watt* (**#36**); the French text (35) describes it as "Enigme" and what the soprano sang as "Mystère." Preparing a text for the French translation (1967-68) Beckett in his Jupiter text (32-34) marked the entire song to be deleted, despite having left in the first drafts (Ohio NBI) and in the typescript (Ohio TS, 22) a place for the two verses.

The subject of the first verse, "fifty two point two eight five seven one four," represents the days (366) in a leap year divided by seven, to give the number of weeks. The intricate composition of the song is worked out in NB3 (34-37); the two contrapuntal paradigms {greatgranma, granma, mama, Miss Magrew} and {blooming, withering, drooping, forgotten} there from the outset, "Magrew" with no apparent import beyond the rhyme. The song reflects the number of days in the year 2080, the date (a leap year), as predicted in the manuscripts, of the likely publication of Arsene's book, *A Clean Old Man* (not mentioned in the final text). The jingle about "The Tuesday scowls" (*Watt* 46) originally appeared at this point, with specific reference to that year.

35.1 [33]: *Fifty-one point one*: the second verse, more obviously following the post-decimal notation of *pi* (.142857. . .), contains a major error, uncorrected in any published text: "Fifty-one point one / four two eight five seven one" should read "Fifty-two point one," the number of weeks in a regular year (365 days divided by seven, as in the year 2079 or 2081). Early drafts (NB3, 37; TS, 223) have "Fifty-two," but the error, apparent in the galleys (G10), was missed by Beckett. The bun was originally a currant bun, with "currant" replaced by "yellow" on the typescript. "Bun" and "man," sad words both, reflect the game of Happy Families (Mr. Bun the Baker, et al). In *Malone Dies* (285), Lady Pedal, discouraged by the response to her singing, tells Ernest to hand out the buns.

35.2 [34]: detained: in Joyce's *Portrait* (187), Stephen Dedalus distinguishes between this word in the literary tradition and its use in the marketplace. Beckett had exploited this distinction in *Murphy* (2).

36.1 [34]: the earth: underlining the parody, "Die Merde hat mich wieder" (**33.8**, **#24**), of Faust's allegiance to the earth. For other reflections on the earth and sky, see **#22**.

36.2 [34]: goat's milk and insufficiently cooked cod: intimations of spiritual insufficiency. On the typescript of the French translation (Ohio TS, 23) Beckett changed the *morue*, or cod, from "saignante" to "bleue."

36.3 [34]: Mr Knott's house: closely modeled on Cooldrinagh, Beckett's family home at the junction of Brighton Road and Kerrymount Avenue, Foxrock, with its wicket gate, larches, chimney stack with four flues, and red-tiled floor (O'Brien 3-6). Cooldrinagh is also the model for Moran's home in *Molloy*; in both works, in the tradition of Irish Big House fiction, it offers a social microcosm. Watt notes the chimneys; when he leaves (**225.1**) he has somehow discovered that on a fine day they are visible from the station.

37.1 [35]: the more beautiful: Watt's conjectures on how the door came to be locked, and his preference of the more elaborate explanation, ignore the basic principle of Occam's razor, to the effect that given a choice between solutions of equal explanatory power the simplest should be assumed. Doherty considers (41) that "the more beautiful" must mean "the more difficult"; yet "beautiful," rather than, say, "logical," points to an aesthetic impulse within Watt that is increasingly overcome by the rationalist prurit, or urge to reason, as immediately in evidence here.

37.2 [35]: Unless he had got in through a window: Watt has half-heartedly essayed a paradigm, but his inability to ascertain how he got into the house does not presage well for his comprehension of more ineffable matters; nor does he seem to recognize how this afterthought undercuts the paradigm offered, as its terms are not embraced within that logical structure. More pertinent is the word "threshold," or *limen*, with the sense of crossing from one existential state to another.

37.3 [36]: a light was burning: as John 1:5: "And the light shineth in darkness; and the darkness comprehended it not."

37.4 [36]: the ashes grey: the fundamental contrast (as in Synge's *Riders to the Sea*) is that of death and life; Watt's scant hair is "red-grey," placing him somewhere between. Such liminality reflects his spiritual status: one aware of voices and strange intimations, yet unable to "attune" these with his everyday self (Marcel Fernandes to CA). The ashes are an emblem of the coenaesthetic experience that Arsene will describe and Watt will later experience (**39.6, 232.2**). Moran has similar intimations (*Molloy* 123), when he finds his kitchen in darkness save for a faint reddish glow, also called the "gloaming" (Beckett is recycling material from *Watt* [**38.2, 40.7, 216.2**]). In *Murphy* (275), "greyen" was used of the "dayspring"; while earlier (78) the archaic "dayspring" was used of the Zodiac, "il Zodiacal rubecchio" (*Purgatorio* IV.64); here, the flames might "spring." Compare the cockatoo (*The Unnamable* 301), gray shot with rose, in the dim light. Rabinovitz (131) suggests an analogy with Descartes's use of illumination as a metaphor for thought: the coal, the mind as object; the lamp, the mind as subject; and the paradox of futility arising as a consequence of the way that the more light one directs towards the mind the more difficult it becomes to discern its inner glow (**64.2**).

38.1 [36]: redden: unlike "greyen," common in colloquial Irish; as in Joyce's *Portrait* (182), where Davin stops once or twice to "redden" his pipe. Watt's business with his hat, "an innocent little game," intimates Freud's *fort* and *da*, as a mechanism for coping with his new situation (compare Krapp playing with the ball as his mother is dying).

38.2 [36]: a gentleman: the perspective will be later reversed, when Watt find Micks sitting "in the gloaming of an expiring range" (216); like Watt, then, Arsene (in his green baize apron) is neither expecting nor surprised by the arrival of the next man in the series of servants. Like the Nixons in part I (**9.8**), the gentleman is not immediately named; he does not identify himself until well into his speech (**56.5**). Watt is later (143) assimilated to the class of Mr. Knott's young gentlemen.

39.1 [37]: Watt put his forefinger in his nose: as noted in **#12**: "Watt snites." Note the distressing effect of the comma, before "to-night."

39.2 [37]: short statement: as Coe notes (44), this unbroken paragraph "constitutes the first of those great Beckettian monologues which, later on, are to form the substance of the *Trilogy*." Equally, it anticipates Lucky's "word salad" in *Waiting for Godot*. In the tradition of Big House fiction it constitutes a set piece, the head-butler's instruction to the new servant. As an extract from the recent French translation, "Arsene parle," it appeared in *Les Lettres françaises* 1267 (22-28 janvier 1969): 5-9. The piece is remarkable for the variety of rhetorical devices woven into it. John Pilling has labeled some, but his listing is incomplete (stopping, as Mr. Graves his narrative, or Darwin his caterpillar, before the end). Pilling implies that Beckett was knowingly using the terms (*ecphonesis, asyndeton, epanorthosis*) he identifies, pushing rhetorical plums into the pudding much as Joyce had in the "Aeolus" chapter of *Ulysses*. I suggest, rather, that while Arsene's statement is heightened by distress and emotion, and Beckett is playing rhetorical games, the figures are by no means "systematically tabulated" (Pilling, "Long Shadows" 63), so an extended naming of parts is fruitless (no plum intended), unless a particular effect is registered. The Calder text, for no good reason, substitutes a period for the colon.

39.3 [37]: Haw!: Arsene's proclivity for hawing is described in the early drafts (NB3, 17; TS, 193) as "prophetic ejaculation"; here, it forms an expression of the *risus purus* (**48.3**).

39.4 [37]: in his head, in his side, in his hands and feet: as the wounds of the crucified Christ.

39.5 [37]: And all the sounds, meaning nothing: compare, because of the birds, Beckett's "German Letter of 1937" (*Disjecta* 53): "Denn im Walde der Symbole, die keine sind, schweigen die Vöglein der Deutung, die kein ist, nie" ["For in the forest of symbols, which do not exist, the little birds of meaning, which does not exist, are never silent"]. In Robinson's summary (118), Arsene is trying to put the experience of Nothing into words, but Nothing cannot be described except in terms that mean something, while something that describes nothing cannot be something (nor yet nothing). The fall from the ladder of words is thus inevitable.

39.6 [38]: the little sounds come: compare Watt's coenaesthetic experience, on his departure, of the little patter of mice (**232.2, 232.3**). Arsene's retreat from the outer world will be increasingly part of Watt's experience, as it was of Murphy's, although neither Arsene nor Watt shows any desire to articulate that experience as Murphy and Belacqua had done (see "Murphy's mind"; *Grove Companion* 388-89). The "window opening on refuge" suggests a Proustian retreat (Marcel's room at Combray), but also the magic casements of Keats's "Ode to a Nightingale," and the poet's wish for darkness and easeful death. Compare *Mercier and Camier* (52), Mr. Gast's vision of a little window opening on an empty place, where "Not a breath stirs the pale grey air."

39.7 [38]: a stirring beyond coming and going: a paradox anticipating later short prose such as *Still* (1972), "Still 3" (1978), and *Stirrings Still* (1983), which invoke the same apotheosis of tranquility, not unlike Malone's region of calm indifference (*Malone Dies* 198) beyond the tumult and commotion of the mind (**57.4**).

39.8 [38]: so light and free . . . the being of nothing: the sense of the *néant*, or of what Milan Kundera was later (1984) to call the unbearable lightness of being.

40.1 [38]: in a moment: as I Corinthians 15:52: "In a moment, in the twinkling of an eye, at the last trump: for the trumpet shall sound, and the dead shall be raised incorruptible, and we shall be changed" (**104.2**). Arsene is saying that there is no "warrant" for any such expectation, even though a few hours of his "old burden" (his service with Mr. Knott, his life, the Old Adam) yet remain and last-minute forgiveness is possible; "lightening" refers to both the easing of that burden and the incipient dawn. Watt, soon to feel himself the right man in the right place (**40.9**), like Arsene once, will find himself under the delusion that he "is come, to stay. Haw!"

40.2 [38]: the old windings: literally, the paths and lanes that have led to this place and time; metaphorically, the winding staircase of Mr. Knott's house (in early drafts the staircase and its fine newell were features of Quin's house); personally, anticipating Beckett's 1946 poem "Saint-Lô," where the mind winds through the devastated town, "ghost-forsaken." The older Krapp, having failed to fulfill the promise of his younger selves, will find a related metaphor in his reels of discarded tapes.

40.3 [38]: the stairs with never a landing: Doherty notes (37) the likely parody of T. S. Eliot's *Ash Wednesday*, the spiritual ascent of a turning stairway. Earlier in *Watt* (14), Tetty Nixon went up the stairs, wringing the carpetrods. The French text rhymes, rather neatly (40): "les escaliers et les paliers."

40.4 [38]: the long lids of sky: the kenning relates Arsene's sentiment to Old English poems such as "The Wanderer" or "The Seafarer"; while the long country roads with the dead walking beside invokes similar Celtic traditions, or Synge's wanderers of the lonely roads and glens. The ghost of Hölderlin ("Der Spaziergang") is among the dead who walk beside Beckett in this haunted passage (Damian Love, "Art of Madness" 176).

40.5 [38]: the dark shingle: as in Beckett's 1937 poem, "Dieppe," published in the *Irish Times* (9 June 1945): "again the last ebb / the dead shingle / the turning then the steps / towards the lighted town." The poem dramatizes the moment of choice (**7.6**) that Arsene now faces: to go into the dark, or to return to the world of others; here, the realization that there is no choice. The French translation (40) makes no attempt to rework the original quatrain, the only shared detail being the "demi-tour" toward (in the poem) "les vieilles lumières" or (in the prose) "les feux du bourg."

40.6 [38]: exitus and redditus: more accurately, "Laetus exitus tristem saepe reditum parit: et laeta vigilia serotina triste mane facit"; a theme from the *De Imitatione Christi* (I.xx) of St. Thomas à Kempis (1379-1471), that a merry outgoing brings a sad homecoming; or, in the earliest English translation by John K. Ingram (25), that "A glad goinge oute ofte tymes bringith furthe a sorful comyng home, and a glad wakyng ouer even bringith furthe a sory mornyng. So euery flesshly ioy entrith in plesantly, but in the ende he bitith and sleeth." Beckett cited the Latin in the *Dream Notebook* (#576), and summarized it as: "Glad Going out & sorrowful coming home." He used it in *Dream* (16, 129); and in "Ding-Dong" (37), where the narrator sees his sometime friend returned from his little trajectory transfigured and transformed: "It was very nearly the reverse of the author of the Imitation's 'glad going out and sad coming in.'" "Sanies I" is structured on the *laetus exitus* theme, all heaven in the sphincter (going out), but disillusionment (coming home). Beckett used the phrase in *Murphy* (103) to describe Rosie Dew's sad return from the Park. After buying from Jack Yeats a Sligo skyscape called "Morning," he described his elation to Thomas MacGreevy (7 May 1935) as "always morning, and a setting out without the coming home." The increeping and outbouncing house and parlor maids (*Watt* 50) reverse the sentiment; but in "From an Abandoned Work" the narrator's life is ordered by the daily journey and return, "in the morning out from home and in the evening back again" (159), joy and sorrow defining his unhappiness at home (*Grove Companion* 573).

40.7 [38]: this gloaming: that is, the twilight, as in the popular Harry Lauder song (1911), "Roaming in the Gloaming" (**216.2**).

40.8 [38]: masturbating his snout: Beckett recorded in the *Dream Notebook* (#221) from Jules Renard's *Journal* (11 novembre 1893): "La solitude où l'on peut enfin soigner son nez avec amour" ["The solitude in which one can at last lovingly pick one's nose"].

40.9 [39]: the fit is perfect: because of Leibniz's doctrine of pre-established harmony (**134.2**), whereby each monad (or individual unit) is in exact correspondence with all others, thereby constituting a perpetual living mirror of the universe. The man cannot, however, presume to "know" this ("let us remain calm"), as the noumena of things is unknowable, but he may sense it, or have (as here) premonitions, in accordance with the dictum, one of Beckett's favorites, *Nihil in intellectu quod non prius fuerat in sensu* ["Nothing in the mind that was not first in the senses"]. Those sensations are here said to be *irrefragable*, incapable of being refuted, a word made much of in *Murphy* (261).

41.1 [39]: clinging to the perimeter: taking its point from the traditional definition of God as a perfect circle or sphere: having "arrived" at the house of Mr. Knott, Arsene is saying, Watt will experience the delicious sensations of imminent harmony, of being "in the midst," at one with his surroundings.

41.2 [39]: transports: in the usual collocation, "of joy"; but in contrast to the "horrors of joy" (*Watt* 42); then with the etymological sense of "carrying across," as Arsene expresses the mystical experience (43).

41.3 [39]: nature is so exceedingly accomodating [*sic*]: incipient in *Watt*, and driving the *Three Novels*, is the great theme of *King Lear*, that of unaccommodated man, arising from Lear's opening cry that "Nothing will come of nothing" (I.i.87) to his realization that man is but a poor forked animal, his life as cheap as beasts, not worth a button (**63.7**). Moran sees in nature "a superfetatory proof of the existence of God" (*Molloy* 99).

41.4 [39]: like a basin to a vomit: a compelling image of those moments that few are spared, when the dichotomy of self and object is overcome in the cathartic experience, and that which was within one is at one with that which is now without.

41.5 [40]: anguish and disgust: Baudelaire's "Réversibilité" ("Ange plein de grâce, connaissez-vous l'angoisse") invokes the anguish and disgust of fearful nights. Beckett alludes to it in *Dream* (148). The French translation reads (41): "l'angoisse et le dégout."

41.6 [40]: tasks of unquestionable utility: service to a master; less vexatious than the agonies of "Job" Murphy suffered; yet of a kind, as the distractions these tasks impose will keep Watt too busy, most of the time, to worry about the alternative "nothing" that might prove to be of the highest value and significance. He will serve Knott, but in so doing will have no chance to know him.

41.7 [40]: intenerating: from L. *tenere*, "delicately"; in Johnson's *Dictionary*, "softening, or making tender." For "establishment" and "abide," see **134.2** and **57.5**.

41.8 [40]: the celebrated conviction that all is well: the sense that "all [shall be] well" derives from Juliana of Norwich (1342-1413), an anchorite discussed in Dean Inge's *Christian Mysticism* (201-09), from which Beckett recorded her sentiment (DN #673), as celebrated by T. S. Eliot in *Little Gidding*, for use in *Dream* (9).

41.9 [40]: or at least for the best: the contention, mocked by Voltaire in *Candide*, of Leibniz's *Monadology*, that our world is the best of all possible worlds, for God in His infinite wisdom will choose the best, and in His infinite power will make it so. This conviction led Leibniz inexorably to the theory of pre-established harmony (**134.2**).

42.1 [40]: he witnesses and is witnessed: reflecting the orthodox opinion that we are set on this earth by God to bear witness to His glory. But God is a witness (**9.1**) that cannot be sworn, and *Watt* instead offers the sustained conceit (the *reductio* of Berkeley) that God (or Knott) could not exist were he not perceived, and must be witnessed in order to be: "Not that he might know, no, but that he might not cease" (**203.2**). This paradox is sustained in Beckett's writings, most obviously *Waiting for Godot*, where characters and actors cannot exist without an audience; and *Happy Days*, where Winnie senses that somebody is looking at her, giving her the impression she exists. *Texts for Nothing* and *How It Is* cry out for witnesses, to "leave a trace" or "keep the record." The word reflects its etymology: Gk. *martyros*, "a witness," one who testifies to life as a slow crucifixion. Jean-Jacques Mayoux, in his afterword to the French *Molloy* (263), puts it nicely: "On ne sait ce que Knott attend de Watt, un simple témoignage de son existence, semble-t-il, spécialement important pour les entités métaphysiques dont l'existence est douteuse" ["One does not know what Knott expects of Watt, a simple testimony to his existence, it seems, particularly important for metaphysical entities whose existence is dubious"].

42.2 [40]: out of sorts: compare *Molloy* (19): "They are deep, my sorts, a deep ditch, and I am not often out of them."

42.3 [40]: Haw! He feels if possible better disposed than usual: the joke arises from the paradox of the only possible, that one cannot be otherwise disposed. The repetition of this sentence was either added to or omitted from the galleys (G13). Two other major "slips" appeared on this page of the galleys: "There I wall," corrected to: "There I was, warm and bright and smoking my tobacco-pipe, watching the warm bright wall"; and having been transported "to some tobacco-pipe" (*Watt* 42-43), adjusted to: "to some quite different season, in an unfamiliar country. At the same time my tobacco-pipe..."

42.4 [40]: It was a Tuesday afternoon: in the late draft (NB4, 259), neither the day nor the month is mentioned here. A question arises: does a greater specificity (the date, the place, the time, the space) better validate the experience?

42.5 [40]: looking at the light, on the wall: behind this description lies the painting, *View of Delft* (Mauritshuis, The Hague), by Jan Vermeer (1632-75), and a little patch of sunlight on a yellow wall in the center thereof. Bergotte, Proust's artist, drags himself from his deathbed to see once more that "petit pan de mur jaune" (*La Prisonnière* I.255). In "Yellow," named partly for this effect, one last thing Belacqua sees is "the grand old yaller wall" outside the hospital. Molloy (25) sees the "declining sun" on the white wall. Compare Ezra Pound's "Erat Hora," a like invocation of a sunlit moment.

42.6 [41]: a conjuncture of one's courses: that is, where "old windings" (**40.2**) meet. Compare the crossroads of *Waiting for Godot*.

42.7 [41]: an apothecary's slice: like the little plated trowel (*Watt* 89) used by Mr. Knott to eat his poss. A curious topology, given that the essence of a "pipe" is roundness (a torus), but if the third dimension is thus reducible to the second then the fourth (time) may be accessible from the third. The French text reads: "spatule d'apothicaire" (42).

42.8 [41]: like a pelican's: in medieval bestiaries, the pelican (an emblem of Christ) so loves its offspring that if on returning to the nest it finds that they have been bitten by serpents it tears open its breast with its beak and washes them in its blood, restoring them to life. Alfred de Musset's "La Nuit de mai" sustains "Ce n'est au Pélican" (*Dream* 21), where Liebert addresses his beloved Lucien, neither piteous as the pelican nor pure as the phoenix, who might have cured him but has not. See also "Text 2": "My varicose veins take their kneeling thoughts / from the piteous pelican." As these intimate, "a pelican in her piety" is the correct heraldic expression (*Grove Companion* 88).

42.9 [41]: Hymeneal: that is, virginal, with less the sense of dewy forejoys (**12.9**) than impending and irrevocable change.

42.10 [41]: bugger these buttons: parodying the words of the dying Lear (**63.7**).

42.11 [41]: the warm bright wall: added to, or perhaps dropped from the galleys (G13), to accentuate the Proustian echo (**42.3**, **42.5**).

43.1 [41]: Gliss — iss — iss — STOP!: Fr. *glisser*, "to slip"; as the musical instruction, *glissando*; or as echoed in Beckett's poem, "je suis ce cours de sable qui glisse" (1948). The French translation (43) retains "STOP" in English. A critique of the Proustian moment or Joycean epiphany follows; in Arsene's words (45), it was not an illusion and yet he is buggered if he can understand how it could have been anything else. Ideal and real, the moment differs from those of Proust and Joyce in that Beckett refuses to validate it; the experience is not in dispute, but any endorsement of its transcendental value is ruthlessly withheld. A similar ethos is expressed in *Endgame*, for on that extraordinary day, like yet unlike all others, something has changed, as Clov intuits.

43.2 [41]: a great alp of sand: compare Joyce's *Portrait* (132), the evocation of eternity: "Now imagine a mountain of that sand, a million miles high, reaching from the earth to the farthest heavens, and a million miles broad, extending to remotest space; and a million miles in thickness"; to which, every million years, a little bird comes to carry away in its beak, "grain by grain," a tiny bit of sand. The phrase, "one hundred metres high," does not appear in Beckett's final draft.

43.3 [41]: the grains slip: in the early drafts of *Watt* (TS, 47), the young James Quin cannot tell ("Well, well, well") how many wells make a river, nor how many millet grains make a heap. The paradox derives from Windelband (89), who traces several "little catches," usually attributed to Zeno, to Eubulides of Miletus, dialectician of Megaria: "Which kernel of grain by being added makes the heap? Which hair falling out makes the bald head?" Burnet discusses the paradox (*Greek Philosophy* 312), and Beckett's notes consider the noise of one grain falling (TCD 10976, 45r-45v); for "one," read: "tiny packets of two or three millions." Compare *Endgame*: "Grain upon grain, one by one, and one day, suddenly, there's a heap, a little heap, the impossible heap." Clov senses the impossible, an almost imperceptible change to this day, the single extra grain needed to make the heap. Hamm later refers to "that old Greek," and reiterates the paradox in human terms, asking at what point the separate moments of human existence add up to something: "all life long you wait for that to mount up to a life" (*Endgame* 70). See Beckett's Riverside Notebook (*Grove Companion* 661): "C [Clov] perplexed. All seemingly in order, yet a change. Fatal grain added to form impossible heap. Ratio ruentis acervi." This is Horace (*Epistles* II.i 47), the *sortites* puzzle, or grains that constitute the heap: "after the fashion of the falling heap." Compare Big Lambert's wife (*Malone Dies* 214) sorting the lentils, or the sense in *Mercier and Camier* (77) of "every millet grain that falls," that every day brings death a little closer. Consider, too, Leibniz's distinction between *virtual* and *actual*, and his *petites perceptions*, below the threshold of perception: countless imperceptible drops of water finally heard as the splash of a wave, a single grain of millet falling noiselessly to the ground but a bushel poured out making a great sound. Descartes's error, Leibniz said, was that his insistence on the clear and distinct "treats as non-existent those perceptions of which we are not consciously aware" (*Monadology* 224). Arsene's glissando is not just an expression of the *sortites* paradox, the noise of the falling grains of sand, but equally one of apperception, of the mind's incapacity to register the impossible process, the "change of degree" (**44.6**).

43.4 [41-42]: my personal system was so distended: like the pelican's (**42.8**), inflated from within, the mystical intuition of the individual afflatus at one with the oversoul, or divine. Specifically ("I trust I make myself plain"), Arsene insists that the incident is not simply "internal," or subjective, essential if his mystical intuition is not to be dismissed as illusory. Mood critiques Watt's use of *ratio* to measure thought and action, and focuses on Watt's attempts to create an internal and rational "personal system"; attempts that are largely flawed and finally disintegrate, as those who put their trust in them. Yet Arsene's "way up" is much the same as Watt's "way down" (in the words of Heraclitus, echoed by T. S. Eliot in *Four Quartets*), as the direct experience in the sunlit yard (or rose garden) finally leads to no more of a revelation than does that knowledge obtained by the application of the blow-lamp of understanding to the empty tin (or pot) of the self.

43.5 [42]: Lisbon's great day: the earthquake of 1755 (in NB4 [265] Arsene says 1759), which struck on the Sunday morning of November 1 (All Saints' Day) while many were at church, the event moving Voltaire to write *Candide* to attack Leibniz's doctrine of pre-established harmony. In Diderot's *Jacques le fataliste*, Père Ange and Frère Jean head to Lisbon, to be crushed, swallowed, and burned, "comme il était écrit là-haut" (535). Beckett refers to the event in the poem, "ainsi a-t-on beau," and in the essay, "La Peinture des van Velde" (*Disjecta* 131). In the Sottisier Notebook he noted from Voltaire's poem, "La Dést[ruction] de Lisbonne": "Tristes calculateurs des misères humaines / Ne me consolez point, vous aigrissez mes peines" ["Miserable calculators of human misery / Do not try to console me at all, you intensify my sorrows"] (*Grove Companion* 321).

44.1 [42]: some quite different season: contrast the 1947 poem, "vive morte ma seule saison," with its paradox of "vive mort" and sense of life as one long gray autumn.

44.2 [42]: since I was not eating a banana: as Krapp later does in lieu of a tobacco-pipe. Sometimes, as Freud might have said, a banana is just a banana, but on page 123, Watt, could he but find what he wants to know, might then put the matter from him, as one "forgets the peel of an orange, or of a banana."

44.3 [42]: an epileptic's dental wedge: to prevent damage to the tongue in case of a fit; the detail raises, if ironically to reject, the possibility that Arsene's experience is a medical malfunction, like that experienced by Dostoevsky.

44.4 [42]: feathers: as the pelican's (**42.8**). The deleted "Runner Duck" passage (**45.6**) suggests a curious "marriage" between Arsene and his duck, which renders the allusion to Christ (as Pelican) somewhat ambiguous (Marcel Fernandes to CA).

44.5 [42]: Crécy: the battle of Crécy (26 August 1346), where the English longbow gave a small army a famous victory over a larger French force. Beckett first (NB4, 267) wrote "~~Agincourt~~"; the change intimates Proust's Odette de Crécy, object of Swann's obsession.

44.6 [42]: a change of degree: not the thermometer, but the steps of a ladder, or scale, the etymological sense of "degree." There follows a critique of the mystical moment, or epiphany, an attempt to identify the precise moment at which a quantitative change becomes a qualitative change, a change of degree a change of state, as water into ice. As such it constitutes an important critique of the Modernist aesthetic, as in Pound's sense of the image as that which records (in an instant of time) the precise moment when the thing inward and subjective enters or is transformed into that which is outward and objective.

44.7 [42]: existence off the ladder: by which the soul ascends, as Descartes imagined he might climb, by clear and distinct degrees, to truth and the knowledge of God. Inge (*Christian Mysticism* 9-10) notes three stages of the *scala perfectionis*: the purgative; the illuminative; and the unitive, or "state of perfect contemplation." Walter Draffin's "elevated position on Saint Augustine's ladder" ("What a Misfortune" 120) mocks this; but in *Endgame* Clov uses the "steps" on a day when (like Arsene) he experiences a sense of subtle change (**43.3**). See Beckett's later parable, "The Lost Ones" (1966). Invoking Yeats's rag-and-bone shop of the heart and Keats's romantic stasis, Doherty reveals (38-39) the disappointed mystic: even if Arsene has somehow climbed to the place where all the ladders end, he is now back where he was: "He has not arrived anywhere and his rejoicing in his expanded spirit which united him with his outside has deceived him." Metaphysically, as Mr. Hackett physically (**15.8**), Arsene has fallen off the ladder.

44.8 [42]: Do not come down the ladder, Ifor: Jacqueline Hoefer in 1959 argued that this jest refers to the closing passage of Wittgenstein's *Tractatus*: "My propositions are elucidatory in this way: he who understands me finally recognises them as senseless, when he has climbed out through them, on them, over them. (He must so to speak throw away the ladder, after he has climbed up on it.) He must surmount these propositions, then he sees the world rightly. Whereof one cannot speak, thereof one must be silent." Beckett insisted (1961) that the ladder was an obscure Welsh joke, used in *Murphy* (188), and that he had read Wittgenstein "only within the last two years" (Fletcher 88); the late draft (NB4, 261) calls it "The Welshman's dream." In the French *Murphy* (137), "Ifor" is "Louis"; but in the French *Watt* (44) "Ifor" is retained.

44.9 [43]: The laurel into Daphne: the original metamorphosis, or qualitative change, of Daphne into the laurel, in Ovid's *Metamorphoses* I.452-552: Apollo, wounded by Cupid's gold-tipped dart, fell in lust with Daphne, who, wounded by Cupid's lead-tipped dart, ran from him. Losing strength, she called to her father, Peneus, to change her and destroy her fatal beauty. Peneus changed her into a laurel, and Apollo, in recognition, decreed it his sacred tree. Doherty here invokes, if only to reject (38), Rocquentin's vision of Sartre's chestnut tree (**82.1**), the world "refusing the easy assimilation of itself into man in order than man can know himself or define himself."

44.10 [43]: where it always was, back again: compare "Dante and the Lobster" (20): "Where are we ever?" cried the Ottolenghi "where we were, as we were."

44.11 [43]: a woman: desire, as summed up in *Proust* (57): "One only loves that which one does not possess entirely." That is, the inner being of consciousness is a constant striving without end and without rest, the longing of the subject to possess the object of his desire, only to discover the nullity of attainment (**44.13**).

44.12 [43]: or a friend: Beckett in *Proust* defined friendship as "the negation of that irremediable solitude to which every human being is condemned" (63), a social expedient "like upholstery or the distribution of garbage buckets" (63), to be rejected by the artist because "art is the apotheosis of solitude" (64). In his copy of *A la recherche* ("Jeunes filles" II.196), the phrase "irrémediablement seuls" is underlined. But, as Arsene intuits, this does not make the "craving for a fellow" (*Molloy* 15) any less real.

44.13 [43]: And yet it is useless not to seek: as defined by Schopenhauer (*WWI* 1.3 #52, 336): "Now the nature of man consists in this, that his will strives, is satisfied and strives anew, and so on forever. Indeed his happiness and well-being consist simply in the quick transition from wish to satisfaction, and from satisfaction to a new wish. For the absence of satisfaction is suffering, the empty longing for a new wish, languor, *ennui*." Watt's exhaustion reflects Leopardi's "non che la speme, il desiderio è spento" ["Not only the hope, but the desire is extinguished"], which Beckett had used as an epigraph to *Proust*. Mr. Knott, one who abides (**57.5**), who neither seeks nor wants, is equally one free from desire. Consider, too, the biblical injunction: "Seek and ye shall find" (Matthew 7:7).

44.14 [43]: until you begin to like it: that is, when the condition of suffering gives way to the condition of boredom or ennui; or, in a word, *habit*. Beckett defines this insulating condition as the compromise between the individual and his environment, "the ballast that chains the dog to his vomit" (*Proust* 19). Compare Proverbs 26:11: "As a dog returneth to his vomit, so a fool returneth to his folly"; hence, perhaps, "puke."

44.15 [43]: prog: food taken by foraging, as plunder, or as a handout.

45.1 [43]: rung by rung, until the night was over: combining the *scala perfectionis*, or mystical ladder, the pun on "degree" (**44.6**), and the Cartesian methodology (**27.4**) with St. John of the Cross's dark night of the soul, as in Dean Inge's *Christian Mysticism* (223-31; DN #697). Like Belacqua (*Dream* 186), Arsene has come too late into a little knowledge of himself; he, too, is a borderman, a John of the Crossroads.

45.2 [43]: a debt to pay: to nature, or death, before he can depart this world; yet Arsene articulates Beckett's fourth certainty (after birth, existence, and death): the need to express, however irrational that need might seem.

45.3 [43]: it was not an illusion: the experience, in Proustian terms, is both real and ideal, yet Arsene refuses to give it transcendental validation (**44.7**); hence he has ended up where he was (**44.10**). In the galleys (G14), Arsene was "suggered" if he could understand how it could have been anything else.

45.4 [43]: you will leave undecided: the consequence, in Coetzee's formulation (98), reworking Jacqueline Hoefer, of a logical positivist meeting a metaphysical being, as an irresistible force an immovable object.

45.5 [44]: any great chance of its being admitted: a *reductio* of the third contention of Gorgias (**97.1**, **148.2**), that even if Watt could know what has happened to Arsene, if anything has, or if Arsene could know what will happen to Watt, if anything will, that knowledge could not be communicated ("admitted" has the scholastic sense of being accepted after scrutiny).

45.6 [44]: if only we chose to know it: in the Grove Press editions, Arsene's conclusion is followed by a blank line, the next line then indented halfway across the page. On his personal copy Beckett marked the space for closure, and the Calder text is continuous. This conceals a curious textual change. The Olympia edition, the galleys (G14), the typescript (133), and NB2 (60), the original composition, all contain a poem and a commentary on an Indian Runner Duck, Arsene's pet (**#37**). This ended in mid-line, and when the poem and commentary, as marked off by Beckett on his copy of the Olympia text, were deleted by Grove the irregularity was not adjusted. The pagination of the Grove and Olympia editions therefore differs from page 45 until the end of part I (by exactly one page), but from part II (page 67) on the two are again synchronized, Grove allowing an extra blank page between parts I and II. The deleted text reads:

> But what is this, so high, so white,
> And what is this, so black, so low,
> Burning burning burning bright,
> Quenched long ago, cold long ago?
> It is a duck, a duck, a duck,
> An old* East India Runner Duck,   (TS, 133: young)
> On a mat, a mat, a mat,
> A hairy mat, a hairy mat.
> Oh ancient mat, oh hairy mat,
> Oh high white brightly burning duck,
> Cush's* stones are crying yet,   (TS, 133: ~~Ethiop's~~)
> Forth from the wall to Habbakuk,
> And from the wood the answering beam
> Cries yet of the appointed time
> Still tarrying, and of old resolves,
> Of wind, and sand, and evening wolves.

> Impatient to be off, the little rascal, she has crept in and sat down on the mat. See how she opens and shuts, in imitation of her master, her orange bill. How against the fawn the dark eyes flash. But Not Heard, she is saying, in her duck language, it is time we were gone. Like the Jerusalem Artichoke, she was born in Newtown-Mount-Kennedy, and can hardly walk, but she is a true Indian Runner for all that. Her breeding is so high that she can eat nothing but pork scrap, pea meal, boiled bullock's lights, boiled sheep's paunches, and a little grit and gravel well scalded together with thirds and middlings. The lines were to her grandmother, I think. I was living in World's End then, I believe. For I have never been without my India Runner. Where I go, she goes too, and every time I leave she leaves with me. So we all bring something with us. You bring your bags, and I bring my duck. In this way we are sure not to go emptyhanded away. Pretty Nuala! They are the best wives a man ever had. And every Sunday she lays an egg for my breakfast. I wake up in the morning and find it in my bed. A long green egg. Which I gob. But I am worse than Mr Ash . . .

Despite Cohn's skepticism (*Canon* 110: "whatever that might be"), an Indian Runner Duck is a breed of domestic duck, with white, fawn and white, and penciled varieties, small and noted for its eggs; "Indian" from the belief that it originated in India; "Runner" because it typically scuttles. An isolated page in French (HRHRC Carlton Lake Collection 1.13, 55) includes nine lines of a translation begun long before the piece was culled (a full version presumably once existed):

> Mais qui s'en vient là si grande, si blanche,
> Et quoi donc, quoi donc, si noir, si bas,
> Qui flambe, flambe, flambe, flamboie,
> Si longtemps éteint, si longtemps froid?
> C'est une canne, une canne, une canne,
> Une vielle canne de Barbarie coureuse des Indes
> Sur un tapis, tapis, tapis,
> Un tapis poilu, tapis poilu,
> Oh grande canne blanche flamboyante

45.7 [44]: Mr Ash: Joyce's *Finnegans Wake* (35) tells how HCE, one Ides-of-April morning, walking in Phoenix Park "met a cad with a pipe," who accosted him "to ask could he tell him how much a clock it was that the clock struck had he any idea by cock's luck as his watch was bradys"; whereupon "the ten ton tonuant thunderous tenor toller in the speckled church (Couhounin's call!) told the inquiring kidder, by Jehova, it was twelve of em sidereal and tankard time" (Pat McCarthy and David Hayman to CA). The name "Ash" reflects his phenomenal and questions his noumenal reality; the encounter figures Watt's attempts to comprehend the noumenal reality of Mr. Knott, who appears in various phenomenological manifestations.

45.8 [44]: Westminster Bridge: crossing the Thames, near the Houses of Parliament, London. Beckett recorded in the Whoroscope Notebook (49): "Kant's exact description of Westminster Bridge (having never set foot outside Prussia). vol. xi. p. 45." This reference has proved difficult to pin, but the anecdote is familiar: an Englishman in Königsberg referred to Westminster Bridge; he was at fault, "but Kant set him right with as great accuracy as if he had been the surveyor who took out the quantities for the bridge" (Houston, *Immanuel Kant* x). Kant used this in his lectures (1802) to show that an object never *perceived* may yet be *conceived* by other modes of cognition.

45.9 [44]: Securing me with one hand: as the Ancient Mariner his unwilling listener?

45.10 [44]: a crucifix . . . a gunmetal half-hunter: an image of the slow crucifixion of time; compare *Waiting for Godot* (49-50), where Pozzo concludes that he has left his watch ("a genuine half-hunter, gentlemen, with deadbeat escapement") at the manor. A half-hunter is like a "hunter," a pocket-watch with a metal case to protect the dial, but typically (hence "half") with a circle of glass let into the case. Mr. Gorman later has a problem with his watch and fob (**239.2**).

46.1 [44]: as God is my witness: introduced (NB4, 275) for the echo (**9.1**): "God is a witness that cannot be sworn." Seventeen minutes past five is 17:17, a useless symmetry. Beckett asked in the Whoroscope Notebook (83): "Could you tell me what time it was?"

46.2 [44]: Big Ben (is that the name?): technically, yes, since "Big Ben" designates not the clock on the Houses of Parliament, Westminster, but its bell. Designed by Sir Edmund Beckett Denison, later first baron of Grimthorpe, the bell (13 tons, 10 cwt 15 lbs) was cast 10 April 1858, and first rang *in situ* 31 May 1859; it was named for Sir Benjamin Hall (1802-67), chief commissioner of public works. The inquiry appears in the late draft (NB4, 275).

46.3 [44]: If you want a stone, ask a turnover . . . plumpudding: the cliché, to leave no stone unturned; with Luke 11:11: "If a son shall ask bread of any of you that is a father, will he give him a stone?" Earlier drafts (NB2, 69; TS, 141) read "bread" for "stone" and "cake" for "plumpudding."

46.4 [44]: oiled and houseled: in the last rites of the Catholic Church, anointing and shriving. In the late draft (NB4, 275), Mr. Ash dies, more logically, of pneumonia.

46.5 [44]: Not a word, not a deed . . . no time, no place: originally (NB2, 71; TS, 143) set out as verse (the first "quatrain" added later), in anapestic couplets (a final trochaic line); but thereafter as prose. A galley error, "nor a trust" (G14), entered the Olympia text; although Beckett marked it for correction it remained unchanged in Grove. Calder, however, reads "not a trust."

46.6 [45]: an ordure: this, then "An excrement," "A turd," and "A cat's flux" (47), in the later rewriting effects a transition between what in the drafts had been separate passages.

46.7 [45]: sat for Fellowship: Arsene is, or might have been, a recipient of the Madden Prize bequeathed by Samuel Madden (1686-1765), philanthropist and divine, to the runner-up in the Trinity College Fellowship examination, provided he were a candidate of sufficient caliber. In the early drafts, Quin's valet, Arthur, then his butler, Erskine, "pleasantly corrupted into Foreskin," was the "Maddened-Prizeman," a fragment retained into the Addenda (**#14**). The typescript (143) inflames the jest:

> "When I sat for Fellowship" said Arsene, "but for the boil on my bottom. . ."
> "On a zouffent pesoin d'un blus betit que soi" we said.
> But it is doubtful if Arsene appreciated the unusual wittiness of this remark. . .

46.8 [45]: The Tuesday scowls . . . Monday morns: in the manuscripts (NB3, 32) set as verse in two quatrains; then placed as prose (NB3, 35; TS, 219) just before the song of the mixed choir and with reference to the story, *A Clean Old Man*.

46.9 [45]: The whacks, the moans . . . the skelps, and the yelps: a sonnet of iambic monometer (with an anapestic final line), the Shakespearean rhyming scheme (abab cdcd efef gg) carefully laid out (twice) in the first draft (NB2, 87; but with "the" omitted). The typescript (159) sets the words as verse, but omits the explicit rhyming scheme.

46.10 [45]: old earth: the title of "Fizzle 6," and a motif varied in several texts, with the sense of one poised at the edge of the grave: *Dream* (137: "Vieil Océan"); "From an Abandoned Work" (160); *Endgame* (104: "old wall"); *Happy Days* (28: "earth you old extinguisher"); and *How It Is* (46: "old sack old cord").

46.11 [45]: father's . . . mothers' mothers' mothers': four generations, his own then those of others, each rendered exhaustively with twice the terms of that proceeding. The first paradigm repeats "my," while the second uses "other people's" only once, but each has fourteen terms, and is otherwise identical. A similar paradigm of fathers and mothers, including Christ's and Mary's and Adam's and Eve's [?], "to mention only a few celebrities," appeared on an early verso (NB2, 98) and in the typescript (169). The apostrophes are rigorously observed in all editions, but the galleys (G15) and Olympia text substituted an erroneous comma in "mothers, fathers' fathers'" (the Olympia Traveller's edition has both comma and apostrophe). Beckett at first missed the error, but marked it in his Olympia text for Grove, who deleted the comma. A like paradigm appears in *Finnegans Wake* 183.25-28 (Pat McCarthy to CA); and an equally deranged model is offered in the Anglican *Book of Common Prayer*, where a man may not marry, among his less fortunate relatives, his father's father's wife, his mother's father's wife, his wife's father's mother, his wife's son's daughter, and his wife's daughter's daughter.

47.1 [45]: The crocuses and the larch: a return to the vistas of "Walking Out," in Croker's Gallops, near Beckett's boyhood home, and an equally ironic invocation of the pastoral tradition: "one of those Spring evenings when it is a matter of some difficulty to keep God out of one's meditations" ("Walking Out" 101). A "little mound in Croker's Acres" later forms the setting of "Not I" (220). Larches were one of Beckett's many "obsessional" childhood images (**47.5**). In "Sanies I" and "A Piece of Monologue" their coming out is associated with his birth; in *Molloy* (36) the dog, Teddy, is buried beneath a larch, the only tree that Molloy, like Belacqua ("Walking Out" 102), can identify with certainty. Larches also feature in "Draff" (183) and "Serena II" (*Grove Companion* 308).

47.2 [45]: uneaten sheep's placentas: "uneaten" was added (NB3, 5) to the already graphic "pastures red with sheep's placentas" (from "Walking Out" 101), to render the pitiless process of nature, where eat or be eaten is the only law. Beckett explained to an uncomprehending Ludovic Janvier "que c'est le moment que les brebis agnellent, parce que le placenta reste sur le pré jusqu'au moment où les brebis le mangent" (Janvier 60). The landscape (breeders and bleeders) and phrase are repeated in *Company* (25) and "Heard in the Dark I" (247).

47.3 [45]: the corncrake: in "Walking Out" (111), Belacqua hears the first corncrake (land rail) of spring, but fails to heed the death rattle in its zoological name, *Crex crex*. Compare the "corncrakes' Chinese chromatisms" (*Dream* 70), the "rail" and "loud calm crake" of the telephone in *Murphy* (7), and their "awful cries" that Molloy (16) associates with the rattle of his mother (*Grove Companion* 111).

47.4 [45]: wasps in the jam: Arsene's paean to the seasons takes its cue from the popular music-hall song, "The Housewife's Lament," two verses of which read:

> In March it is mud, it is slush in December;
> The midsummer breezes are loaded with dust.
> In fall the leaves litter. In muddy September
> The wallpaper rots and the candlesticks rust.
>
> There are worms on the cherries and slugs on the roses,
> And ants in the sugar and mice in the pies.
> The rubbish of spiders no mortal supposes;
> And ravaging roaches and damaging flies.

47.5 [45]: the larch turning brown a week before the others: Beckett's family home, Cooldrinagh, held a small plantation of larches, one of which turned green, and later brown, a week before the others.

47.6 [45]: the sea breaking over the pier: the East Pier at Dún Laoghaire, as that memorable March equinox when Krapp saw: "the whole thing. The vision at last" (*Krapp's Last Tape* 60).

47.7 [45]: the consumptive postman: identified by Eoin O'Brien (18-19) as Bill Shannon, the Foxrock postman of Beckett's childhood, who appears thus in *Dream* (146). Previously "Shannon" (NB5, 7), he later appears as "Severn" (**69.2**).

47.8 [45]: *The Roses Are Blooming in Picardy*: a detail added to the typescript (175); the usual title of one of the most popular songs from World War I, composed (1916) by Hadyn Wood to lyrics by Frederick E. Weatherley:

> Roses are shining in Picardy
> In the hush of the silvery dew
> Roses are flowering in Picardy
> But there's never a rose like you!
>
> And the roses will die with the summertime
> And our roads may be far, far apart
> But there's a rose that dies not in Picardy,
> 'Tis the rose that I keep in my heart.

The whistling postman is evoked in *Dream* (146), in a paragraph "reverently" set aside as he has since died: "The dead fart, says the Preacher, vanity of vanities, and the quick whistle." For like images of consumption, compare the "bloody rafflesia" of "Enueg I" and *Malone Dies* (317), the flower resembling corrupted tissue.

47.9 [45]: the standard oillamp: the "standard lamp" of "A Piece of Monologue" (265), which invokes similar images of Beckett's childhood (**49.1**). Compare "The Expelled" (57): "I love oillamps."

47.10 [46]: the February débâcle: Leap Year (**34.1**).

47.11 [46]: the endless April showers: as the beginning Chaucer's *Canterbury Tales*: "Whan that Aprile with his shoures soote / The drogth of March hath percèd to the roote."

47.12 [46]: the whole bloody business: earlier, "cursed"; the change accords with the pastures red with uneaten sheep's placentae (**47.2**).

47.13 [46]: And if I could begin it all over again: earlier (TS, 143), this followed directly the "I do not regret" sentiment (*Watt* 46), as a prelude to a sustained lament on "a lamentable tale of error, folly, waste, ruin" (**#6**).

47.14 [46]: a third time: marked by Beckett when preparing his Calder text for the French translation to be changed into "2nd"; an ambiguity derives from whether "again" includes the original instance.

47.15 [46]: *We shall be here all night*: in the early drafts, sung by "we" and Arsene, in NB2 (83) "to the air of [blank space]"; in the typescript (155) "to an air not heard before nor likely to be heard again": and with "pure laughter" (the *risus purus*) at the thought that one could ever be understood by another. Yet the opening lines echo Hymn #242 (*Hymns Ancient and Modern*), "We Love the Place, O God"; words by William Bullock (1854) to the music ("Quam dilecta") of Henry Jenner (1861):

> We love the place, O God,
> Wherein thine honor dwells,
> The joy of thine abode
> All earthly joy excels.
>
> It is the house of prayer
> Wherein thy servants meet;
> And thou O Lord art there
> Thy chosen flock to greet.

The first four lines of the poem in *Watt* intimate a logical series, with elements of "We shall," "be here," and "all night"; but the variation is neither exhaustive nor rigorous (there could have been six combinations), and in line four "be here" is broken into its binary parts (opening the way for other permutations).

48.1 [46]: resting on the flight: not without reference to Rembrandt's *Rest on the Flight to Egypt*, in the Dublin National Gallery; but in his notes on Dutch art, taken from Wilenski (BIF 5001, 7) Beckett discusses Adam Elsheimer's *Flight into Egypt* (Vienna), seeing the escape from defined darkness into infinite light equally as a flight from defined light into darkness and mystery. Compare Molloy's "flight and bivouac, in an Egypt without bounds, without infant, without mother" (*Molloy* 66).

48.2 [46]: Like Tyler?: as in Wat Tyler, leader of the Peasant's Revolt (1381). Also ("Watt") the nickname of Tyler, a one-eyed market gardener with a small farm at Tyler's Gate, on Cornelscourt Hill Road, near Foxrock (O'Brien 360). Like Murphy, Watt has no Christian name. The French translation (48) alludes to a different Watt (James Watt, inventor of the stream engine): "Plaît-il? Comme la machine à vapeur?"

48.3 [46]: the bitter, the hollow and the mirthless: these three "modes of ululation" (L. *ululatus*, "a howling, a shrieking"), Arsene says, correspond to successive *excoriations* (L. "having the hide flayed off") of the understanding; the early drafts (NB3, 29) had "stages"; the typescript (213) preferred "unwindings." It reminds "us" of the story, never told, of the rabbi's trousers (NB3, 31; TS, 215). The galleys (G15) omitted: "They correspond to successive, how shall I say"; this contributed to the Olympia error, "successives," marked by Beckett for correction by Grove. Compare the ditty of Mrs. Williams in "Human Wishes" (*Disjecta* 157): "Madame, for mirth, for my part, / I never had the heart. / Madame, for my part, to mirth / I have not been moved since birth." The passage proposed (lesser to greater, lower to higher, outer to inner [a later addition], gross to fine, matter to form) reflects classical doctrines of the tripartite soul (rather than Murphy's description of his mind), rising from the mundane to the divine. In the words of Brett (*History of Psychology* I.93): "as the soul is itself intermediary between Pure Forms and the Formless, so the process of development through which it goes is threefold: for there is first the process of moulding the material, irrational nature; then the intermediary stage in which concrete embodiments of law are studied; and finally the highest stage in which the laws of nature are made the subject of thought and the mind thinks over the last great law of all things, the Good in which they live and move and have their being." In place of the soul, consider the three excoriations of the laugh: the ethical, in response to irrational nature; the hollow, the intellectual, in respect of the law; and the dianoetic, the mirthless, in relation to processes of thought and mind. This precise hierarchy (ethical, intellectual, and dianoetic) is recorded in Beckett's Philosophy Notes on Aristotle (TCD 10967/109; Windelband 154), which conclude that: "The highest perfection of its development is achieved by the rational nature of man in knowledge. The dianoetic virtues are the highest"; indeed, they attain the realm of "pure thought." The dianoetic force explodes in *Murphy* (246) as the laugh of Democritus, the "guffaw of the Abderite" who contended that "Nothing is more real than nothing"; the sentiment in echoed in *Texts for Nothing* (XII): "the long silent guffaw of the knowing non-exister." This is the *risus purus*, the pure laugh or laugh of laughs, the comic equivalent of apperception, the laugh laughing at itself. Beckett advances the jest in the French translation (49), by footnoting the *risus purus*: "(1) Locution latine signifiant à peu près rire (*risus*) pur (*purus*)." Hesla (59) offers a further gloss, from Fritz Mauthner (*Beiträge* III.632): "Reine Kritik ist im Grunde nur ein artikuliertes Lachen. Jedes Lachen ist Kritik, die beste Kritik" ["Pure criticism is at bottom simply an articulated laugh. Every laugh is criticism, the best criticism"]. Watt, by contrast, does not laugh, which makes him what Rabelais calls an *agaleste*, the best known instance of whom was, of course, Christ.

48.4 [47]: Not a word, not a—: Arsene went "over that" a little earlier (**46.5**).

49.1 [47]: before the cock crows: the religious echo (John 18:16-27) intimates Arsene's sense of betrayal as he leaves the place on which his hopes so long were fixed.

49.2 [47]: the weary little fat bottom: see **61.1** for the two types of servant preferred by Knott; Arsene is in the mold of Hardy, but Watt is more like Laurel.

49.3 [47]: three hundred and sixty directions: those of the circle, or compass; a greater choice than Mr. Hackett had on the first page of the novel (**7.6**).

49.4 [48]: a cromlech: a prehistoric stone structure, consisting of one flat slab raised and supported by two others; O'Brien (20) identifies this as that at Glen Druid, near Foxrock. The sentiment was earlier (NB3, 40; TS, 228) at the final point of Arsene's leaving, with the longing for metamorphosis more obvious. The galleys (G16) and the Olympia text, corrected by Beckett for Grove, read: "for lovers to scatch their names on." The French translation (49) prefers "statue de pierre."

49.5 [48]: sorrow: compare Isaiah 53:3: "a man of sorrows, and acquainted with grief."

49.6 [48]: luxurious: in the fallen sense of "wanton" or "sensual."

50.1 [48]: Yes: in a world of negation, less an affirmation than a transition from individual experience to that shared by others, with a distant echo of the end of *Ulysses*. Added to the late rewriting (also on page 48) as conversational lubricant.

50.2 [48]: we are no longer the same: as Beckett argued in *Proust* (13), for all time, we are other, "no longer what we were before the calamity of yesterday." Aspirations of yesterday were valid for yesterday's ego, but not for today's.

50.3 [48]: whereas sorrow is a thing you can keep on adding to: compare the comment, attributed in the Whoroscope Notebook (61v) to Gentile: "In coming to know itself by thinking about itself, mind is adding to itself & so making the self which it knows." The word "sorrow" (**49.5**) replaced the earlier "wisdom"; the "stamp or egg" collection started as "egg or shell." The passage was rewritten in early 1945 (NB5, 1) for insertion into an existing version. The sentiment was earlier Watt's (NB3, 41, 43; TS, 227, 229), after hearing the angelic choir. The typescript here marks an important transition, for "we" is crossed out and "Watt" is insinuated for the first time. "Quin" is still there, and although "Watt" is/was not present (his name written in later) first-person narrative references are crossed out, and "he" replaces "we."

50.4 [48]: is it not: despite the missing question mark, there is an echo of the French "n'est-ce pas?" In the sentence following, Beckett restored to the galleys: "of another man . . . who takes the place."

50.5 [49]: procuration: management of the affairs of another. Previous drafts (NB3, 45; TS, 230) read more simply: "it may be direct or it may be indirect." Watt will feel no curiosity about whoever takes his place.

50.6 [49]: the increeping and outbouncing house and parlour maids: the "Laetus exitus tristem" motif of St. Thomas à Kempis's *Imitation of Christ* (I.xx), that a merry outgoing brings a sad home-coming (**40.6**). No attempt is made to replicate the jest in the French translation (50). Arsene pedantically means "housemaids" rather than "house."

50.7 [49]: or canal: suggesting casual prostitution, the Grand Canal (famously in Joyce's *Portrait*) being a favored pick-up place ("canal knowledge"). The phrase, "bar parlour or canal," was added to the original (NB3, 44).

50.8 [49]: Mary . . . Ann: as Mary, the mother of Jesus, and Ann, the mother of Mary, hypostatized as the generic servant-girl, Mary Ann (compare "Draff" 189). Buck Mulligan celebrates her propinquity in the opening chapter of *Ulysses*.

50.9 [49]: let there exist a third person: reflecting the "Third Man" argument, a variety of the ontological "proof" of the existence of God, as in the title of Flann O'Brien's *The Third Policeman*: that Mary and Ann cannot exist without "some such superior existence" of the Platonic form of the "house" or "parlour maid," or the Idea of a Mistress or Master to reify their existence. But that form or Idea is in turn contingent upon another for its existence, and so ad infinitum, or until the unchanging First Cause (a necessary postulate for other forms to exist) is reached. Beckett's notes on Philosophy (TCD 10967, 93) identify the "3rd man argument," commenting thus: "If a man is a man in virtue of his participation in the form as αυτοανθροπος there must be a man who will have his being relatively to the form. Now this is not the autoanthropos who is the form, nor the particular man who is so in virtue of participation in the form." Alexander's *Short History of Philosophy* (67) states this more succinctly: "if the idea 'man' exists as something apart from actual men, we must have a higher idea to embrace both the ideal and the actual man." The Platonic theory of knowledge asserts that the only things of which we can have certain knowledge are propositions of logic and mathematics that are necessarily true, a doctrine contrary to Beckett's dubious affirmation of demented particulars as the only straws that the mind might grasp. This important sentiment was present virtually from the outset (NB3, 45; TS, 230).

51.1 [49]: Jane: another generic name for the servant girl, the apparently casual error reflecting the lack of particularity implicit in the Third Person theory of knowledge; in the typescript (231), a second "Ann" is crossed out and "Jane" is written in.

51.2 [49-50]: onions and peppermints: the effect of eating peppermints after onions extreme pungency, the peppermints unbearably hot. There are nine repetitions, of first onion then peppermint; an open series with no implicit significance or termination—that is, assuming that the supply of onions and peppermints is infinite, and the ideal paradigm unrestricted by empirical constraints.

51.3 [50]: figments of the id: in a note on the "Id, Ego & Superego" (TCD 10971/7, 6), Beckett records: "Id: Instinctual cathexes seeking discharge - that in our view is all that the id contains"; blind, instinctive impulses battling within what Neary calls the pudenda of his psyche (*Murphy* 47), fighting against the demands of the physical world, but called to rational account with the coming of the light. Earlier versions (NB3, 47; TS, 231) read "a nightmare vision."

51.4 [50]: had so bravely born: for a curious echo, see **#37**, the match that so bravely burns: "Then it went out." One might have expected "borne."

51.5 [50]: the dust: behind this passage is the paradox expressed in Diderot's "Le Rêve de d'Alembert," of life generated from the plane of inert sediment, only to return to that state—his literal interpretation of the injunction, *momento quia pulvis est, et in pulverem reverteris*, one of Beckett's obsessive biblical sentiments (Genesis 3:19): "for dust thou art, and unto dust shalt thou return."

51.6 [50]: Daltonic visualisations: after John Dalton (1766-1844), the English chemist who first enunciated the theory of definite molecular proportions in atomic combinations (this, rather than the tests for color-blindness named after him, seems to be what is intended; winning combinations rather than racing "colors"). The French translation (51) is vaguely Platonic: "Relecture par l'oeil de l'esprit de la page hippique du jour?"

52.1 [50]: vitamens: spelled "vitamines" in NB3 (46); then "vitamens" in the typescript (232), and galleys (G17), and so into the Olympia text; but Beckett marked the word in his copy of the Olympia for correction by Grove. As it remained unchanged, Beckett again noted it in his copy of Grove for correction ("vitamins") by Calder.

52.2 [51]: then eats again, then rests again: eight repetitions, in the same order; again (**51.2**) an open series without any anomalies.

52.3 [51]: coprophile: one who loves dung; Beckett noted on the typescript (232) his preference for "coprophage" (an eater of dung), but the change was not made. In NB3 (48), the list was extended to include a boa-constrictor or an Aran islander, but these changes did not appear in the typescript, which, however, added "naturist," or nudist. The French translation (53) reads "coprophage." In the Whoroscope Notebook (38), Beckett recorded: "phagomanie (envie de manger sans en avoir besoin)" ["phagomania (desire to eat without the need)"].

52.4 [51]: Jane: this "Jane" is present in the early drafts (NB3, 49; TS, 232), and may have suggested the previous revision (**51.1**).

52.5 [51]: catatonic stupor: a vacancy that is the consequence of dementia praecox or schizophrenia; a state attributed in *Murphy* (193) to the patient Clarke.

52.6 [51]: to turn for his sustenance to the clyster: that is, to receive nutrition by means of liquid injected into the intestines; compare the "clysterpipe" of the hypostatical enema (*Dream* 81, 185).

53.1 [51]: or in an upward direction: added to the manuscript (NB3, 49); that is, in the manner made notorious by J-K. Huysmanns in *A rebours* (1844), usually translated as "Against Nature" (by means of an enema). In *Murphy* (182), the patients in the MMM are fed in a manner "highly irregular"; the French translation (133) specifies: "alimentation par l'autre bout."

53.2 [52]: metabolic exchanges: as in food to energy, in digestion.

53.3 [52]: the great sympathetic: a node of nerves originating from the cervical, thoracic and lumbar regions, controlling activity and increasing the heart rate; the active survival mode (fight, flight); as opposed to the parasympathetic, which lowers the heart rate and attends the sedentary needs (digestion, excretion) when not under threat. In the Whoroscope Notebook (Interpolations 4), Beckett wrote: "synalgia (sympathetic pain)."

53.4 [52]: chyme, or chile, or both: *chyme* is the semi-liquid pulp to which food is reduced by action of the stomach acids; *chyle*, lymph milky in appearance, thanks to the presence of emulsified fats, which pass to the blood and tissues by way of the lacteals and thoracic duct. NB3 (49) reads, oddly, "chime, or chile"; the typescript "chime, or chyle" (233); and the galleys (G17) "chyme, or childe" (Beckett struck out the "d"). Beckett noted the correction to "chyle" on his Olympia Press copy for Grove, and, since the change was not made, on his Grove copy for Calder. The French text has (54): "du chyme, ou du chyle."

53.5 [52]: a piano or cello: the typescript reads (213) "strings" for "cello." In his 1969 review of the French translation (5), Alain Jouffroy recalled a passage in Stendhal: "un homme vêtu de noir touchant du piano et se retournant vers un homme qui tient un violoncelle: c'est l'homme de génie, perdant son temps à vouloir faire sentir un passage sublime à la médiocrité."

53.6 [52]: a dangerous and detestable practice: since conducive to masturbation.

54.1 [53]: vegetables,nuts: the lack of spacing, unnoticed by Beckett, persisted into the Grove editions, but was regulated in Calder.

54.2 [53]: the coal-hole: an opening in the wall, leading to a chute, to deliver coal to the basement. See **#18** for the "sempiternal penumbra" of Mr. Knott's coal-hole.

54.3 [53]: the American Bar: typically one built into the wall, for concealment during Prohibition. O'Brien suggests (7) that Beckett has conflated his family home, Cooldrinagh, with Glencairn, the nearby mansion of "Boss" Croker, whose house had a conservatory (a glass-walled room for growing plants), an oratory (a small chapel), and an American Bar.

55.1 [54]: on its way down to be filled . . . on its way up to be emptied: related to the image in *Murphy* (58) of humanity as a well with two buckets: "whilst one comes up full to be emptied, another goes down empty to be filled" (John Marston, *The Malcontent* III.iii.60-61). This is inaccurately cited in the Whoroscpe Notebook (Interpolations 11): "A well with 2 buckets. Whilst one comes up to be filled another goes down to be emptied. Such is the state of all humanity." This defines a principle of equilibrium in the Newtonian universe, with respect to the closed circle of desire (*Grove Companion* 181). The effect is comic, but like the byplay with Malone's two pots (185), one for soup and the other for his bodily needs, the second filling as the first is emptied, intimates a mechanical universe (Mary's actions having the regularity of piston rods). Yet the local equilibrium of such machines is subject to the Second Law of Thermodynamics (Malone's decline is signaled when one pot remains full while other is filling), which insists on inevitable heat loss until homeostasis is obtained (compare *Endgame*).

Mary's limbs will therefore presumably continue thus (Arsene's sentence is unfinished) even as the machine of her body is winding down.

55.2 [54]: Winter and summer: NB3 (55) at this point states: "Roussillon Nov. 18" [1942], then (with little between) "March 1st" [1943]; it begins: "Continuing then again . . ."; that is, when Beckett resumed writing after having arrived at Roussillon. There is thus a coincidence between the conditions of writing and the pattern of narrative, at this point interrupted and then resumed, in a different direction. Arsene's break in the narrative anticipates that of Arthur (197): "But here Arthur seemed to tire, of his story."

55.3 [54]: the long days when the sun was a burden: blending Ecclesiastes 1:9: "there is no new thing under the sun," with Ecclesiastes 12:5: "and the grasshopper shall be a burden, and desire shall fail: because man goeth to his long home."

55.4 [54]: I shall rise: as in Yeats's "The Lake Isle of Innisfree": "I shall arise and go now . . ."

56.1 [54]: a bun: compare page 35: "*a big fat bun / for everyone*"; the French translation (57) offers "une brioche."

56.2 [54]: or a hat to my head: Molloy fears losing his hat (90), for how, when lost in the dark wood, might he salute a lady? Compare the narrator of *Fizzle* 1, "He is barehead," making his way through a dark and issueless labyrinth without the protection, however social and symbolic, that the hat affords. A curious gloss is offered in *Mercier and Camier* (111): "Were I not without desires, said Mercier, I would buy me one of those hats, to wear on my head." See also **26.1**.

56.3 [55]: a passing man in blue: a British bobby, rather than the Irish *Garda* (see **9.2**). In the early drafts (NB3, 29; TS, 211), Arsene laughs mirthlessly: "A little gritty, perhaps" (*Grove Companion* 448). The collocation, "black and blue," is suggested.

56.4 [55]: It was summer: the French translation offers a nice rhyme (54): "C'était l'été."

56.5 [55]: Arsene: the first mention of his name (**38.2**). He was earlier "a professional cook-general," his name "affectionately corrupted into But-Not-Heard" (TS, 67). Hesla (63) suggests that it derives from Arsenius (d. 450 AD, an anchorite called out of seclusion by the Emperor Theodosius before becoming again a resolute eremite; but a more likely precursor is the servant of Julien Sorel in Stendhal's *Le Rouge et le noir*. Another Arsene is a butler in "Play"; in the drafts thereof he was first Erskine.

57.1 [deleted]: *Now the day is over*: a "Child's evening hymn" (1865), by Sabine Baring-Gould (1834-1924), music by Joseph Barnaby; in *Hymns Ancient and Modern*, #346. Beckett on his copy of the Olympia text marked the passage for deletion; no change was made in Grove, but it was again marked on his copy of Grove, and deleted in Calder, the sense running "from the earth" to "and the door open" without a break. The French translation follows the Calder changes. Arsene's "a little low" replaces the previous "a little high" (NB3, 59; TS, 237), the change attuning him to Watt and Murphy, each of whom hears a tone flat. The hymn is mentioned in *Dream* (134, 156), and is sung by Krapp (*Krapp's Last Tape* 59), a passage Beckett also omitted in his own productions.

57.2 [55]: Hallow's E'en: the evening of October 30, or, in Ireland, *Samhain*, when the spirits of the dead communicate with those yet alive. Beckett marked this in his Olympia text to be changed to "Hallow-e'en," but Grove did not make the change, which, however, appears in Calder. The French text (58) reads "la Toussaint."

57.3 [55]: Guy Fawkes: November 5th, celebrating the attempt, or rather the failure, to blow up the British parliament in 1603, the conspirator, Guy Fawkes, found in the cellars amidst barrels of gunpowder that he was planning to ignite. The event is celebrated with firecrackers and bonfires, and the burning of a stuffed effigy, or guy (as in Eliot's *The Hollow Men*). The French text (58) has "des Trépassés" (1 November, All Souls' Day).

57.4 [55]: one who neither comes nor goes: the early drafts (NB2, 87; TS, 159) record that Arsene could say: "Go! and the duck went, and Come! and the duck came, and Do this! and the duck did that. So extraordinary is the effect of God's image." Later (NB3, 59; TS, 238) a small ditty appeared: "Let him not to / Who will not fro, / Nor him come / Who will not go." The biblical text implicated in this, Beckett's most persistent motif, is Psalms 121:8: "The Lord shall preserve thy going out and thy coming in from this time forth, and even for evermore." The verse underlines less the Lord's preservation of His servants than their transitional nature in a phenomenal world, governed by the laws of motion. This also derives from the pre-Socratics, Windelband noting (111) that the two characteristics of corporeality are the filling of limited space and the quality of being in motion in the void (see the entry for "motion" in the *Grove Companion* [384-86]). All Beckett's early characters accept the principle affirmed by the cyclist of "Serena III": "keep on the move / keep on the move." Belacqua in *Dream* and "A Wet Night" is urged to move on, and in "Ding-Dong" he must set himself in motion to give the Furies the slip. Murphy embodies the monad in motion. His statement (105), "When he came to, or rather from," is more than a quibble, for it reflects the Occasionalist ethos of Geulincx (*Metaphysica* II.11 176): "Motus enim duas habet partes: *abesse* et *adesse*" ["Motion thus has two parts, *from being* and *to being*"]. Thus the Unnamable addresses all the dogs to come (379): "adeste, adeste, all you living bastards." In the phenomenal world, the alternative to motion is the homeostasis of a world running down, as in *Endgame* or *Happy Days*; but in *Watt* the alternative contemplated, if not attained, is the quiet still world where Mr. Knott abides.

57.5 [55]: abide: unlike his servants, Mr. Knott is said to *abide*, as one in the house of the Lord. Consider Psalms 61:7: "He shall abide before God for ever"; or Ecclesiastes 1:4: "One generation passeth away, and another generation cometh: but the earth abideth forever"; or Malachi 3:2: "But who may abide the day of his coming?" To "abide" entails freedom from desire (Leopardi's "il desiderio è spento"), the end of the constant striving without end or rest that is the condition of those who come and go; yet Mr. Knott still needs (desires?) to be witnessed, that he might not cease to be.

57.6 [55]: Yet come he did . . . and go . . . he must: touching on the crucial question, a surprisingly late formulation given its final importance in the text with respect to problems of witnessing, perception, permutations, and order, as to whether Mr. Knott is sempiternal, having a beginning but no end; or serial, part of an order or a series but one imperceptible from the human perspective, and so immortal only relatively. In *Proust* (21): "The mortal microcosm cannot forgive the relative immortality of the macrocosm. The whisky bears a grudge against the decanter." Or "Draff" (191), the rose to the rose: "No gardener has died, comma, within rosaceous memory." Beckett's "comedy of an exhaustive numeration" (*Proust* 92) arises in *Watt* from the sense of a physical universe in which crocuses flower then fade, larches turn green then brown, and the whole bloody business of the earth's renewal begins all over again. Over the next few pages Arsene will enunciate the theme to be explored more fervently in part III, that of the servants who come and go, into the house on the ground floor, up to the first floor, then out of the house, a sequence which began with those unknown, through those known from Walter to Micks (**59.2**), to others as yet unknown. Their coming and going is of a different order to the seasons, but has its own sequential logic and timing, so that eventually Watt who came, served on the ground floor, then moved to the first floor, must go. Such motion is in marked contrast to the stasis of Mr. Knott, "who neither comes nor goes," but rather "abides." Like the whisky decanter or gardener he seems immortal, but that may be only because he is witnessed from a different serial perspective. See also **#26** and **#29**.

57.7 [55]: for I am not illegitimate: as in *Murphy* (251): "(for he was not illegitimate)."

58.1 [55]: a coming to . . . a going from: a central metaphysical concern (**57.4** to **57.6**); compare *King Lear* (V.ii.9-11), Edgar to Gloucester: "Men must endure / Their going hence, even as their coming hither; / Ripeness is all." One *mirlitonnade* is like a brief "Breath": "On entre, on crie, / et c'est la vie. / On crie, on sort, / et c'est la mort."

58.2 [56]: this shadow: compare Psalms 144:4: "Man is like to vanity: his days are as a shadow that passeth away"; or, for the sense of withering, Psalms 102:11: "My days are like a shadow that declineth; and I am withered like grass." The Anglican Burial of the Dead intones: "He fleeth as it were a shadow, and never continueth in one stay." As he was compelled (or free) to come, Watt will be obliged to leave; his coming to and presence in the house of Mr. Knott, his conviction that he is at last the right man in the right place, must exist in the shadow, the certain knowing, of his departure to come.

58.3 [56]: though in purposelessness: an intimation of Kant's *Zweckmässigkeit ohne Zweck*, as recorded by Beckett in the Whoroscope Notebook (60): that, even though we know the world lacks purpose, we must act as though it had. The language has a Pauline intonation; compare (for tone, rather than text) I Corinthians 13:2: "And though I have the gift of prophecy, and understand all mysteries, and all knowledge; and though I have all faith, so that I could move mountains, and have not charity, I am nothing."

58.4 [56]: the English . . . the Irish: a "confusion" not noted in the typescript (239). Beckett, asked if he were English, reputedly replied, "Au contraire."

58.5 [56]: obliged to have someone: to exist, to be witnessed (**42.1**), which is, in a sense, "looking after" oneself. The Olympia and Grove texts refer to "Knott," but the Calder edition dignifies him as "Mr. Knott."

59.1 [57]: to fuss over him . . . to make much of him: Harvey (365) hears an echo of "give glory," which is not the language of the King James Bible; better, perhaps, is the sequence impressed on young Anglicans, to magnify the Lord: "We praise thee, we bless thee, we worship thee, we glorify thee; we give thanks to thee for thy great glory."

59.2 [57]: For Vincent and Walter were not the first: NB3 (62) includes here in large letters Beckett's self-instruction, "Walterise selon P. 81" (**#33**); that is, in conformity with his page 81 (in the HRHRC numeration, 162), after having finalized the names of the servants who come and go and the sequence in which they do so: Vincent, Walter, Arsene, Erskine, Johnny. NB3 (62-65) makes the changes; the typescript (239-42) gets them into the final order. The sequence finally became: Walter, Vincent, Arsene, Erskine, Watt, Arthur, and Micks. Mood has noted ("Personal System" 259) that there are seventeen items, that the first listing is complete, but that only nine are listed the second time, "though correctly." If by "items" he means individuals the count is inexact, as, according to my tally of sequential and completed "moves," the lists correspond and are exhaustive. The difference is that the first goes back in single units, beginning with Walter (I have added two later sets to indicate how exactly they correspond); whereas Watt, Arsene, and Erskine have entered the second series, and the "oustings" each skip one servant (that is, the new one in ousts not his predecessor but the one before him):

                    List A (the two servants tending Mr. Knott)
  a. *Erskine and Arsene
  b. *Arsene and Walter
  1. Walter and Vincent
  2. Vincent and another whose name Arsene forgets
  3. that other whose name Arsene forgets and another whose name he also forgets
  4. that [other] other whose name he also forgets and another whose name he never knew
  5. that other whose name he never knew and another whose name Walter could not recall

6. that other whose name Walter could not recall and another whom Walter could not recall either
7. that [other] other whose name Walter could not recall either and another whose name Walter never knew
8. that other whose name Walter never knew and another whose name even Vincent could not call to mind
9. that other whose name even Vincent could not call to mind and another whose name even Vincent could not call to mind either
10. that [other] other whose name even Vincent could not call to mind either and another whose name Vincent never knew

List B (servants ousted as others come in)
a. Watt ousted Arsene
b. Erskine ousted Walter
1. Arsene ousted Vincent
2. Walter ousted that other whose name Arsene forgets
3. Vincent ousted that other whose name Arsene also forgets
4. that other whose name Arsene forgets ousted that other whose name Arsene never knew
5. that [other] other whose name Arsene also forgets ousted that other whose name Walter could not recall
6. that other whose name Arsene never knew ousted that other whose name Walter could not recall either
7. that other whose name Walter could not recall ousted that other whose name Walter never knew
8. that [other] other whose name Walter could not recall either ousted that other whose name even Vincent could not recall to mind
9. that other whose name Walter never knew ousted that other whose name even Vincent could not recall to mind either
10. that other whose name even Vincent could not recall to mind ousted that other whose name even Vincent never knew

60.1 [59]: the vanity of human wishes: as Ecclesiastes 1:2: "Vanity of vanities, saith the Preacher, vanity of vanities; all is vanity"; or Samuel Johnson's poem, "The Vanity of Human Wishes" (1749), his imitation of Juvenal's tenth satire; but equally the final line of Leopardi's "A se stesso": "e l'infinita vanità del tutto."

60.2 [59]: to the next but one: from grandparent to grandchild, as seems appropriate given the *modus operandi* of the second paradigm.

61.1 [59]: two types of men: Quin's predilection was for "small, bald, fat, pale, clean-shaven and bandy-legged men" (NB1, 87; TS, 67), like Arsene and Erskine, rather than big, bony ones like Watt, Vincent, and Walter. Compare Neary and Wylie in *Murphy*; or Vladimir and Estragon in *Waiting for Godot*. This is the "Hardy Laurel" genotype (*Grove Companion* 246), Oliver Hardy (the "little fat one") and Stan Laurel (a "long hank"), as Camier and Mercier are called (48). Arsene and Erskine are of a type, and consecutive in their coming and going, which means that the small fat type does not alternate with the big bony kind; with only seven known servants, the sequence {B B S S B S B}, where "S" is short and fat, and "B" is big and bony, offers no obvious pattern.

The French text offers an impressive "rhinorutilants" (red-nosed). Arsene's corrected slip, "with you and Arsene, forgive me, with you and Erskine," is likely (on the pattern of similar instances in the drafts of the *Trilogy*) to have been Beckett's inadvertent error, subsequently retained in a text that thus reflects the process of its composition (**115.3**).

61.2 [60]: never knew never knew: despite Beckett's writing "never knew" again in the margin of the galleys (G20), the Olympia text did not repeat the phrase; Beckett noted it in his copy for Grove, who made the change.

61.3 [60]: in tireless assiduity turning: as the angels turn, with care and attention, about the throne of God Dante's *Paradiso* (X); compare how heaven goes "rowan an' rowan an' rowan" in "Ding-Dong" (45). The allusion is repeated overleaf: "eternally turning about Mr Knott in tireless love." Compare *How It Is* (123): "we do not revolve." See also **74.3**.

62.1 [63]: Not that space is wanting . . . time lacking: earlier said (NB1, 89; TS, 69) of the "countless separate dissimilitudes" between Arsene and Erskine, despite their being of a type; then later (TS, 225) of listeners to the angelic choir, "too numerous to mention"; and again (NB4, 81; TS, 443), of Louit's duplicity. The statement became something of a refrain, reiterated then excised and placed variously in the drafts; this is the sole survivor.

62.2 [61]: I hear a little wind: in broadly biblical terms, the Holy Spirit, as in Acts 2:2, the descent of the Holy Dove on the apostles at Pentecost. Compare "The wind in the reeds" (*Waiting for Godot* 15). In the earlier drafts (NB3, 41; TS, 227), it was a sign for Arsene to go, after a long night in Mr. Quin's hallway (**#37**), as it may later be for Watt (**223.3**). The phrase was then placed before the onions and peppermints. Molloy as he leaves Lousse feels a "little wind," whence he cannot tell (*Molloy* 60); that passed by the young Jacques Moran (118) forms its ironic counterpoint.

62.3 [61]: that fire . . . that shall never be snuffed: echoing Latimer to Ridley, as they awaited burning (16 October 1555), as in Beckett's notes of English literature (TCD 10970, 6r): "Be of good comfort, Master Ridley, & play the man; we shall this day light such a candle by God, here in England as I trust shall never be put out."

62.4 [61]: as you perhaps will do for another: compare **45.4** for a similar moment of skepticism; in the event (222), Watt departs without even taking leave of Micks.

62.5 [61]: ineffable: of the incapacity of human understanding to comprehend God. Geulincx uses "ineffabile" in his *Ethica* of the conjunction of body and mind, glossing it in the "Annotata" (242-43) as the hypostasis, or dual nature of God and man in Christ. Geulincx wrote, and Beckett recorded (TCD 10971/6, 23): "Ineffabile . . . id est dicitur, non quod cogitare aut effari non possumus (noc enim nihil esset: num nihil et non cogitabile idem sunt" ["Ineffable

. . . is that which we cannot understand and grasp (which is <u>nothing</u>; in fact, <u>nothing</u> and <u>not thinkable</u> are the same thing)"]; it is rather that modality that we either cannot think of or cannot completely grasp through reason. Malone (218) contemplates conating and ineffing. Despite Arsene's clear warning that the attempt to utter or to eff is doomed to fail, Watt will persist in his attempts to do so, even as his world becomes unspeakable.

62.6 [61]: from the crown of my head to the soles of my feet: Job 2:7: "So went Satan forth from the presence of the Lord, and smote Job with sore boils from the sole of his foot unto his Crown."

63.1 [61]: do my doodles: *purissimavirgoemendacormeumetcarnemmeam*. Or, perhaps, as Beckett does throughout the *Watt* notebooks.

63.2 [62]: like Theseus kissing Ariadne: as he was about to abandon her on Naxos. Ariadne, the daughter of Minos and Pasiphae, fell in love with Theseus, who carried her away, only to forsake her on the shore.

63.3 [62]: hither and thither: like the wading girl in of Joyce's *Portrait* (172), stirring the water with her foot, "hither and thither," and stirring equally a profane joy in the mind of Stephen Dedalus. The connecting link with Theseus and Ariadne is "on the seashore." Arsene's dawdling suggests the inertia of Proust's tante Léonie (*Swann* I.242-43), like a water-lily driven from bank to bank, "refaisant éternellement la double traversée" ["eternally repeating the double crossing"]; reaching its point of departure only to repeat the antithetical manoeuvre, "pareil aussi à quelqu'un de ces malheureux dont le tourment singulier, qui se répète indéfiniment durant l'éternité, excitait la curiosité de Dante" ["also like one of these unhappy ones whose particular torment, repeated indefinitely throughout eternity, aroused Dante's curiosity"]. Beckett had made this association in *Murphy* (56). Either nuance is lost in the French translation (64): "par ci par là."

63.4 [62]: by your side, to be your guide: in the medieval mystery play, *Everyman*, Knowledge says (lines 522-23): "Everyman, I will go with thee, and be thy guide / In thy most need to go by thy side." This is the epigraph to the Dent Everyman series. Cohn notes (*Canon* 396) the anticipation of *Company*: "only shades to keep you company."

63.5 [62]: for what I have not said, I ask you: echoing the Anglican Confession: "We have left undone those things which we ought to have done; And we have done those things which we ought not to have done; And there is no health in us." In his copy of the Grove text prepared for Calder, Beckett deleted the comma.

63.6 [62]: for what I have done ill: further echoing the Anglican confession: "We do earnestly repent, and are heartily sorry for these our misdoings; the remembrance of them is grievous unto us; the burden of them is intolerable." The penitent seek forgiveness; but Arsene's affirmation that personally it is all the same to him whether he is thought of "with forgiveness or with rancour" does not improve his chances. That sentiment was present in the early drafts (NB3, 67; TS, 243-44), but there lacked dramatic impact.

63.7 [62]: bugger these buttons: as Doherty has noted (39), a gloriously banal echo of the dying Lear's "Pray you undo this button" (*King Lear* V.iii.309), repeated from earlier in the scene (see **42.10**); Arsene is clearly having major problems with his greatcoat. The phrase does not appear in the early drafts (TS, 244), where Arsene simply rises and, buttoning his coat, leaves the house; but it is present in the late draft (NB4, 245).

63.8 [62]: Goodbye: Doherty notes (39) throughout Arsene's short statement a sustained situational echo of the Anglican service of Evensong, and especially of the *Nunc Dimittis*, from Luke 2:29-31: "Nunc dimittis servum tuum, Domine" ["Lord, now lettest thou thy servant depart in peace"], Simeon's song of petition, thanks-giving, and prophecy.

63.9 [62]: he appeared again, to Watt: a devastating use of the comma, transforming the pedestrian prose of the late draft (Arsene "appeared again to Watt") into a tragedy of *percipere*. Arsene at the kitchen door strikes the same pose as Clov in *Endgame*, when the latter is (or is not) about to depart from Hamm.

63.10 [62]: became two men: less the experience of alterity than an anticipation of the strange figure to appear to Watt on his departure (**225.2**).

64.1 [63]: a firm unhurried hand: like the sudarium (**32.8**), anticipating (by several decades, and less gently) the action of the dreamt self in "Nacht und Träume" (1982).

64.2 [63]: turning towards the lamp: perhaps, the attempt to switch off the inward glare that the thing-in-itself might be more readily discerned (see **37.4** for the Cartesian paradox of light directed toward the understanding). In vain: in the darkness Watt is "no whit better off than before."

64.3 [63]: little by little: from the proverb, "little by little the bird builds its nest" (**194.4**); one of Beckett's "true sayings," but associated with the *sortites* problem of the millet grains (**43.3**, **182.4**, **235.2**). This ending is not in the early drafts, but the typescript (244) presents a crude version; the poetic passage (from "already in the kitchen" to the end) first appears (early 1945) in NB5 (2).

64.4 [63]: gold and white and blue: with liturgical significance, the gold and white of Easter combined with the blue and white of the Virgin Mary. This "day without precedent" signals a new dispensation, whereas the sky in *Molloy* (129) is simply "that horrible colour which heralds dawn."

II

67.1 [64]: II: in the galleys, a single blank line marks the end of the previous section and the start of this. Beckett marked "Chapître 2" (then "II," changing the figure from Arabic to Roman), and added (much as he would for parts III and IV): "Commencer avec 20 l., en belle page" (that is, begin on a new page with a twenty-line break). The Olympia and Grove pagination is hereafter re-aligned.

67.2 [64]: Mr Knott: earlier drafts (NB3, 69; TS, 245) begin: "Then the years passed, it seems to Watt now a great number of years, though they cannot have been so many, each in all essential particulars closely resembling the other." The intuitive assumption, that Watt spends a year on each floor, (a) has nothing tangible to confirm it, and (b) is the consequence of later revision where the category of time is unmarked (and space and causality, in Schopenhauer's sense, similarly obscured). The typescript comments (269, crossed out) that Watt "~~entered Quin's service on the 26th of June~~" (**104.1**). Mr. Knott is a good master, in a way, but the qualification matters, for Watt has few direct dealings with him and by the end of a (presumably) two-year tenure will know him little better than he does now. Mr. Knott is a God-figure, and the novel is fundamentally an allegory; in Christian terms (the mythology with which Beckett claimed to be most familiar), of mankind's quest for salvation, and the inevitable frustration of that quest. The opening of part II, up until "the old credentials" (*Watt* 85) appeared in John Calder's 1983 *A Samuel Beckett Reader* (71-84); despite the same title, a selection differing from his 1967 Reader.

67.3 [64]: for reasons that are not known: compare "for reasons unknown" of Lucky's short statement in *Waiting for Godot*. At the end of Watt's sojourn in Knott's house, as in the beginning, the reasons (even those offered to the understanding) remain unknown. The hope, entertained here, that the "time would come for him, as he thought it had ended for Arsene, and for Erskine just begun," that is, of some clarification during "the second or closing period of Watt's stay in Mr Knott's house" (*Watt* 165), is doomed to frustration; indeed, little narrative attention will be given to that period.

68.1 [64]: seakale: a hardy headless variety of cabbage, with dark green curly leaves (*Brassica oleracea acephala*). The late draft (NB5, 5) crosses out "~~strawberries~~."

68.2 [64]: on the dunghill: the late draft (NB5, 5) read: "on the scrap heap." The final instructions undermine Ecclesiastes 3:1: "To every thing there is a season, and a time to every purpose under heaven."

68.3 [65]: remarkable: with the French intonation, "worthy of notice"; the late draft (NB5, 5) reads: "a shame." Nothing is said about the "second floor slops" (those of Mr. Knott, presumably), save this cryptic comment that both Watt and Erskine are responsible for their disposal, and that (a parody of the Cartesian mingling of vital and animal spirits in the conarium?) their commixture with those of the first floor is not encouraged.

68.4 [65]: that complex and delicate matter, Mr Knott's food: said (*Watt* 87) to give very little trouble. The typescript (247) led directly into the preparation of Mr. Quin's food, but in the late draft the passages concerning the Galls and the pot were assigned their final positions.

68.5 [65]: to be sure: the casual assertion uttered when one is uncertain. The typescript noted of Arsene (199): "a Gallic tinge creeping into his style as a result of his chagrin."

69.1 [65]: please God: not in the late draft (NB5, 7); the lack of commas accentuates its cliched nature. The matter is "described" at the end of part II.

69.2 [65]: Severn: in the late draft (NB5, 7) the postman is named "Shannon" (**47.7**). The change intimates Joseph Severn, the physician attending Keats (who died of TB); one westwards river replacing another. O'Brien (18) documents Bill Shannon's love of greyhounds and dancing; the French text (62) adds: "grand danseur devant l'Eternel."

69.3 [66]: Mr Graves: earlier (NB4, 10) "Mr Gomez"; in the later draft (NB5, 7), simply "the gardener" (**142.5**).

69.4 [66]: no light for Watt: faintly ironic, given wattage as the measure of illumination.

69.5 [66]: his mouthpiece: the first distinct intimation of Sam, whose presence becomes increasingly evident. NB5 (9), written in early 1945, reads "~~his amanuensis~~"; this is crossed out and "his mouthpiece" written on the verso opposite (8). See **79.1** and **125.1**.

69.6 [66]: the fishwoman: Mrs. Gorman (**138.1**). Not present at this point (NB5, 9), but a reference added as an insert on the opposite verso (NB5, 8v).

70.1 [66]: it's: having overlooked it in the galleys (G22), Beckett noted the error, his from the late draft (NB5, 9), on his copy of the Olympia text, but as it remained uncorrected he again marked it for change on his copy of Grove for the Calder edition.

70.2 [67]: This fugitive penetration: "fugitive" invariably possesses for Beckett the echo of Dante's "così l'animo mio, ch'ancor fuggiva, / si volse a retro a rimirar lo passo / che non lasciò giammi persona viva" [*Inferno* I.25-27: "thus my soul, ever fugitive, turns back to look at the pass [the *selva*], which none has ever left alive" (Beckett's under-lining; TCD 10966, 2r); Cary translates the phrase as "that yet failed"]. The incident with the Galls father and son assumes increasingly this aspect of failure.

70.3 [67]: the Galls, father and son: one piano-tuner was present in the drafts of *Watt* virtually from the outset (NB1, 13, 21). This blind man was first Hicks; this was crossed out (TS, 2) and replaced by Green, composer of "To Nelly" (**11.2**).

NB5 (11) replaces "tune" with "temper" (in the French [63], "accorder"); but Beckett finally chose "choon." By so doing, Heath Lees suggests (185), he sought not merely to imitate the Dublin accent but to do so in a manner itself slightly off-key. The episode appeared (with minor variations) as a pre-publication "Extract from *Watt*" in *Irish Writing* 22 (March 1953): 16-24. Culik argues (101) that "Gall" derives from Franz Joseph Gall, father of phrenology, noting the way that Mr. Gall in *Mercier and Camier* claims to know the secrets of the skull. This is supported, obliquely, by Garnier's *Onanisme* (83): "le célèbre phrénologiste Gall, en vertu de son ingénieux système des localisations de toutes les facultés dans la boître crânienne"; the piano as a box of mis-firing synapses. A collateral relative, Lord Gall of Wormwood, features in "Echo's Bones" and *Murphy* (99). Consider, too, the blind stripling, the piano tuner of *Ulysses*. Further references in *Watt* to "the Galls father and son" invariably lack the comma.

Lees explores a different "comma": that arising in Western music as a consequence of the disparity between the mathematical ratios of the notes of the octave and their acoustical realities. He cites early references about the bells that ring at the end of Watt's first period (**149.1**): "a chord, a charming chord, a charming charming second a comma sharp, a charming charming third a comma flat" (TS, 459). The "Pythagorean comma" is, Lees says (175), the difference between tuning twelve perfect fifths as opposing to seven perfect octaves, which piano tuners overcome by "tempering" the instrument, spreading the anomaly imperceptibly over the other notes within the octaves (*Grove Companion* 78). The discrepancy, he concludes, lies at the heart of Western music, and this acoustical fact offers a sustained metaphor for Watt's untuning: "inevitable not just because Watt is what he is, but also because Western music is what it is" (184).

70.4 [67]: we are come: appropriately Gallic ("nous sommes venus").

70.5 [67]: but he might have done this: a brief flirtation with the Cartesian method and the potential absurdities arising from such inquiry.

71.1 [67]: Or were they not: the question mark was deliberately dropped, before the galley stage, having been present in the late draft (NB5, 11). In the next paragraph, "disposition" was crossed out in the galleys (G22) and "command" substituted; and in the one following, the definite article was added to Olympia's "to music room."

71.2 [68]: deserved to be admitted: a Pelagian rather than an Augustinian perspective.

71.3 [68]: Buxtehude: Dietrich Buxtehude (1637-1709), Danish-born organist and composer, whose *Abendmusik* Bach once walked fifty miles to hear. The name is written in large letters in NB2 (12v). He represents, Heath Lees suggests (177), composers turning from old vocal modes to new tunings, the well-tempered scale overcoming the "Pythagorean comma" (**70.3**). This description of the music room was earlier (TS, 97) part of Art Conn O'Connor's picture of Mr. Alexander Quin at his piano (**#26**).

71.4 [68]: a ravanastron: identified by Lees (178) as an ancient Indian instrument of the banjo family, with a long neck, a tuning peg, and rounded sounding board; in the early drafts (NB3, 12; TS, 97), it hangs from a red nail, grey-green, with a green-grey bamboo bow. In the typescript (45), Mr. Alexander Quin spent the leisures of a lifetime on the ravanastron, neglecting James in its favor. The crucified plover appears in the galleys, but is anticipated in *Dream* (205), the Alba's back like "a bird crucified on a wall."

72.1 [68-69]: The mice have returned: later associated (**232.3**) with a patter of sensation in Watt's mind. In the early drafts (NB1, 21; TS, 9) Quin and Green discoursed:

> "The mice have returned" said Quin.
> "Nine dampers remain" said Green, "and a like number of hammers."
> "Not corresponding, I hope" said Quin.
> "In one case" said Green.
> "Not successive, I trust" said Quin.
> "No, sir" said Green.
> Quin had nothing further to say.
> "The piano is doomed, in my humble opinion" said Green.
> "The pianist also" said Quin.
> "The piano-tuner also" said Green.

Nine hammers remain, and an equal number of dampers, corresponding in one instance only; this parodies notions of harmony and synchronicity, and intimates a serial universe, in which systems and patterns exist, and must upon occasion coincide, and yet do so in a manner that finally lacks meaning (**93.4**, **134.2**, **136.5**).

72.2 [69]: incidents of note: the typescript meditates (125): "The things of note, the things of less note. / The things of little note, the things of no note." The pun becomes a refrain (**128.4**). The late draft (NB5, 13) crosses out "various incidents" and writes "incidents of note." In the preceding paragraph, the galleys offered an intriguing hypostasis (G23), corrected without comment: "Mr Wnott's house."

72.3 [69]: in a sense not: the late draft (NB5, 11) clarifies the implied syntax: "and in a sense it differed from them"; the minor change renders the text more "knotty."

73.1 [70]: purely plastic: Gk. *plasma*, "a thing molded or formed"; hence, malleable, lacking in structure or form, particularly (in light of the discussion to come) that imposed upon language by semantics and semiotics. In the same line, *nice* is used in the literal sense of "precise" or "scrupulous."

73.2 [70]: gradually lost . . . its sound . . . all meaning: this is the experience, later marked in Beckett's writing, of the *diminuendo al niente*, or fading into nothing. Heath Lees has indicated Beckett's precise sense of this pattern, describing Watt's experience, or "untuning," in terms of his diminishing response to the musical stimuli around him, to the things that might have attuned his world had he been able to hear them (**#34**). The musical experience generated by that "incident of note," the Galls, thus corresponds to Watt's experience of diminution with the pot (*Watt* 75ff.), meaning fading until language is purely plastic; and to his visual experience of the picture, or colored reproduction (128-30), which likewise fades in time. The tragedy may be defined in terms of the Gestalt: with repeated familiarity the figure, as an organized whole, becomes one with the background against which it earlier stood out; so that when the various stimuli no longer provoke Watt to re-form the Gestalt and so distinguish it from the homogenous surface, or ground, the figure becomes increasingly impaired, until no differentiation is possible.

Damian Love offers a complementary reading, in terms of Beckett's fascination with schizophrenia: "A brain disease affecting attentional mechanisms, it disrupts the ability to integrate perception and behavior in a coherent narrative. Familiar features may become drained of secure meaning; trivia may seem uncannily significant; the whole world undergoes a sinister, infinitesimal slip into unreality. It is akin to the common experience of derealization whereby prolonged fixation renders a word or object 'peculiar' (*unheimlich*). These phenomena indicate an inward focus of attention, albeit not consciously undertaken, upon cognition itself, until consciousness, not designed for such hyper-reflexivity, becomes lost in a mental mirror-world and begins to fragment. An example of such confusion is the inability to distinguish between external voices and the inner voice of one's own thoughts; the latter may be objectified into the 'voices' of typical schizophrenic hallucination. The resulting 'madness' raises problems, in that psychotic reason cannot be equated with irrationality or incoherence. Bizarre as schizophrenic behavior can seem, it rarely lacks a logical basis. It tends rather to reflect the fact that the schizophrenic's reasoning is no longer grounded in the *implicit* framework of practical orientations and shared cognitive skills developed and maintained by social existence. Schizophrenics often try to mitigate the instability of their radically subjective world by holding fast to very *explicit* principles, and reasoning from them inflexibly until reason itself becomes a path to 'insane' beliefs. Watt is a case in point . . . [He] strives sincerely to hang on to normal cognizance of the outside world but fails through the very strain of his efforts. Desperate attempts to make the absurd incident of the Galls father and son yield a meaning leave Watt baffled as it 'gradually lost, in the nice processes of its light, its sound, its impacts and its rhythm, all meaning, even the most literal' (73). This is one of Watt's many perceptual fluxes. His relentless scrutiny of experience has effects similar to those of the reflexive focus of schizophrenia, although genuine psychosis sets in at a level of cognition prior to conscious intentionality. Watt's horror at this chaos drives him to more rigorous applications of logical scrutiny, which lead only to such absurdities as the famished dog hypothesis. As schizophrenia demonstrates, logical reasoning, divorced from the implicit scaffolding of 'normal' socialized orientation, is itself the surest path to insanity" (*Grove Companion* 504). As Love suggests in his Oxford D. Phil (22), this is not the fanciful "slap-up" psychosis of *Murphy* (104) but the nightmare experience of alienation. That process is accentuated in *Watt* hereafter.

73.3 [70]: comment: with a sense of the French *commenter*, "to interpret."

73.4 [70]: This fragility of outer meaning: Watt's purely literal readings of experience reflect an oddly prelapsarian view of language, in which words mean only, and precisely, what they seem to say. But *now* the "outer meaning" is lost (**73.2**), which causes Watt to search for a substitute (symbolic, allegorical) meaning (**73.5**), and in that process literal meaning deteriorates altogether. This speculation, and that which follows, first appeared in the late drafts (NB5, 15ff.), with a fleeting error in the galleys (23), Watt having not seen a symbol since "the sage of fourteen."

73.5 [70]: a symbol: *Watt* ends with a flourish: "No symbols where none intended." "Symbol" is best understood in the sense of *allegory*, which, as Beckett noted in his "Dante" essay (1929), implies a three-fold intellectual operation: "the construction of a message of general significance, the preparation of a fabulous form, and an exercise of considerable technical ingenuity in uniting the two" (*Disjecta* 26). Watt, to his credit, does not attempt this, but is unable even to cope with face values, the "direct expression" Beckett affirmed in that early essay (29). Beckett had noted in *Proust* (11) that the Proustian equation is never simple; but the key to its resolution is what he calls *the ideal real*, "at once imaginative and empirical, at once an evocation and a direct perception, real without being merely actual, ideal without being merely abstract, the ideal real" (*Proust* 75; *Le Temps retrouvé* II.872-73). This underlies the sense of particularity, of the straws and flotsam that constitute the only things that the mind might grasp. By the time he was writing *Watt*, however, Beckett's distrust of even the ideal real had hardened, largely due to Fritz Mauthner, who contends that though there can be no thought without words, words themselves are inane, *verba inania*, lacking substance or sense, and so our thoughts are inane, empty, never "obviating the void" (*Grove Companion* 359). Beckett's acceptance of Mauthner's "Nominalist irony" (*Disjecta* 173), and his qualified affirmation of demented particulars (*Murphy* 13), opens the way for the "inane" verbal comedy, much of it cast in Proustian terms, that follows here.

73.6 [70]: when his father appeared to him in a wood: a vision (**91.1**), but also an involuntary memory, so immediately present (**73.5**); thus, in Watt's understanding, an ordinary occasion, ideal and real rather than allegorical. Compare Murphy's vain attempts to invoke voluntary images of his father.

73.7 [70]: a voice: soon to become insistent (**91.1**).

74.1 [70]: flowering currant: the late draft (NB5, 17) reads "violets." Compare images of hawthorn (in *Dream*, "The Expelled," and *Molloy*) and verbena (*Dream*, *Molloy*, *How It Is*, *Film*), in terms of the Proustian experience of past time. In *Swann* (1.207), Marcel, his autoerotic passion spent, sees the trace of a snail among the sprays of "cassis sauvage" [wild black-currant] outside his window, and senses that he is alone, with night falling on a sterile land. As this memory is involuntary, the past returns in its full radiance. Compare Krapp's experience in the punt (61). In the French translation of *Watt* (74), Beckett suppressed the allusion, preferring "une bouffée de groseiller en fleur."

74.2 [70]: an old lady: later named as "Mrs Watson" (**80.4, 139.1**). The galleys (G23) erroneously rendered her "young"; Beckett recorrected this to "old." In the late draft (NB5, 17), the first encounter, she is "a lady of delicate upbringing and advantageous person" (though amputated above the knee), who leads Watt to understand, with characteristic delicacy, that, all things considered, she had no objection.

74.3 [70]: assiduities: constant attentiveness (well, three distinct occasions). Johnson's *Dictionary* defines *assiduity* as: "Diligence, closeness of attention"; giving as its example (Rogers): "Can he, who undertakes this, want conviction of the necessity of his utmost vigour, and *assiduity*, to acquit himself of it."

74.4 [70]: no tendency appeared: a phrase used to describe apparently habitual activity in a pseudo-objective manner, in parody of the language of psychiatry. In particular, it is used of Watt's various manifestations of aphasia (**165.3**).

74.5 [71]: fistular: a *fistula* is an abnormal passage between two internal organs, or from one to the surface of the body, as literally in *Mercier and Camier* (58), or metaphorically in *Murphy* (219): a "psychosomatic fistula." The Unnamable (353) considers himself a network of fistulae. Watt's father's trousers are, more simply, full of holes.

74.6 [71]: in the farce of their properties: that is, in the particular instance of his father, Watt is able to go beyond "face values" (as it were), and perceive not simply the externals (the trousers, gray, flaccid, and fistular) but that which is not obviously perceptible (the legs within the trousers). The incident with the Galls, on the contrary, cannot be thus sustained in his mind; indeed, even the superficial significance fades.

74.7 [71]: in his time . . . on the contrary: although correct in the proofs (G24), this line was misplaced in the Olympia edition, and entered four lines later; Beckett marked the error on his Olympia text, and the adjustment was made by Grove. The grammatical distinction between nouns of mass and number is here abused by "quantity."

74.8 [71]: ill told, ill heard: intimating the narrative consequences of how the story will be relayed (imperfectly) by Watt to Sam, and thence (imperfectly) to the reader; but also anticipating stories later told, such as *Ill Seen Ill Said* (1979-81), where seeing is always ill seeing, saying always ill saying, and images ill seen and ill said worsen in the haze into "collapse" (78). Asserting broad similarities (alienation, the quest, prose that goes on like a steam-roller) rather than ascribing direct influence, Ruby Cohn hears here an echo of *The Castle* (1922), the only large work of Kafka (she suggests) that Beckett might have read in German: "Es war mir, als sei es vor vielen Jahren geschehen, oder als sei es gar nicht mir geschehen, oder hätte ich es nur erzählen hören, oder als hätte ich selbst es schon vergessen" ["To me it was as if I had heard it many years before, or as if it had really not happened to me, or that I might only have heard it, or that I might myself have already forgotten it"] (*Das Schloss*; in Fletcher 88). However, Beckett probably did not read Kafka in German before World War II (Matthew Feldman to CA).

74.9 [71]: and more than half forgotten: insofar as memory, in the Cartesian paradigm, represents an extension of self into the past, and to the extent that Mauthner is correct in saying that memory and language are synonymous, it follows that the unreliability of the one entails the inevitable failure of the other. As a consequence of such impairment of memory, Watt is incapable of reconstituting a unified self. Memory, like voice, finally becomes a trace, the half-remembered, half-forgotten difficult music of echoes ill-recalled and selves fugitively united (*Grove Companion* 361-66).

74.10 [71]: to unroll its sequences: Watt's mind is likened to a movie, giving the credits after the action is over. In *Murphy* (252), also as he is trying to recreate an image of his father, Murphy's mind reels upward off a spool. The common source is part IV of Henri Bergson's *Creative Evolution* (1907), with its metaphor of the cinematographical mind, conceptual thought likened to the cinematograph. Beckett used Bergson's metaphor in the fragment, "Lightning Calculation" (1934), where Quigley systematizes his feelings: "Item: He could not forget his father's death, the entire process of which, from the falling ill to the internment, had become a talkie in his brain of almost continuous performance featuring himself, in postures that impressed him as ignoble." The reference suggests a technique and metaphor for Watt's perceptual fluxes, for the schizophrenic eye that pays attention too closely has affinities with the camera and thus depicts effects that can be achieved through close-ups, stills, and slow-motions, which break down our sense of normal functions and actions, and confront us instead with their "properties" (Damian Love to CA). Compare *Malone Dies* (194): "The turmoil of the day freezes in a thousand absurd postures."

75.1 [71]: the simple games that time plays with space: compare Mr. Hackett's sense of "the frigid machinery of a time-space relation" (**21.2**), and the painting of the circle and [its] center, in boundless space, in endless time (**129.5**). Watt, the reader will be told (129), knows nothing about physics, but clutches to the perimeter of a classical Newtonian universe where laws of reason, harmony, and equilibrium hold sway, unaware of developments in contemporary physics (atomic fission, quantum mechanics, relativity, and uncertainty) that have changed the rules.

75.2 [71]: toys: in the Cartesian sense of a mechanical device or machine; compare the "ethical yo-yo" of *Murphy* (108). Watt's toys (logic, reason) are outworn (**75.1**).

75.3 [72]: not into what they really meant: I cite Kenner (58), who notes Jacqueline Hoefer, who quotes Wittgenstein (*pereant qui ante*): "to distinguish between what can be said about an event and what the event *really* means is sheer nonsense." The reasoning is Kantian: the distinction between the *noumenon*, the *Ding-an-sich* that cannot be known; and *phenomena*, that may be apprehended by the senses. The "oh" was added in the late rewriting to accentuate this enormity.

75.4 [72]: induced: compare Murphy's "maieutic saw" (*Murphy* 71), the contention of Socrates (whose mother, Phaenarete, was a mid-wife) that he was incapable of giving birth to wisdom, but was an excellent man-midwife, skilled in the art of bringing thought to birth (*Grove Companion* 532-33). Here, however, meaning "induced" gives way to things "elicited" (*Watt* 77), "saddle[d]" (79), and finally "foisted in" (126).

75.5 [72]: the notorious difficulty: the Proustian equation, resolved through the agency of involuntary memory, when the past returns in its full radiance; the appositional phrase, "at will," implies instead the conscious monochromate agency of voluntary memory. The late draft (NB5, 19) reads "intellectually"; the French translation (75): "a volonté."

75.6 [72]: the material conditions . . . the scant aptitude: that is, the imperfect mode of communication, advanced by Watt in the asylum to Sam, as described in part III.

75.7 [72]: litigious: in the scholastic sense of inviting controversy or logical disputation (a *summa* of the preceding cases of "Add to this"), rather than with any legal implication.

76.1 [72]: the first and type of many: in the words of Thomas Vaughan, from his "Poimandres" in the *Corpus Hermeticum*: "Nature that was so fair in the *type* could not be a *slut* in the *Anaglyph*. This makes her ramble hither to examine the medall by the *Flaske*, but whiles she scanns their *Symmetrie*, she *forms* it. Thus her *descent* speaks her *Originall*: God in love with his *owne Beauty*, frames a Glasse to *view* it by *reflection;* but the *frailety* of the matter excluding *eternity*, the *composure* was subject to *dissolution*" (Rudrum, ed., *Thomas Vaughan* 598). The distinction is Platonic, that between the Idea and the particular, but, in printing, the type is the matrix from which all anaglyphs take their form (imperfect, since copies). The frailty of Watt being what it is, to say nothing of eternity, the image formed is subject to inevitable deterioration, and finally dissolution.

76.2 [73]: a thing that was nothing had happened: that is, not nothing, but a thing that was nothing; a distinction reflecting the sentiment of Democritus, so important in chapter 11 of *Murphy*, that non-Being (the Void) has an equal right with Being to be existent; that that which Is Not is equally as real as that which Is: "Naught exists as much as Aught" (**77.5**). Watt intuits this proposition, but its subtlety is too much for him.

77.1 [73]: In a culture-park?: where mass-products and artifacts of the social contract are displayed. The use of "one" adds to the hauteur, uniting Sam and his dear reader in scorn of the world; the French "Dans un centre culturel?" (77) softens the scorn.

77.2 [74]: or the door become a door: in his Grove copy, Beckett changed "or" to "on" for the Calder edition, which made the change. In the galleys, he had twice changed "became" to "become," but apparently did not notice the "or." In the late drafts (NB5, 182), Beckett had noted: "Gall incident. Not a ring but a knock"; the sense of opportunity [not ever] knocking is more pronounced in the drafts.

77.3 [74]: I remember: such memories (**74.1**, **75.5**) would be voluntary.

77.4 [74]: he could never have spoken at all of these things: as Molloy might say: "You must choose, between the things not worth mentioning and those even less so. For if you set out to mention everything you would never be done" (*Molloy* 41).

77.5 [74]: For the only way one can speak of nothing: in the galleys (G25), this sentence, until "termite," was enclosed in square brackets, which Beckett marked for deletion. It picks up Watt's previous speculations (**76.2**) about the nature of nothing, and extends them in the direction of negative theology: the contention that it can be said of God only that he has no qualities known to man, that "no name names him," and that "we can predicate of God only what he is not" (Windelband 237, 290). Hesla (77) cites Spinoza's *omnis determinatio est negatio*, unaware that Beckett had earlier done so in the Whoroscope Notebook (59; from Dean Inge's *Christian Mysticism* 121), to the effect that the perception of a figure is not the determination of its being, but of its non-being (consider Watt's problems in "determining" the elusive figure that appears, to him, at the end of the novel). The deity thus conceived is above or beyond reason and being: "it has no determination or quality, it is 'Nothing'" (Windelband 335). In Alexander's summary (189), positive determinations would reduce His substance to something finite; it must, therefore, be described in negative terms: "We do not know what God is; we can only say what He is not." This conception passed in Greek thought through Philo to the gnostics and early Christian apologists, especially Augustine, to inform medieval scholasticism and the *via negativa* of mysticism with the *docta ignoranta*, the stripping of knowledge so that the deity-as-Nothing might be apprehended as not-knowing, a step toward not-being, or the Not-I. Such matters were recorded extensively in Beckett's early notes on Philosophy (TCD 10967), but the *via negativa* retained its attraction long after its rejection as "all balls" in *How It Is*. Hence his partial acceptance of "The Way" (1981), an unpublished prose-poem now at the HRHRC, Austin, that forms a distillation of all the journeys undertaken by his various characters (*Grove Companion* 637-38).

77.6 [74]: as though he were a man: the qualifications of this simple proposition ("which to be sure he was, in a sense, for a time") were even more devastating in the late draft (NB5, 23), which added: "in part." Compare *Molloy* (39): "What I liked in anthropology was its inexhaustible faculty of negation, its relentless definition of man, as though he were no better than God, in terms of what he is not."

77.7 [74]: anthropologists . . . termite: to be studied in terms of its social behavior, a perspective with which Beckett had little sympathy; indeed, he took issue with any theory of anthropomorphism, such as that of Protagoras, that assumed man ("Homo mensura") to be the measure of all things. To a short note on Geulincx and the theory of the two clocks (TCD 10967, 189r), Beckett added in annoyance: "What anthropologism!" He copied Mauthner's attack upon "Anthropomorphismus" (TCD 10971/5, 1; *Beiträge* II 474), underlining the sentence: "Der mittelalterliche Nominalismus ist der erste Versuch der wirklichen Selbstzersetzung des metaphorischen Denkens" ["The nominalism of the Middle Ages is the first attempt at a genuine self-destruction of metaphorical thinking"]. This passage concludes (10971/1, 4; *Beiträge* II.479) with a sentiment that informs this section of *Watt*: "Das letze Wort des Denkens kann nur die negative Tat sein, die Selbstzersetzung des Anthropomorphismus, die Einsicht in die profunde Weisheit des Vico: homo non intelligendo fit omnia" ["The last word of thought can only be the negative act, the self-destruction of anthropomorphism, the insight into the profound wisdom of Vico: not everything is intelligible to man"].

78.1 [74]: a hypothesis: an equally ancient error, that to explain is to exorcise. Watt may have failed with the Galls father and son, but a more elaborate instance is soon forthcoming, with the hypothesis needed (then needing to be replaced by another, and yet another) to account for the famished dog. Even so, this is not a bad definition of scientific method and its recurrent need to reformulate hypotheses, although Beckett does not acknowledge the principle of falsifiability (in the Whoroscope Notebook [18], he was more cynical: "function of hypothesis 'to save the appearances', i.e., over the facts"). Beckett's earlier notes on Socrates (TCD 10967/52ff) indicate the general provenance of this passage within pre-Socratic thought and with explicit reference to what he called "Limits of Knowing": that hypotheses have nothing to do with ethics but rather reflect the "essential nature of science" and conceptual thinking, so are not considered within the eudaimonistic principles of Socrates. The narrative perspective here is thus curiously in sympathy with that of Socrates, an anthropomorphic ethic that is also [above] rejected.

78.2 [75]: variously interpreted: in the late draft (NB5, 24), "variously hypostasized"; assuming (like Christ) the dual nature of man and God.

79.1 [76]: to me: the first direct admission by Sam (as yet unnamed) of his authorial presence. Not in the late draft (NB5, 25/27), and thus indicative of the surprisingly late decision by Beckett to render retrospectively, and only gradually, the narrative of part II as (perhaps) having been presented through the mediation of Sam (**69.5, 125.1**).

79.2 [76]: posterior to the phenomena: that is, after-images (see *Demented Particulars* #246.1), formed by the continuance of the process in the sense-receptor after the stimulus has ceased, and explicable only by subsequent hypothesis (**78.1**); but with a Proustian tinge with respect to the initial meaning lost and then recovered, or the reversal of that process, the return to the inchoate. This long paragraph does not appear in NB5 (25-27). The inchoate was furthered when the Olympia text introduced "penomena," overlooked in the proofs (G25) but marked on Beckett's Olympia text for correction by Grove. Another error five lines later ("throught") was corrected ("thought") without comment.

80.1 [77]: one more word: rather, a short statement; but compromising the "Finally" (added later) of the previous paragraph.

80.2 [77]: Watt learnt . . . to accept: a sentiment that Beckett found significant (**#9**): nothing (a nothing) had happened, but was that not, perhaps, something?

80.3 [77]: flowering currant: a detail relating this passage to the wider Proustian debate about voluntary and involuntary memory (**74.1**).

80.4 [77]: Mrs Watson: similarly, in Watt's mind, an "ordinary occasion" (**73.6**), rather than a memory, voluntary or in—, and so not losing its definition. The "old lady of delicate upbringing" was so named in the later draft (NB5, 29), but the latent Oedipal implications of the earlier "capitulation" (**74.2**, **139.1**) are now manifest.

80.5 [77]: Watt thought sometimes of Arsene: the text from this point to "loss of species" (*Watt* 85) was included in John Calder's 1967 *A Samuel Beckett Reader* (43-57), but not in the 1983 selection with the same title. In his introduction (41), Calder calls it: "an amusing excursion into a kind of philosophical doodling that occurs often in Mr. Beckett's work and no doubt is part of the process by which . . . the soul grows wiser." The issue is more intricate than this suggests.

80.6 [deleted]: what had become of the duck: as a consequence of a previous excision (**45.6**), Beckett marked his Olympia text to cut this line and to adjust the following text: "He wondered ~~also~~ what Arsene had meant. . . ." Since regulation would have entailed a major resetting, Grove Press left the lines as they were, thus creating a major anomaly (for details of the duck, see **#37**, the Olympia original, or the 1958 Travellers' Companion edition). The Calder text omits these lines, and reads: "Watt sometimes thought of Arsene. He wondered what Arsene had meant. . . ." The French translation (81) follows suit. Salman Rushdie cites (55) a similar example in *The Wizard of Oz*, where the witch says, as she dispatches the Winged Monkeys to capture Dorothy, "I've sent a little insect ahead to take the fight out of them." There is no insect in the film, but there had been, for she refers to a musical sequence, by the Jitterbug, finally excised (Ralph Crane to CA).

81.1 [78]: if they consented to be named: as by Adam, in the Garden of Eden (**73.4**). The phrase appears, again, on page 84.

81.2 [78]: Pot, pot: Beckett in the galleys (G26) was particular about this capitalization, the two "forms" intimating the Idea and the particular, the latter evading by a hairbreadth the nature of a true Pot. The discrepancy reflects Plato's polemical argument in the *Cratylus* about naming, in turn anticipating the scholastic dispute between Nominalism and Realism, against Heraclitus and the notion of eternal change: "all things are like leaking pots." This might be rephrased in terms of *langue* ("Pot") and *parole* ("pot"). Equally, the pot represents what Beckett in "Peintres de l'empêchement" (1948) called resistance of the object, or "l'empêchement-objet" (*Disjecta* 136), the absence of rapport between the subject and the object. Watt's awareness of the pot as pot, as individual and not as a class, goes beyond the *quidditas* of apprehension in *Portrait* (212), yet may echo Joyce's phases of aesthetic apprehension (Pat McCarthy to CA). James Knowlson indicates that to Beckett the image in its greater accuracy and precision was superior to the word (*Images of Beckett* 49). Watt's dilemma thus exemplifies a central crux of the Modernist aesthetics of the Image.

81.3 [78]: be comforted: as Matthew 5:4: "Blessed are they that mourn: for they shall be comforted." Watt is attempting to make a pillow out of old words (**117.3**).

81.4 [78]: that is was: an error ("it") overlooked in the galleys (G26) and introduced into the Olympia text; despite Beckett's marking the error, "is" remained unchanged in all Grove editions, although it was corrected in Calder. Olympia's "alway hope" (line 38), also marked, was corrected by Grove.

81.5 [78]: It was in vain: the rest of this paragraph was a late verso insert (NB5, 30v), as was the earlier sentence, "He had realised . . . being meant" (NB5, 28v), the meditation thus intensified after the structure was in place.

82.1 [79]: the pot remained a pot: that is, it exists in its own being, at a level of reality beyond that experienced by the individual perceiver. Beer notes (63) the comical rhyme with "knott," and the "elaborate word game" (pots, hats, heads, chamber-pots) that ensues as Watt tries names on things, "as a woman hats" (*Watt* 83). Robinson (125) compares the experience of Roquentin, in Sartre's *La Nausée*, putting his hand upon the park bench (like Mr. Hackett) to insist that it is a seat, but in vain, the word staying upon his lips. Looking at the root of a chestnut tree, he sees it mere undifferentiated existence without meaning or purpose: "Knotty, inert, nameless, it fascinated me, filled my eyes, repeatedly brought me back to its own existence. It was no use my repeating: 'It is a root'—that didn't work any more . . . The root, with its colour, its shape, its frozen movement, was . . . beneath all explanation" (186). *La Nausée* reads *noueuse*, "knotty." Damian Love defines this effect as *anti-epiphany*, experience without the meaning, with Mr. Knott as the supreme example: "hypnotically fascinating yet utterly banal" ("Art of Madness" 68).

82.2 [79]: Watt is a man: echoing the paradigm of being which began the novel (see the Introduction), Beckett's disposition of Aristotle's categories, as recorded ("with some appearance of reason") in his early notes on Philosophy (TCD 10967, 99r: "Aristotle of Stagira"): "10 modes of mental representation corresponding with 10 capital modes of existence [compare Mr. Knott's piano—CA]: Substance, Quantity, Quality, Relation, Place, Time, Position, Condition [bracketed with 'Possession'], Active, Passive." These lead to the exemplum (Beckett's underlining): "<u>Socrates is a man, 70 years old, wise, teacher of Plato, in prison, sitting on his bed, having fetters on his legs, teaching his disciples, being questioned by them</u>. First 4 modes alone essential, rest being qualifications of them. In practice only 2, substance & accidence, or, subject & predicate." Also cited in NB1 (3). Alexander's *Short History* (65) offers a summary, differing in too many specifics (and lacking the application to Socrates) to be assumed as a direct source. Beckett adds a marginal note: "at cock sparrow fart"; that is, he later noticed that he had left out the category of Time ("sparrow fart": the crack of dawn).

82.3 [79]: his last refuge [footnote]: Psalm 46:1: "God is our refuge and our strength, a very present help in trouble." Compare "Fingal" (33): "A land of sanctuary, he had said, where much had been suffered secretly. Yes, the last ditch." The footnote protests too much; Watt is again oblivious to what Arsene is saying. The note, a late verso addition (NB5, 30), does not appear in the extract in *Irish Writing* (22), nor in the galleys (G26), Beckett reminding Olympia: "note manque."

83.1 [80]: semantic succour: Watt seeks a precise reference (or denotation) for "Knott"; as Mood points out (256), he wants to make a "pillow of old words" (117), "to be pacified" (123), "comforted" (81), and even "tranquillized" (82).

83.2 [80]: It is a raven: in the late draft (NB5, 31), first "~~something~~" and then "~~Grail~~" was crossed out, before "raven" was added, perhaps for the pun (in French) on "pot" and "Poe." The galley (G27) and Olympia's "It it a raven" persisted into Grove, but was silently corrected on reprinting; however, Beckett marked it on his copy of the Grove for correction by Calder. As Robinson notes (126), Sartre's Roquentin in the midst of the nameless plays the game of trying names upon things: why not *centipede* instead of *tongue*? As for *raven*: why not (a nod to Lewis Carroll) a *writing-desk*? Or (J. Jurms, haw! germs choice, ha!) a high-grade *po* (**27.8, 226.2**).

83.3 [80]: as his mother had taught him: not without irony, given that Beckett's mother, as Celia to Murphy, had been determined to make a man out of him (*Murphy* 65). Knowlson says (215) that Celia is quoting the exact words that Beckett's mother had used to him, and that Murphy's reply vents Beckett's own frustration and tension. Beer (43) deftly makes the link between this and the "mother language" of *Watt*. Alfred Adler's discussion of the neurotic constitution defines as "the fictitious goal" of masculine protest the wish to be "a complete man"; this goal is not shared by Murphy or Watt, neither of whom is "a man's man," nor a woman's man (**139.2**). Beckett, who had dismissed Adler as "Another one truth mind," was at least spared John Robert Keller's psychoanalytic reduction of *Mr.* Knott to a mother fixation, and such, er, stirring insights as: "a pot, perhaps the very one in which he lovingly prepares his Knott/mother's needs in the vain hope of sharing a nurturing experience" (Keller 103).

83.4 [80]: as a box, or an urn: or, to be sure, a pot. Many of Beckett's protagonists are trapped metaphorically, like Molloy (49) or literally: in an urn, like the Unnamable (9), those in "Play," or Nagg and Nell in *Endgame*; or in a box ("All Strange Away"). Proust's equivalent is a vase, his metaphor for the past imprisoned within the self, guarded by forgetfulness against the occasion of involuntary memory.

83.5 [80]: the extraordinary newell lamp: a survival from the earliest drafts, where Mr. Quin's house featured a splendid staircase turning about a magnificent newel (the pivot of a turning staircase). The "tutelary newell" is celebrated in the typescript (125). See **#37**.

83.6 [80]: the number of steps seemed to vary: when the Expelled is thrown down the steps, he is less concerned about "the fall" than about how many steps there are, and he arrives at three figures, uncertain which is "right" ("The Expelled" 46). That depends on whether the top and/or the sidewalk should be counted, which parodies the debate as to whether integers begin with 1 or 0. The dilemma recurs in *All That Fall* (29), as Dan Rooney, uncertain of the number of steps, wonders irritably if they do not change in the night. But counting, he adds, is "One of the few satisfactions in life!"

83.7 [80]: the various sorts: *cirrhus*: thin and wispy clouds, at the highest and coldest point of the cloudy region; *stratus*: a low-lying, flat and gray cloud formation; *cumulus*: a mass of large white or gray clouds with a flat base and a rounded fluffy top, created by rising hot currents. The Olympia and first Grove editions have the misprint, introduced but overlooked in the galleys (G27), "tumulus"; this was silently corrected in later Grove reprintings, but persisted into the Calder text. It was corrected in the French translation (76), which offers the cliché resisted here: "quand il faisait un temps divin." Kenner (90) cites Geulincx (*Ethica* I.ii.2): "Video nubes, saepe candidas, nonnunquam atras" ["I see clouds, often white, sometimes black"]; the point being that perception resides, not in the sky and empty space, but in the inner self.

84.1 [81]: his last rats, at last: when marking his copy of the Grove text for the Calder edition, Beckett proposed a paragraph break at this point. Rats abandon a sinking ship; but Watt, when he leaves the house of Mr. Knott, will find himself, or his mind, assailed by a patter of mice, a flurry of little gray paws (**232.3**).

84.2 [81]: this dereliction: Harvey notes (356) the anguish of this experience for Watt, in contrast with the deliberate attempts by Murphy to cultivate something of the same effect. Compare the sentiment "ex Derelictione me" in the Annotata of Arnold Geulincx's *Ethica*, that one is worth nothing, and has no value, until dead (*Grove Companion* 595).

85.1 [82]: the old credentials: that is, beliefs that have offered credence.

85.2 [82]: the gardener: reflecting the philosophical dilemma as to whether the existence of the garden proves that of the gardener; but Mr. Graves cannot speak to this. The sun's being "well up, in the sky" is, presumably, a like anthropological impertinence.

85.3 [82]: keck: in Johnson's *Dictionary*, "to heave the stomach, to reach at vomiting." From hawking: a hawk does not cough, but rather kecks.

85.4 [82]: unspeakable: literally, with reference to Watt's loss of speech; emotionally, with terror; theologically, a mystery that cannot be articulated, as in the proud Pentecostal praise: "Thanks be unto God for his unspeakable gift" (see II Corinthians 9:15). For Watt's aphasia, the degeneration of his spoken language, see part III. See also **215.5**.

85.5 [82]: Kate: the famished dog, introduced but not explained, like Mr. Graves and the fishwoman on page 69, until "much later" (**112.3**).

85.6 [82]: loss of species: a phrase recurrent in *How It Is*, where it implies Darwin's *On the Origin of Species*, as in the Unnamable's sense (387) of caged beasts born of caged beasts born and dead in a cage. Windelband's *History of Philosophy* (126) argues that the ethical ideal of Platonism lies not in the ability and happiness of the individual "but in the ethical perfection of the species"; thus, loss of species constitutes loss of form, of what makes one One with others (*Grove Companion* 261).

85.7 [82]: The song that Erskine sang: Beckett's instructions on the galleys (G27) were to leave a gap ("composez cette signe avec beaucoup d'espace dessus et dessous") and put in the "Point d'interrogation" with "blanc avant et après." The typescript (254) read "Page 42," an instruction to include details from NB3 (84), where a few bars of music are given and a theme suggested: the lament of *Candide*'s eunuch: "O che sciagura d'essere senza [coglioni]!" ["Oh what a shame, to be without [balls]"] (**8.4, #35**). For further instances of this theme, see the *Grove Companion* (94). The song, as later sung by Erskine alone (NB5, 37), is different and unmusical: "I was as happy as the day was long / I played on the sand and in the sea all day / Making pies with my spade and pail / Under the yellow cliffs on the sand / in the sand / I recall this period now with pleasure / The summer has changed and the sea too."

85.8 [82]: But Watt was not so far gone as all that: as Rabinovitz suggests (125), Watt still has faith in the Cartesian tenet that the only things that can be relied on are those that can be clearly and distinctly beheld, which precludes recourse to the opinion of others. The extract from *Irish Writing* 22 effectively ended (24) with "the old credentials," but this paragraph was included, to round it off.

86.1 [83]: the nature of the object: in Kantian terms Watt was able to penetrate beyond the merely phenomenal to an understanding of the noumenal, the *Ding-an-sich*.

86.2 [83]: Mr Knott sometimes rose late and retired early: intimating (a point not developed) Mr. Knott as some kind of sun-god. He is later glimpsed through "an eastern window at morning, a western window at evening" (**147.2**); he disappears behind bushes then reappears, as if they were clouds (**169.7**); and his head and feet complete, "in nightly displacements of almost one minute [degree]" a circuit of his bed (**207.4**). In the early drafts (NB3, 69; TS, 245), this passage, then the preparation of his food, immediately followed the sentiment that Mr. Quin was a good master.

86.3 [83]: on Sunday he did not rise at all: as in the first book of Genesis, where the Lord, after six days of creation, on the seventh day rests. In the typescript (245), Quin rose late and retired early on Monday, Tuesday, Friday, and the Sabbath; rose early and retired late on Wednesday and Saturday; and neither rose nor retired on Thursday (a day unaccounted for in the published text), whatever state of negative capability this might require. His is a state "neither sleep nor vigil" (NB3, 69; TS, 245). The repeated sequence of days matches that of the opening sentence of the paragraph, but other than a diminution of the order of {3, 2, 1} there seems no complexity to the paradigm, save that it fails, because of the missing Thursday, to match the empirical world. Quin's aboriginal inactivity on Thursdays may reflect Archbishop Ussher's calculation that the world was created on that day.

87.1 [84]: very little trouble: yet the disposal of the remnants of Mr. Knott's meals will occupy some thirty pages. Early drafts (NB3, 69; TS, 245) refer to Earle's remarkable work on the preacher, "that he preached once a year and twice on Sundays"; that is, that "the stuff is still the same, only the dressing a little altered." The theological analogy is made with Quin's poss. The first remark is recorded in the Whoroscope Notebook (Interpolations 2); this is John Earle (1601-65), Anglican clergyman and author of the *Microcosmographie, Or A Peece of the World Discovered in Essays and Characters* (1628), 78 short studies, mentioned in Beckett's notes on English Literature (TCD 10970, 11r) and ticked as having been read. Beckett mentioned Character II, "A Young Raw Preacher"; but Earle influenced the early *Watt* (NB1, 7) in the initial statement of intent (see my Addendum 2) and in the anticipated book, *A Clean Old Man* (**#23**), that title echoing Earle's Character LXV, "A Good Old Man."

87.2 [84]: foods of various kinds: NB3 (71) and the typescript (246) offer a detailed list of the ingredients of this "invariable Eintopf" [hot-pot], the details not in all cases corresponding (major differences only noted):

1 large tin asparagus soup,* hot.	*Heinz* (NB3)
1 lb. potatoes, boiled, mashed, with skins, hot.	
1 tin sardines, with oil and bones, pulped.	
4 red onions, peeled, raw; sliced, cold.	
2 garlics, ditto.	
6 fat rashers, fried, with rind, diced, cold.	
Yokes of 3 duckegges [sic], whipped.	
1/4 mediumsized ram's testis, raw, hashed.	
1/4 lb. butter, melted.*	*drizzling* (NB3)
1/2 lb bread, hot, shredded.	

1/2 pint salad cream, cold.
1/2 pint clotted cream, iced.
1 tablespoon Alpa anticancer salt.
1 tablespoon Cayenne pepper.
1 tablespoon mustard* powder.   * *Coleman's* (NB3)
1 tablespoon curry powder.
1 tablespoon salt of celery.
3 tablespoon Demara sugar.
100 grammes Stilton or other blue cheese, with rind, mashed.
Juice of 6 blood oranges, with pips.
1 dockglass dry sherry.
1 pint stout.*   **1 bottle Beamish 4X* (NB3)
1 tailor rye whiskey.*   * *Canadian* (NB3)
1 dock glass white rum.*   * *Bacardi* (NB3)
1 breakfast cup camp coffee.
1 snipe tonic water.*   * *Indian*
4 aspirins, powdered.
2 tablespoons #Sanatogen.
2 tablespoons bicarbonate of soda.
4 liver pills.
anthelmintic; insulin; digitalin; etc etc.

         #"*a high protein powder*" (NB3)

These quantities were multiplied (TS, 248-49) by 14 (double-yoke duck eggs counting as one) each Saturday night, to supply the two full meals (lunch at noon, dinner at 6 pm) that Quin required (NB3 multiplied by 7, to suggest a daily amount). The cooking was done, in a big black cauldron and a big black jug, stirred with a stout black rod, by Erskine and "Johnny" Watt between 7 pm and midnight every Saturday (in the late draft, NB5 [39], "Sunday"). Having simplified this in the later rewriting, Beckett added on the galleys (G28): "tea, coffee, milk, stout, beer, whiskey, brandy, wine and water."

87.3 [84]: meat . . . camomille: Beckett's requests when marking his Olympia text for Grove for a comma after "meat" and for the accurate spelling of "camomile" were over-looked, just as he had overlooked them in the galleys (G28); he repeated the request when marking his Grove text for Calder, who made the corrections.

87.4 [84]: absinthe . . . salicylic acid: to cater to a wide variety of conditions:
absinthe: a distillation of wormwood, otherwise the "fairy" or "green poison"; a later insert into NB5 (39).
whiskey: the spelling indicates Irish rather than Scotch, but NB3 (71) specifies Canadian.
insulin: an extract from the isles of Langerhans in the pancreas, used in the treatment of diabetes to aid the uptake of glucose into the tissues.
digitalin: a glucoside made from foxgloves, for treatment of the heart.
calomel: mercurous chloride, for the relief of irritation; formerly used as a purgative.
iodine: added to salt for prevention of goiter.
laudanum: an opiate, for treatment of pain.

mercury: the "silver bullet" used in the treatment of venereal disease; Mr. Knott's teeth, like those of Oscar Wilde, may be blackened.

coal: to prevent coughing; perhaps as the Bishop of Cloyne's elixir, tar-water.

iron: to increase haemoglobin in the red blood cells (Mr. Knott may be a "bleeder").

camomille: a plant related to the chrysanthemum, used as a herbal tonic. The misspelling was introduced in NB5 (39), and remained in the galleys G28), the Olympia text, and all Grove editions, until corrected in the Calder text.

worm-powder: for, well, the treatment of worms; not in the earlier drafts.

salicylic acid: a crystalline phenolic acid, of sweetish acrid taste, used as an antiseptic and disinfectant, and in the treatment of skin diseases; originally prepared from willow bark to treat rheumatism. Here ("of course"), aspirin; NB3 (71) recommends "4 Bayer aspirins, ground to a powder."

87.5 [84]: poss: a *posset*, a drink made by the blending of ingredients.

87.6 [84]: inextricably mingled: Beckett wrote in large letters on the verso of the early draft (NB3, 78): POINCARÉ, as if to suggest the French mathematician's insistence upon the irreversibility of time's arrow, the ingredients "never again to be divided." He also wrote, on the same page, "bubble bubble," as if to suggest the witches' brew in *Macbeth*.

88.1 [85]: tears would fall . . . into the pot: a detail of concern in the early drafts, lest the precise measurements and exact volume of the pot be jeopardized. Watt's exertions and calculations constitute an image of the Newtonian universe in which the laws of the conservation of mass, work, and energy are not yet upset by the Einsteinian equation.

88.2 [85]: at twelve o'clock noon sharp and at seven p.m. exactly: in the typescript (246) the hours are noon and 6 p.m. In the early drafts (NB3, 80; TS, 251), Mr. Quin drank the poss with an appreciative "ñum ñum."

88.3 [85]: If the bowl still contained food: this detail, and the next paragraph, are not in the late draft (NB5, 40, 41), but in the final writing they anticipate the famished dog and "explain" why Watt, who serves the poss, does not see Mr. Knott at meals. Watt earlier rang a little bell to tell Mr. Knott that his poss was ready, and Mr. Knott rang it when he wanted Watt to clear away; this hint of the Eucharist was not sustained (**#13**, **#37**).

89.1 [86]: a little plated trowel: in a note at the end of NB5 (182), Beckett records: "Knott's meal eaten with a little silver trowel like the trowel that the tea merchant uses, to trowel the tea out of the caddy, into the pot." In the early drafts (NB3, 85; TS, 254) Quin ate with a soup spoon.

89.2 [86]: Coal was also economized: Beckett indicated when marking his Olympia text for Grove that he preferred "also was"; but as it remained unchanged he repeated the request when marking his Grove edition for Calder.

89.3 [86]: Twelve possibilities occurred to Watt: there are apparently four terms: whether Mr. Knott was responsible for the arrangement; whether he knew he (or who) was responsible; whether he knew such an arrangement existed; and whether he was content. These may be displayed as a truth table: {A or -A}, {B or -B}, {C or -C}, and {D} (for Mr. Knott, like the God of Genesis, seems always content, so {D} is not negated; in the table, it is irrelevant). Beckett offers a 12-point schema (NB3, 42v), but its logic is not compelling; nor is Mood (259) quite right to see 24 possibilities, figured as 4! (factorial four, or {4.3.2.1}), let alone to assume that the twelve omitted relate to "was not content," for the paradigm is not combinatory. D being irrelevant, it rather entails three elements and their negatives, the pattern comprising {A B C}, {A B -C}, {A -B C}, {A -B -C}, {-A B C}, {-A B -C}, {-A -B C}, and {-A -B -C}, or eight sets in all. Thus, in the order presented in *Watt*:

	A	B(b)	C	D
1.	t	t (b)	t	t
2.	f	t	t	t
3.	t	t (b)	f	t
4.	f	t	f	t
5.	t	f	f	t
6.	f	f	f	t
7.	t	f	t	t
8.	f	f	t	t
9.	t	t	t	t
10.	f	t (b)	t	t
11.	t	t	f	t
12.	f	t (b)	f	t

The apparent complication (eight logical sets, but twelve representations) has arisen with respect to {B} and {-B}, between "Mr Knott knew that he was responsible" {B or -B} and "Mr. Knott knew who was responsible" {b or -b}. Without this distinction, there would be an identity between possibilities 1 and 9, figured as {t t t t}; possibilities 2 and 10 {f t t t}; possibilities 3 and 11 {t t f t}; and possibilities 4 and 12 {f t f t}. This option is not allomorphic, that is, its distribution is not restricted by other conditions; so there are logically eight further possibilities (numbers 2, 4, 5, 6, 7, 8, 9, and 11 [below]). Other sequences (13 to 16) might logically complete the pattern, with either {B} or {-B}; those (marked *) are absent from the text:

1. {A B C D}	2. {-A b C D}
3. {A B -C D}	4. {-A b -C D}
5. {A -b -C D}	6. {-A -b -C D}
7. {A -b C D}	8. {-A -b C D}
9. {A b C D}	10. {-A B C D}
11. {A b -C D}	12. {-A B -C D}
*13 {A -B -C D}	*14 {-A -B -C D}
*15 {A -B C D}	*16 {-A -B C D}

Despite Watt's admission of "Other possibilities," there seems no logical reason why these last should have been put aside as "unworthy of serious consideration." #13, for instance, would read: "Mr Knott was responsible for the arrangement, but did not know who was responsible for the arrangement, but knew such an arrangement existed, and was content"; #14: "Mr Knott was not responsible for the arrangement, but knew he was not responsible for the arrangement, but did not know that such an arrangement existed, and was content"; #15: "Mr Knott was responsible for the arrangement, and did not know who was responsible for the arrangement, but knew such an arrangement existed, and was content"; and #16: "Mr Knott was not responsible for the arrangement, and did not know who was responsible for the arrangement, but knew such an arrangement existed and was content." There are problems with some options as given: in #12, terms {-A} and {B}, and {B} and {-C}, are mutually contradictory, while #11 and #16 require "and" instead of "but" (logically but not semantically equivalent?) between terms {A} and {b} to make sense. The various options were worked out in NB3 (72), and again in NB5 (42), while in the typescript (247), a "brief analysis" was offered, but with Quin responsible (or not) for the arrangement, and knowing (or not knowing) "who or what was or were" responsible for it; one instance of "Quin" (instead of "Knott") survived into the late draft (NB5, 41). Earlier, when Quin was responsible, but did not know who/what was/were responsible, the phrase "but forgot it" had to be interpolated; and possibilities #3 and #4 were there reversed. In short, the paradigm as it evolved is and always was a bit of a mess, semantic considerations affecting the strictly logical, which may (or may not) be the point.

90.1 [87]: Other possibilities occurred to Watt: the typescript noted that further than this it is impossible to go, "in the present state of our knowledge"; the later draft (NB5, 42) tidied up the earlier paradigm and deleted a couple of options.

91.1 [88]: a little voice: this anticipation of the *Three Novels* was a late addition, first appearing (without "little") in NB5 (45). The next paragraph, the voice as joking or serious, was even later. The voice reflects a case study of the type discussed by Jung in his third Tavistock lecture (2 October 1935), which Beckett had attended, where Jung had suggested that complexes breaking from conscious control may form personalities of their own: "They appear as visions, they speak in voices" (**73.6**). Consider, too, the voices of *How It Is* (within or without), and the outset of *Company*: "A voice comes to me in the dark. Imagine." But unlike Augustine (*Confessions* 11:6), for whom such voices are a revelation, Beckett's narrators remain as they were, in the dark.

91.2 [88]: a canon: previously (TS, 254) "a man of parts," a musical pun asserting itself. The earlier "privates" became "crotch," retaining the consonance.

91.3 [88]: inarticulate bipedal brothers and sisters in God: man as a featherless biped capable of speech, compared with, usually, the parrot, but here the (inarticulate) ostrich.

91.4 [88]: shat on, from above, by a dove: more euphonic (and blasphemous) than the earlier: "defecated on, from above, by a pigeon" (TS, 255; NB5, 47); the change to "shat" was made in the galleys (G30). In *The Criminal Prosecution and Capital Punishment of Animals* (168), Evans tells of a lascivious priest castrated by a divine thunderbolt. Consider, too, the third verse of "We Love the Place, Oh God" (**47.15**): "We love the sacred font / For there the Holy Dove / To pour is ever wont / His blessings from above."

91.5 [88]: So it was necessary: the saga of the famished dog is introduced by what Kant would call a hypothetical imperative, as defined by Windelband (552): "If you will this or that, then you must proceed thus or so"; it concludes several pages later (112) with a categorical statement: "The name of this dog . . . was Kate." This, the most outrageous parody of scholasticism in an impossible treatise, derives from the simple premise that if a dog's dish is put outside at evening full or partly so, and is brought in the next morning empty, then someone or something must have wrought that change. A dog. A famished dog. A dog kept famished to eat the food. A family that owns the dog. A family that (necessarily) must breed dogs so that there is always a famished dog. And so on, each premise yet fresh premises begetting, until, from the simple statement that "it was necessary" that a dog from outside call at the house and several hypothetical propositions, there finally comes into being (112) an empirical declaration that the name of this dog "was" Kate, and that the family necessary for her being "was" the Lynch family (100). The reification is purely linguistic, Nominalist, but by the end of the sequence the image of Kate eating from her dish with the dwarfs standing by (117) *is* substantive; the conditional has become the indicative. In like manner, perhaps, have countless human societies reified their nominalist "gods."

92.1 [89]: it was more usual: the early drafts (NB3, 86-89; TS, 255-56) calculated the odds by echoing the earlier song of the mixed choir (*Watt* 34-35), and becoming increasingly entangled in long, recurring decimal places, the point being to sustain in mathematical terms the futility of Watt's exhaustive rendering of his experience.

92.2 [89]: attendance: perhaps in the French sense of *attendre*, "to await." It remains uncertain exactly how one might define an "average" dog.

92.3 [89]: in which case the dog got nothing: a partial paradigm follows, the two terms being "lunch" ("L") and "dinner" ("D"); each with three possible outcomes: all ("A"), or part ("P"), or none ("N"). Mood (260) correctly identifies nine possibilities, figured as 3^2, but gets one excluded variant wrong. The outcomes are: {LA DA}, {LA DN}, {LA DP}, {LN DA}, {LN DN}, {LN DP}, {LP DA}, *{LP DN}, {LP DP}. The text offers the following, from the dog's perspective, which assumes that all or part of the lunch is identical to all or part of the dinner, the poss being consistent (were it not, there would be more variables and a more complex set of outcomes):

{LA DA}: Mr. Knott eats all his lunch and all his dinner; the dog gets nothing

{LA DN}: Mr. Knott eats all his lunch but none of his dinner; the dog gets half

{LA DP}: Mr. Knott eats all his lunch and part of his dinner; the dog gets less than half

{LN DA}: Mr. Knott eats no lunch but all of his dinner; the dog gets half

{LP DA}: Mr. Knott eats part of his lunch and all his dinner; the dog gets less than half

{LN DP}: Mr. Knott eats no lunch but part of his dinner; the dog gets more than half

{LP DP}: Mr. Knott eats part of his lunch and part of his dinner; the dog gets half, or more than half, or less than half, depending on how much is uneaten

{LN DN}: Mr. Knott eats no lunch nor any dinner; the dog gets all (a wonderful day, for the dog)

One outcome is not mentioned; there is no way of determining whether the omission is inadvertent or deliberate (I suspect the former):

*{LP DN}: Mr. Knott eats part of his lunch but no dinner; the dog gets more than half

93.1 [90]: his arrival: thus in the Olympia text, and, despite Beckett's request to change "his" to "its," also in the Grove. Most instances of "his" on the previous page were changed to "its" on the galleys (G30), but Beckett overlooked this one, which persisted until Calder made the change.

93.2 [90]: By what means then were the dog and the food to be brought together: as Robinson notes (123), Watt does not ask why the scraps are given to a dog, but instead must find the right combination of meaning and words to construct a web so exhaustive that he can be sure to have imprisoned the solution to his question within it. The galleys (G30) read: "For left over, the food left over," having omitted: "Watt's instructions were formal: on those days on which food was"; Beckett restored this in a marginal note.

93.3 [90]: at the moment of his setting up house: "establishment" is here intimated, but carefully avoided (**134.2**); it appears, however, thirteen lines later.

93.4 [90]: or if not Mr Knott, then another: the first intimation that the universe of Watt, and perhaps that of Mr. Knott, may be serial. This theme was hinted at in the early drafts (NB3, 89; TS, 258): "Or if not him [Quin], then another, of whom all trace is lost"; but it was not given detailed expression. Beckett's earlier writings toy with intimations of a serial universe, that is, one in which the perceived order of existence is subject to other orders, perhaps unperceived. Thus in *Proust* (21): "The mortal microcosm cannot forgive the relative immortality of the macrocosm. The whisky bears a grudge against the decanter"; or in "Draff" (191), the words of the rose to the rose: "No gardener has died, comma, within rosaceous memory." This is the "storiette" of Bernard de Fontenelle (1657-1757), in his *Entretiens sur la pluralité des mondes* (1686), as appropriated in Diderot's "Le Rêve de d'Alembert" (1769), that within the memory of the rose the gardener is immortal. This is invoked in "Echo's Bones" (19) and parodied in *Draff* (179), where the stolen "rose" is the perforated nozzle of the gardener's hose. Intimations of seriality in *Watt* anticipate not only the pre-established arbitrary (**72.1**, **93.3**, **134.2**), but also the various series of dogs, pictures, servants, and frogs. The suggestion that Mr. Knott might be serial (that is, immortal only from Watt's perspective, and part of a different series which he cannot perceive) is reiterated in the Addenda, notably **#25**, the portrait of Mr. Knott's father, and **#29**, where Arthur encounters an old man who used to work for Knott's father. This might once have pleased Watt, but he is "an old rose now, and indifferent to the gardener."

94.1 [91]: those solutions that did not seem to have prevailed: logically, they might have prevailed in an alternative "universe." Even so, each solution proposed meets with a larger number of objections, each introduced by "But." The number of solutions and hence the number of objections becomes increasingly complex, but they can be tabulated (*Watt* 97-98), and the operation reduced to a formula (**98.1**).

95.1 [92]: This person: only part of this parenthesis ("This messenger might have been further employed to clean the boots, either before leaving the house with the pot of food, or on returning to the house with the pot empty") appears in the early draft (NB3, 93; TS, 259 ["~~keg~~" reverting to "pot"]); the first sentence is extended in NB5 (53). It echoes the old man's "I cleaned the boots" (*Watt* 252), a task first carried out by Mr. Hackett (NB1, 43). "Mr Graves" is not named. The latter part ("And is it not strange . . .") is even later, added in the final rewriting. The passage responds to the turgid writing around it "with a kind of fury"; this final phrase enacts the pent-up emotion behind the logical constraint.

95.2 [92]: And is it not strange: words earlier attributed (TS, 252) to Watt's stirring the poss, with the danger (were the cauldron completely full) of it overflowing from his tears and sweat and beads of moisture.

96.1 [93]: when ten o'cluck strock: the phrasing in the early draft (NB3, 93), Beckett indicating nowhere any wish to normalize it, as the Olympia Traveller's Series decided to do (105). Earlier drafts read "the old church clock."

96.2 [93]: was a dog the same thing as the dog: underlined in the typescript (260), where it echoes the (or an) earlier distinction: "waiting for the tram, for a tram" (**8.2**). A limerick used by linguists generates 720 {6!} subtle variations arising from the choice of the definite or indefinite article:

> *A prominent protestant preacher*
> *Called the hen a most elegant creature,*
> *A hen pleased with that*
> *Laid an egg in his hat,*
> *And thus did the hen reward Beecher*

The galleys (G31) note, oddly: "in Katt's instructions there was no mention of the dog."

96.3 [94]: the dog too: a Daltonic visualization, for dogs (as Beckett knew) are color-blind. The later draft (NB5, 57) offered a simple contrast of green [go] and red [stop]; but the change from red or green [go] to violet [stop] was noted (NB5, 56v). This is less an allusion to the infra red/ultra violet spectrum than a curious echo of Nordau's *Degeneration* (28-29) (DN #621): "Red a dynamogenous colour / Violet an inhibitive."

97.1 [94]: if he did, and he were found . . . might he not confound: the rhetorical model (compounding the rhyme of *found*, *confound*, and *bound*) seems to be, again, that of Gorgias (**45.5, 148.2**): that there is nothing (no such man); even if there were, we could not know it (he could not be found); and even if we could know it that knowledge could not be communicated (he might confound, in his mind).

97.2 [94]: homeward bound . . . outward bound . . . if bound he be: nautical terms, hence green (port) and red (starboard). As the setting out and the return home constitute a "necessary journey" (*Grove Companion* 402), another sense of "bound" is present, as in Geulincx's image of delusory freedom, the ship heading towards the Pillars of Hercules and the galley-man crawling towards the rising sun (*The Unnamable* 336).

97.3 [94]: his faithful emaciated dog: in the early drafts (NB3, 95; TS, 261) "lurcher" was used (as "in the lurch"). The French text (98) improvises with "son fidèle sac d'os."

98.1 [95]: *Number of Solutions . . . Number of Objections*: the "numbers" refer back to the four numbered solutions that have been ventured (94-97), and consequent objections, each introduced in a separate paragraph with "But." The first set of numbers tabulates for each solution (n) the number of objections (n + 1); the need in the fourth instance for five explains why the final objection, "But would not this greatly add . . ." (97), was added to the late draft (NB5, 57). The second table calculates the cumulative objections, these growing geometrically. Early drafts (NB3, 96-99; TS, 262) discuss the relationship between the two sets, the one ordinal, the other cardinal, to reach the formula: $n(n + 3)/2$. Thus, the 8th solution would entail 9 objections, with $8(8 + 3)/2$, or 44 objections in total. Or, to use the instance in the typescript (262-63), a hundred solutions would generate 6,150 objections, "incredible as that may appear" (Beckett's answer [NB3, 99], rather too incredible as the correct figure is 5,150, but the error entered the typescript). Errors notwithstanding, the discovery of the mathematical formula seems to confirm a principle of reason operating at the heart of the pre-established arbitrary.

98.2 [95]: nature's debt: compare the exchange in "Human Wishes" (*Disjecta* 161):

> Miss C. His debt to nature?
> Mrs W. She means the wretched man is dead.

98.3 [96]: the second local's man: earlier correct (TS, 264), but the error was introduced in the galleys (G32), and appears thus in the Olympia and (despite Beckett's attempted correction) Grove texts. Beckett's request ("the second local man's") was repeated when marking his Grove text for Calder, who made the change. The "annuity of fifty pounds" was earlier (TS, 263) a "mensuality" of £3.3.4, paid on the first of every month.

99.1 [96]: a kennel or colony of famished dogs: a fantasia developed at length in the early drafts and typescript (**111.1**).

99.2 [97]: in block: imitating the French "en bloc" (Beer 53).

100.1 [97]: or a sixpence: an error, "sixpense" appeared in the galleys (G33), and entered the Olympia text. Beckett marked it in his Olympia copy and Grove made the correction.

100.2 [97]: castoff clothes: (NB3, 105; TS, 266) lists most of these, but has "a breeches" instead of "a knickerbockers"; the brothers van Velde make up "un pantalon," singular yet twain. See **14.6** for the suggestion ("a scissors") of the dual.

100.3 [98]: a half-crown . . . a halfpenny: coins in common currency during most of Beckett's life, in descending order from the silver coins, the half-crown (two shillings and sixpence, eight to the pound), florin (two shillings), shilling (twelve pence), sixpence, and threepence ("thruppence"), to the coppers, the penny and the "ha'penny." Although Irish coins were redesigned after independence, the British structure was retained.

100.4 [98]: The name of this fortunate family was Lynch: the necessary and sufficient conditions established (the famished dog, so the family to tend it), the family has changed from one hypothetical to one that exists (**91.5**). Beckett records of Mrs. Thrale in his "Human Wishes" notebooks (I, 69): "Lynch the maiden name of her maternal grandmother Lady Cotton of East Hyde."

101.1 [98]: Tom Lynch: Beckett offered in the early draft (NB3, 104ff) several charts and/or calculations of the different generations, the relations between, and the ages of the Lynch family, in their attempt of the millennium, a process parodying Malthusian mathematics. This culminated (NB3, 108) in a chart depicting the family Lynch at the moment of Watt's entering Mr. Knott's service: five generations; twenty-eight souls; and 980 years (but see **103.3**).

Ackerley 113

The diagram that follows is based on that chart, but with the age of each individual added and minor adjustments to take account of small differences, such as changes of name, in the final text:

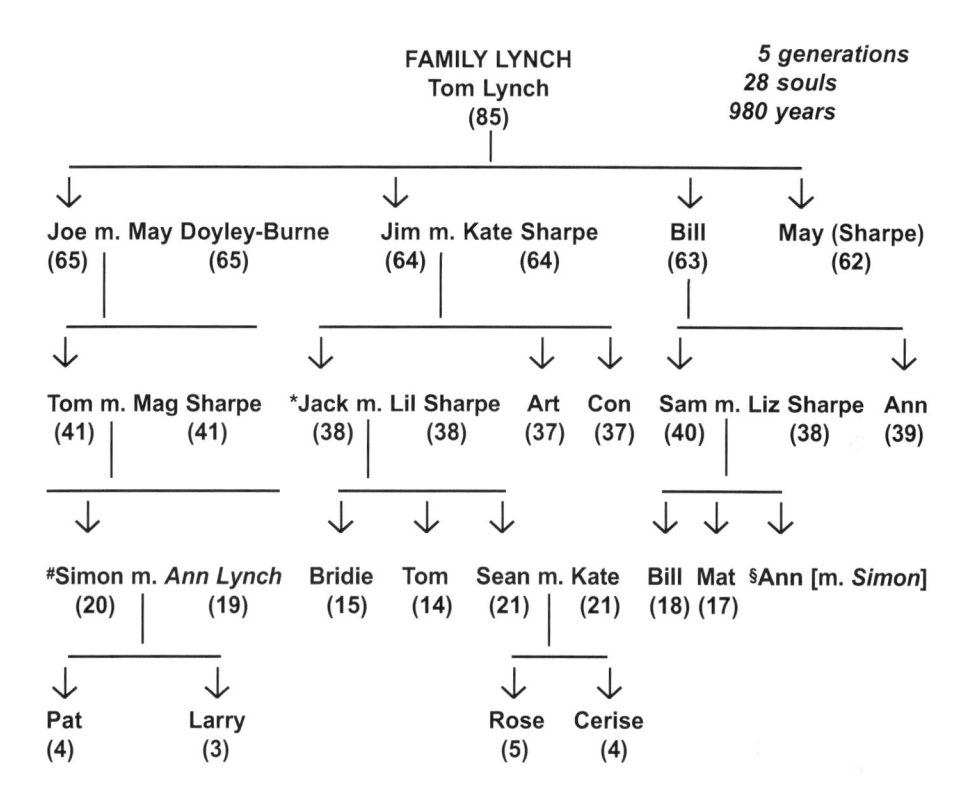

FAMILY LYNCH
Tom Lynch
(85)

5 generations
28 souls
980 years

↓ Joe m. May Doyley-Burne (65) (65)
↓ Jim m. Kate Sharpe (64) (64)
↓ Bill (63)
↓ May (Sharpe) (62)

↓ Tom m. Mag Sharpe (41) (41)
↓ *Jack m. Lil Sharpe (38) (38)
↓ Art (37)
↓ Con (37)
↓ Sam m. Liz Sharpe (40) (38)
↓ Ann (39)

↓ #Simon m. *Ann Lynch* (20) (19)
↓ Bridie (15)
↓ Tom (14)
↓ Sean m. Kate (21) (21)
↓ Bill (18)
↓ Mat (17)
↓ §Ann [m. *Simon*]

↓ Pat (4)
↓ Larry (3)
↓ Rose (5)
↓ Cerise (4)

***Jack**: also referred to as Frank.
Simon: earlier known as Doyley.
§ **Ann**: her age recorded with Simon

101.2 [98]: caecum: the blind gut, part of the large intestine; earlier (TS, 266) "stomach."

101.3 [98]: Bill: not without vague reference to William Beckett, whose son by a merciful providence was named Sam, aged about forty years.

101.4 [98]: Doyly-Byrne: echoing "burn with Byrne" (**11.5**); or simply Gilbertian. Here she lacks a Christian name, but is identified later (109), and in the charts (NB3, 104, 108), as another "May." In the French translation (103), she is "Flo née Doyly-Byrne."

101.5 [99]: Parkinson's palsy: a wasting disease characterized by uncontrollable palsy; a contributory cause of the death of Beckett's mother (25 August 1950), also named May.

101.6 [99]: Jim's lad Jack: in the drafts (TS, 266), he is named Frank (**102.6**).

101.7 [99]: Art and Con: the inseparable or "boon" twins, a pseudocouple (**13.4, 102.4, 103.2**) responsible for bringing the famished dog to the house of Mr. Knott, to consume any food left on his plate. They have done this since they were twelve; thus, relative to the dogs (Kate is the sixth) they are immortal, as d'Alembert's gardener to the rose. So alike that no-one could tell the difference between Art and Con (except, perhaps, a Pro), they have degenerated from Art Conn O'Connery, who painted the portrait of Alexander Quin (**#2**). They are, presumably, the Lynch twins who jeer as the Rooneys shuffle home (*All That Fall* 31).

101.8 [99]: as least as: this error ("at least as") was overlooked by Beckett in the galleys (G33), and from the Olympia text to the Grove; but Beckett requested the correction when marking his Grove edition for Calder.

101.9 [99]: young Tom's wife Mag: perhaps, the matrix of Molloy's mother, another Mag, who does not have the same afflictions but is confined to her bed. The subepilectic seizures of monthly incidence imply that her abnormal electrical discharges in the brain, and consequent convulsions and impairment of consciousness, are triggered by menstrual irregularities. Mag, Lil, and Liz are probably sisters, but their relationship to "Jim's wife Kate née Sharpe" is presumed rather than proven; it is likely that a dynasty of Sharpes exists, and that their series intersects (indeed, largely coincides) with that of the Lynches.

102.1 [99]: Lil née Sharpe aged thirty-eight: Beckett's request on his Olympia text that Grove remove the italicised "*e*" (G33) was ignored; the change was made by Calder. Liz Sharpe's good fortune in being more dead than alive reflects Beckett's frequent sentiment, *Optimum non nasci aut cito mori*, that it is best not to be born but to die quickly; a tag copied from Schopenhauer, Burton, or Geulincx into the Whoroscope Notebook (85v).

102.2 [99]: Simon: in the early draft (NB3, 104), "Doyly" [*sic*], but changed to "Simon" on the second chart (NB3, 108).

102.3 [99]: ? : the hiatus and question mark were omitted in the galleys (G33), and since the passage was at the bottom of the page Beckett restored the latter and insisted: "hiatus in MS." The typescript (267) has no hiatus, and continues: "[whose] effeminacy and pusillanimity shrank form all the active offices of life."

102.4 [100]: Blind Bill and Maim Mat: an obvious pseudocouple (**13.4, 101.7, 103.2**), linked in the symbiotic relationship best known from W. B. Yeats's play, *The Cat and the Moon*, but developed by Beckett from a sketch entitled "The Gloaming" into a one-acter entitled "Rough for Theatre I," where a crippled vagrant, B, is drawn to the violin melodies of a blind beggar, A. The relationship is developed more artfully in *Endgame*.

102.5 [100]: a bleeder: the typescript of *Murphy* finds Mr. Willoughby Kelly advising Celia: "sever your connexion with this ~~bleeder~~," with "Murphy" written in (*Demented Particulars* #32.4). In like vein, the Whoroscope Notebook (26; dated "4/12/35") offers a maieutic saw: "The wise man will not marry the sister of a bleeder." See **102.8**.

102.6 [100]: Frank: the name of Beckett's brother, but not obviously a member of the Lynch family since mentioned nowhere else. The name appears thus (instead of "Jack") throughout the early drafts (**101.6**), but at this point only in the galleys (G34) and all published texts; other references to "Frank" were carefully changed to "Jack," but Beckett missed this one. Mood is thus wrong (260) to say that Frank is "never identified," and to consider Bridie "unplaced in the genealogy." Preparing his Calder text for the French translation, Beckett crossed out "~~Frank~~" and wrote in the margin "Jack," with a question mark below. Hence the draft of (Ohio NBIII) records: "la fille de Frank (?) Bridie"; this entered the galleys and final text (105), as an oddity arising from careless proofing. The German translation (122) reads: "Franks Tochter Bridie."

102.7 [100]: the toolshed: in early drafts (TS, 102) the outhouse; the change accentuates a mild sexual jest. Compare *Happy Days* (18): "within a toolshed."

102.8 (footnote) [100]: Haemophilia: a sex-related, hereditary disease characterized by delayed clotting and uncontrolled bleeding, even after minor injuries. It is not, despite the note, an exclusively male disorder, but the condition in women is extremely rare. The comparison with the prostate is invalid, not because (as Beckett famously observed) women don't have prostates, but because haemophilia among women requires the inherited deficiency on both sides. The footnote was perhaps added when Beckett was alerted to the incongruity; it parodies the many notes and diagrams of medical textbooks in which Queen Victoria's condition (she was a carrier) is traced through the royal houses of Europe. It was omitted from the galleys (G34), Beckett indicating in the margin: "Note manque." The mis-spelling of "enlargement" as "enlargment," despite Beckett's correction on his Olympia text, was ignored by Grove, so Beckett marked it again on his Grove text for Calder.

103.1 [100]: excema: Beckett corrected the mis-spelling to "eczema," which he had overlooked in the galleys (G34), when marking the Olympia text for Grove, but the error remained uncorrected until the Calder edition. The Olympia Traveller's Series erupted with "exzema." The *sacrum* is a triangular bone of five fused vertebrae at the lower end of the spine; Celia's final customer (*Murphy* 278) is afflicted by the condition.

103.2 [100]: Rose and Cerise: another pseudocouple (**13.4**, **101.7**, **102.4**). The language used of their begetting is pseudo-biblical: "conceived and brought forth."

103.3 [101]: nine hundred and eighty years: the footnote overleaf says that the figures are incorrect; simple addition gives 978 years. The discrepancy is "explained" on page 105, where Liz is 40, whereas she was previously said to be 38.

104.1 [101]: when Watt entered Mr Knott's service: perhaps, on the 26th of June (**67.2**); from whence the millennium was calculated to fall in the following March.

104.2 [101]: Then a moment passed and all was changed: as in I Corinthians 15:52 (**40.1**): "In a moment, in the twinkling of an eye, at the last trump: for the trumpet shall sound, and the dead shall be raised incorruptible, and we shall be changed."

104.3 [101]: puff puff: compare "wol fup, wol fup" (*Watt* 165). See **44.6**, for an attempt to identify the precise moment that a quantitative change becomes a qualitative change, or a change of degree a change of state ("be it liquid, be it solid"), as water into ice.

104.4 [101]: Till changing changing: "eight months and a half approximately" is calculated by *taking the twenty years yet remaining* until the millennium and *dividing it among the twenty-eight members of the family, resulting in* (Beckett in the early drafts [TS, 269] worked out the calculations in full, along the lines indicated): *five-sevenths of a year each from the current moment, or* "[five] times twelve [months] equals sixty [months] over [divided by] seven" equals eight and four-sevenths months (exactly sixteen days for February [excepting the debâcle], a little more in the other months), call it *eight months and a half approximately*, if all are spared, which they are not. This assumes that there are no birthdays as such, a sudden qualitative advance of a year, but rather a steady quantitative process. Preparing his Calder text for the French translation, Beckett noted "fois 12 egale [*sic*] soixante / divisé par sept égale."

104.5 [102]: expelled: in an early version (NB3, 109), Liz "was delivered of" a child; the typescript (269) changed this to "expelled a child." Compare "The Expelled"; or the image of forcible ejection at the outset of "Act without Words I," where the protagonist, deprived of the intrauterine primal pleasure, is flung across the stage.

104.6 [102]: exsanguious: deficient in blood. Beckett ignored the spelling in the proofs (G34), but preferred "exsanguine" when marking the Olympia text for Grove; however, the passage remained unchanged until the Calder edition.

104.7 [101]: (1) the figures given here: for the mistake, see **103.3**; the footnote, again, was omitted from the galleys (G34), Beckett indicating: "Note manque." Having checked the figures Sean Lawlor asked Beckett if the errors were intentional or inadvertent, and received the reply (1968): "Thank you for your letter and for going to all that trouble, but sorry past caring. See also note p.101 Calder's Jupiter edition" (Sean Lawlor to CA).

105.1 [102]: Tom and Jack: in earlier drafts, Tom and Frank (**102.6**). The list of relatives (including Liz) adds up to twenty-four; Larry and Pat, Rose and Cerise, and (to be sure) the new arrival do not express their astonishment.

105.2 [102]: anyth-ing: the curious hyphenation occurred on the galleys (G34), and was overlooked; Beckett's request when editing his Olympia text for Grove that it be corrected being ignored, it was repeated on the Grove text for the Calder edition.

105.3 [103]: the Lynch millenium [*sic*] was retarded: although the birth of the baby means that the number of "souls" remains at twenty-eight, the loss of Liz means that the burden of her forty years (as the text specifies) must be assumed by others. This adds, Beckett (or Sam) calculates, almost a year and a half to the expected day, if all are spared. There are no indications as to how this figure was arrived at, but if Liz's forty years is divided by twenty-eight each survivor will be responsible for one and three-sevenths years. Hence the "17 months" recorded in an early draft (NB3, 111). If that is added to the "mere five months" that remain, the millennium is retarded by something under two years (a better figure would be 22 months). Beckett crossed out "17 months" and wrote in "19"; a figure derived from "roughly two years" minus the five months already budgeted. Thus the extra time necessitated by Liz's death; but the variables are vague, and in the shadow of so many comings and goings the figures are impossible to calculate in any meaningful way (**106.2**).

105.4 [103]: since the death or Liz: Beckett corrected the error ("of"), which he had overlooked in the galleys (G35), when marking his Olympia text for Grove, but it remained uncorrected until the Calder edition.

106.1 [103]: souls: although used casually previously (*Watt* 103), through repetition and changing dynamics the word assumes greater irony.

106.2 [103]: nearer by twenty-four days: as a consequence of the time remaining now being shared among 30 souls, rather than 28. That is (crudely), Liz's 40 years (or rather, since two months have passed and their onus assumed by each of 28 souls, her 37 years and four months) can now be divided by 30 instead of 28, the difference by so doing being (by my crude calculations) some 33 days, rather than the 24 stated. But any precise calculation must guess at what Beckett's "almost" and "roughly" means, and whether one accepts the "good nineteen months" as valid (**105.3**).

106.3 [104]: self-propelling invalid's chair: perhaps from Lourdes; in earlier drafts (NB1, 95; TS, 75), precisely such a chair was offered as a prize (**27.8**).

106.4 [104]: a son and a daughter: the error, "daugter," overlooked in the galleys (G35), entered the Olympia text; noted by Beckett, it was corrected in the first Grove edition.

107.1 [108]: dressing up for the night: in an early draft (NB3, 112), "taking off her clothes"; but this is crossed out on the typescript (272) and the final version substituted.

108.1 [105]: in a fit of depression, or in a fit of exaltation: a simple paradigm, with two terms, depression (D) and exaltation (E) as singularities, and the interval (I) between the four binary combinations of (d) and (e), thus permitting six possibilities: {D}, {E}, {dIe}, {eId}, {dId}, or {eIe}. Mood's "6 possibilities, figured as 2 + 2 + 2" (260) is imprecise.

108.2 [106]: her uncle Jack: "Frank" persisted into the galleys (G35), where Beckett caught the error, which went no further (**102.6**).

108.3 [106]: so white: as a whited sepulchre (Matthew 23:27).

109.1 [106]: Joe, Bill and Jim: the names of Bill and Jim have been reversed, but according to the genealogy (**101.1**) Jim is Joe's junior by one year, and Bill their junior by two years and one year respectively. The pattern of deprivation ("lessness") is otherwise accurate and complete.

109.2 [107]: one hundred and ninety-three years: the sum of the ages of Joe, Bill, and Jim, according to the original figures (**101.1**), is 192, but if the extra months lapsed since then are taken into account the sum could be "more than" 193 years.

109.3 [107]: seventeen years: a figure derived by calculating the figures (the burden of 193 years shared by those who remain) if all are spared; but a counter-calculation (TS, 274), based on the ratio of recent deaths to births, indicates over that period a likely "clear loss of twentytwo souls, leaving only five Lynchs [sic] alive, with an average age, if the tot were to be attained, of two hundred years." Hence the collective despair.

109.4 [107]: gripes: spasmodic pains in the intestine or (here) the caecum.

110.1 [107]: Then they were sorry for what they had said: with a liturgical echo of the Anglican Confession: "We do earnestly repent, and are heartily sorry, for these our misdoings; the memory of them is grievous unto us, the burden of them is intolerable."

110.2 [107]: her uncle Joe: mistakenly recorded in the galleys (G36) as "Jim," but the error was caught by Beckett and went no further. The paragraph is not in the late draft (NB5, 59), which jumps directly to "This little matter" (*Watt* 111). The paradigm of Joe, Bill, and Jim acts as the departure point (**109.1**) for a set of variations, three terms combined in factorial three (3!) ways, for six combinations: {A B C}, {A C B}, {B A C}, {B C A}, {C A B}, {C B A}. *Watt* prefers the following order: {Jim, Bill, Joe}, {Joe, Bill, Jim}, {Bill, Joe, Jim}, {Jim, Joe, Bill}, {Joe, Jim, Bill}, {Bill, Joe, Jim}. The last term, {Bill, Joe, Jim}, repeats the third, omitting {Bill, Jim, Joe}, presumably due to Beckett's carelessness as the galleys are also wrong. In the draft of the French version, Beckett got this right, writing out the sequence in full (Ohio NBIV, 8v), and correcting a further error (Ohio G106); yet the French text (113) still repeats the mistake.

110.3 [107]: in agreement . . . in disagreement: a simple paradigm of agreement (A) and disagreement (D), with four binary combinations, the first term in the pluperfect ("had been"), the second in the imperfect ("were"): {A D}, {D A}, {A A}, {D D}. Mood's "6 possibilities figured as 2 + 2 + 2" (**108.1**) is awkward. The simplicity is complicated by new terms, *amity* and *enmity*, "as before, only redistributed"; then *for* and *against*; and finally, fatally, by *objection* and *answer*, "as before, only in other mouths." While the first set(s) and their new terms initially conform to the conditions, that correlation does not hold for the last, for empirical reasons expounded at length. Truth tables, it seems, are of limited use in coping with human mendacity or verbal evasiveness. The argument gets more contorted until, at the end of the paragraph, when it apparently returns to the original two terms (agreement, disagreement), the logic that generated the paradigm has been rendered irrelevant.

110.4 [108]: no, not one: with the force of Romans 3:10: "As it is written, There is none righteous, no, not one." Malone accordingly forgives no-one (180).

110.5 [108]: Bill, Joe and Jim: a similar paradigm to that earlier (**110.2**), presumably its model, as it repeats (*Watt* 111) the same error, the repetition of {Bill, Joe, Jim} as the third and sixth terms, instead of completing the pattern with {Bill, Jim, Joe}. Mood (260) misses the error, calling the pattern complete.

111.1 [109]: This little matter of the food and the dog: at this point in notebooks (NB3, 119 ff) and typescript (275 ff.), there is a long, entertaining passage (later ruthlessly cut back) concerning the "best breed of dog," a cross between the Irish Setter (which copes with inanition over a long period) and the Palestine Retriever; and how that breed might be established and purchased (not from Joffa, for the messengers might not return, but from Cork, for they surely will the moment their business is done). Difficulties include: the reluctance of the Palestinian Retriever dog to cover the Irish Setter female (TS, 277), but not of the Irish Setter dog to cover the Palestinian female (NB3 first used "bitch," but this changed, Beckett deciding [130] on "female dogs"); a gallery of boxes and crates that paying spectators might view the process (TS, 278-82; diagrams in NB3, 120, 122); ensuring that the numbers of Retrievers and Setters, males and females, be equal, lest one be (as it were) "at a loose end" (TS, 283-86); the permutations by which various Setters and Retrievers might unite (TS, 287); the odds for betting (TS, 289). One unfortunate after-image (TS, 280) was that Watt for a long time could not see a crate without associating it with dogs copulating and (a curious reference) the thought of his mother, wife, and/or little girl. See **#27**.

112.1 [109]: very natural: death as the inevitable outcome of any natural process, the ultimate debt to nature (*Grove Companion* 399-401; **98.2**).

112.2 [110]: Add to [t]his: Beckett corrected the error, which he had overlooked on the galleys (G37) when marking his Olympia text for Grove; but as it persisted into the first Grove printing (later corrected) the request was repeated on his Grove copy for Calder. The phrase, "Add to this" (**75.7**, **147.3**) invariably indicates a later addition to the text.

112.3 [110]: The name of this dog . . . was Kate: the virtual ("it was necessary" [91]) has become actual. Unlike the Galls father and son, whose existence is "long posterior to the phenomena" (79), the mental phenomenon has generated the tangible. In the French text (115) "Kate" is declared a "chien" ("pour ne pas dire chienne").

113.1 [110]: Cis: possibly "called after" Beckett's Aunt Cissie, a "near and dear friend." *But this is a mere conjecture*. Cis in the French text (115ff) is also a "chien."

113.2 [111]: he lost interest in it: less Berkeley's *percipi* than Neary's Gestalt experience (*Murphy* 48), whereby, the stimulus fading, the figure sinks into the ground.

113.3 [111]: to witness: an intimation (dog/God) of a crucial theme (**42.1**, **203.2**); hence Watt's fear of retribution when he neglects this office. In the French translation Beckett preferred "d'assister à son absorption par le chien" (Ohio NBIV, 13).

113.4 [111]: an atom: in the typescript (263), a "crumb"; the revision sets the deistic story of creation against the atomist tradition of dissolution. The same change was made elsewhere (NB5, 59; *Watt* 98).

114.1 [112]: touched it with one's stick: as Mr. Hackett does (**8.1**), in possible imitation of Stephen Dedalus in the "Proteus" chapter of *Ulysses*, to verify its existence. The stick exemplifies self-extension: the problem, discussed at the outset of Schopenhauer's *World as Will and Idea*, of the body in immediate or intermediate relationship to the self with respect to the space through which it moves (*Grove Companion* 542).

115.1 [113]: greatly lightened: an egregious pun, yet not entirely without the Christian sense of a burden enlightened.

115.2 [113]: This refusal: the "refusal" intimates Dante's "lo gran rifiuto" ["the great refusal"] (*Inferno* III.60), the abdication of the papacy by Celestine V (13 December 1294) in favor of Boniface VIII, as mentioned in "What a Misfortune" (136), *Eleuthéria* (159), and a letter to George Duthuit (9 March 1949): "Pour ma parte, c'est le gran rifiuto qui m'intéresse" (*Grove Companion* 87).

115.3 [113]: I beg your pardon: the narrator (Sam?) signals his presence; but see **61.1** for the suggestion that the slip may have been Beckett's, and deliberately retained.

115.4 [113]: to assist at the meeting: the verb has the French sense of "to be present at"; the "gravest consequences" reflect the refusal to bear witness.

115.5 [113]: As is was: Beckett corrected the error ("it"), which he had overlooked on the galleys (G38), when marking his Olympia text for Grove, but as it remained uncorrected he marked it in his copy of Grove for the Calder edition.

115.6 [113]: No punishment fell on Watt: as Doherty observes (43), man needs the fiction of punishment for a crime uncommitted to withstand the burden of an emptiness and isolation which are unbearable but must be borne. Punishment would be a solace for it would imply that "someone would be observing and taking account of his action."

116.1 [113]: a precedent of rebelliousness: the figure of Prometheus is implicit.

116.2 [114]: transgression: as Doherty notes (42-43), Watt's offence is against prescribed immemorial rites as rigid (and as devoid of substantial reality) as the Old Testament laws; nothing happens because finally there can be no transgression. The late draft (NB5, 67) retains the earlier "disobey," and adds only as an inset "grace."

117.1 [114]: mecanism: a mis-spelling introduced in the galleys (G39); overlooked by Beckett, the error entered the Olympia text, and although noted by Beckett was repeated in Grove; Beckett again marked it in his Grove copy for Calder. The "mechanism" is pre-established harmony (**134.2**); one manifestation of that is the cliché, "in this connexion."

117.2 [115]: the forms: as the Platonic; a late draft (NB5, 69) reads: "appearances." The sense is not unlike that expressed in Joyce's *Portrait*, a world apprehended by words.

117.3 [115]: a pillow of old words: compare *How It Is* (134), for the oakum of "words ill-heard, ill-remembered." Kenner comments (59-60) that Watt "bears the Cartesian cross, the discursive intellect, with its irremediable itch to think explicable worlds into existence, stumbling through corridors of exquisite absurdity toward some talismanic formula with which it can be temporarily at rest." See **81.3**.

117.4 [115] the veronica: a perennial or annual bush (or shrub) of the figwort family, that bears clusters of small, typically blue flowers; by implication, the sudarium (**32.8**), suggesting the relief of suffering.

118.1 [116]: the pleasure garden: the park and gardens surrounding the asylum of St. John of God, Stillorgan; the setting of part III of *Watt*, the beginning of "The End," and the end of *Malone Dies*. The phrase insinuates a link between Knott's mansion and the cells of Bedlam (**151.5**), and is used of Lousse's garden (*Molloy* 48).

118.2 [116]: from the ground floor to the first floor: the galleys read (G39): "from the ground to be sure"; but Beckett in a marginal note restored: "floor to the first floor, for no reason that Watt could see, though." In the late draft (NB5, 71ff), the text is substantially there but very fragmented, with instructions to add passages at various points: Watt's duties (from TS, 300); Erskine flying up and down the stairs (from NB3, 159); and the obscure keys as a new insert (NB5, 175).

119.1 [117]: to make sure that nobody is coming: originally, "than nobody was coming"; the error, overlooked in the galleys and Olympia text, persisted into Grove, where it was silently corrected on reprinting. Beckett marked it in his Grove text for Calder, who made the change.

120.1 [118]: to support the middle depths: Fletcher (92) hears the French intonation of *supporter*, "to tolerate"; the French reads (123): "supporter les profondeurs moyennes."

120.2 [118]: do such fish exist?: Coetzee comments (247-48): "Watt's creation of a fish out of words (120) is a maneuver which, however translated into other words, evacuates all that precedes it of certainty. While not necessarily a stylistic maneuver, it acts to reduce all communication to the level of playing with words." Perhaps, but the text has already created from words alone a famished dog and a dynasty of Lynches to "support" it. The fish is an image of Christ, who perhaps "exists" in this way, now.

120.3 [118]: a bell: the detail gives logical truth value to one proposition only: if the bell is in Erskine's room, then Erskine could have pushed it. Yet, when Watt gets into Erskine's room (128), for his "essential" examination (123), he finds the bell broken.

121.1 [118]: his great big white chamber pot: the Calder edition inexplicably omits "white"; the French translation (124), follows suit.

121.2 [119]: that so perplexed him: the typescript (304) reads "under consideration"; "dissembled" in the same sentence reads "hidden." Watt, who responded to the problem of the left-over food, is frustrated by his inability to form a necessary (or even sufficient) hypothesis to explain the anomaly. Hence his need to examine Erskine's room, for an empirical explanation.

122.1 [120]: off the hooks: Beckett in the typescript (307) crossed out "a little deranged" in favor of "a little demented." The further change anticipates Watt's taking the picture off its hook (*Watt* 130).

122.2 [120]: qui vive: compare "on the alert" (119); the phrase often intimates the mind's vigilance on the frontiers of consciousness (*Grove Companion* 475).

122.3 [120]: the sound of the bell came always on the stillness: echoing the carol, "It Came upon the Midnight Clear," with its sentiment: "Then sang that bell more loud and clear, / 'God is not dead, nor doth he sleep.'" The typescript (307) reads "silence."

123.1 [121]: always locked: scrupulousness demands that this assertion, and its contrary, "never unlocked," be qualified, as the door must be on occasion locked and unlocked.

124.1 [122]: simple keys: the distinction between "simple" and "obscure" keys (and locks) is one of degree: the five notches of a typical cylinder key may be cut to eight depths, so that eight to the power of five (32,768) different keys are possible. The more intricate (master keys) may lift the pins of many locks, especially those with fewer internal pieces ("simple locks"), but most are attuned to one pattern only ("simple keys") and are unlikely (Watt retracts "never") to open anything other than the pattern to which they are matched. The first draft (NB3, 167) replaced "~~complex~~" with "obscure."

125.1 [123]: I should never have known it either: the early drafts (NB3, 169; TS, 311) read "we," yet the pronoun is not employed in the earlier sense of "we" as a character (**#37**), but with an irritating omniscience. "Watt" first entered the early draft (NB3, 157; TS, 299) about this point, in relation to Erskine; he was not obviously the narrative focus, but soon (NB3, 160) dominated the perspective. The typescript of the earlier parts of NB3 reads "we"; this suggests that the typing was done shortly after the drafts were written, not as an independent later recension. At this point on the typescript (TS, 311), "~~we~~" is crossed out and "n" (an algebraic unknown, like the "n" or "m" of the Anglican catechism) is substituted, so that the phrase reads: "n would never have known it either." Other adjustments followed: "For all that n knows"; "And if n does not appear to know a great deal"; and "he assured n at the time" (the passage otherwise unchanged). The paragraph from "And so always" to "in one way or in another" (*Watt* 127-28) made similar changes. "Sam" (or "I") was thus not a direct introduction; rather, at this intermediate stage, Beckett had resolved on a (third person) narrative voice, as yet unnamed. (In like manner, when writing *The Unnamable*, he determined that a voice would begin with M, so deployed "M—" until "Mahood" was decided upon). The narrator ("Sam") is now explicitly here, in the first person, for the first time. He has been hinted at, in self-conscious footnotes, textual lacunae, ironic authoritative comments (**37.2**), and curious commas, all of which suppose (in a perhaps fallacious argument from design) an organizing presence; and, more openly, in such details as Watt's "mouthpiece" (**69.5**) and "me" (**79.1**). His presence will become more insistent (**151.4**). Even without any awareness of the textual history and of Sam's late introduction, his presence is a problem, perhaps an insoluble one, as little of the first chapter and not much of the fourth implies his mediating voice, and even in parts II and III, where that voice is more explicit, there are textual features that can be credited to him only with difficulty.

126.1 [124]: foisted: the typescript's original "~~put in~~" (313) was crossed out and "foisted" written in (**75.4**). Following the introduction of Sam (**125.1**), this paragraph was vastly elaborated, Beckett adding, by hand and upside down on the verso (TS, 312-13), several sentences, notably those indicating a narrative self-consciousness or referring to "I" or "me" or "one's little notebook." The late decision to provide another narrative voice led to much new material being foisted in, to justify the new perspective.

126.2 [124]: were not, or rather were: this phrase was either omitted from or added to the galleys (G42), this accounting for the exaggerated spacing of the next few lines, Olympia not wishing to reset more type than was necessary. Olympia introduced a new error, "or rather weres," which Beckett had no chance to correct until preparing his Olympia text for Grove, who made the correction.

126.3 [125]: never told: the galleys (G42) introduced a felicitous "never old," which Beckett corrected in the margin.

127.1 [125]: in putty, or butter: an earlier draft (NB3, 171) reads "dripping"; Beckett made the change by hand (TS, 313).

127.2 [125]: a trouser's pocket: Beckett removed the apostrophe, not present in the typescript (313) but ignored in the galleys (G43), when marking his Olympia text for Grove. The "error" (compare **230.3**) persisting in Grove, it was marked again for Calder, where the change was made.

127.3 [125]: Lachesis: second of the three Moirae, or Fates, who measures with her rod the thread of a man's life (spun by Clotho, to be cut by Atropos). Earlier versions (NB3, 170) read, less imaginatively, "chance," the change made on the typescript (315).

128.1 [126]: might have aroused: the drafts (NB3, 171; TS, 315) have "would have aroused"; the comic change of modal verb was made on the galleys (G43). A "crow" is a crowbar, or jemmy.

128.2 [126]: Ruse a by: the first instance of the first phase of Watt's aphasia (see **164.1**); a late change, earlier versions reading (NB3, 173; TS, 319): "By a ruse."

128.3 [126]: a bell . . . but it was broken: how, then, does Mr. Knott summon Erskine in the night (**120.3**)?

128.4 [126]: The only other object of note: the phrasing echoes the earlier incident of note (*Watt* 72), concerning the Galls father and son, and raises similar questions about the "fragility of outer meaning" (73) and "the simple games time plays with space" (75). "[O]ther object of note," appears neither in NB3 (173) nor in the typescript (317), which read "The only other thing"; but it is present in NB5 (77) and in the galleys. The description of the picture remains constant, offering an echo of Kandinsky's *Punkt und Linie zu Fläche* ["Point and Line to Surface"], 1926, invoked in *Murphy* (112): "a point in the ceaseless unconditioned generation and passing away of line." The French translation (133) reads: "Le seul autre objet digne de remarque," and calls the picture (NB5), or colored reproduction (NB3, TS), "un tableau."

128.5 [126]: Was it receding? Watt had that impression: NB5's "Did it approach? Watt thought it did" (77), is absent in the galleys. Similarly: "Was it receding? It gave Watt that impression" (NB5, 77), was changed to adjust the relationship of object and perceiver: "Was it receding? Watt had that impression."

128.6 [126]: the eastern background: that is, to the observer's right. The crucial difference between orientation by points of the compass as opposed to "left" and "right" is that the former are not dependent upon subjective alignment (**129.7**). NB5 (77) has "western" crossed out and "eastern" written over; earlier drafts (NB3, 173; TS, 317) had noted: "Far behind." The Evergreen Original, once the standard Grove Press edition, represented on the cover circle and point in a curious greenish-beige color, with an incongruous cut in the canvas to denote the breach; it also misplaced the point, to the northwest [our left] when it should be in the east [our right], relative to the breach.

128.7 [126]: blue, but blue!: the phrase appears thus in NB5 (77). The point was first blue (NB3, 173), but this was crossed out and "almost black" proposed; then, on the typescript (317), "almost black" is crossed out and "blue" returned. Blue and white are associated in Beckett's writing with the sense of ineffable longing, but the change curiously echoes Nordau on Maeterlinck (*Degeneration* 229): "but blue! blue!"

129.1 [127]: upon the same plane: the painting is an emblem of Beckett's reflections on the visual arts, notably "La Peinture des van Velde ou le monde et le pantalon" (1946; written 1945), "Peintres de l'empêchement" (1948), and "Three Dialogues" (1949). In the typescript (317), it is a colored reproduction, or an original, "by the Dutch painter X," presumably Bram van Velde (David Hayman to CA). Beckett was dissatisfied with the kind of art that remains on the plane of the feasible, that improves the result with a lick of Euclidean geometry, or strains to "enlarge the statement of a compromise" ("Three Dialogues" 138-39). The picture moves Watt quite literally to tears and induces a kind of metaphysical anguish, but his tragedy, ultimately, is that he does not possess the "violently extreme and personal point of view" advanced by B in Dialogue 1 (the need to express), and so must turn away in disgust, to do a little worse "the same old thing," and go a little further along the "dreary road" that leads not to sanctuary but to the asylum.

129.2 [127]: perhaps even mingle: the verb is incongruous, and if one hears an absurd echo (most would not) of the "Ithaca" chapter of *Ulysses*, where Bloom and Stephen pass water (L. *mingere*, "to urinate"), an attenuated sense arises with respect to "pause and converse" in a world of cosmic loneliness; "mingle" is used in this Joycean manner at the end of part III (**213.3**). But one might equally hear the echo of Thomas Hardy's "The Convergence of the Twain" in the image of ships in the night that might collide. *Who knows*, indeed.

129.3 [127]: what the artist had meant to represent: the painting first appears as a sketch on the back outside cover of NB1. In the early drafts

(NB3, 173; TS, 317), it is mounted, but not framed, and attached to the wall by four tin-tacks, raised from the skirting, bulging a little from the wall. Thus Watt (who did not examine it closely) took it for a reproduction rather than an original. He wonders (TS, 323) what the painter could have intended to "portray." Watt's knowledge of painting in the drafts is extensive (in the typescript [329] he is able to date the painting to the month), but the lengthy satire of academia and academy is eroded in NB5, where "intended" and "represented" are matters of distaste. The diminishing process continues in the galleys, which introduces: "Watt knew nothing about painting" (**129.6**). Beckett noted from Wilenski (BIF 5001, 12): "But for Rembrandt the universe was essentially boundless, not only in space but in time . . . For him the universe was not a miraculously functioning organisation, but a boundless & eternal mystery, & the fragments in it were emotive in relation to that mystery."

129.4 [127]: a circle and its centre: point and circle clearly correspond, in some kind of way, to the relationship of Watt and Knott, and testify to Watt's inability to find stability in a world where figure and ground do not form a firm Gestalt. Watt's schizoid tendencies manifest themselves in a narrative impulse that fastens on the unimportant and ignores or distorts the significant; some elements remain perceptually stable, but others dissolve. Early drafts (NB3, 177; TS, 319, 321) contain much detail about circles, arcs, sectors, segments, and tangents, but these were eliminated. Technically, the major figure is not a circle but, as early drafts note, "rather an arc of three hundred and fifty or three hundred and fifty-five degrees, for it was nothing more, a wide mathematical arc" (compare the 360 intervals of the Frog Song). To the extent that the figure is not a circle, then the premise that the point is the center of the (or a) circle is (logically) invalidated. However, the Gestaltist impulse is to complete the simplest figure, so Watt does not entertain this possibility, but rather tries to ascertain the relationship of figure and ground (either circle or point may constitute the foreground). Nor does he acknowledge the non-Euclidean possibility that the point could be the centre of an infinite number of circles, including or not including that depicted. He prefers rather to accept the circle as a circle, to assume that centre and point must each "search" for the other, and to differentiate merely between "a centre" and "its centre" (and the negations thereof).

Faced with the inexplicable, Watt takes refuge in Cartesian methodology, the attempt to enumerate, to exhaust every logical possibility. He therefore tries (NB3, 175; TS, 319) to determine the relationship of circle and dot (see facing page for figure) by accepting "a circle" but exhausting the possibilities of "a centre" and/or "its centre" in one paradigm, and "not a centre" and/or "not its centre" with another (TS, 318):

1. a circle & its centre in search of each other (1)
2. a circle & its centre in search of its centre & a circle (3)
5. a circle & a centre not its centre in search of its centre & its circle (5)
6. a circle & a centre not its centre in search of its centre & a circle (7)
3. a circle & its centre in search of a centre and its circle (4)
4. a circle & its centre in search of a centre & a circle (2)
8. a circle & a centre not its centre in search of a centre & a circle (6)
7. a circle & a centre not its centre in search of a centre & its circle (8)

```
                    its     its
                    its     a
                    a       its
                    a       a
            its     its
            a       a
            its     a
            a       its
```

The numbers on the left represent the order in the table that follows; the numbers on the right (circled by Beckett) indicate the order in which they would appear in the published text. The galleys (G43) omitted #2, {a its its a}, which Beckett restored in a marginal note. The truth-table and the conclusions that derive from it first appear in the typescript (not as part of the text), but the table is presented precisely in NB5 (76) and the conclusions added to the text:

circle & its centre	circle & not its centre
its its	its its
a a	a a
its a	its a
a its	a its

Such a truth-table is reductive. While it may explain a relationship of two dimensions, it is of dubious efficacy with three (space), and cannot cope with four (time). Watt's simple games with space and time (called in the early drafts the "autology of autoscopy") render it irrelevant, but Watt nevertheless persists with his Method, despite the tears that flow down his fluted (earlier, "hollow") cheeks, unchecked. If the circle is in any sense an emblem of God, like Miss Counihan's bust, "All centre and no circumference" (*Murphy* 60), it is here incomplete, broken, a violation of the perfection that is not of this world (*Molloy* 90). Either way, the logic of the truth-table cannot apply.

129.5 [127]: in boundless space, in endless time: not in the early draft (NB3, 175); the typescript (319) reads "limitless time." The addition, with small changes from "motion" to "movement" and "limitless time" to "endless time" (NB5, 77) are less corrections of "a mathematically meaningless description," as Coetzee suggests (115), than intimations of a movement away from the pre-Socratic concerns of *Murphy*, with its Atomist paradoxes of Motion (112-13) and the Doctrine of the Limit (50), with their more recent analogues of Uncertainty and Relativity, toward the realm of impotence and ignorance that Watt increasingly inhabits. Even so, the later phrasing reflects the pre-Socratic notion of *to apeiron*, "the Unlimited": the central problem being to show how the Limited gave form to the Unlimited; in the words of Anaximander, that becoming might not fail. Similar notions inform Schopenhauer's sense of the *Ding-an-sich* (*WWI* 1.2, #25, 168): "true wisdom is not to be gained by measuring out the boundless world, or, what would be more to the purpose, by actually traversing endless space. It is rather to be obtained by the thorough investigation of any individual thing, for thus we seek to arrive at a full knowledge and understanding of its true and peculiar nature."

129.6 [127]: (Watt knew nothing about physics): like the earlier comment, "Watt knew nothing about art" (**129.3**), this phrase first appears in the galleys. Coetzee (124) comments: "If [Watt] knew anything about the theory of relativity, he would be aware that it runs counter to the notion of infinite space and time coexisting together."

129.7 [128]: on its right side . . . on its left side: there is a curiosity about this description: the relationship of point and breach, as defined by the compass, makes sense only as a mirror image. That is, "its" relates not (as one assumes, with what Beckett terms elsewhere an anthropomorphic insolence) to the perspective of the viewing subject but to that of the picture; of the object perceived rather than the perceiving subject. This was a gradual evolution through the manuscripts, beginning in NB3 (177):

> Watt wondered also how the painting, which was painted
> *and slightly buckled*
> on a square board, would look upside down, with the point
>   *west*   *north*
> ~~on the left~~ and the breach ~~above~~, or on its right side, its right
>
> right side that is from the point of view of Watt, with the point
>   *south*   *west*
> ~~at the bottom~~ / ~~below~~ and the breach on ~~the left~~, or on its left
>   *north*   *east*
> side, with the point ~~above~~ and the breach ~~on the left~~

These possibilities are depicted (NB3, 176), not in precise correspondence with the text:

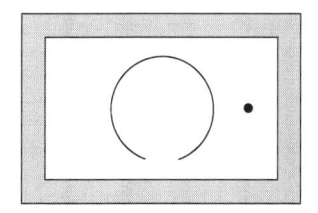

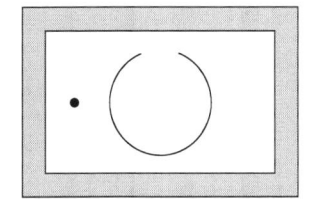

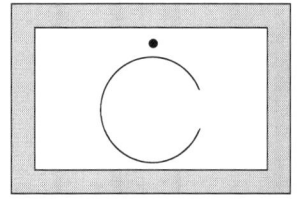

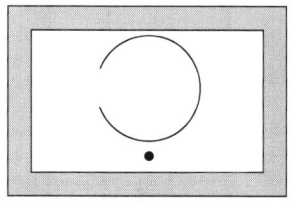

The movement is from the anthropomorphic perspectives of "above" and "below" to the more universal (non-subjective) directions of the compass. This process was taken further in the typescript collation (TS, 323), where the explicit comment about Watt's point of view was deleted:

> Watt wondered also how the painting, which was ~~painted on~~
> a square ~~and slightly buckled board,~~ would look upside
> down, with the point west and the breach north, or on its
> *left side*
> ~~right side, its right side that is from Watt's point of view~~,
> *right*
> with the point south and the breach west, or on its ~~left~~ side,
> with the point north and the breach east.

Two illustrations only are offered (TS, 323), again not in the sequence of the text:

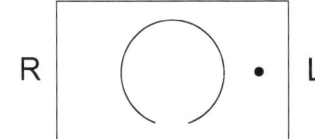

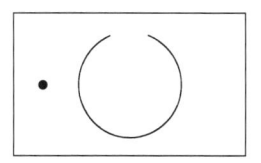

There is at this point no reference to Watt's taking down the picture, nor to the hook, nor to the erosion of the painting's significance. The difference between the compass directions, "East" and "West", and "left" and "right", is that between the objective mapping of external reality and one's subjective orientation. But even this mapping is conventional, based on the assumption that North is "above" and South "below." Compare the figure of North in "The Lost Ones": like Polaris, the North Star, she offers direction and fixity in a featureless cylinder/universe, but her position is determined by nothing other than the place at which she chooses to sit. Such complexities do not enter here, but the movement from the subjective perspective to the objective (that is, the left or right *of the picture*) is marked. NB5 (79) consolidates these changes:

> Watt wondered how this picture would look upside down, with the point west & the breach north, or on its left side, with the point south & the breach west, or on its right side, with the point north & the breach east.
> So he took it from its hook and held it before his eyes, at arms' length, upside down, and on its left side, and on its right side. . . .

The mirror inversion is unambiguous, and although the final sentence differs from the published text all co-ordinates are in their final form. Tin-tacks are replaced by the hook (or nail), that Watt might more easily take it down. That's it, one might assume. Yet, oddly, in marking his Calder text for the French translation in 1967, Beckett crossed out all the compass points, and wrote in their opposites, "north" becoming "south" and so on. That is, there was a curious reversion to the viewer's perspective from that of the object, from "left" to "droit," and "right" to "gauche," before the galleys (Ohio G126) and published text (134) restored the final perspective.

130.1 [128]: for ever in vain: the galleys (G43) read "for even in vain"; overlooked by Beckett, this entered the Olympia text, but was marked for correction by Grove, who made the change.

130.2 [128]: by the nadir: consider Job 1:21: "Naked came I out of my mother's womb, and naked shall I return thither." This relates the picture to the exigencies of birth and death: "It is by the nadir that we come and by the nadir that we go." The pun on "breach" and "breech birth" ("the point slipping in"?) was finally irresistible, as the abstract form was induced to mean something. The phrase was a late insertion in NB5 (78), which added: "circle did not reassure."

130.3 [128]: Did the picture belong to Erskine?: apparently not, for when Erskine left he did not take it with him. The early drafts (NB3, 177; TS, 323) long consider how the painting came to be there, and who brought it, with the tentative deduction that as the Dutch painter X, "still a comparatively young man," has painted it only Walter could have done so. The Addenda describe (250-51) a "Second picture in Erskine's room," not mentioned in the body of the text yet present from the outset (NB1, 110; NB2, 7; TS, 93) as a portrait of James (later Alexander) Quin, in the Chinnery-Slattery tradition, the work of the Master of the Leopardstown Half-lengths. Its inclusion in the final text, even as an appendix, complicates matters, for if this is a portrait of Mr. Knott's father (as various manuscript details affirm) then Knott must be serial, one who comes and goes rather than abides. Only in the final Addenda is the picture placed in Erskine's room, having previously occupied a place of honor above the fireplace in Mr. Quin's dining room. Even as these fragments affirm the serial theme, the relegation of the once-prominent portrait to the dusty coal-cellar of the Addenda foregrounds the enigma of ignorance and impotence reflected in the abstract depiction of circle and point.

130.4 [128]: Prolonged and irksome meditations: Coetzee (103) sums up the textual history of this phrase as a response to Watt's changed reasoning on the ownership of the picture, from one once a connoisseur to one finally ignorant of art. That reasoning could not last, yet its conclusion was essential—the painting belongs to Knott's establishment, this a crucial link in the chain of evidence leading to the conclusion that Knott is eternal yet may change—so it could not be omitted: "Beckett's solution is to summarize." To consolidate that conclusion, a new paragraph was added, beginning: "There were times when Watt could reason rapidly" (**131.3**). "Mr Knott's bed" was a late insertion (NB5, 80v), its roundness intimating eternity.

131.1 [129]: a term in a series: in the drafts (NB4, 8; TS, 331), Watt, then a connoisseur, reflects that if the painting was not the first object of its kind to be so favored then it must have been preceded by others. Wondering what these might have been, he forms images of images on the narrow white-washed wall: Kaspar David Friedrich's *Men and Moon*, a Hercules Seghers colored engraving, and an Elsheimer pen drawing (brought to the house wrapped up in brown or tissue paper or an old newspaper, and attached with tintacks to the wall [Watt searches for the holes, but not one does he find {but the walls could have been plastered and distempered anew}]). Richard Coe notes (50): "Watt's first instinctive reaction is to 'tame' the seemingly inexplicable by postulating a 'series' of which any present phenomena is a part." Watt grows dissatisfied with this solution as he becomes increasingly aware of a disquieting fallacy in the law of cause and effect, that not only does the "cause" determine the "effect," but, equally, the position and nature of the "cause" are limited by the "effect": "Every beginning determines the ending of that which preceded it, just as tyrannically as every ending determines a beginning" (Coe 51). As Robinson says, more succinctly (129): "In the series 1-2-3, 2 is as constricted by 3 as it is by 1"; an idea Watt finds "too horrible to contemplate" (**134.6**). This reasoning leads, irrefragably, to the doctrine of the pre-established arbitrary (**134.2**).

131.2 [129]: pod of eternity: the word missing (a favorite) is *dehiscence*, the natural force by which a seed is projected from the pod.

131.3 [129]: Mr Nackybal: this paragraph added as an insert to the late draft (NB5, 80), for reasons suggested above (**130.3**), Beckett dropping in, without explanation, the name of Mr. Nackybal (**174.1**). Coetzee notes (104) that the complex argument carried on in Watt's mind and reported, "in oratio recta and obliqua, in a self-effacing way," has been replaced by a summary "composed by an editor who makes disparaging remarks about his subject and mystifies his readers by referring to a character who will not be introduced for another forty-three pages."

131.4 [129]: and yet it moved, like Galileo's cradle: drawn from the example of Geulincx to support his contention that motion is not possible save through the agency of God (and according to His volition), that of the child, wanting the cradle to rock, and finding it does so, because the mother has imparted motion to it (*Ethica*, "Annotata" 227-28, nn. 6-7). This analogy, with its paradox of stillness and motion, is that of the Cartesian "earthball"; in Mahaffy's words (61): "The earth did indeed move, but it was like a passenger on a vessel, who, though he was stationary, is nevertheless carried along by the motion of the larger system which surrounds him." This derives from Geulincx's *Ethica* ("Annotata" 167, n. 9); cited in Beckett's notes on Geulincx (TCD 10967/6). Compare *Dream* (134): "he moves forward, like the Cartesian earthball, with the moving ship"; repeated in *The Unnamable* (336), the ship heading toward the Pillars of Hercules and the galley-man crawling toward the rising sun. Krapp recalls lying in the punt without moving: "But under us all moved, and moved us, gently, up and down, and from side to side" (*Krapp's Last Tape* 61). See also "Les Deux besoins" (*Disjecta* 55). These analogies intimate Galileo's "eppur se muove" ["yet it moves"], before, or rather after, the inquisitional hearing of 22 June 1633, his celebrated (if apocryphal) *sub voce* recantation of his public abjuration of the *Dialogo dei due massimi sistemi del mondo* (1632), which had cautiously affirmed the Copernican theory of the earth's movement about the sun.

131.5 [129]: nothing could be added . . . nothing taken away: reflecting less the physical law of the conservation of mass than its metaphysical equivalent, the principle of equilibrium within the closed system of the Newtonian universe (*Grove Companion* 181-82). Yet, as Coe notes (52), over and above the structure of cause and effect (**131.1**) there seems to be a core of reality that is outside time and space (that "abides"), and that eludes the powers of time and space and logic to determine its existence, so that human existence both belongs to and yet evades the series (**134.3**). The "solution" to this paradox, which pervades *Watt* and is explored in **#29**, is the haunting possibility that Mr. Knott may be serial, but (like the decanter to the whisky, the gardener to the rose, the dwarfs to the dogs) of an order imperceptible from the human perspective.

131.6 [129]: as it was now, so it had been in the beginning: as the refrain from the various Anglican services of prayer: "As it was in the beginning, is now and ever shall be, world without end. Amen."

131.7 [129]: Mr Knott's face ever slowly changed: undermining the theological equivalent of a steady-state universe, in which Mr. Knott eternally abides, with one running down in time, in which even he might change at an imperceptible rate. Compare *Molloy* (164), Gaber to Moran about Youdi:

"Changed . . . no, he hasn't changed, why would he have changed, he's getting old, that's all, like the world." This is an argument against the God of Spinoza, as rehearsed in "Le Rêve de d'Alembert" (317), for if He is immanent then He too must grow old and die.

131.8 [129]: This supposition . . . was to be strikingly confirmed: if so, that striking confirmation is never relayed to the reader. This paragraph was a late insert (NB5, 80v).

132.1 [130]: nothing came or went, because all was a coming and a going: the differentiation between action that is complete, or incomplete, in time; in grammatical terms, that between the perfective and imperfective aspect; *genesis*, or becoming, rather than *ousis*, or being (**133.2**). Otherwise, the Heraclitean flux (**57.6**).

132.2 [130]: this tenth rate xenia: in the drafts (NB5, 81),"explanation" is crossed out and "xenia" substituted. The word, from Martial, means presents made to departing guests. Thus in the galleys (G44), but in his copy of the Olympia text Beckett marked for Grove a proposed change to "xenium?"; the detail remaining unchanged, he repeated the request when marking his Grove text for Calder, who made the change. The word suggests a "flower of thought," as in Goethe's "Xenien" (1796), satirical epigrams written as a classical distich, hexameter and pentameter, denouncing the platitudinous intellectual world. Beckett copied one from the *Walpurgisnachtstraum* scene of *Faust* ("Als Insekten sind wir da...") into his "Black Notebook" (BIF 5004, 103), and imitated the form in "Gnome." The French translation (136) explains: "cet aphorisme de dixième ordre."

132.3 [130]: Yet what: the galleys read (G44): "Yes what"; this was overlooked by Beckett until he marked his Olympia text for Grove, who made the change.

132.4 [130]: such a correspondence: the observance of rhythm and periodicity within phenomena (or the imposition of rhythm and periodicity upon phenomena) to discern (or to create) form. As Doherty notes (46), to construct an hypothesis of the general law of duration for the servants of Mr. Knott we need first to know how long Watt (then, how long other servants) spend on each floor. But, as it turns out, Watt is never to know how long he spent in Mr. Knott's house, nor how long on either floor. There is, finally, no conclusion to be drawn from the length of days, as the "light of the day" (133) may differ (logically and empirically) from the first floor to the ground floor.

132.5 [130]: this monstrous assumption: not in the early drafts, but added to NB5 (83). Yet the "following considerations" point to the likelihood of this *perfectly reasonable* assumption, not because it is impossible that the "distribution of service" might vary (ten years or two [**134.3**]), but because, by Occam's razor, the simplest hypothesis is assumed to be correct; in Beckett's words, the obvious reading is always right. But...

134   *The Annotated* Watt

133.1 [131]: the first could not out till the second up: a fragment from the early drafts (NB3, 183), which indicated "an infinity of servants" (and so a Prime Mover). A diagram was offered (182), the variants at the right being those proposed in the typescript (333):

1st	can't	out	until	2nd	up	
2nd	"	up	"	3rd	in	
3rd	"	in	"	1st	out	
4th	"	in	"	3rd	up	*1st can't out till 3rd in
3rd	"	up	"	2nd	out	*2nd can't up till 1st out
						*3rd can't in till second up

The revision entailed the elimination of the original verbs ("the first could not ~~be~~ out until the second ~~came~~ went up"), replaced by the preposition only; and the elimination of the "4th" in favor of a more exhaustive set of {1 2 3} with six (instead of five) moves.

133.2 [132]: every going, every being, every coming: the early draft (NB3, inside front right cover) offered "1 The Coming 2 Downstairs 3 Upstairs 4. The Going," to define the Coming, Being and Going paradigm ("Downstairs" and "Upstairs" combined in "Being"; a tripartite schema embracing the novel's four-part structure). This section, from "For the service" to the "blowlamp," does not appear in the late draft but was taken from the earlier one (NB3, 182ff). Kenner notes (88) the presence of Geulincx's *Physical Vera* (II.12): as in all bodies there are three tendencies, *abitus, transitus, aditus*, so in all movement is there a parting from somewhere, a passage somewhere, a going to somewhere. This insight he shares with Coetzee (146), who adds (147) that the starting-point for the parody of *Watt* is seventeenth-century philosophical prose, that of Descartes in the *Meditations* and Geulincx in the *Ethica*. The three terms form a paradigm, going (G), being (B), and coming (C), these corresponding to the three prepositions, "out," "up," and "in"; combined in a universe of six binary selections: {BC}, {BG}, {CB}, {CG}, {GB}, {GC}. Noted correctly by Mood (260). Each term is dependent on (but see **133.3**) all the others being enacted simultaneously; but each servant, in time, forms part of three such universes, and so part of the "long chain of consistence."

133.3 [132]: consisting with: earlier (NB3, 183) "depending on"; but the typescript (333) qualifies this: "no, not depending on, for depending on suggest[s] the idea of dependence, but conforming to, yes, conforming to." This was then crossed out, and "consisting with" written in. The drafts thus explain the curious choice of preposition, and the phrasing on the next page: "this long chain of consistence," earlier alternatives reading (in order of choice): "necessity," "dependence," and "conformance."

134.1 [132]: from the long dead to the far unborn: Joseph Conrad's "Preface" to "The Nigger of the Narcissus" invokes "the latent feeling of fellowship with all creation" that "binds together all humanity—the dead to the living and the living to the unborn." Compare *The Unnamable* (389): "the ancient dead and the dead yet unborn."

134.2 [132]: a pre-established arbitrary: finally (since the only possible, or because maximal disorder implies its identified contrary) identical to *harmonia praestablia*, or pre-established harmony, the doctrine of Leibniz who contended that all things have been harmonized by God for all time, a harmony established before creation, with each monad, or unit of existence, so pre-arranged that any changes in it are accompanied by corresponding changes in all others. As Hesla notes (75), Leibniz's expression of the monad as "a perpetual living mirror of the universe" accounts for why things connected with Mr. Knott are subject to continuous change and yet kept in strict order: "the greatest variety possible, but with the greatest possible order" (*Monadology* #58). Voltaire in *Candide* mocked Leibniz's contention that all was for the best in the best of all possible worlds (see **43.5**, Lisbon's great day), and Diderot insisted mockingly throughout *Jacques le fataliste* (1773), whatever the provocation, that "il était écrit là-haut." Beckett parodied this in the "niggling curriculum" of "Dante and the Lobster" (10), in the "little adjustments" of the First cause in "Fingal" (32), and in the principle of all things hobbling together for the only possible that structures *Murphy*. In "The Expelled" (48), the time comes for the narrator to buy his hat, "as though it had pre-existed from time immemorial in a pre-established place." The "Organisation" for Moran implies such harmony; but in *How It Is* a love that deposits sacks all along the track at the right places (to be "met" at the right times) is rejected as inconceivable. The word "establishment" has been used in *Watt* several times (41, 69, 70, 85, 115, 130, 131), as if to anticipate this moment. The arbitrary was an early presence in the drafts (NB3, 183; TS, 333), before the implications of seriality had been worked through (**72.1**, **93.4**). The doctrine implies, primarily, that the existence of a series, or any number of interacting series, does not entail causality (**134.3**), but rather that (as in Romans 8:28) "all things work together for good to them that love God, to them who are the called according to his purpose." Watt, alas, is not one of these, and his world becomes increasingly less harmonious.

134.3 [132]: Tom, Dick, Harry: as in "any old Tom, Dick or Harry." The passage offers an intricate critique of seriality, or cause and effect, in that the structure of determinism and the notion of the pre-established arbitrary here explored (**131.1**, **131.5**, **134.2**) asserts that the various movements of Tom, in time and place, are not dependent on, or *because of*, those of Dick or Harry, but occur because Tom is Tom. As Richard Coe concludes (52), an impossible paradox is entailed: "For either Tom is temporal, in which case his whole existence is determined by his place in the series; or else he is a-temporal, a-spatial, and independent of the series—he cannot very well be both. *And yet*, says Beckett, *this is precisely what he is*. Human existence is a logical impossibility. It belongs to the series and yet evades the series; it is at once in time and out of time."

134.4 [132]: then Dick serves two years on the ground floor: elaborating the fallacy of the "monstrous assumption" (**132.5**), and clarifying the notion of "consistence" (**133.3**). The galleys (G45) read: "ten years on the first floor"; but Beckett firmly corrected this to "two" and "ground," and added in the margin: "and then Harry comes, and if Dick serves ten years on the first floor..." A little later, he also entered in the margin, after the repetition of Dick's "two years on the ground floor" [the "change" in place]: "or if Harry's coming then, and Dick's two years on the ground floor..." Without access to a final typescript there can be no certainty, but the galley changes probably correct an omission rather than register a change of intent. Beckett apparently approved "ground floor" and similar phrases but in a letter to John Calder (12 February 1963) he indicated a preference for the hyphenated form.

134.5 [132]: tired of underlining this accursed preposition: and yet it was necessary to have done so, *because of* the logical contradictions and monstrous assumptions of human existence as noted above, and below.

134.6 [132-33]: that would be too horrible to contemplate: an echo surviving virtually intact ("too appalling") from the earliest drafts (NB2, 72-73; TS, 145), of the relationship of life and experience; it questions the contention that the whole (here, the pre-established arbitrary) is greater than its parts (here, Tom, Dick, or Harry), while yet asserting that there are limits to the part's equality with the whole (**#6**).

135.1 [133]: Mr Knott was haven: added to the early draft (NB3, 184), perhaps from Psalms 107:28-30: "Then they cry unto the Lord in their trouble, and he bringeth them out of their distresses. / He maketh the storm a calm, so that the waves thereof are still. / Then they are glad because they be quiet; so he bringeth them unto their desired haven."

135.2 [133]: Haw!: the typescript (335) reads "Bah!" and "Pah!," but the late change accords with the prophetic ejaculations of Arsene.

135.3 [133]: calm and free and glad: initiating a simple reversed paradigm, beginning with the three terms, {calm, free, glad}, repeated thrice but without variation; considering then the binary pairings that might derive from this: {calm, free}, {free, glad}, and {glad, calm}; then the singular units: {calm}, {free}, or {glad}. I do not understand what Mood means (260), when he says this represents "7 possibilities; figured as $3 + 2^2$; twice."

135.4 [133]: a conception of which for the moment he had no need: without reference to the exchange between Napoleon and the Marquis de Laplace, when the Emperor reproached the author of the celebrated *Méchanique céleste* (1796) for his failure to have mentioned *le bon Dieu*.

>Laplace: "Sire, I had no need of that hypothesis."
>Napoléon: "But it is a fine hypothesis. It explains so many things."

135.5 [134]: any other flower of the field: as in Psalms 103:15-16: "As for man, his days are as grass: as a flower of the field, so he flourisheth. / For the wind passeth over it, and it is gone." One of Beckett's favorite biblical sentiments, it reappears in "Enough" (191), *Endgame* (42, of Mother Pegg), and "From an Abandoned Work" (155).

136.1 [134]: the white sweetness: lilies lack any overpowering odor, yet the detail throbs with a Proustian sense of the pre-madeleine experience in *Du côté de chez Swann*, where Marcel returns home along a path engulfed with the fragrance of white hawthorn.

136.2 [134]: the Tomness of Tom: the subject of a long digression (NB3, 189, 191), in the typescript (339-43) mercifully crossed out, concerning the relation ("not of the least importance") of his Tomness, his thereness, and his thenness. Rabinovitz (130) usefully glosses this with reference to Schopenhauer's sense (*WWI* II.404ff) of the inner nature of the self as a noumenal reality, a thing-in-itself that is the essential center of that self and unaffected by causality. More simply, Watt confronts the conundrum of life in a present that both is and is not conditional upon (ordained by) the long chain of consistence from the past to the future.

136.3 [134]: the ancient labour: the application of reason to the fundamental enigma of existence, in particular, to the dilemma of being both in and out of time, part of the series yet independent of it (**134.3**); a futile endeavor as nothing will come of it (however that "nothing" might be construed). Fred Miller Robinson (150) describes Watt's mental processes in terms of Buster Keaton's nut-cracking machine. The three brief paragraphs here are later inserts (NB5, 84v), facilitating the transition to the frog song. The drafts read (NB3, 191; TS, 343): "With the notion of the preestablished arbitrary I have no fault to find. The man habitually opening his tin of sardines, or his tin of condensed milk, with an acetylene blow-lamp, has my sympathy and even my esteem." This early "I" is nebulous, certainly not Sam; and any sympathy is soon (as it were) evaporated.

136.4 [135]: the time and the place and the loved one: from Petrarch's "Sonetta in vita di M. Laura," line 12: "I benedico il loco, e'l tempo e l'ora" ["I bless the place and time and hour"], punning on "l'ora / Laura." Browning's "Never the time and place / And the loved one together" in "Jocoseria" (Senneff 142) surely derives from this. Anticipated in *Dream* (191): the Alba "quietly delivered herself up to the place and the hour."

136.5 [135]: Krak!, Krek! and Krik!: the paradigm is meticulously laid out in NB4 (5) and the typescript (355), but Olympia Press messed up the typesetting, with only one interval between each "Krik!" and three convergent chords. On the galleys (946) Beckett insisted that it be redone completely: "Impossible à corriger. A refaire complètement d'apres MS. Voir note explicative p. 110." An explicative note (placed at the end of the Washington University file), or "note pour l'imprimeur . . . pas a imprimer" reads: "Il s'agit ici de 3 voix, parties ensemble et se repetant à des intervalles differents, et de leur déroulement jusqu'au moment où elles se font entendre de nouveau ensemble. Les petits traits represent des secondes. Entre deux krak 7 secondes, entre deux krek 4 secondes, entre deux krik 2 secondes. [New paragraph] Il faut souligner ce déroulement par groupes de trois voix au moyen d'une interligne après chaque groupe. Voir MS." He added: "S'il vous plaît, utiliser Bodoni 8 petit ou gros oeil pour avoir l'alignement exacte." The Grove setting of eight intervals, while it aligns every "Krak!," is arguably not as pleasing as the 11 by 11 setting (121 beats, the last as the first) in the typescript (355). Mood atonally perceives (260) "30 possibilities of continuous 4-beat measures"; Kenner inclusively identifies (86) "nine-beat, six-beat and four-beat intervals"; and Cohn (*Canon* 116) hears them as seven, five, and three. The intervals are precisely eight, five, and three beats respectively, a Fibonacci sequence (each the sum of the two previous) that completes its cycle after 120 intervals (the lowest common multiple of the constituent terms, 8 x 5 x 3); were there two more frogs ("Krok!" and "Kruk!") their intervals could be two and one; a sixth would croak at each thirteenth interval, but the final chord would not sound until 2,560 intervals had passed (13 x 8 x 5 x 3). Were the Fibonacci series extended {21, 34, 55 . . .}, the pattern of coincidence would be equally inevitable, but at increasingly greater levels (17,930; 304,810; 3,352,910...). The intervals of 3, 5, and 8, correspond, Heath Lees suggests, with the first inversion (E, G, and C) in the scale of C-major, as exemplified by the second picture in Erskine's room (**#26**) and the chapel bells at the end of the chapter (**149.1**). The song, Lees comments (12), acts as "an agent of transition between the inevitability of separateness (the individuation of Tom, Dick and Harry) and the possibility of meeting" (Watt and the fishwoman). Better, perhaps, is the sense of individuated notes finally resolved in a chord, as this creates a parable of periodicity and comments on the Law of Series as invoked by the individual series of dogs, pictures, and servants (to mention only these): when two or more independent series (here, three individual frogs) operate periodically in a given universe, coincidence is a mathematical inevitability. But (to echo Arsene), to conclude from this that the universe is harmonious would, I think, be rash, as the attribution of significance to interval 360, when the three series coincide, may say more about the human mind that reveres such symmetry than about the distinct phenomena that have (willy-nilly) created the pattern. The frog song illustrates, in a ruthless *reductio*, the machinery of the Joycean epiphany or Proustian moment, but one terrifying difference between Beckett on the one hand, and Joyce and Proust on the other, is the refusal to attribute transcendental value to such synchronicity.

138.1 [137]: the fishwoman: in the early drafts (NB4, 82-89; TS, 445-59), this interlude took place after the Louit story; in the final text, the transition is abrupt, less a reflection of the time and the place and the loved one than the realignment of previous material.

138.2 [137]: hold a candle: an effective use of the casual commonplace, not present in the typescript (445). The Freudian innuendo disappears in the French text (136): "aucune ne pouvait se comparer aux yeux de Watt."

139.1 [137]: Mrs Gorman: originally Mrs. Piscoe, the change made on the typescript (449). The drafts (NB4, 82; TS, 447ff) mention Watt's few adventures, "leading up to and away from his adventure with Mrs Watt"; this may be the genesis of his amours with the one-legged "Mrs Watson" (**74.2**, **80.4**). Mrs. Piscoe had her admirers "before" and "after" her husband in the early drafts (NB4, 82; TS, 449); "during" is a later innovation.

139.2 [137]: a man's man: Alfred Adler in *Individual Psychiatry* defines as "the fictitious goal" of masculine protest the wish to be "a complete man" (TCD 10971/7, 14); this is not a goal shared by Watt. Beckett in the early drafts (NB4, 84) outlined the paradigm based on "man" (M) and "woman" (W), where {MM} represents "man's man": {MM}, {WM}, {WW}, {MW}; one complete set that leads into another more complex: {MM + WM}, {MW + WW}, {(M + W)M}, {(M + W)W}. This finds expression on page 139: "a man's man and a woman's man . . . men's and women's women." The same paradigm in its negative form is reiterated on page 142.

140.1 [139]: his post-crucified position: the characteristic response of many of Beckett's characters, to intimate and escape from a world of pain; compare the sigmoidal position adopted by Watt at the station (233), with its similarity to the embryonic position. Consider, too, the sense of crucifixion in Otto Rank's *The Trauma of Birth* (138) as "the prevention of the embryonal position"; that is, of constraining the desire to return to the womb, of assuming the fetal position (*Grove Companion* 114).

140.2 [139]: velleitary: weakly volitional, or merely inclined.

141.1 [139]: But it was not Mrs Gorman on Watt: Beckett having overlooked the error, the galleys (G47), Olympia, and first Grove editions read: "if was not." This was silently changed on the Grove reprinting to "it was not," one error replacing another, until Calder made the correction: "But if it was not..." Mrs. Gorman's prepositional flexibility (**139.1**) is further compounded: Watt draws her down "among" his lap. Molloy, similarly, finds true love "in" another (*Molloy* 7).

141.2 [140]: interversion: Johnson's *Dictionary* defines *intervert* as: "to turn to another course"; here, to change positions.

141.3 [140]: on more than one occasion: the galleys (G47) omit "on"; the error entered the Olympia text, where Beckett noted it for correction by Grove, who made the change.

141.4 [140]: ancient error: that of Adam, of wanting to know (**136.3**), compounded with the tradition that carnal knowledge was a consequence of the Fall.

141.5 [140]: clonic gratification: pleasurable spasms (sullied by "cloaca," or sewer) deriving from muscular contractions and relaxations; as in "Serena I" and *Murphy* (139).

142.1 [140]: some endocrinal Bandusia: a blockage of the *vas deferens*, the duct that carries the sperm from the testes to the urethra, preventing completion of the sexual act; *tractable* has the sense of "easily treated," the opposite of *intractable*; *endocrinal*, relating to hormones. The jest arises from Fr. *bander*, "to have an erection," with the *fons Bandusiae* (*Odes* III.13), a spring near the birth-place of Horace. See "Bando" (**170.1**). NB4 (88) has a "probably tractable ? "; the typescript (455) fills the gap with "disturbance"; both have "endocrinal fountain." The galleys (G47) omitted one line, "not unworthy of the occasion. Whereas as things stood, with Watt's"; this Beckett restored.

142.2 [140]: the Hellespont: the ancient name of the Dardenelles, separating the Sea of Marmara from the Aegean and Leander (on the Asian side) from Hero (on the European). Leander would swim from Abydos to Sestos, but one tempestuous night (compare Watt's "languid tides") he drowned, and Hero, in despair, threw herself into the sea.

142.3 [141]: a man's man: an extension of the previous paradigm (**139.2**), with all the sets negative, and the binary pairings of man (M) and woman (W) themselves paired, as in {MW}, a "man's woman." The possibilities are limited because the first term must finish in "M" (Watt is not a woman) and the second must finish in "W" (Mrs. Gorman is not a man): {-(MM) -(WW)}, {-(WM) -(MW)}, {-(MM) -(MW)}, {-(WM) -(WW)}. One further set is offered: {-([MM WM] [MW WW])}: Watt neither a man's [man] nor a woman's man and Mrs. Gorman neither a man's [woman] nor a woman's woman. Mood's "5 possibilities, figured as 2^2+1" (261) reflects this. The galleys (G48) omitted: "Between Watt not a man's man and Mrs Gorman not a man's woman?"; the wide spacing in the Olympia and Grove texts is a consequence of its re-insertion.

142.4 [141]: conglutination: in Johnson's *Dictionary*: "The act of healing wounded bodies; reunion; healing." Olympia and Grove place a period, rather than a comma, after "dying perfume"; Beckett did not note the error, but Calder made the correction.

142.5 [141]: Mr Graves: in earlier drafts (NB4, 10, 13), the gardener was Mr. [Kevin] Gomez, whose ancestor arrived in Ireland in 1555; a long passage (13-23) about the Armada and other matters was quite literally (with a scissors) excised from the typescript (365). A miserable man, he was made more so by Watt's tendency to pronounce his name correctly, in the Spanish manner (NB4, 11; TS, 363). He gave way, first to "the gardener" (NB5, 7) (**69.3**), and only later to "Mr Graves" (the changes made on the typescript [398ff] probably post-date NB5). The existence of a garden presumes that of the gardener; but Mr. Graves's name presages the fate of all natural things. In *Mercier and Camier* (47), a Mr. Graves enters the pub; he may or may not be one of the Graves brothers of *Texts for Nothing* 2, whose farm the narrator passes on his winter journey.

142.6 [141]: four times a day: the galleys (G48) and Olympia edition read "three times a day." The error was missed by Beckett when marking his Olympia text for Grove, so the first Grove edition reproduced "three"; but on reprinting silently changed "three" to "four." When he marked his Grove text,

Beckett requested that Calder do likewise. The French translation (148) has: "quatre fois par jour."

143.1 [141]: the key and the bottle: the galleys (G49) read: "he bottle"; Beckett overlooked the error, which persisted into the Olympia text, but he marked it for correction by Grove, where the change was made.

143.2 [141]: a feeling little short of liking: not in the early drafts, but a long, deleted description of the breeding of the famished dogs (**111.1**) included (NB3, 143; TS, 291) the similar pronunciation of the gateman, Frith. In preparing his Calder text for the French translation, Beckett marked for deletion this paragraph and these venerable saxon words; so that the French translation (148) runs from "et la bouteille vide . . ." to "Monsieur Graves avait beaucoup à dire."

143.3 [142]: prostituting himself to some purpose: in Murphy's words, *quid pro quo*; the late draft (NB5, 87) is more mundane: "had not demeaned himself altogether in vain." Mr. Graves's "what," "that," and "with" (NB5, 89) became "wat," "tat," and "wid."

143.4 [142]: His father had worked for Mr Knott: a detail directly linked to one of the earliest passages in the novel, the encounter in his garden between Quin and an old man who claimed to have worked for his father (**#29**). The encounter predates any suggestion that Quin/Knott is serial; indeed, the [too] explicit sentence, "Here then was another series," does not appear in the late draft (NB5, 87), which omits the "tavern companions" to record that Mr. Graves's words were "without interest."

143.5 [142]: like a house on fire: an unfortunate cliché, given that in "Dante and the Lobster" and "Draff" the gardener murders several of the family and sets the house on fire. The French translation (149) reads: "Tout au long de sa vie conjugale il s'était entendu avec sa femme, comme l'ormeau avec la vigne"; but the traditional entwining of the elm and the vine lacks the irony of the original.

144.1 [143]: floccillating: from L. *floccullus*, a lock of wool or wool-like substance; in the Whoroscope Notebook (78) Beckett writes: "floccillation (picking the bedclothes)." This is taken from the *OED*; the unique citation (from Brande's *Scientific Dictionary*) adds: "this is an alarming symptom in many acute illnesses." Molloy's hands floccillate his sheets (*Molloy* 66).

144.2 [143]: Judge Jeffreys: George Jeffreys (1648-89), Baron of Wem and infamous persecutor of the Popish Plot. He headed the "bloody assizes" at Winchester after Monmouth's insurrection (1685), and was rewarded with the office of Lord Chancellor. On the death of James his position became perilous. Fleeing the country disguised as a seaman, he was recognized in a Wapping pub and taken to the Tower, where he died of the stone, a condition said to have affected the severity of his judgments. A pupil of "the celebrated Busby"

(*Murphy* 97), his excesses are outlined in Cooper (*Flagellation* 156-60). Mentioned as if presiding [over] the Ecclesiastical Commission, a body responsible for the revenues of the Established Church; but this was not instituted until 1835.

144.3 [143]: their missile flights: is Watt, a university man, engrossed in the problem of self-extension, as manifest when a stick becomes a stone: how the self (or bird) occupies the space through which it moves (**8.1**, **32.2**)? Probably not.

144.4 [143]: their canorous reloadings: nothing to do with the canon earlier peppered (*Watt* 91); but rather the tendency of birds to repeat their songs.

145.1 [144]: in the vestibule: the early drafts (NB4, 6; TS, 357) told how Watt would ring the bells when it was time for Quin's meals; and how Quin would ring the bells as a sign to Watt to clear away.

146.1 [144]: a little blue flower: an image from *Heinrich von Ofterdingen*, by the German poet Novalis (Freidrich von Hardenberg, 1772-1801), for the later Romantics and Symbolists an emblem of longing and transcendence, as the green carnation would be for the Decadents. Beckett had taken notes on Novalis (TCD 10971/1, 33v) in which he defined the blue flower as the "Romantic ideal." The flower is invoked at the end of "Assumption" (7), in *Dream* (70), and in a 1934 review of some Rilke translations (*Disjecta* 66); Beckett parodied it in "Calvary by Night," where it mingles with Leopold Bloom's languid floating flower. The "fat worm burrowing into the earth" is an emblem of the earth-bound soul, with affinities to many of Blake's images. The galleys (G49) read: "until the worm was gone and only the worm remain"; Beckett changed the second "worm" to "flower," and added: "One day the flower would be gone and only the worm remain," probably to restore an omission rather than to make a change.

146.2 [145]: assuming that the ground was level: added to the early draft (NB4, 9), perhaps to prevent Mr. Knott being defined by any such attribute as height.

146.3 [145]: face to face: I Corinthians 13:12: "For now we see through a glass, darkly; but then face to face: now I know in part; but then I shall know even as I am known." Watt catches a few glimpses of his master, not clearly, "but as it were in a glass" (147). Also Genesis 32:26: "And Jacob called the name of the place Peniel; for I have seen God face to face, and my life is preserved."

146.4 [145]: and even from behind: Exodus 33:23, the Lord's words to Moses: "and thou shalt see my back parts: but my face shall not be seen." The early draft (NB4, 9) read: "positively from behind." See also **211.3**.

146.5 [145]: so many other sorrows: the galleys (G49) read "so many others sorrows"; Beckett overlooked the error, which made its way into the Olympia text, where it was marked for correction by Grove, who made the change.

146.6 [145]: abandoned all hope: an echo of Dante's *Inferno* III.9, the words above the entrance to hell: "Lasciate ogni speranza / voi ch'entrate" ["All hope abandon, ye who enter here"].

147.1 [146]: another to diminish: according to the principle of equilibrium (**55.1**).

147.2 [146]: in a glass: darkly, as in I Corinthians 13:12 (**146.3**). Compare the shimmering windows, western and orient, of the examination hall (195).

147.3 [146]: Add to this that the figure: the second such paragraph was later added to the typescript by hand (358), to anticipate the changing accidents of Mr. Knott (Beckett lists them here as: tall, thin, sturdy; fat, small, middle; pale, flushed, yellow; and dark, fair, ginger) that determine the final paradigm (**209.7**) and accentuate the Augustinian theme, that one cannot know what God is but only what he is [K]not.

147.4 [146]: PLOPF: in the early drafts (NB4, 9), the sounds have no final "F" and the phrasing is more explicit: "once he had heard him break wind." This becomes (TS, 461 [mis-numbered]): "once he had heard him make a strange noise." The sequence offers a *diminuendo al niente* effect, but, as Mood notes (261), the sequence of alternating italics is imperfect (or Watt's hearing diminished), there being no "*plop*," "*plo*," nor "*pl*"; while a final "p" (and "*p*") is lacking.

147.5 [146]: a teaser: an antimony, or logical contradiction; with the sense, as first recorded (NB1, 5, 7; TS, 1), of "the well-known teaser of the suffering."

148.1 [147]: A friend: at one early point (NB4, 10), the conversation unfolded in more detail, the call to Quin coming at precisely 12:15 p.m. from a "disciple" named "Mr Keith Jones" who insisted that "Mr Quin is always in."

148.2 [147]: What had he learnt? Nothing: one possible model for Watt's final speech is suggested by the Abbé Sieyes's famous pamphlet (Paris, 1788), which began: "Qu'est-ce-que le Tiers État? . . . Tout"; and proceeded: "Qu'a-t'il été jusqu'a présent dans l'ordre politique? . . . Rien"; the basic pattern being: "Qu'est-ce que . . . tout" / "Qu'a t-il . . . Rien." Another is that outlined in John Burnet's *Greek Philosophy* (120), of Gorgias of Leontini (483-375 BC), who affirmed that (1) there is nothing, (2) even if there were anything we cannot know it, and (3) even if we could know it we could not communicate that knowledge. Thus, Knott has no real existence; if he did he could not be known; if he could be known that knowledge could not be communicated. For other instances of this paradigm, see **45.5** and **97.1**. Despite its centrality, Büttner insists (154) that the key "gnosiological" problem must be how we can grasp or get to know Mr. Knott: "If he really does exist, there must be a way of reaching him."

148.3 [147]: Sicker, aloner: the early drafts (NB4, 90; TS, 461) read: "So sad, so alone," and "Sadder, aloner." That Watt is exhausted reflects the futility of his attempt to comprehend his master by the rational technique akin to "proof by exhaustion"; that is, by calculating the area of an ever-refined polygon inscribed within a circle, the point being that this may be done without using *pi*, yet, however exhaustive, such a calculation can be approximate only, an infinitesimal gap remaining between the perfect circle (God) and human reason (*ratio*). Thus Descartes, in Beckett's first footnote to *Whoroscope*, is said to have proved God. [*Note*: here, and until the end of part II, I observe the HRHRC mis-numbering of pages 459/460 and 461/462].

148.4 [147]: Was not that something?: as if mocking in despair the Socratic principle that the beginning of knowledge is the recognition that one knows nothing.

148.5 [147]: yellowist: the "wistful" superlative is presumably not in error, as it is spelled "yellowest" in the early draft (NB4, 90), but thus in the typescript (461) and galleys (G50); Beckett chose not to "correct" it for either the Grove or Calder editions. On the galleys, the next line read: "half ender, ended"; this was overlooked, but Beckett marked the Olympia text for correction by Grove, where that change was made.

148.6 [147]: on arising, on descending: the galleys (G50) are correct, but the Olympia Press added another "on arising"; this may have been done to fill the space (and avoid realigning the type) created by Beckett's removal from the galleys of "one morning" (G50 read: "But at last ~~one morning~~ he awoke").

149.1 [148]: the sound of bells: identified by O'Brien (22) as coming (in Beckett's boyhood world) from the nearby Tullow Parish Church, near Cooldrinagh, also the original of Moran's "beloved church" in *Molloy*. In a letter to Susan Manning (21 May [1955]), Beckett noted: "Xmas morning in the fields near Glencullen, listening to the chapel bells." The typescript (459) waxes lyrical about the bells, in such a way as to suggest an echo of the frog song: "It was to the sound of bells, of church bells, of chapel bells, ringing deep and slow, ringing high and swift, in commemoration of some memorable occasion in the life of their Lord, or of His family, or of His numerous followers. Deep and slow, high and swift, so that for every three peals of the former there were no fewer than five of the latter, and that the third and fifth, the sixth and tenth, the ninth and fifteenth, the twelfth and twentieth, etcetera, strokes, on the one hand of the reformed, on the other of the aboriginal clappers, produced as chord, a charming chord, a charming charming second a comma sharp, a charming charming third a comma flat, assuming that the bell-ringers began to ring their bells at precisely the same moment, and that they continued to ring them at intervals in each case identical with the initial interval, and that Quin's residence was precisely equidistant from the two [blank space] of worship, a combination of circumstances seldom united." Heath Lees argues (172) that the "Pythagorean comma," or disjunction between mathematical and acoustical realities (**70.3**), is indicative of Watt's psychological untuning, manifest at the end of this chapter. The final and reduced version appears in the typescript, written in by hand on the final verso (462); here, the stranger's name is Martin.

149.2 [148]: the milkboy: O'Brien (19) identifies him (in Beckett's boyhood world) as coming from the small dairy owned by Mr. Tully, close to Cooldrinagh.

149.3 [148]: Arthur: one of the small fat seedy shabby type (**61.1**). Earlier drafts (TS, 459) are strangely anticlimactic: "The strange man's name was Phelps. He resembled Arsene in structure." He was briefly called Martin (**149.1**). In the final text, the simple repetition of "Arthur" is unutterably poignant. In "Avant *Fin de partie*," a forerunner of *Endgame*, F (the factotum) happily responds to any other name; he objects only to Arthur: "tout sauf Arthur" (*Grove Companion* 32).

III

151.1 [149]: III: in the galleys (G50), after the end of part II, Beckett deleted "111" (Arabic) and insisted on "III" (Roman), adding (much as he had for part II and would for part IV): "20 l:—en belle page."

151.2 [149]: about this time: not when Arthur came and Erskine went, as narrative sequence implies; but the time, undefined, when Watt told Sam about Arthur. There is a distinction between *récit* (the sequence of textual events), *histoire* (the order in which events occurred before being narrated), and *narration* (telling the story): here *narration* overlaps *histoire* and *récit* (Pat McCarthy to CA). The beginning of part III, up to "from time to time" (*Watt* 164), and the final paragraph were pre-published as an "Extract from *Watt*" in *Irish Writing* 17 (December 1951): 11-16; Beckett told Mania Péron (4 August 1951) that this "mauvaise revue" had requested a contribution, and ("dans ma grande bonté") he had agreed, choosing these because he could not find anything "moins scandalisant" (*Grove Companion* 278). Large chunks are omitted from this extract; these are indicative of the text as it must have been at a late stage, some parts not yet composed and others not moved into their final position. These are:

- the footnote (153)
- the paragraph beginning: "When Watt spoke" (156)
- part of the paragraph beginning "This garden was surrounded" (156), from "For a big-bottomed man" to the end (157)
- the passage from "How hideous is the semi-colon" (158) to "and so looking about me" (with "And" capitalized)
- both references concerning Watt's resemblance to the Christ believed by Bosch (159)
- the passage about the hole (160-62), the text reworked: "Wait, wait, I am coming, I cried, and closed my eyes. But when I opened them again Watt was no longer there . . ."
- two paragraphs, from "For us moving so" to "in the way described" (164)

Beckett suggested to Barney Rosset (30 August 1956) that his *Evergreen* selection should include the beginning of part III; in the event it was not included.

151.3 [149]: pavilion: Robinson (106) senses an heraldic association with "The Field of Gold" (in contrast with the fallen natural world). Beckett uses "pavilion" in the German Diaries for museum and gallery rooms associated with distinct periods or themes. For "pavilion" as the bell of a wind instrument, see **#26**.

151.4 [149]: me: the implied narrator, Sam, incrementally hinted at in part II, is now the defined voice of the novel, which purports, rightly or wrongly, to be his rendering of Watt's words, told haltingly with many a hiatus, reversed and entangled, over a long period of time, within (or, rather, without) the asylum, their meetings taking place on the infrequent occasions that the conjunction of their meteorological preferences has permitted an exodus. Smith suggests (116-18) that just as *Watt* represents a transition between the aborted "Human Wishes" fragment and later fiction, so Sam exemplifies "something" of the quality of Samuel Johnson in matters of temperament, such as his need for conversation, moodiness, periodic depression, and fear of going insane.

151.5 [149]: mansions: John 14:2: "In my father's house are many mansions"; also, the "mansions of Bedlam," or cells of Bethlem, the London asylum visited on 8 May 1775 by Boswell and Johnson, with Arthur Murphy. The jest was an 18th-century commonplace. Beckett cited Boswell in his "Human Wishes" Notebook (BIF 3461/1, 29): "He calls the cells in Bedlam the 'mansions' (& the corridors the galleries)." Malone awakes in an asylum, thinking he might be dead, "expiating my sins or in one of heaven's mansions" (*Malone Dies* 182). Compare the desire to escape "into the spacious annexe of mental alienation" (*Proust* 19). The original of Watt's asylum is St. John of God's, at Stillorgan, near Foxrock, housing the docile rather than the criminally insane (*Murphy* 43); also the setting of *Malone Dies*.

152.1 [150]: windowlessness: less a feature of the padded cells, as in *Murphy* (181), than the condition of the monad, for Leibniz the unit of elementary being, which, since hermetically enclosed, offers no window to the world. Hence their "separate soundless unlit warmth." In his Philosophical Notes (TCD 10967/191; Windelband 423), Beckett noted: "Each monad is, with reference to the rest, perfectly independent, unable to exercise or experience influence. Their 'windowlessness' is expression of their 'metaphysical impenetrability'." An error, "windowlesness," unnoticed by Beckett, entered the galleys (G50) and the Olympia text, where it was noted for correction by Grove. Two lines later, "come" was mis-spelled as "some"; Grove made both changes.

152.2 [150]: just as well, if not better: compare *Waiting for Godot* (31.b): "That passed the time." / "It would have passed in any case." / "Yes, but not so rapidly."

153.1 [151]: No truck: a paragraph added later (NB4, 95), the surge of violence distinguishing Sam from the milder patients in "Fingal," "kicking a football" (30). The final "back as we went" reverses the more clichéd "back as we came" of the addition.

153.2 [151]: important thing was the wind, the sun was the: a line dropped from the galleys (G51), but restored by Beckett in a marginal note.

153.3 [151]: For when on Sam . . . deepest night: embedded here is a quatrain of iambic tetrameter (Marcel Fernandes to CA); NB4 (97) reflects this:

> For when on Sam the sun shone bright,
> then in a vacuum panted Watt,
> and when Watt like a leaf was tossed,
> then stumbled Sam in deepest night.

153.4 [151]: this volte-face: for Watt's earlier dislike of the sun, see page 33. The footnote is not in the late draft (NB4, 99). The galleys (G51) omitted the footnote; the error, "in known," appeared in the Olympia text, Beckett marking it for correction by Grove.

154.1 [151]: the garden: a forsaken Eden, whence grace has fled and luxuriance is barren, where Sam and Watt walk like desolate Adams, their awkward embraces adding to the ironies. The French text avoids edenic overtones, consistently using "parc." The grounds of St. John of God's at Stillorgan (**151.5**) comprised mainly the "pleasure garden" (O'Brien 243), some fifteen acres adjacent to wilder terrain. The galleys (G51) and Olympia text read: "Not that the garden as so little"; the error was overlooked by Beckett until he marked his Olympia text for Grove, where the change was made.

154.2 [151]: tropical luxuriance: incongruous, given the temperate clime. The aspens are associated with the crucifixion (**213.3**), and the yews, as at the end of part II, intimate death.

154.3 [152]: the pissabed: an ancient term for "dandelion," the word Beckett used (NB4, 98) into the galleys; as Fr. *pissenlit* ("pisser en lit"), from the plant's diuretic virtues.

154.4 [152]: a rustic bridge: compare *Dream* (27): "hyphen of passion"; bridges analogous to the hyphen as links between separate entities. In NB4 (98), "crown" was "ridge."

154.5 [152]: and Watt on his at his: as Ann Beer notes (56), the pedantry suggests "that all group or plural experience is an illusion: the individual and his language are alone."

155.1 [152]: (I could hardly do otherwise): the galleys (G51) and Olympia text read: "hardly to otherwise"; Beckett overlooked the error until marking his Olympia edition for Grove, where the change was made.

155.2 [153]: the overarching boughs: added to the late draft (NB4, 99); perhaps intimating the purple prose cited in the "Aeolus" chapter of Joyce's *Ulysses*: "the overarching leafage."

155.3 [153]: We were attached: originally in parenthesis, until the galleys (G51), where Beckett deleted the brackets.

155.4 [153]: vestige: NB4 (98) reads "suggestion"; *vestige* is pedantically correct, there having once been such seats but now no longer.

155.5 [153]: properly so called: see **#29** for the jest about the passing bush, or shrub. The vacuous sentiment, "properly so called," suggests a joke that only linguists find funny: the farmer looking into the sty and wrinkling his nose: "Roightly is they called pigs."

155.6 [153]: Birds of every kind: in Eden, Adam was granted dominion over the fowl of the air (Genesis 1:26). Robinson (109) cites *King Lear* IV.i.36-37: "As flies to wanton boys are we to the gods; / They kill us for their sport." The "peculiar satisfaction" reflects the arbitrary nature of grace and suffering in this created world, where it is the pleasure of the gods to destroy the helpless; in that sense Sam and Watt come "nearest to God" (*Watt* 156).

155.7 [153]: ordinary: the dining room, and so the meal served there; also, the exercise of ecclesiastical jurisdiction over a specified territory.

156.1 [154]: Gomorrha: the final writing fills a blank in the late draft (NB4, 101), Beckett for once not preferring the hiatus (Cork as a City of the Plain too much to resist?).

156.2 [154]: manner .: marking his Olympia edition, Beckett noted the inadvertent space from the galleys (G52); but it persisted into the Grove text and was closed only in Calder.

157.1 [155]: broad-shouldered . . . big-bellied . . . broad-basined . . . big-bottomed: four sets, which, since the order of the terms is irrelevant, offer six binary combinations: {AB}, {AC}, {AD}, {BC}, {BD}, {CD}. Representing "shouldered," "bellied," "basined," and "bottomed" by "A," "B," "C," and "D," the text offers: {AB}, {CD}, {CB}, {AD}; missing are {AC}, "broad-shouldered and broad-basined"; and {BD}, "big-bellied and big-bottomed" (the latter perhaps implied in one perforated by a rusty barb in both the stomach and the arse). The phrase, "or perhaps both," is not in the late draft (NB4, 102). Nor are the missing elements equivalent to two others introduced, "big-bosomed and broad shouldered," and "big-bosomed and broad-basined"; as missing are two further options of "big-bosomed and big-bellied" and "big-bosomed and big-bottomed" (the obese wet-nurse satisfies the latter condition). The incompleteness is probably intentional, as the paradigm is not difficult; Mood's description (261) of "14 possibilities, figured as 5+4+3+2+1," with one missing element, is curious. The sequence from "For a big-bottomed man" to the end of the paragraph was absent from the pre-publication extract in *Irish Writing* (**151.2**).

157.2 [155]: running with the scissors, the brandy and the iodine: the late drafts (NB4, 102) read: "running with brandy and iodine"; the definite article makes a small difference (compare **8.2**, **96.2**).

158.1 [156]: How hideous is the semi-colon: a comment not present in the late draft (NB4, 105); nor are the following semi-colons, new sentences preferred. To John Calder (12 February 1963), Beckett wrote: "I started to suppress colons & semi-colons having forgotten 'how hideous is the semi-colon' page 156. So they all go back as indicated. Sorry for this stupidity." The French translation (162) retains them as in English.

158.2 [156]: if possible what follows: the galleys (G52) offer no punctuation but Beckett in marking the Olympia edition requested a comma after "possible"; as no change was made, he repeated the request when marking his Grove edition for Calder, who added it.

158.3 [156]: croaking: the galleys (G53) read "singing," as in the late draft (NB4, 105); but Beckett crossed it out and wrote in the change.

158.4 [156]: touched it with a stick: as Mr. Hackett his seat (**8.1**, **32.2**, **82.1**, **144.3**).

159.1 [156]: doubts . . . in a reasonable mind: the Cartesian philosophy of doubt, whereby Descartes rejected all evidence of the sense (hence "one deprived of his senses"), dreams, and hallucinations, there remaining one thing (he asserted) that could not be doubted, the consciousness of thought and thus of the self that thinks. This led to the famous *cogito, ergo sum* ["I think, therefore I am"], on which foundation he raised his structure of knowledge and thought. The phrases, "beyond all possibility of error" and "with a distinctiveness that left no room for doubt" assume a Cartesian clarity, reflecting the principle that all things conceived as clear and distinct are true. Sam, in doubting the sanity of the person responsible for the lay-out, is following the *Méthode*.

159.2 [157]: advancing backwards: Coetzee adds (221): "In *Through the Looking Glass* the White Queen also moves backwards, and finds that it helps her memory work both ways."

159.3 [157]: believed by Bosch: a painting in London's National Gallery, *Christ Mocked (the Crowning with Thorns)*, by Hieronymus Bosch (1450-1516), Catholic painter of the Spanish Netherlands whose works are characterized by elements of fantasy and the grotesque (see the cover). In his notes to Dutch art (BIF 5001, 43), Beckett cited an unidentified German source: "London (N. G.) *Dornenkrönung*)." The late draft (NB4, 106) reads "supposedly by Bosch," with "supposedly" an afterthought; it locates the picture in "the National Gallery" rather than "Trafalgar Square." The final ambiguity ("believed by Bosch" and "supposed by Bosch") is deliberate; the sentence beginning "For if anyone," was added late (not in NB4, 106). The French translation added an extra hiatus: "le Christ dit de Bosch (National Gallery No ?)." Macmillan ("Visual Arts" 36), links the circular crown of thorns in the Bosch painting to the circular race course seen from Watt's window, the painting in Erskine's room, and the pattern formed by the barbed wire fences as they bulge toward each other: "The relationship of the series of pictures is first of all visual. They all represent circularity." Perhaps; but suffering and pity are of greater concern.

159.4 [157]: standing before a great mirror: anticipating the mirror dance, which Sam and Watt engage in (168). Nicola Ramsay describes the "mirror gag" as part of the "clown routines" of the circus, silent movie, and music-hall traditions.

159.5 [159]: in the ravine: the late draft (NB4, 106) is more direct: "in the fleshy part of the posterior." Thus did Dr. Watson receive his wound in the

Khyber. Watt's "handkerchief" (NB4, 106) became "panky-hanky," to accentuate the coming inversions.

160.1 [158]: a pole, or perch: a jest arises because, in English measurement of length, a pole is five and a half yards; equally, it is a perch (in Irish measurement, seven yards make a pole, or perch). The phrase, "or a perch," was not present in the late draft (NB4, 115) but appears in the galleys (G53). The French text (164) struggles gamely: "sans le secours d'une lame, en gaule [a fishing rod], ou en perche [a jumping pole]."

160.2 [158]: by a bull, or by a boar: the existence of the hole presumes a maker of holes, as that of the garden presumes a gardener. However, two holes complicate matters, given the premise here advanced that both could not have been made by one animal, however infuriated. It therefore follows that the holes were caused by the weather ("numberless winds, numberless rains"), and the usual ingenuity is applied to the refutation of the alternative premise ("the" implying definition) concerning the bull and/or boar.

160.3 [158]: my pretty uniform: presumably a euphemism for a straitjacket.

160.4 [158]: the couloir: French for "corridor"; earlier (*Watt* 158) "channels or straits" was preferred.

160.5 [158]: their normal acuity: given that the second hole is a bare yard away, and that Sam passed through the first some ten or fifteen minutes before (the numbers echoing the increase of acuity, or sharpness [Gk. *axios*, "sharp"]), there is every probability that ten or fifteen times his spatial and temporal norms is still not much.

160.6 [158]: the infuriated mass: what follows are assumptions derived from basic physics and mechanics, such as force equals mass times acceleration, or that increases or reductions of velocity are consequent upon the rate of acceleration in relation to the resistance met.

161.1 [159]: by a bull: among some details taken from Wilhelm Stekel's *Psychoanalysis and Suggestion* (1923), Beckett noted (TCD 10971/8, 24): "A man chased over the fields by a mad bull cannot be expected to appreciate the botanical specimens (Bion)."

161.2 [159]: an infuriated bull . . . boar . . . cow . . . sow: apparently initiating a simple paradigm of six binary pairs (since two holes) selected from these four elements: {AB}, {AC}, {AD}, {BC}, {BD}, {CD}; but complicating this by the admission of {AA}, {BB}, {CC}, {DD}, to allow ten choices in all; and permitting four singularities, {A}, {B}, {C}, {D}, these considered (*Watt* 162) as {A C B D}: "the bull, the cow, the boar, the sow." This may be what Mood means (261) by "14 possibilities, figured as 4+4+(3+2+1)." Assuming "A," "B," "C," and "D" to represent, respectively, "bull," "boar," "cow," and "sow," the text legitimizes the following pairings: {AA}, {BB}, {AC}, {BD}; and rules out two others: {AD},

{BC}. Four options, then: {CC} (cow and cow), {DD} (sow and sow), {AB} (bull and boar), and {CD} (cow and sow) are not considered, although {bull and boar} appears previously. The paradigm is rehearsed at the end of the paragraph (*Watt*, 162): {A}, {B}, {AA}, {BB}, {CC}, {DD}, {AC}, {BD}; but omits the same four combinations: {AB}, {AD}, {BC}, {CD}. The logical possibilities, then, are constrained by the empirical world.

162.1 [160]: an infuriated cow: the galleys (G54) and Olympia text read "sow," an error (overlooked by Beckett, yet the same mistake nine lines later was corrected) that persisted into the first Grove text but was silently changed on reprinting. In his notes to the "trueborn jackeen" (TCD 10971/2/7), Beckett noted: "the black cow, or sow, meaning misfortune." The French translation (165) loses the euphony of "bull, boar, cow, sow"; offering: "sanglier, taureau, laie [wild sow], vache." Curiously, Beckett's fence at Ussy was broken down some years later by wild boars (Knowlson 460-61).

162.2 [160]: the fury of love, the fury of hate: as of Empedocles, advocate of the "strife of opposites," or universal dynamic of hate and love. The late draft (NB4, 110) read: "in the heat of hate, the heat of love." The pairings are problematic, in that they imply (the syntax is uncertain) "the bull, the cow" and "the sow, the boar" [why the chiasmus?], and "the bull, the boar," but not "the cow, the sow." The fury of hate has one coupling; that of love has two.

163.1 [161]: with a cloth: the echo of the sudarium (**32.8**) is more explicit in the French translation (168), which uses the earlier word (34): "un petit linge."

163.2 [161]: I anointed his face: as Mary, brother of Lazarus, the feet of Jesus (John 12:3).

163.3 [161]: And so we paced together: again (see **159.4**), a mirror-dance, face to face, perhaps indicative of Watt's recession to the narcissistic, to Lacan's mirror stage. Their movements suggest puppets, as in Kleist's essay, "Über das Marionettentheater" (1810), which intrigued Beckett: consciousness destroys the dynamics of motion, so that movement is translated into a stiffness lacking natural grace or charm. The galleys (G54) complicated the movement by repeating, in the wrong order, two lines; these Beckett firmly crossed out.

163.4 [162]: perhaps something: echoing the end of part II (**148.4**).

164.1 [162]: Watt's manner, at this period: the seven following paradigms have each an example of Watt's language (indicated in various drafts by Arabic numbers, 1 to 8); an explanation of that language, ending with a variation of "Beg pardon" (referred to in capital Roman numbers, I to V); and the consequences of "Thus I missed" as variations of "I suppose," "I suspect," and "I presume" (capital letters, A to G). Beckett retained this schema when marking his Calder text for the French translation. Although no errors are noted in either his Olympia or Grove text, several appear at one point or another. The paradigms were first "translated" into English in Ruby Cohn's *Comic Gamut* (309-10).

164.2 [162]: *Day of most . . . moved I so*: on a presumably discarded page of an early translation (HRHRC Carlton Lake Collection 1.13, 55v), Beckett noted:

> *Most of day, part of night, now with Knott*
> *Up till now, oh so little seen, oh so little heard*
> *From morning till night*
> *What then, this I saw, this I heard*
> *Dim, quiet thing*
> *Also now ears, eyes, failing*
> *In hush, in mist, so I moved*

The imperfect inversions, here as in the final text, are the "little seen" and "little heard" of the third line, and the "ears" and "eyes" failing of line seven. Watt's "pardon beg" (165) reflects the process in miniature.

164.3 [163]: the inversion affected: in the late draft (NB4, 121), Beckett outlined the pattern of inversion ("a" to "g"), then revised it for the actual text ("1" to "7"):

> (a) *words only* (1)
> (b) *letters "*   (2)
> (c) *words & letters* (4)
> (d) *sentences only* (3)
> (e) *sentences & letters* (6)
> (f) *sentences & words* (5)
> (g) *sentences & words & letters* (7)

The late draft (NB4, 114) capitalized the "T" of each following "that."

164.4 [163]: face to face: an imperfect paradigm begins: "breast to breast"; "notwithstanding our proximity"; "belly to belly"; "pubis to pubis"; but no example is given thereafter.

165.1 [163]: Thus I missed I suppose . . . I suspect . . . I presume: the three terms, "suppose," "suspect," and "presume," are distributed over the next few pages. A logical problem arises as there are only six {3!} possible permutations: {ABC}, {ACB}, {BAC}, {BCA}, {CBA}, {CAB}; but eight desired outcomes. One way of dealing with this, toyed with in the late draft (NB4, 128), where the sequence was composed, was to add a fourth term, "I take it"; but this allows twenty-four variations, which is too many. The compromise with seriality was to have the seventh repeat the first, and the eighth (potentially) repeat the second. The late draft (NB4, 128) outlines the proposed full set (see overleaf):

1.	*suppose*	*suspect*	*presume*
2.	*suppose*	*presume*	*suspect*
3.	*suspect*	*suppose*	*presume*
4.	*suspect*	*presume*	*suppose*
5.	*presume*	*suspect*	*suppose*
6.	*presume*	*suppose*	*suspect*
7.	*suppose*	*suspect*	*presume*
8.	*suppose*	*presume*	*suspect*

This was followed, but not religiously, as the Olympia and Grove texts have "presume" twice as the third instance, and the fourth omits "suppose" (see **166.2** and **166.5**). There is no reason to suspect that these are teasers rather than inadvertent errors as they were correct in the galleys; besides, an error in the late draft (NB4, 129), the omission of "suppose" in the sixth pattern, is corrected in the text. Corrected versions were restored without comment in the French drafts, typescript, and final translation (Ohio NBV; Ohio TS, 119-21; 171-73); but these observe a different order, using "imagine," "suppose," and "présume": "Ainsi je perdais (j'imagine) des choses fort intéressantes (je présume) touchant le quatrième stade (je suppose)"; in the sequence of {ISP}, {SPI}, {PIS}, {IPS}, {SIP}, {PSI}, then back to {ISP}, with no eighth instance. The change from "je me trompe" to "j'imagine" was made in the typescript (Ohio TS, 119-21), to avoid the plethoric reflexive pronoun.

165.2 [163]: his dislike of battology: futile reiteration in speech or writing; the text earlier read (NB4, 133) "repetition." Beckett "Human Wishes" notebook (I, 71) offers a curious gloss: "Erasmus distinguishes <u>battologia</u> (vain repetition Matt. vi.7) from <u>iteratio</u>, & defends 'My God! My God!' as <u>justifiable earnestness</u> !" [Beckett's *exclamatio*]. That Watt's sense of chronology was strong merely means that he could distinguish the various stages of his stay.

165.3 [163]: until Watt began to invert: in the late drafts (NB4, 131ff), this and other instances of the phrase read: "until a tendency appeared in Watt to invert" (see **74.4**).

165.4 [163]: *Ot bro . . . trat stews*: the five senses: *bro* => orb (sight); *murd* => drum (ear); *niks* => skin (touch); *lems* => smel (smell); *gnut* => tung (taste). Touch was earlier "palp" (NB4, 118). The galleys (G55) cite "(1)"; but Beckett has crossed this out with a marginal "Note suprimée" (with no indication of what the note might have said). On a discarded page of an early translation (HRHRC Carlton Lake Collection 1.13, 55v), he noted:

To orb, pale blur, dark bulk   Pour l'oeil pale voile, sombre masse
To drum, low puff, low puff   Pour le tambour
To skin, gross mass, gross mass
To smell, stale smell, stale smell
To tongue, tart sweets, tart sweets

Thus: "To see a pale blur, a dark bulk. To hear a low puff, a low puff. To feel a gross mass, a gross mass. To smell a stale smell, a stale smell. To taste tart sweets, tart sweets." A freer version of the final line (compare Molly Bloom) might read: "To say, sweet-heart, sweet-heart." Watt's "Geb nodrap" mirrors the process in miniature.

166.1 [164]: *Of nought*: a significant passage, perhaps the one moment in the text (the end of part II might be another) that Watt expresses directly (!) his expectations and the consequences of his stay at Mr. Knott's house. "[S]entences" is best understood as "units of sense" within the "period," or more complex analytical unit. With "my little" standing for "all," as in the advice of Saint John of the Cross that the soul seeking the divine union must first divest itself of the love of earthly things, and "ignoring" in the French sense of not-knowing, the passage might be "translated" thus: "To find him, I abandoned all; to learn him, I forgot all; to have him, I rejected all; to love him, I reviled all. To him I brought this homeless body, this unknowing mind, these emptied hands, this emptied heart. To the temple, to the teacher, to the source—of nought." As Michael Robinson notes (120): "This uncharacteristic utterance, comparable in form and language to a religious incantation, is almost the only occasion on which Watt admits the extra-rational aspect of his quest. It belies his frequent assertion that he has lost all desire to understand his surroundings, that he passively accepts the irreconcilables of his servitude. He reaches the asylum not in resignation but in despair and anguish, knowing that what he sought, what he offered his whole self to, is 'nought.'"

166.2 [164]: Thus I missed I presume: the galleys read (G55): "Thus I missed I suspect." This makes sense as the pattern of "suspect," "suppose," and "presume" is otherwise violated. The error entered the Olympia text (and so others) after having been correct in the proofs. The French text conforms to the proper paradigm.

166.3 [164]: Deen did taw? . . . Ton wonk: on a discarded page of an early translation (HRHRC Carlton Lake Collection 1.13, 55v), Beckett offered a "translation" ("Taw" with the sense of both "Watt" and "what"), as he essayed a version in French:

What did need? Knott	quoi besoin	Iouq nioseb. Tonk
What had got? Knott	quoi avait	Iouq tiava. Tonk
Was cup full? Pah!	Était tasse plein	Tiatée ssat nielp. Heup
But did need? Perhaps not	mais besoin ptet pas	Siam tiava nioseb tetp sap
But had got? Know not	mais avait	Sais pas Siam tiava Sias sap

The "cup full" runs over in Psalm 23, and "Deen did tub" is a serendipitous reminder that Jonathan Swift wrote *A Tale of a Tub* (Smith, "Epistemology" 667). Watt's "Nodrap geb" reflects the process in microcosm. It is possible that "Quin" finally became "Knott" at this point (NB4, 119, 121), "tonk" being preferable to "niuq"; the passage records the first instances (other than later typescript emendations) of "Knott," which is used thereafter.

166.4 [164]: so much wind: the late draft (NB4, 134) read: "empty sounds."

166.5 [164]: touching the fourth stage: "I suppose" is omitted from all current texts; nor was it in the galleys (G55). It was present in the final draft (NB4, 134), so the omission is presumably an error. Beckett restored the complete paradigm without comment (but in parentheses) in the French translation (Ohio NBV; Ohio G164; 172).

166.6 [164]: But I soon got used to these sounds: the pattern of "and then I understood as well as before" is no longer present, and remains absent until the final set of variations (169).

167.1 [165]: *Say he'd, No . . . Say he'd, Shave*: a "translation" might read: "He'd say, Shave. When [he] had got things ready to shave, the bowl, the brush, the powder, the razor, the soap, the sponge, the towel, the water, he'd say, No. He'd say, Wash. When [he] had got things ready to wash, the basin, the brush, the glove, the salts, the soap, the sponge, the towel, the water, he'd say, No. He'd say, Dress. When [he] had got things ready to dress, the coat, the drawers, the shirt, the shoes, the socks, the trousers, the vest, the waistcoat, he'd say, No." The items of ablution and dress, here, are in alphabetical order; in Watt's original that order is reversed, Beckett having adjusted the items in NB4 (122).

167.2 [165]: pubis to pubis: the late draft (NB4, 134) originally read: "stomach to stomach"; "so much balls" was added to that draft (137), perhaps suggesting the change.

167.3 [165]: Until Watt began to invert: missing from this is the preceding "So all went well," the phrasing present in all previous instances at this point.

167.4 [165]: *Lit yad mac . . . rof mit*: A "translation" might read: "So [he] lived, for [a] time. Not sad, not gay. Not awake, not asleep. Not alive, not dead. Not bod[y], not spirit. Not Watt, not Knott. Till [the] day came to go." A late draft (NB4, 137) read "Ton bod" (as in a mirror?). On a discarded page of an early translation (HRHRC Carlton Lake Collection, 1.13, 55v), Beckett essayed a preliminary French translation:

Jusque jour départ	*Pas Wat pas Knot*	*Pas corps pas esprit*
Till day came to go	Not Watt not Knott	Not body not spirit
pas vif pas mort	*pas veille/eveille pas dort/endormi*	*pas triste pas gai*
not alive, not dead	Not awake, not asleep	Not sad, not gai
ainsi vécut un temps		
So lived, for time		

Calder introduced an error, "don yag" for "ton yag" (noted by Beckett in his personal copy, but not corrected in print).

167.5 [165] This meant nothing to me: thus in the galleys (G56), but the late draft (NB4, 137) was more like the earlier instances: "These were words that at first, though we walked fused [? *illegible*] together, sounded quite inane to me. / Nor did Watt follow me."

168.1 [165]: words in the sentence ... sentences in the period: the late draft (NB4, 131) concludes: "of the sentences in the period & of the words in the sentences." This reversal occurs (twice) in the next paragraph, with respect to the eighth paradigm. Other than this reversal, which reflects the normal linguistic hierarchy, the passages are as in the notebook.

168.2 [165]: *Dis yb dis*: a "translation" reads: "Side by side, two men. All day, part of [the] night, all day. Dumb, numb, blind. [Did] Knott look at Watt? No. [Did] Watt look at Knott? No. [Did] Watt talk to Knott? No. [Did] Knott talk to Watt? No. What then did [we] do? Nix, nix, nix. Part of [the] night, all day. Two men, side by side." Hesla (83) glosses this with respect to Spinoza's *determinatio negatio est* (**77.5**), suggesting that it reflects the final breaking of Watt's heart and spirit, and describing it as "the formulation of the fact that in my being I am alienated from every other being. Between myself and the other there lies the abyss impassable even to intuition." The two men, side by side, echoes Stephen Dedalus in the "Aeolus" chapter of *Ulysses*: "Rhymes: two men dressed the same, looking the same, two by two." On a discarded page of an early translation (HRHRC Carlton Lake Collection 1.13, 55), Beckett essayed a version in French:

Side by side, two men	Côté à côté, deux hommes	Toc à toc xeud semmo
All day, part of night	tout le jour, partie de nuit	tuot el rouj, itrap ed tuin
niks		
what then did us do? No		
Watt talk to Knott? No	Watt parle à Knott non	Taw elrap à Tonk. non.
Knott talk to Watt? no		Tonk elrap à Taw. non
Watt look at Knott? No	Watt regarde Knott	Taw edrager Tonk non
Knott look at Watt? no		Tonk edrager Taw non
Dumb, numb, blind	Muet, gourd, aveugle	Teum, droug, elgueva
Part of night, all day	Two men side by side	

168.3 [166]: It took me some time to get used to this: thus in the galleys (G56), but the late draft (NB4, 139) reflected the earlier instances: "These were sounds that at first, though we walked united [?*illegible*] together, conveyed very little to me. / Nor did Watt follow me."

168.4 [166]: Then he took it into his head to invert: in the late draft (NB4, 136), this paragraph began with "Until a tendency appeared" (**165.3**); the final text varies the expected "until Watt began." The paragraph recapitulates the previous seven conditions of inversion, then attempts to combine them in one ultimate aphasic rendition, "in the brief course of the same period," sequentially rather than simultaneously, (1) the words in the sentence, (2) the letters in the word, (3) the sentences in the period, (4) the words in the sentence and letters in the word, (5) the words in the sentence and sentences in the period, (6) the letters in the word and sentences in the period, and (7) the letters in the word, words in the sentence, and sentences in the period. This eighth paradigm became too complex because of the nature of the inversions (**164.3**) and the difficulty of assimilating it into a logically exhausted set of variations (**165.1**). In the late draft (NB4, 136), however, Beckett offered "an example of Watt's manner at this period": "yats reve. Tossed bed ever. Reve erif. Raja rood reve. Open window ever. Fro ever. Reve to"; this may be "translated": "Ever to. Ever fro. Window ever open. Door ever ajar. Ever fire. Bed ever tossed. Ever stay." This is difficult to match with the final description, although the broad principles can be seen both here and in the final "Beg nodrap . . . .nodrap, pardon geb." The attempt may have been too much; hence the cop-out (*Watt* 169): "I recall no example of this manner."

168.5 [166]: ho no: compare "'Omer, 'Orace & Hovid" (Whoroscope Notebook 68v); or Professor 'Iggins's cure for a 'orrible 'eadache (a couple of haspirates). Not in the late draft (NB4, 136); but the phrase appears on page 116, also for the first time. Here, "together" (NB4, 136) was eight times replaced by "simultaneously."

169.1 [167]: so much Irish to me: Molloy (37) and Murphy (5) reflect on sounds that are so much Gaelic to them; that is, somewhere between Chinese and double-Dutch.

169.2 [167]: tympan: the tympanum, or membrane separating the middle from the inner part of the ear; compare *The Unnamable* (383). The late draft (NB4, 138) has "ear."

169.3 [167]: myopia: short-sightedness.

169.4 [167]: the faculties so called of: the hiatus appears in the galleys thus, but in the late draft (NB4, 138) a reference to [John] "LOCKE" is spelled out. The missing word, or words, might be anything from "sensation" to "human understanding."

169.5 [167]: the following information: in the late drafts (NB4, 138), that "information" concerns what little Watt has to say on the subject of the second or closing period of his stay, the text there continuing without pause to the passage now on page 199: "Watt had little to say . . . ." The description there of the senses (**199.2**) is directly related to the "LOCKE" hiatus (see **169.4**). In the final rewriting, the discussion in the garden was reallocated to this point, and the misadventures of Louit were elaborated to fill the intervening thirty pages.

169.6 [167]: One day they were all four in the garden: the decision to reallocate this material of an earlier provenance (**169.5**) from the garden scene at the end of part II to here was made on the late draft (NB5, 93), where Arthur was named Martin and Mr. Graves was Mr. Gorman. The transition is awkward, but the two parts are thus aligned, as if to imply a continuity in the second or closing period of Watt's stay in Mr. Knott's house and garden with the first or opening period. There is also a narrative convenience, in that the gathering offers Arthur an excuse to tell his tale.

169.7 [167]: disappearing now behind a bush, emerging now from behind another: a process of obnubilation (**169.9**), as befitting a sun-god (**86.2**). Büttner, curiously, thinks that Mr. Knott is in a tree (100), and that the tree is therefore Yggdrasil.

169.8 [167]: Watt was sitting on a mound: compare the opening of *Waiting for Godot*, where the latent theological implications are developed. Consider, skeptically, the phrasing of "roll away" in the distant context of the empty tomb (Luke 24:2).

169.9 [168]: obnubilated: in Johnson's *Dictionary*, "to cloud, to obscure"; compare Burton's *Anatomy* (I.iii.2.ii): "So doth the melancholy vapour obnubilate the mind." In the early drafts (NB4, 25; TS, 361), Watt offered this consolation to Mr. Gomez.

169.10 [167]: I means a ------: Mr. Graves alludes to a little-known set of short stories, the title of which alludes to Saul's Road to Damascus experience (Acts 9:5).

170.1 [168]: Bando: Fr. *bander*, "to have an erection"; as in the "Eumaeus" episode of *Ulysses*: "bandez." Beckett toyed with "Bandavita" (NB4, 25), the "warm milk" suggesting "Bournvita" (a chocolate drink); and "Bandavagita" (TS, 367; too obvious). See "some endocrinal Bandusia" (**142.1**). The "3 weeks" of NB4 (12) became "five or six years."

170.2 [168]: squames: flakes of dead skin.

170.3 [168]: Ostreine: an oestrogen supplement, derived from oysters.

170.4 [168]: Spanish Flies: cantharides, reputedly a potent aphrodisiac; an unusual plural. *Dream* invokes (20): "ardente cantharide, gratte, je te l'ordonne"; an unpublished poem, "To My Daughter," notes "*impurée* of cantharides."

170.5 [168]: on a Saturday afternoon: anticipating Saturday night, the conjugal rendez-vous of the once-weakly; with particular reference to "the Saturday B. and I." (*Murphy* 129), the British and Irish Steam Packet ships that sailed between Liverpool and Dublin (**170.6**).

170.6 [169]: It cannot enter our ports: because of the intransigency of the Irish republic toward birth control and the importing of contraceptive devices (in Beckett's belief, payback for clerical support in the new "free" state). Beckett had mocked this in his TCD satire, "Che Sciagura" (**85.7**), which depicts "the B & I boat threading the eye of the Liffey on Saturday night," smuggling in contraceptives. The "northern frontier" is the boundary between Eire and Northern Ireland.

170.7 [169]: hasardous: the spelling, based on Fr. *hasard*, is in the galleys (G57) as well as the Olympia and Grove editions; whatever Beckett's wish (the pertinent page in his marked Grove copy is missing), Calder preferred "hazardous." A poem, "Antipepsis," has "hasard." Compare "palissades" (158).

171.1 [169]: at ten or even fifteen times: it may be coincidence that the dimensions of the "pleasure gardens" of the asylum (**154.1**) are ten or fifteen acres; and there is no significance in Sam's heightened acuity that lasts ten or fifteen minutes (**160.5**); yet a meaningless arithmetical motif is asserted.

171.2 [169]: Mr Ernest Louit: what follows was, originally, part of Watt's consolation to Mr. Gomez (NB4, 26; TS, 369). Mr. Louit's prize was reduced from an earlier "~~fifty pounds~~" (TS, 369) to £3.10.0, then to the final £3.7.6. The parenthetical details, "(from which he emerged . . . seven and sixpence)," are missing from the Calder edition and French translation (176). Beckett's Grove copy, on which he typically marked such changes, lacks these pages, but it was presumably his decision to delete these lines.

171.3 [169]: *The Mathematical Intuitions of the Viscicelts*: earlier (NB4, 26; TS, 369), those of the "~~Primitives~~," with "Visicelts" written in. Beckett's coinage mocks the distinction between two ancient Germanic tribes, Ostrogoths ("eastern Goths") and Visigoths ("western Goths"), the latter pillaging as far as the Iberian peninsula.

171.4 [169]: £. s. d.: in the galleys (G57), Beckett insisted: "signe pour livres anglais. Si necessaire utilisez L." The French translation did so (177). On his Calder copy, Beckett changed "months" to "weeks"; the French text thus reads (177): "six semaines de recherche."

171.5 [169]: Coloured Beads: added, insultingly, to the early draft (NB4, 29).

171.6 [170]: ferocious plethora: playing on the etymology, Gk. *plethora*, "fullness"; more simply, an exorbitant appetite.

172.1 [170]: sweet-smelling hay . . . straw: added as an insert to NB4 (28v); with reference to bumpkin army recruits who have to be taught left from right by a hank of hay on the left foot and a wisp of straw on the right; hence in Joyce's *Portrait* (22): "Hayfoot! Strawfoot!" Alternatively, academics who cannot distinguish hay from straw.

172.2 [170]: further great hilarity: explained in the drafts (NB4, 29; TS, 373), as indicating the committee's familiarity with the region and its paucity of either hay or straw.

172.3 [170]: Handcross: unlocated in Ireland (there is a town of that name in West Sussex); the name may have been suggested by the image of bog-oak crosses (**#1**). A gap was left in the draft (NB4, 30), and the word added to the typescript (373) by hand.

172.4 [171]: and then roast him: Beckett omits the ending of this old chestnut, to the effect that having roasted and eaten his faithful hound, Louit should have shaken his head sadly and added: "A pity O'Connor isn't here; he'd have loved these bones."

172.5 [171]: flags: reeds, as in *Krapp's Last Tape* (61): "We drifted in among the flags."

173.1 [171]: cotton-blossoms: *Eriophorum*, a bog grass with cotton-like balls of fiber.

173.2 [171]: medullars: the *medulla* [sic] is the innermost part of an organ; specifically, the marrow, as in "chilled to the medulla" in "Embers" (96), Louit having sucked this from the bones. Having overlooked the error on the galleys (G58), Beckett noted it when marking his Olympia edition for Grove; the correction, ignored by Grove, was made by Calder.

173.3 [171]: Ennis: Gaelic, *innis*, "an island"; county town of County Clare, on the river Fergus, some 25 miles from Limerick; Leopold Bloom's father committed suicide there. A gap was left in the draft (NB4, 30), the word added to the typescript (375) by hand. Louit's departure from the west is dated as "December the 3rd."

174.1 [172]: Mr Thomas Nackybal: as the drafts testify, the name is a partial anagram of "Caliban," the gross material being of Shakespeare's *The Tempest*; that name an anagram of "can[n]ibal." Earlier (NB4, 33) "Con[n]an"; "Nacibal" (NB4, 47; TS, 377); then "Nakibal" (TS, 395ff.). He hails from the Burren, the stony waste in Connemarra invoked by Lucky in *Waiting for Godot*, but his real name (198) is Tisler and he lives in a room on the [Grand] canal. Mr. Nackybal can extract from the ancestral half-acre of moraine (the residua of a retreating glacier) nourishment for himself and his "perennial" pig (one lasting two seasons), and from six-figure sequences their cube roots. This emulation of the idiot savant suggests Vito Mangianele, son of a nineteenth-century Sicilian shepherd (*Grove Companion* 398).

The art of the con reflects the fact that each digit between 0 and 9 has a unique final digit when cubed: 0, 1, 8, 7, 4, 5, 6, 3, 2, and 9 (from 0 to 9, respectively). In a four- to six-figure perfect cube, then, the final digit can be derived by inspection. To find the other figure (for the root must lie between 0 and 99), it is necessary to learn the cubes from 0 to 9 (0, 1, 8, 27, 64, 125, 216, 343, 512, 729), and to apply the following scale: less than 1000, **0**; 1 to 7, **1**; 8 to 26, **2**; 27 to 63, **3**; 64 to 124, **4**; 125 to 215, **5**; 216 to 342, **6**; 343 to 511, **7**; 512 to 728, **8**; and 729 to 999, **9**. Beckett notes this in NB4 (67, 68), and on a typescript verso (418) works out some examples in full. Thus, Mr. Nackybal's first problem (186), 389,017 easily gives "sivinty-thray" (Beckett having worked this out longhand [NB4, 55]). Because the trick does not work in reverse, Mr. Nackybal does well to make only twenty-five "slight" mistakes out of forty-six attempts (190), compared with four "trifling errors" in the extractions. Unpleasantness ensues (190) when Mr. O'Meldon calls out 519,313, for this number is not a perfect cube and so is not on the sheet (*Grove Companion* 352).

174.2 [172]: the rock-potato: a species unknown; presumably a potato coaxed from the terminal moraine.

174.3 [172]: the clover-thatch: not, I suggest, the use of clover in thatching (making roofs from grass), but the art of coaxing it to cover the rocky moraine, with the aid of . . .

174.4 [172]: every man his own fertiliser: entered on the typescript (377), echoing Buck Mulligan in the "Scylla and Charybdis" chapter of *Ulysses*: "Every man his own wife" (a sentiment Beckett applied to "the spiritual Kandinsky" in "Three Dialogues" III). NB4 (34) reads, more simply, "manure"; while the French text has (180): "l'art du fumier maison."

174.5 [172]: turf versus combustion: perhaps, whether turf should be used for thatching, or burnt as peat.

174.6 [172]: the fly-catching pig: a dig at curiosities reported by anthropologists obnubilated in the Celtic twilight.

174.7 [173]: On the dais they were five: in the early drafts (NB4, 36), designated by responsibility: A, President; B, Vice President; C, Treasurer; D Correspondence Secretary; E, Recording Secretary. They were not then named, but NB4 (76, 79) records in red pencil: "Stern, Mr O'Wein, Mac Meldon, Baker"; on the typescript (380), their functions were crossed out and replaced by their names: the President (Mr. Fitzwein); the Vice President (Mr. Kelly, changed to Mr. Magershon); the Treasurer (Mr. O'Meldon); the Correspondence Secretary (Mr. MacStern); and the Record[ing] Secretary (Mr. de Baker). The names are in their final form in the later draft (NB5, 92). In NB4 (36) Beckett outlined the movements of the various heads, and there, but also on the verso of the typescript (380), drew a diagram of the (twenty) ways that the five looked each at the others, that is, the most economical way that each can be sure of having looked at, and having been looked at by, each of the others. This activity occupies the next six pages:

NB4 (36):

```
A —> B —> C —> D —> E —> A
A —> C —> E —> B —> D —> A
A —> D —> B —> E —> C —> A
A —> E —> D —> C —> B —> A
```

TS (380) (see next page); a modification of the above:

```
    T          VP         P          RS         CS
o ←——— o ←——— o ←——— o ←——————→ o

o ↙——→ o ↙——→ o ↙——→ o ————→ o ————→ o

o ↙——  o ↙——  o ———→ o ———→ o ————→ o

o ↙——→ o ———→ o ———→ o ———→ o ————→ o
```

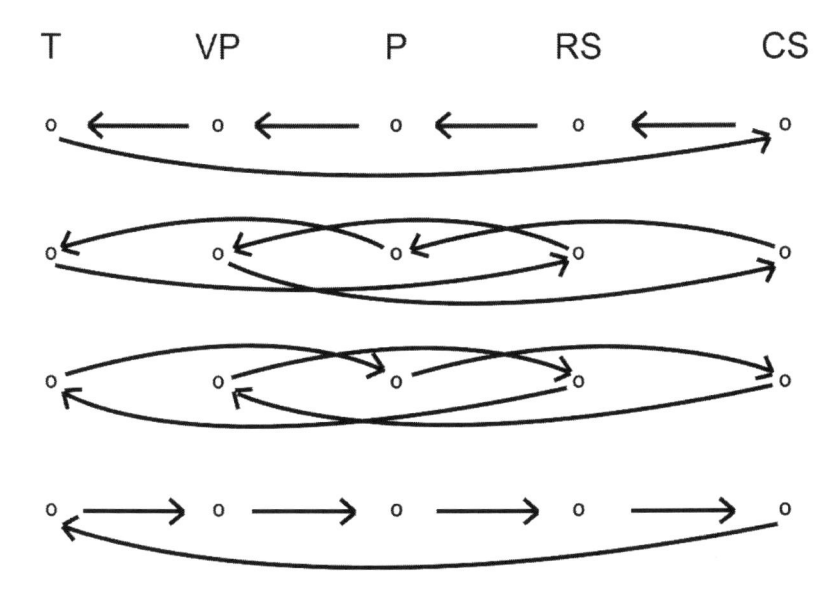

The order of seating, as Louit and Mr. Nackybal would see it, is as follows:

C	B	A	E	D
Mr. O'Meldon	Mr. Magershon	Mr. Fitzwein	Mr. de Baker	Mr. MacStern
Treasurer	*Vice President*	*President*	*Record Secretary*	*Correspondence Secretary*

The first set of moves (middle of 175), one to their right, matches the typescript (1); the second set of moves (175-76), two to their right or three to their left, matches the typescript (2); the third set of moves (top of 176), three to their right or two to their left, matches the typescript (3); the fourth set of moves (middle of 176), four to their right or one to their left, matches the typescript (4). There are no errors. Neatly, each set begins and ends with Mr. Fitzwein, yet encompasses all five members, none of whom in the "five times four or twenty looks" delineated meet the look of another. In *Mercier and Camier* (82), the pseudocouple and the giant barman look at each other, three versions of self creating nine images; this is (96) "Mercier's contribution to the controversy of the universals" (*Grove Companion* 508). Compare, too, the "situation circle" of unrequited love at the outset of *Murphy*.

174.8 [173]: the cerebellum: the most reptilian portion of the brain, the back and lower part that correlates voluntary movement, as opposed to the more intellectual cerebrum; hence the source of unvocalized agricultural ideation.

175.1 [173]: an ecstasy of darkness, and of silence: compare, if ironically, the third part of Murphy's or Belacqua's mind, the "matrix of surds" imaged as the embryonic state of primal pleasure and thus the ultimate bliss; compare, too, Malone's desire to reach the "great calm" that lies beyond the words and images that run riot in his head (*Malone Dies* 198).

175.2 [173]: Mr Fitzwein looked: in the Calder text, "looked" and "is looking" is changed consistently to "looks"; the relevant pages are missing of Beckett's Grove copy, on which he marked the changes for Calder, so there is no way to confirm whether these were sanctioned by Beckett or initiated by John Calder.

175.3 [174]: the back of Mr Fitzwein's head, is now craning forward looking at: these words were dropped in the galleys (G59), but restored by Beckett in a marginal note.

176.1 [174]: sinciput: the forepart of the head or skull; the forehead or brow.

176.2 [175]: corollae: the circles or whorls of flowers, here applied to the ear.

177.1 [176]: turned towards heaven: in the typescript (385), "~~otherwise employed~~" is crossed out and this written in.

177.2 [175]: Nor is this all: the ensuing description, made at greater length and with much digression, repeats the first cycle (**174.7**), as in (5) of the typescript diagram. There are no errors. Projecting this forward ("And so on"), the outcome of the "five times eight or forty looks" (178) is thus precisely the same as that of the first set of twenty looks, that is, nothing.

177.3 [176]: pneumogastric: an elaborate fart (*pneuma*, air; *gastric*, of the stomach); balancing Mr. Magershon's mental travails. Consider Mr. Fitzwein's lunch of kidney-beans.

178.1 [177]: its setting out: the "laetus exitus tristem" motif of Thomas à Kempis, that a merry outgoing brings forth a sad homecoming; but echoing the theme of Joyce's *Ulysses*, Stephen Dedalus setting out to meet the self that he is ineluctably preconditioned to become. The phrase is commonly used of the soul's journey, complemented by "its coming forth."

179.1 [178]: Then it will be found: the earlier method (NB4, 45; TS, 391) of alloting these numbers was to have two inverted hats or mortar-boards, or one inverted hat and one inverted mortar-board, into which might be placed as many slips of paper, bearing numbers, as members of the committee.

179.2 [178]: no number of the committee: although Beckett nowhere notes the anomaly, present in both the Olympia and Grove texts (his Grove is missing these pages), Calder's change is appropriate: "no member of the committee." The penultimate citation on this page mis-spelled *number* as "numbr" in the galleys (G60) and Olympia text; Beckett originally overlooked the error, but noted it for Grove, who made the change.

180.1 [179]: boracic solution: sodium tetraborate, dissolved, for eye relief.

180.2 [179]: to say x squared minus x: "say" appears neither in the galleys (G60) nor the Olympia text, but Beckett added it when marking his Olympia text for Grove, Grove making the change [so, why did they not make others?]. The formula may be checked mechanically: Number One is looked at four times, and looks four times (8); Two, having looked and been looked at by One, is looked at and looks thrice (6); Three, etc etc, is looked at and looks twice (4); Four, etc etc, can only be looked at and look once (2); and Five, etc etc, is neither looked at nor needs to look (0). The total of looks is twenty; when $x = 5$, $(x^2 - x) = (25 - 5) = 20$. Mood's explanation, "figured as 5 x 4" (260) seems simpler, that is, five examiners each gives four looks; but it ignores Beckett's process and does not guarantee that each receives four looks. Compare **94.1** for the satisfaction of finding a mathematical formula that seems to confirm a principle of reason at the heart of the pre-established arbitrary.

180.3 [179]: The physical: Louit, emboldened, continues where he had left off on page 174, in much shorter time in his world than it has taken you, dear reader, to get there, in yours.

180.4 [179]: t— t— tolerable: Mr. Fitzwein's stutter questions Mr. Nackybal's sobriety, "t.t." intimating a teetotaller.

181.1 [179]: deject: in the archaic sense of "to cast matter from the bowels" (*dejecture*), "to excrete." The French text (179) is more explicit: "même pour excréter il n'a besoin de personne." One might wonder which single hand is used to absterge the podex.

181.2 [179]: Hence the squint: chiroplatonism (*Dream* 43); in common parlance, it makes you blind. Contrast the committee's reaction to Mr. Nackybal's scratching (*Watt* 183).

181.3 [179]: a different crawl of life: the draft (NB4, 46) offered "walk"; this was crossed out and "crawl" written in. The anticipation of *How It Is*, with hindsight, is obvious.

181.4 [179]: collaborators: the error in the galleys (G61), "colloborators," overlooked by Beckett, entered the Olympia text; noted there for correction, it persisted into the first Grove edition, but was silently corrected on reprinting.

181.5 [180]: prodigal: wasteful and extravagant, Louit having returned with nothing, like the prodigal son (Luke 15:11-32).

181.6 [180]: If I tell you this in such detail: NB4 (46) reflects the change of topic with a change of ink; the relationship between the "text" and the circumstances of its writing is a thesis in itself.

181.7 [180]: punctilio: with strict adherence to the nicer points of etiquette; compare the "punctilious placing" (182).

181.8 [180]: to prosper and multiply: II Corinthians 9:10: "multiply your seeds sown, and increase the fruits of your righteousness."

182.1 [180]: thirty-fold: a retelling of Christ's parable of the sower of seed (Matthew 13:8): "But other fell into good ground, and brought forth fruit, some an hundredfold, some sixtyfold, some thirtyfold."

182.2 [181]: dust, or ashes . . . committing: as in the Anglican service of the Burial of the Dead, when the body is "committed" to the grave: "Ashes to ashes, dust to dust"; but with the sense of dust and ashes used not simply as fertilizer but also mixed with the seed, to "thin" them (those mentioned are tiny), so that they are not sown too closely.

182.3 [181]: the plumb: the plumb line, a leaded weight to ensure perpendicularity; its use in the sowing of seed (as Arthur later admits) is not obvious. The "board" refers to a length of wood, to ensure a trench of consistent depth and straightness.

182.4 [181]: little by little: with reference to the recurrent motif of the heap of millet (or seed), built up or taken away grain by grain. At this point in the early draft (NB4, 49), Mr. Gomez was asleep. See **64.3**, **194.4**, and **235.2**.

182.5 [181]: left hand, nor his right: as in Christ's injunction (Matthew 6:3) to let not thy left hand know what thy right is doing.

182.6 [181]: a diffuse ano-scrotal prurit: an urge to scratch the spot that itches, around the scrotal and anal regions. Beckett entered "prurit" from Garnier into the Dream Notebook (#443), using it twice in a sexual sense in *Dream* (19, 108), and later of the mind (181): "the prurigo of living." Murphy invokes (193) "the rationalist prurit," or desire to know.

183.1 [181]: Ego autem: the footnote was not in the galleys (G61), Beckett indicating in the margin: "<u>Note manque</u>." The draft (Ohio NB5) and typescript (Ohio TS, 134) of the French translation read: "(1) Locution latine signifiante: moi (ego) aussi (autem)"; Beckett added to the galley (Ohio G181) "à peu près," to match this phrase with other French footnotes.

183.2 [182]: the right old hairy mottled hand . . . the left old blue old bony knee: in preparing his Calder Jupiter text for the French translation, Beckett marked this passage for deletion; it is omitted from the French text. The pose assumed is similar to that assumed by the Citizen in the "Cyclops" episode of *Ulysses*.

183.3 [182]: a cupola, a dome, a roof, a spire, a tower, a treetop: in the typescript (401), "a roof, a cupola, a spire, a dome, a treetop, a tower"; marked (3, 1, 4, 2, 6, 5) for reordering alphabetically. No attempt was made to duplicate this in the French translation (190).

183.4 [182]: Four hundred and eight thousand one hundred and eighty-four: according to Beckett's workings (NB4, 52; see inset), the cube root of which is 74; however, in multiplying 74 by 74 the first time he made a mistake.* In the French translation, Louit first advanced (Ohio, BB5), "Quatre cent huit mille cent quatre vingt quatre" [408,184], but this was overwritten on the galleys (G182) as "Quatre cent trente-huit mille [438,976, the correct cube of 76, as worked out by Beckett in long multiplication on a verso inplication on a verso in Ohio (NB5)]. As well as correcting the inadvertent error, the change was generated by the need for a more convincing phonic ambiguity in French, the by-play that follows (191-92) deriving from the confusion between "soixante-TRRREIZE" and "soixante-SSSEIZE."

```
    74
    74
   ___
   296
  *522
   ____
  5516
    74
   _____
 22064
 38612
 _____
408,184
```

*518 is correct; Beckett seems to have multiplied (4 x 8 = 32), 2 and carry 3

183.5 [182]: a gazelle: as in Thomas Moore's *Lallah Rookh*, the lines a byword for banality: "I never nurs'd a dear gazelle / To glad me with its soft black eye, / But when it came to know me well, / And love me, it was sure to die" ("Fire-worshippers" I, 279-82). Compare: "throttled gazelle" (*Dream* 214).

184.1 [182]: an old quinch: NB4 (53) reads "an old goat!"; the typescript (403), "puckaun" (as at the end of the novel). The French translation (190) has "bique" (nanny-goat).

184.2 [182]: Not another word . . . not a word more: an exact echo (also in the context of an examining committee) of the *Mus eventratus* (**28.9**): "McGilligan," said the 3-Vow-Man, "not another word, not a word more." The early draft (NB4, 52, 53) toyed with "Fine, said the R. S." [text] and "or Fuck" [verso]; this became (TS, 403): "Not another word, Mr Louit" said the Record Secretary Mr de Baker"; the final connection made only as the *ridiculus mus* disappeared.

184.3 [183]: M. de Baker . . . M. Fitzwein: the errors were introduced in the galleys (G62), and although Beckett in marking the Olympia text for Grove drew attention to the second anomaly (he missed the first), both remain in the Grove printings. Calder made the change. A curiosity marked at this point is that the American Grove text observes the British usage of no period after "Mr" but Calder's British text prefers the American mode.

184.4 [183]: His eyes coil into my very soul: unidentified as an allusion, but vaguely suggestive of *Othello* or *Hamlet* (Gertrude's reaction to Hamlet's chastisement?), or Keats's *Lamia*. The French text is unhelpful (191): "Sa prunelle coule jusqu'à tréfonds de mon âme."

184.5 [183]: the angelus: a Catholic devotion to honor the Annunciation, from the opening words, *Angelus Domini nuntiavit Mariae*, a bell rung thrice daily (and on the radio), at 6 am, noon and 6 pm. It is heard by Molloy (15). Here, a euphemism for passing wind, as in the query, "Did an angel speak?" The offence was more audible in the drafts (NB4, 53; TS, 405): "a slight unpleasant sound was heard."

184.6 [183]: as with wet bands: as preparing a broken limb for a splint.

184.7 [183]: (the French extraction): marked by Beckett for extirpation when preparing his Calder text for the French translation. The comment draws attention to Mr. de Baker's Huguenot roots.

184.8 [183]: Three hundred and eighty-nine thousand . . . and seventeen: indeed, the cube of sivinty-thray .

185.1 [184]: Not at all, not at all: a confused extra line in the galleys (G62) was crossed out by Beckett: "Not at all, not at all, Mr Louit, said Mr de Baker, said Louit."

186.1 [184]: Is that all? said Mr Magershon: marked in Beckett's Calder edition for deletion in the French translation.

186.2 [184]: better seated: the choice reflects Chamfort's Maxim #155, that it is better to be seated than upright, lying down than seated, dead than all that (**232.1**).

186.3 [185]: sweet seventeen: the change to "soixante-seize" (**183.4**) created a small problem for the French translation, which Beckett resolved neatly (193), Mr. Magershon saying: "Pensez à vos soixante-seize printemps" ["Think of your seventy-six spring-times"].

187.1 [186]: I believe you: echoing Mr. Hackett's "I choose to believe you" (22).

187.2 [186]: The best of us may make a slip: in the French text (194), "Errare humanum est (1)," with an explanatory footnote in the drafts (Ohio NB5): "(1) Locution latine signifiant: errer (errare) humaine (humanum) est (est)"; and, again, a handwritten "à peu près" (**183.1**).

187.3 [186]: the long turkey cucumber: on the analogy of the Jerusalem artichoke, about which Beckett speculated in the Whoroscope Notebook (26): "Jerusalem artichoke neither from Jer. nor an artichoke but a Canadian sunflower (girasol). Irish potatoe [sic] neither Irish nor a potatoe [sic], but a Peruvian tuber." Not in the typescript (413). In the French translation (195): "le concombre géant d'Istambul."

188.1 [187]: only once by a horse: a celebrated hoax in which a horse ("Clever Hans") stamped out answers to simple sums in response to hidden signals from its master.

188.2 [187]: the Kulturkampf: the "cultural struggle" as defined by Bismarck, the German Iron Chancellor, against the Church to support Catholics who refused to accept the decisions of the Vatican Council (1870). Marriage and education were declared civil matters, and monastic teaching was placed under state regulation (*Grove Companion* 306). The typescript (415) read, "~~In the Victorian epoch~~"; with "Kulturkampf" written in.

188.3 [187]: Not horsey, fishy: Mr. de Baker's witticism was marked for deletion when Beckett prepared his Calder text for the French translation, Beckett presumably unable to find an equivalent pun; the French text (196) uses "louche." The galleys (G62) offer an unfortunate reading: Mr. Nackbal lies on his "aide."

189.2 [188]: Thank you, Mr Louit, said Mr O'Meldon. Not at all, Mr O'Meldon, said Louit: marked for deletion when Beckett prepared his Calder text for the French translation.

190.1 [189]: an occasion of some unpleasantness: the French translation reads (197): "un ange passa." The unpleasantness is caused by the fact that this number is not a perfect cube. In the French translation, "~~Cinq cent dix-neuf mille trois cent treize~~" is crossed out on the galleys (Ohio, G189), and "Six cent cinquante-neuf mille quatre cent treize" written in; as this (659,413) is the perfect cube of 87, the point is lost. The confusion was recurrent: Beckett had underlined the original number in his Olympia copy, put a question mark in the margin, then, presumably later (as the pen is different), wrote in large letters: "Stet."

190.2 [189]: Don't keep us waiting here all night: echoing Arsene's lament (**47.15**). In the galleys (G64) a line of type was lost, Beckett restoring it in a marginal note: "all night. Louit turned around and said, Is the number."

191.1 [190]: in the galleys (G64) another line was lost, Beckett restoring it in a marginal note: "best, out of friendship to me, to—to—who is doing his best." A little later, to compensate, another was repeated: "What can I have been thinking of, said Mr Magershon."

191.2 [190]: malice prepense: archaic (Anglo-Norman) legal terminology; with malice aforethought. The French translation offers (199): "avec prémé—mé—méditation." Like God, heaven is a witness that cannot be sworn (**9.1**). In the early draft (NB4, 65), the Treasurer shifts his weight, "like a bear" (compare **31.5**).

191.3 [190]: I can well believe that, said Mr de Baker: not in the typescript (423). The Olympia edition introduced the error, "belive," even as another mistake in the galleys (G64) was corrected ("sai" for "said"). Beckett on his Olympia copy noted "belive" for correction by Grove, who made the change.

191.4 [190]: the western windows: the galleys (G64) and Olympia text read "eastern," the error at first overlooked by Beckett, who noted it on his copy of the Olympia text for Grove, who made the change. For a photograph of the Trinity College examination hall, its raised dais, and its western windows, see Eoin O'Brien, *The Beckett Country* (125).

191.5 [191]: Mr Fitzwein said . . . of the square root, said Louit: most of this long passage was marked for deletion when Beckett prepared his Calder text for the French translation, but the transitional passages were retained (199).

192.1 [191]: extirpation: on the typescript (423) "~~extraction~~" is deleted and "extirpation" written in, with the literal sense of "being pulled out by the roots."

192.2 [191]: Louit said nothing: in the typescript (423), "Louit lifted, spread his arms, let them fall, to his sides~~, the right arm to the right side, the left arm to the left side~~." The gesture is like that of Neary (*Murphy* 4), seeking his sublation of the Hegelian synthesis.

192.3 [191]: It was question-time: the repetition of this phrase introduces a longish passage (until "Enough!") not present in the typescript (425).

192.4 [192]: Enough! cried Mr Magershon: ample, said the reader.

193.1 [192]: Column of cubes: the French translation (200) of the verse is faithful until the last two lines, in response to "Que veux-tu boire, ma chère?": "Je boirais bien un pot, dit colonne racines, / De ton extrait mortuaire." The Calder text introduced an erroneous comma (instead of a period) after the preceding "said Louit."

194.1 [193]: Darwin's caterpillar: a parable from Darwin's *On the Origin of Species* (VIII, 208), on Instinct, likened to habit and repetition. A caterpillar, interrupted in building its "hammock" [NB4 (69) has "~~nest~~"] and returned to it or to another at a similar point, would normally complete the work; but if taken to one at a further state of completion would get confused and attempt to start not from the point given but from where it had left off. Belacqua tells the story in "Echo's Bones" (23), but Doyle, the gardener, does not "smoke" the reference, so it is taken further: "'He was working away at his hammock' said Belacqua, 'and not doing a damn bit of harm to man or beast, when up comes old Monkeybrand bursting with labour-saving devices. The caterpillar was far from feeling any benefit.'" "Monkey Brand" was a soap, for washing pans, according to their slogan, "For bright and happy reflections." In *Murphy* (218), Miss Counihan stops in mid-flow, and seems likely to go back to the beginning, "like Darwin's caterpillar"; here, Mr. Magershon begins to spin the yarn, but, appropriately, is disturbed as he does so (*Grove Companion* 125-26).

194.2 [193]: Raise your point: the point raised is perfectly valid, as it concerns the limits of the con, proof by inspection (**174.1**) being restricted to six figures (roots of 1 to 99).

194.3 [193]: bringing down his fist with a thump: the galleys (G65) read, rather nicely: "bringing down his fist with a thumb" (this corrected); but the galleys (and hence all published texts) read: "What I have just said"; whereas the typescript (429) has: "What I hae said"; since ticked by Beckett this was (presumably) intended.

194.4 [194]: Little by little: in the typescript (429), the proverb is complete: "'Little by little the bird builds its nest,' said Louit." See **64.3** and **182.4**.

195.1 [194]: nine hundred and seventy three million two hundred and fifty-two thousand two hundred and seventy one: Mr. O'Meldon, having done some homework, is slightly in error; he presumably intends 973,242,271, which, as Mood points out (262) is the cube of 991, but, as such, outside the permissible range of 0 to 99. Mood further notes that the next figure cited, 998,700,129,999, is not a cube; however, his figures are wrong as the cube root of that figure is closer to 9999^3 than (as he suggests) "randomly between 9995^3 and 9996^3, closer to the former." The cube of 9999 is 999,700,029,999; this, clearly, was Beckett's intention, as both cubes are worked out accurately in NB4 (67); the error in verbal transmission is "explained" (but is the more inexplicable) by Beckett working it out again (NB4, 71) and getting it wrong (998,700,129,999; two "small" errors of addition in the long multiplication); the written text (NB4, 70) cites the erroneous form. Beckett's usage reflects the American "billion" (a thousand million) rather than the British (a million million); the distinction, or confusion, is significant in *Company* (55), where "seventy American billion" seconds represent some 22,000 years, and "million" seems the logical alternative.

195.2 [194]: while in the orient night is falling fast: Mr. de Baker, wittingly or otherwise, is mocking Dante's cosmology, where Jerusalem and the Pillars of Hercules mark the span of the known universe, day rising in the one as it is setting in the other.

195.3 [194]: turned them round: the galleys (G66) and Olympia text have "found"; Beckett missed the error, but noted it in on his Olympia text for Grove, where the change was made.

195.4 [195]: in this order: in the typescript (437), the five leave in inverted alphabetical order, "as chance would have it"; reworking on the early draft (NB4, 77) indicates that this was an afterthought rather than the original intention, but it was forsaken in the final writing, so that any subsequent re-ordering is indeed the consequence of chance; Mood's imperfect permutation, with "3 possibilities; 4 times" (261), misses the point of the pattern. The initial order in relation to the typescript schema (**174.7**) is {A C D E B}, but Mr. Fitzwein, {A}, immediately disappears from the sequence.

196.1 [195]: like something out of Poe: not in the typescript (439); the analogy is perhaps suggested by a general gloom not unlike the House of Ussher.

196.2 [195]: the first was last: not entirely so, as Mr. Fitzwein is by now in the tram; the permutations henceforth exclude "A" and have four terms only; in the order: {B E D C}. The effect is that of a full shuffle, with the first element placed last in the following steps: {C D E B}, {D E B C}, {E B D C}, {B E D C}. Scripture is thus unwittingly fulfilled (Matthew 20:16), for the last are now first and the first are last.

196.3 [195]: the eleven tram: passing the gates of Trinity College, the Clonskeagh line; recalled by the narrator of *That Time* (228): "no, no, trams then all gone long ago."

196.4 [195]: but hardly had Mr O'Meldon: the present order, {B E D C}, changes, not in ordered steps but in several (four) independent movements that effect a simultaneous arrival at the door, the outcome of which, {D C B E}, is either the product of chance, or of some "other agency" (such as an unacknowledged principle of precedence: rank, age before beauty, pearls before swine . . .). The passage was scrambled in the galleys (G66), Beckett having to reorder the positions.

196.5 [195]: accompanied by: Beckett "restored" to the galleys (G66) at this point, before "ceasing," a line that had dropped from the type; and also part of the following line: "by Mr O'Meldon and Mr MacStern, towards Mr Magershon. But hardly had Mr O'Meldon and Mr MacStern and Mr de Baker." The effect is confusing, but the Olympia typesetters managed to sort it out.

197.1 [196]: the customary coagulation: as in the clotting of blood. The crowded doorway is a standby of the silent movies; Beckett had drawn on it in *Murphy* (259), and would again in *All That Fall*, where Miss Fitt and Mrs. Rooney get stuck at the top of the stairs.

197.2 [196]: the little landing along: imitating the German construction with a final preposition ("entlang"); earlier in the sentence, the present participles "resisting," "stepping," and "urging" are used adjectivally, as post-modifiers, in the French manner.

197.3 [196]: the bitter stout porter Power: the typescript (441) reads: "the stout porter Power"; this builds on the early draft (NB4, 78): "~~small~~ porter" (with "stout" written in above); the joke extending, little by little. "Power" (an Irish whiskey) was there from the outset. The jest appears in *Murphy* (139): "Why did the barmaid champagne? . . . Because the stout porter bitter"; it was anticipated in "Echo's Bones" (12), where Lord Gall of Wormwood gives the right answer, impatiently. In the French text (204), Beckett tried to duplicate the effect: "Et comme Louit descendait l'escalier il croisa l'appariteur Power, moins aigre-doux que doux-amer, qui montait" (the pun on "bittersweet" and "bitters").

197.4 [196]: they had passed: not the pluperfect, but a complex conditional: "they would have passed." Earlier in the sentence, the modal "had" is twice used as a simple conditional, but is followed each time by the more complex mood.

198.1 [198]: (he merely knew . . . nought nought): the explanation of the con (**174.1**) was marked by Beckett for deletion when preparing his Calder text for the French translation. The French (206) omits the explanation, but changes "He lived in a room on the canal" to "il pourrissait dans une chambre sur le canal" ["He rotted in a room on the canal"]. In earlier drafts (TS, 443),

Louit's duplicity is spelled out explicitly (he had never gone west), as is his subsequent disgrace.

198.2 [198]: his fall and subsequent ascension: in the early draft (NB4, 81) and in the typescript (443), Louit was "sent down" in disgrace; he became a traveler for Arola soap; married a rich widow; augmented his earnings by smuggling Bandavagita across the border; was happy in his home; and "a hundred and one other thinks [*sic*] too tedious to relate."

199.1 [198]: there was no other place: echoing T. S. Eliot's *Little Gidding*, or perhaps the traditions on which Eliot draws, in its sense of "fixity" (the still point of a turning world) and of the mystical experience intricately related to place ("here, now, and always").

199.2 [199]: Watt had little to say: in the late draft (NB4, 138), this passage continued directly after "the following information" (*Watt* 169), and continues, then concludes the interrogation concerning the eighth and final stage of the second or closing period of Watt's stay in Mr. Knott's house (**169.5**). The description of the senses relates back to the hiatus in which Locke is the significant absence (**169.4**). Yet a pre-publication "Extract from *Watt*" in *Merlin* 3.1 (winter 1952-53): 18-26, began at precisely this point and continued, without omissions, until "on the other foot" (*Watt* 213). As Richard Seaver tells the tale ("Beckett and *Merlin*" 23-24), he and Alexander Trocchi were given permission by Beckett to publish an extract in their fledgling Paris-based magazine, *Merlin*, subject to the condition that it was to be the following inventory of Mr. Knott's attire and the stations of the furniture in his room (Seaver later suggested to Beckett, who did not contradict him, that this indigestible portion was chosen as a test of their good faith). The publication led indirectly to the Olympia Press *Watt* under the imprint of "Editions Merlin."

199.3 [199]: exiguity: in Johnson's *Dictionary* as: "Smallness; diminutiveness; slenderness."

200.1 [199]: this ambience followed him forth: as a source of light in a world of darkness, Mr. Knott's radiance by comparison dims all about him.

200.2 [199]: as often his head was bare: compare "Fizzle I," "He is barehead," for one making his way through a dark, issueless labyrinth, his direction random or impulsive. The nucleus of that *foirade* may be the being of Mr. Knott. There is the hint of a rhyme between "dowdy" and "gaudy," Beckett having changed the latter on the galleys (G67) from "showy."

200.3 [200]: As for his feet: what follows constitutes the first of four increasingly large paradigms, the extension and the *reductio* of all those given earlier. A mere five lines and/or trifling sequences were confused on the galleys (G68), but carefully restored by Beckett; this paradigm and the longer and more pointless two to follow are almost perfect in their meticulous and relentless iteration. Mood notes (261) that there are 78 possibilities, complete and correct; his sense of these "figured as 12+11+10+9+8+7+6+5+4+3+2+1" conforms to (or derives from) the diagram sketched by Beckett in the manuscript (NB4, 154-55) where each term and/or combination is outlined in a manner that allowed him to check them all. Thus, "sock" combines with twelve other terms; "stocking" with eleven ("sock and stocking" already accounted for); "boot" with ten, etc. Hence, the seventy-eight possibilities represented, in logical order beginning with "sock" and ending with "bare" [below]. There is, however, a crack in this apparently pristine formulation, for while the terms are limited by the condition of Mr. Knott's two feet (each column represents one), no differentiation is made between left and right; his world seems curiously unaware of such parity. Were this a factor, another seventy-two possibilities—that is, the existing seventy-eight, plus these laterally reversed, but minus the five instances of the same item or combination, {sock sock} or {boot boot}, that can be differentiated only if one distinguishes between, say, a left boot and a right boot and permits the left also to be placed on the right foot, the way, presumably, that a sock or stocking might be (with the further complication that "barefoot," or {bare bare}, cannot be so distinguished). That is, there might equally be a gross paradigm of 150 possibilities, or more, or less, depending upon what combinations are decreed admissible:

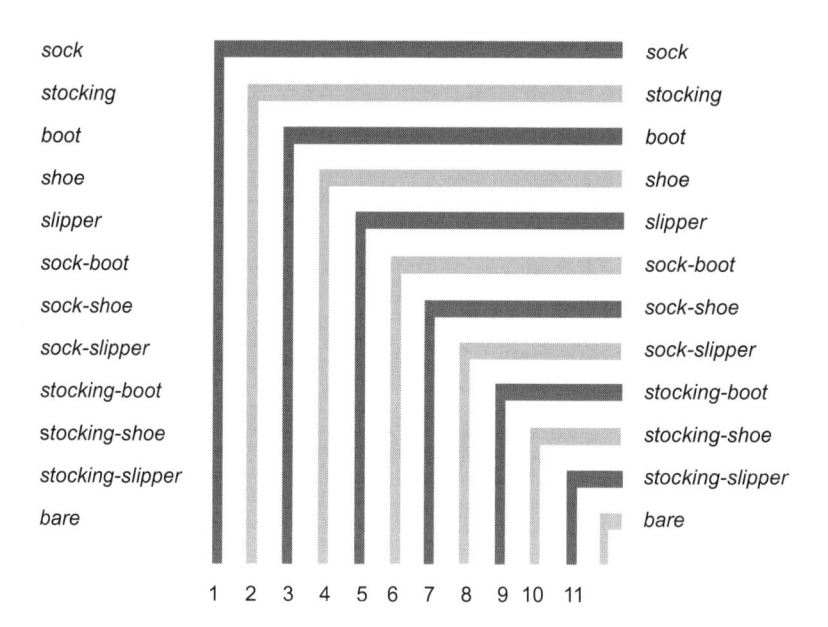

sock		sock
stocking		stocking
boot		boot
shoe		shoe
slipper		slipper
sock-boot		sock-boot
sock-shoe		sock-shoe
sock-slipper		sock-slipper
stocking-boot		stocking-boot
stocking-shoe		stocking-shoe
stocking-slipper		stocking-slipper
bare		bare

1 2 3 4 5 6 7 8 9 10 11

201.1 [201]: when one is no longer young, when one is not yet old: entered, almost as an independent prose-poem, into the late draft (NB4, 157). Harvey notes (351) its thematic link to Dante's "Nel mezzo del cammin di nostra vita," the opening line of the *Commedia divina*. Beer suggests (55) this as the core of the onion, the "one passage where the underlying narrator seems to speak in his own voice." The phrase, "perhaps something," echoes Watt's despair from the end of part II: "But was not that something?" (148).

202.1 [202]: an anthropomorphic insolence: echoing the earlier conviction that the only way to speak of God is to speak of him as though he were a man, and affirming Beckett's rejection of the Protagorean assertion that man is the measure of all things (**77.7**); perhaps the most direct intimation in the novel of the metaphysical being of Mr. Knott.

203.1 [202]: The better to witness, the worse to witness: in the galleys (G69) this line was repeated inadvertently, constituting, perhaps, a mild irony.

203.2 [203]: that he might not cease: the sustained conceit (**42.1**) that God (or Knott) could not exist were he not perceived, and so must be witnessed in order to be. A late draft (NB4, 92) states: "Quin in need of witness." This is a *reductio* of Berkeley's celebrated *esse est percipi*, "to be is to be perceived," the keystone to his work. This asserts that objects of sense perception, such as the tree in the quad or Mr. Knott, have no knowable existence outside the mind that perceives them, from which Berkeley reasons that all reality exists ultimately in the mind of God. The sense of being is sustained by being perceived as an object by another: *esse est aut percipi aut percipere*, "to be is both to be perceived and to perceive." The conclusion is inevitable: Mr. Knott cannot exist unless he is perceived, and hence his need for servants, however imperfect, so that (to twirl the text) even if he "ever almost" ceases he never quite does so. Ruby Cohn notes (*Canon* 396): "Mr. Knott's two needs differ from those of *Les Deux Besoins* [*sic*], but they remain binary."

203.3 [203]: as one unfamiliar with the premises: a fossil from the earliest drafts (NB1, 31; TS, 19), where Quin, woken in the night, cannot find the lavatories in his own house (**#15**), and pauses irresolute before going down the stairs to meet Mr. Hackett.

203.4 [203-04]: Here he stood . . . from the door to the bed: the terms of the paradigm are initially misleading: Mr. Knott may be standing, sitting, kneeling, or lying; near the door, the window, the fire, or the bed. In principle, he could adopt one of four postures at the end of each move; that is, each posture may be manifest in four locations, giving a total of 64 positions (that is, {posture + place}). What follows describes only the movement, so the paragraph might have been four times as long. Let {A} = door; {B} = window; {C} = fire; and {D} = bed; there are thus twelve single moves possible. However, Mr. Knott moves in a double sequence, from (for example) A to B, then B to C. Each of the twelve single moves, then, may be paired with any of the others, ringing up the changes on the figure {ABCD}, but limited by the conditions that each must begin where the previous one ended, and that the middle terms must be identical (it is impossible, even for Mr. Knott, to move from where he is not). A sequence such as {AAAB} is inadmissible, since {AA} entails no movement; and {ABAB} is also ruled out, as the middle terms are not identical; however, sequences such as {ABBA} or {ABBC} are legitimate. There are from each location nine legitimate double-moves, such as that for A: {ABBA}, {ABBC}, {ABBD}, {ACCA}, {ACCB}, {ACCD}, {ADDA}, {ADDB}, {ADDC}, a total of 36 legitimate sequences in all. Beckett worked out a diagram to this effect (NB4, 125), the movements numbered in their order in the text:

From	door	to	window,	from	window	to	door	1
"	"	"	fire	"	fire	"	"	5
"	"	"	bed	"	bed	"	"	12
"	"	"	window	"	window	"	fire	13
"	"	"	"	"	"	"	bed	21
"	"	"	fire	"	fire	"	bed	20
"	"	"	"	"	"	"	window	29
"	"	"	bed	"	bed	"	fire	26
"	"	"	"	"	"	"	window	32
From	window	to	door,	from	door	to	window	2
"	"	"	bed	"	bed	"	"	7
"	"	"	fire	"	fire	"	"	10
"	"	"	door	"	door	"	bed	15
"	"	"	"	"	"	"	fire	23
"	"	"	bed	"	bed	"	fire*	18
"	"	"	"	"	"	"	door	31
"	"	"	fire	"	fire	"	bed	28
"	"	"	"	"	"	"	door	30
From	fire	to	bed,	from	bed,	to	fire	3
"	"	"	window	"	window	"	"	9
"	"	"	door	"	door	"	"	6
"	"	"	bed	"	bed	"	window	17
"	"	"	"	"	"	"	door	25
"	"	"	window	"	window	"	"	14
"	"	"	"	"	"	"	bed	33
"	"	"	door	"	door	"	window	24
"	"	"	"	"	"	"	bed	36
From	bed	to	fire,	from	fire	to	bed	4
"	"	"	door	"	door	"	bed	11
"	"	"	window	"	window	"	"	8
"	"	"	fire	"	fire	"	door	19
"	"	"	"	"	"	"	window	27
"	"	"	door	"	door	"	"	16
"	"	"	"	"	"	"	fire	35
"	"	"	window	"	window	"	door	22
"	"	"	"	"	"	"	fire	34

* *as in Beckett's original (no quotation marks)*

This diagram was followed by another (NB4, 127), a diamond-shaped schema of the four points (door, window, fire, bed) with vectors; this was to check that the movements [above] were sequential. The galleys (G69, 70) have minor errors of spelling ("windox"), but the paradigm is perfect. In preparing his Calder text for the French translation Beckett re-numbered the moves; the drafts of the French translation (Ohio NB5) equally reflect the care taken to ensure that they are complete and sequential.

204.1 [203]: trom the window: Beckett marked the error, which he had overlooked in the galleys (G69), on his copy of the Olympia text for Grove; but as it remained uncorrected he noted it again when he marked his Grove text for Calder, who made the correction.

204.2 [204]: This room was furnished solidly: this, the penultimate large paradigm, is the most obsessive so far; compare Beckett's *Proust* (46-47): "the attempt to communicate where no communication is possible is merely a simian vulgarity, or horribly comic, like a madness that holds a conversation with the furniture." It has the following terms:

> a. seven days of the week, from Sunday to Friday fortnight, twenty days, if one counts inclusively (the published text says "nineteen" [**206.1**]).
> b. tallboy, dressing-table, night-stool, and washhand-stand, these being. . .
> c. on their feet, head, face, or back (then, from Thursday to Friday fortnight, on their side)
> d. by the fire, by the bed, by the door, and by the window.

Moody contends (261) that the pattern is incomplete, and that what is offered here is a selection of twenty options (for the first twenty days) from a logical "80 possibilities, figured as 4 (pieces of furniture) x 5 (positions) x 4 (places in the room." This is misleading, as each of the twenty days must have each of the four pieces of furniture in one position or another, so there are of necessity four paradigms for each day. In this sense, the pattern is complete, and there are, indeed, eighty listings. However, each of the defined positions (e.g., the first, the tallboy on its feet near the fire) could be associated with any other combination of the furniture, and not merely that given, the possible permutations thus being {20.19.18.17} (this assumes that only one piece can be near the fire, or bed, or door, or window at any one time, but that all can be on their heads, or in any other position, at the same time), for a total of 116,280 (not merely eighty) days in all, or almost 320 years. Beckett offered a twenty-day diagram (see overleaf) in NB4 (160), the numbers reflecting the day as included in the final text, thus: Sunday = 1; Monday = 2; Tuesday = 3; Wednesday = 4; Thursday = 5; Friday = 6; Saturday = 7; Sunday week = 8; Monday week = 9; Tuesday week = 10; Wednesday week = 11; Thursday week = 12; Friday week = 13; Saturday week = 14; Sunday fortnight = 15; Monday fortnight = 16; Tuesday fortnight = 17; Wednesday fortnight = 18; Thursday fortnight = 19; and Friday fortnight = 20:

		Fire	Bed	Door	Window
Tallboy	Feet	1	6	11	16
	Head	17	2	7	12
	Face	13	18	3	8
	Back	9	14	19	4
	Side	5	10	15	20
		Fire	Bed	Door	Window
Dressing Table	Feet	4	5	10	15
	Head	20	1	6	11
	Face	16	17	2	7
	Back	12	13	18	3
	Side	8	9	14	19
		Fire	Bed	Door	Window
Nightstool	Feet	3	8	9	14
	Head	19	4	5	10
	Face	15	20	1	6
	Back	11	16	17	2
	Side	7	12	13	18
		Fire	Bed	Door	Window
Washhand-stand	Feet	2	7	12	13
	Head	18	3	8	9
	Face	14	19	4	5
	Back	10	15	20	1
	Side	6	11	16	17

There is one error only: the pattern for the first Monday (top of 205) reads, "the tallboy on its back by the bed," as the Saturday week (14); whereas it should be, "the tallboy on its head by the bed" (noted by Mood 262). The galleys (G70), apart from minor misspellings, were almost as accurate, only one sequence being omitted and that carefully restored in Beckett's marginal note. Again, the drafts of the French translation (Ohio NB5), contain a list of all the permutations, rigorously crossed out as they were checked off (the total came to seventy-nine, but there should have been eighty, hence a recheck, and one numbered 69A).

206.1 [206]: nineteen days: a curious error, given the detailed calculations, so perhaps deliberate, to underline the difference between casual and inclusive counting (from Sunday to the following Friday fortnight could be considered nineteen days). The figure was changed to "twenty" when Beckett marked his Calder text for the French translation.

207.1 [206]: unspecified: the paradigm might be further complicated (**204.2**) by moving the chairs and filling the corners, and interrogating the "sides" on which other items might fall. One might ask how many "sides" a night-stool and washhand-stand might possibly possess.

207.2 [206]: not at all rare: this phrase does not appear in the late draft (NB4, 162), but completes the sentence begun some two pages earlier.

207.3 [207]: the illusion of fixity: compare the fixed bed of Odysseus in Homer's *Odyssey* (Pat McCarthy to CA). The bed is a relic from the early drafts, Quin's round table (NB1, 35) its prototype: "It was seated at this table that Quin conceived the round bed" (TS, 25).

207.4 [207]: almost one minute: in error for "one degree," there being sixty minutes to a degree; Mr. Knott in the course of twelve months would move little more than six degrees. The error appears in all the English texts, but Beckett changed "minute" to "degree" when preparing his Calder text for the French translation. The precession is "almost" one minute [degree] because of the slight incommensurability between the 360 degrees of a circle and the 365 (366) days of the year. Compare the stopwatch of *Ill Seen Ill Said* (76-77), its "sixty back dots" each set to a point of the compass. See **86.2**.

207.5 [207]: coccyx: the terminal, triangular vertebral bone, mentioned later (233) in the context of a possible fall; here, the fulcrum, or pivot, of Mr. Knott's revolving body.

207.6 [204]: Saint Patrick's Day: March 17th; a detail not in the late draft (NB4, 162).

208.1 [207]: ataraxy: likened a vegetable growth: stoical indifference, or imperturbability, as associated with Epicurus. Beckett observed in the Whoroscope Notebook (82v): "The Stoics aspired to apathia, the repression of all emotion, & the Epicureans to ataraxis, freedom from all disturbance." His Philosophy notes (TCD 10967, 122), consider the only obtainable: "Happiness is the highest good zwar, but happiness pre-supposes a knowledge of the nature of things which cannot be acquired. Hence happiness is not possible, or only possible in a non-committed condition of suspense, suspension of judgment, reserve of opinion. Only possible happiness ataraxy." This note is followed by another, a skeptical critique of the alternative of skepticism, of imperturbability arising from such suspension: "the sceptics were called 'The Suspenders'" (TCD 10967, 123). Watt's "utmost serenity" is followed by despair as his changed situation becomes apparent to him (in the late draft [NB4, 166], he vomits on leaving the house); Molloy, in contrast, is restored to his "old ataraxy" (*Molloy* 42).

208.2 [207]: the vegetable-garden: Calder drops the hyphen, which is a common feature of house and garden. A little later, Calder introduces the error: "be reckoned."

208.3 [208]: the weather was fine: picked up as a refrain in *Molloy* (20, 93, 157), where it links the Molloy and Moran sections of the narrative.

208.4 [208]: its significance diminished: a detail that accentuates the break-down of the Gestalt, of figure and ground, and the increasing deterioration of Watt as he fails to respond to his world (see **128.4** to **130.2**). The phrase, "coloured reproduction," was used in the early drafts, when Watt failed to take it for an original work; but when the typescript was revised for

Notebooks 5 and 6 "picture" and "painting" were used, so when "reproduction" appears here (or, more precisely, is added, between commas) it acts as an index of Watt's failure to respond to earlier stimuli. The spacing of the third and second-last lines is accounted for by the deletion of "rather" ("or ~~rather~~ coloured reproduction") from the galleys (G70).

208.5 [208]: explosives: that is, *plosives*, consonants such as [b], [p], [g], or [k], articulated with a conspicuous expulsion of air (the linguistic term derives from *explosive*, so Watt is not entirely wrong). Compare Watt's later pleasure in Micks's fricatives (**216.7**). In the late draft (NB4, 169), Watt was an "excellent" linguist. Despite their "extraordinary vigour," Mr. Knott's dactylic ejaculations are not noticeably dominated by plosives.

209.1 [209]: rain on the bamboos: in the late draft (NB4, 169), "bamboos" is a later addition, the words crossed out perhaps "~~dry earth~~." Beckett had used the image in his poem "Alba," where the "singing silk" and the "areca" [wooden sounding board] of the *kîn*, or Chinese lute, invokes a sacred music (desecrated in "Dortmunder"), like "la pluie sur les bambous" (Laloy, *La Musique chinoise* 75; DN, #498). Harvey notes (359) associations with "Alba" and "Dortmund," but his "contemplative ataraxy produced in both poems through the influence of music," while applicable here, hardly applies to the latter.

209.2 [209]: solitary dactylic ejaculations: not entirely verbal, if account is made of a note in the Whoroscope Notebook (68v), with reference to onanism: "Ce qu'Aristophanus appelle 'le rythme par le dactyl' (*Nuées* II.i" [the French translation of *The Clouds*]); from Gk. *dactylos*, "finger," the structure of that digit (long-short-short) determining the metrical term. The first draft (NB4, 170) included "kakaka" and "quaquaqua."

209.3 [209]: Exelmans!: René Joseph Isidore Exelmans (1775-1852), Marshal of France who distinguished himself during the retreat from Moscow (*Grove Companion* 185). His name is also used as an expletive in "The End" (80).

209.4 [209]: Cavendish!: Sir Charles Cavendish (1591-1654), eccentric mathematician and friend of Descartes, with whom he disputed on geometry and on whose behalf he petitioned Charles I to offer a post in England. He was the first to calculate the weight of the world. Mentioned in Baillet (153). Mahaffy (86) tells how his library of mathematical manuscripts, gathered during his extensive travels, was sold by his wife to the pasteboard makers.

209.5 [209]: Habbakuk!: more accurately, Habakkuk, the Old Testament prophet who asks God to account for the burden of sin and the iniquities about him: why doth the wicked devour the man more righteous than he? The Lord replies that the vision of iniquity is for but an appointed time, and the just shall live by faith; the prophet is made aware of his shame and rejoices in the midst of desolation (*Grove Companion* 241). Invoked in "Dortmunder," as the "mard of all sinners"; in the poem in the Olympia *Watt* deleted from the Grove text (**45.6**), "East India Runner Duck" is rhymed with "Habbakuk."

209.6 [209]: Ecchymose!: a discoloration, such as a bruise, from the extravasation of blood; defined by Ruby Cohn (*Comic Gamut* 81) as "a term of pathology that may be translated as 'bloody blotch.'" In Garnier (*Onanisme* 455), the consequence of self-abuse.

209.7 [209]: Mr Knott's physical appearance: a monstrous paradigm characterized by the following terms:

> *figure*: {fat, thin, sturdy}
> *stature*: {tall, small, middlesized}
> *skin*: {pale, yellow, flushed}
> *hair*: {dark, fair, ginger}

Out of these simple features (four attributes, each with three variants) eighty-one combinatory sets emerge, precisely tabulated in the manuscript, but finally presented in apparently random rather than obviously sequential order. They might be written out, although Beckett chose not to do so [see below], as a series beginning with {A1 B1 C1 D1}, that is {fat, tall, pale, dark}, and ending, after eighty further increments, with {A3 B3 C3 D3}, or {sturdy, middlesized, flushed, ginger}. Mood (262) errs (see **204.2**) in suggesting that there are 1944 possibilities, of which the text offers but one twenty-fourth; in multiplying the 81 possibilities by {4!}, or 24, he fails to acknowledge the constraints afforded by the fact that each set *must* include one term from each category. There can therefore be only 81 sets; the paradigm is complete. There are two minor errors of punctuation common to all texts: the paradigms "dark, thin, yellow, and small" (209:31) and "tall, fat, yellow, and fair" (209:38) have an extra comma (Laura Lindgren to CA). The late drafts testify to the huge amount of work Beckett put into creating and checking the paradigm, but on a loose leaf included with the late draft (NB4, 143), and on a horizontal axis, he painstakingly wrote out his fair copy of the 81 sets. I have regularized Beckett's capitalization (most items are capitalized, but a few are not), but have retained his general use of "Yell" for "yellow," "Ging" for "ginger," "Flush" for "Flushed," and "Mid" for "Middlesized" (occasionally spelled out in full, or followed by a period). I display the paradigm (see overleaf) in units of nine (the loose-leaf draft aligns them in fifteens), so that the structural relationships between the different sets is more readily apparent:

1	2	3	4	5	6	7	8	9
1 Fat	1 Thin	1 Sturdy	2 Fat	3 Thin	4 Sturdy	1 Fat	2 Thin	3 Sturdy
2 Tall	2 Small	2 Mid	1 Small	1 Mid	1 Tall	2 Mid	1 Tall	1 Small
3 Pale	3 Flush	3 Yell	3 Pale	2 Flush	2 Yell	4 Pale	4 Flush	4 Yell
4 Dark	4 Fair	4 Ging	4 Fair	4 Ging	3 Dark	3 Ging	3 Dark	2 Fair

10	11	12	13	14	15	16	17	18
4 Fat	1 Thin	2 Sturdy	3 Fat	4 Thin	1 Sturdy	2 Fat	3 Thin	4 Sturdy
1 Tall	3 Small	3 Mid	2 Small	2 Mid	3 Tall	3 Mid	2 Tall	2 Small
3 Pale	2 Flush	4 Yell	4 Pale	3 Flush	4 Yell	1 Pale	1 Flush	1 Yell
2 Ging	4 Dark	1 Fair	1 Dark	1 Fair	2 Ging	4 Fair	4 Ging	3 Dark

19	20	21	22	23	24	25	26	27
1 Fat	2 Thin	3 Sturdy	4 Fat	1 Thin	2 Sturdy	3 Fat	4 Thin	1 Sturdy
4 Tall	4 Small	4 Mid	3 Small	4 Mid	4 Tall	4 Mid	3 Tall	2 Small
2 Flush	3 Yell	3 Pale	2 Flush	3 Yell	1 Pale	1 Flush	1 Yell	3 Pale
3 Ging	1 Dark	1 Fair	1 Dark	2 Fair	3 Ging	2 Fair	2 Ging	4 Dark

28	29	30	31	32	33	34	35	36
2 Fat	3 Thin	4 Sturdy	1 Fat	2 Thin	3 Sturdy	4 Fat	1 Thin	2 Sturdy
1 Tall	1 Small	1 Mid	2 Small	1 Mid	1 Tall	1 Mid	3 Tall	3 Small
3 Yell	2 Pale	2 Flush	4 Yell	4 Pale	4 Flush	3 Yell	2 Pale	4 Flush
4 Fair	4 Ging	3 Dark	3 Ging	3 Dark	2 Fair	2 Dark	4 Fair	1 Ging

37	38	39	40	41	42	43	44	45
3 Fat	4 Thin	1 Sturdy	2 Fat	3 Thin	4 Sturdy	1 Fat	2 Thin	3 Sturdy
2 Tall	2 Small	3 Mid	3 Small	2 Mid	2 Tall	4 Mid	4 Tall	4 Small
4 Yell	3 Pale	2 Flush	1 Yell	1 Pale	1 Flush	2 Yell	3 Pale	2 Flush
1 Dark	1 Fair	3 Dark	4 Fair	4 Ging	3 Dark	3 Ging	1 Dark	1 Fair

46	47	48	49	50	51	52	53	54
4 Fat	1 Thin	2 Sturdy	3 Fat	4 Thin	1 Sturdy	2 Fat	3 Thin	4 Sturdy
3 Tall	4 Small	4 Mid	4 Small	3 Mid	2 Tall	1 Mid	1 Tall	1 Small
2 Yell	3 Pale	1 Flush	1 Yell	1 Pale	3 Flush	3 Yell	2 Pale	2 Flush
1 Ging	2 Dark	3 Fair	2 Dark	2 Fair	4 Ging	4 Fair	4 Ging	3 Dark

55	56	57	58	59	60	61	62	63
1 Fat	2 Thin	3 Sturdy	4 Fat	1 Thin	2 Sturdy	3 Fat	4 Thin	1 Sturdy
2 Tall	1 Small	1 Mid	1 Small	3 Mid	3 Tall	2 Mid	2 Tall	3 Small
4 Pale	4 Flush	4 Yell	3 Pale	2 Flush	4 Yell	4 Pale	3 Flush	4 Yell
3 Fair	3 Ging	2 Dark	2 Ging	4 Dark	1 Fair	1 Dark	1 Fair	2 Ging

64	65	66	67	68	69	70	71	72
2 Fat	3 Thin	2 Sturdy	1 Fat	2 Thin	3 Sturdy	4 Fat	1 Thin	2 Sturdy
3 Tall	2 Small	3 Mid	4 Small	4 Mid	4 Tall	3 Mid	4 Tall	4 Small
1 Flush	1 Yell	1 Pale	2 Flush	3 Yell	2 Pale	2 Flush	3 Yell	1 Pale
4 Fair	4 Ging	3 Dark	3 Ging	1 Dark	1 Fair	1 Dark	2 Fair	3 Ging

73	74	75	76	77	78	79	80	81
3 Fat	4 Thin	1 Sturdy	2 Fat	3 Thin	4 Sturdy	1 Fat	2 Thin	3 Sturdy
4 Tall	3 Small	2 Mid	1 Small	1 Mid	1 Tall	2 Mid	1 Tall	1 Small
1 Flush	1 Yell	3 Pale	3 Flush	2 Yell	2 Pale	4 Flush	4 Yell	4 Pale
2 Dark	2 Fair	4 Ging	4 Fair	4 Ging	3 Dark	3 Ging	3 Pale	2 Fair

The numbers to the left represent a grid, or pattern of repetitions, which Beckett had used to order the permutations and ensure that each was correct (A =1, B = 2, C = 3, and D = 4). *Note*: the numbers in the first column do not correspond to the sets above, but represent the template to set the paradigm in motion; with the exception of "1" and "2" they all appear, accurately, in the other columns. For reasons unknown, Beckett often chose to reverse the third and fourth terms, for example {CBDA} preceding {CBAD}. His paradigm (NB4, 149) is not complete; I have silently filled out the missing elements:

ABCD	1	3	27	51	75
ABDC	5	7	31	55	59
ACBD	9	11	35	59	
ACDB	13	15	39	63	
ADBC	17	19	43	67	
ADCB	21	23	47	71	
BACD	2	4	28	52	76
BADC	6	8	32	56	80
BCDA	10	12	36	60	
BCAD	14	16	40	64	
BDCA	18	20	44	68	
BDAC	22*	24	48	72	
CABD	3	5	29	53	77
CADB	7	9	33	57	81
CBDA	11	13	37	61	
CBAD	15	17	41	65	
CDBA	19	21	45	69	
CDAB	23	25	49	73	
DABC	4	6	30	54	78
DACB	8	10	34	58	
DBCA	12	14	38	62	
DBAC	16	18	42	66	
DCBA	20	22	46	70	
DCAB	24	26	50	74	

22: Beckett mistakenly has "20"

On the verso of the loose leaf (NB4, 143v), Beckett indicated a closer relationship between the sets, distributed more randomly in the published text. Numbered as above, they may be read off, horizontally, as nine groups of nine, each with the first two elements in common:

```
 1 55 73 46 28 10 64 19 37 76  4 58 13 49 31 40 67 22
61  9  7 34 16 52 25 43 70 71 26 44  8 62 80 53 35 17
38 65 20 74  2 56 11 47 29 23 41 68 59 77  5 32 14 50
51 33 15 69 24 42  6 60 78 18 54 36 45 72 27 81  9 63
30 12 48 21 39 66 57 75  3
```

Although the paradigm is complete and the process apparently "exhaustive," Watt still does not know his master: Mr. Knott's essence is not deducible from his attributes. Watt needs to recall St. Augustine's dictum, that one cannot know what God is but only what he is not (**77.5**, **147.3**). Were other attributes included (carriage, expression, shape, size, feet, legs, hands, mouth, nose, eyes, ears, blood-type), and/or the variants increased, the paradigms would become increasingly (geometrically) impossible, and Watt still no better off. The galleys again handled this set of variations well, with a few minor mis-spellings (*giger* for "ginger") but only three erroneous sequences; these were carefully crossed out by Beckett. Calder's use of the hyphen in "middlesized" is a transgression. Preparing his Calder text for the French translation Beckett numbered the moves from 1 to 79, that is, taking the first as given and "moving" from the second; but finding he had missed one, he inserted "2A" (this was a check only, but not an aid to composition, as it had been originally).

211.1 [211]: or so it seemed to Watt: the comment, apparently casual and not in the late drafts, reduces the largest and most obsessively complete of the logical paradigms to the status of impression.

211.2 [211]: thay they: Beckett marked the error, overlooked in the galleys (G72), on his copy of the Olympia text for Grove; but as it remained uncorrected he noted it again for Calder, who made the correction ("that they").

211.3 [211]: (1) For the guidance of the attentive reader: who remains curious as to precisely what Mr. Knott's "veritable aspect" might be (like unto the hind quarters of the Lord as revealed to Moses in Exodus 33:23 [**146.4**]?). Beckett indicated the absence of the footnote from the galleys (G72): "Note manque"; perhaps because he had no chance to proof the footnote the second, "Mr Knott" appeared in the Olympia text as "Watt." In his Olympia copy, Beckett noted the correction for Grove, but this appeared only in later reprintings. Beckett, working from his Grove first edition, marked the change for Calder.

212.1 [212]: when dying in London: the galleys (G72) register the change from "living" to "dying." Neither detail appeared in the late draft (NB4, 169). Murphy (188) looks out his skylight toward the coal-sack and the stars. Harvey identifies (349-50) the "curiously autobiographical note" behind this reference, noting the obvious connection with the years 1933-35 when Beckett was "living" in London, and suggesting the ambiguous relationship between Beckett and his character, but equally that between Murphy and Watt as parts of the same fictional "self." Watt makes a later appearance in *Mercier and Camier*, wearing a huge bowler hat and a heavy greatcoat, under which he is probably naked, drinking excessively, and telling such sentiments as "fuck life." He is large, foul-mouthed, argues with policemen, and abuses others in the pub (the "real" Watt drinks only milk). He recalls someone called Murphy, who came to a bad end. This Watt is "quite unrecognizable" (111), and not easily reconciled with the earlier one; he is not obviously the man who sought to comprehend the mysteries of Mr. Knott. His "place in the series" is analogous to that of Malacoda in "Draff," where the intensity of a first appearance (the poem, "Malacoda") is rendered into pastiche, turned to swill (the "series" for Beckett also encapsulates its own negations and absurdities).

212.2 [212]: a fascia of white light: a broad band of color, with the medical sense of a thin sheet of connective tissue connecting a muscle or organ. The word has echoes of Leopardi's "fascio" from "Canto noturno di un pastore errante dell'asia" (line 23), with its sense of "burden" beneath the *candida luna* ["white moon"] (**217.1, 222.6**).

212.3 [212]: obturation: in Johnson's *Dictionary*: "The act of stopping up anything with something smeared over it." Hesla observes of such promotion of intellection (81), "This is about as close as you can get to an adequate anthropomorphic image of Nous nousing nous."

213.1 [213]: or put it in a drawer: the galleys (G72) either dropped the next words, or Beckett made a late insertion, punning on the cliché, a foot in one's mouth: "or put it in his mouth." Again, no distinction is made between right and left leg.

213.2 [213]: Continuing then: the final paragraph, with the beginning of part III, were pre-published as an "Extract from *Watt*" in *Irish Writing* (see **151.2**). The finale is identical to the published text save that after "the aspens" *Irish Writing* adds a comma, then "and the yews."

213.3 [213] aspens: trees that tremble, from an engrained memory of having been used for the crucifixion of Christ (**154.2**). The repetition of brambles, briars, thistles, and nettles reiterates the image of a fallen world.

213.4 [213]: the issuing smokes: the image of reconciliation from *Cymbeline*, appropriated by Joyce to end the "Scylla and Charybdis" chapter of *Ulysses* with the anticipation of reconciliation between Bloom and Stephen, is here further appropriated. For the possible Joycean echo in "mingled," see **129.2**. A "pine of smoke" rises at the end of *Murphy*; and at the outset of Moran's narrative, before his world is shattered, the smoke from his neighbors' chimneys rises "straight and blue" (*Molloy* 93).

IV

215.1 [214]: IV: in the galleys chapter IV is unmarked and only an indentation (not even a blank line) separates "to vanish" from "As Watt told"; Beckett marked "Chapître IV" and added (much as for II and III): "En belle page 20 l. de texte."

215.2 [214]: As Watt told the beginning of his story: the opening of part IV, until the end of page 219 (in the French translation, 223-28), appeared as "L'Histoire de Watt," a pre-publication, "Traduit de l'Anglais par Ludovic et Agnès Janvier en collaboration avec l'auteur," in *Les Lettres nouvelles* (septembre-octobre 1968): 11-16.

215.3 [214]: Two, one, four, three: Beckett wrote in large letters in NB4 (139): "Watt tells 4 before 3"; this decision was reached before the late rewriting of chapter 4 in NB6. Heroic quatrains, or elegaic stanzas, are four-line stanzas of iambic pentameter with an *abab* rhyming scheme; they are not notably elaborated thus. Coe's comment (191) is apposite: "the more one tries to puzzle this out, the more one's thoughts take on the cast of Watt's own, and that, it seems to me, is the major and comic point."

215.4 [214]: not quite cold: NB6 (1) reads "warm." Beckett's final rewriting of part IV retreats from obvious irony toward simple statement (**222.6**). The phrasing, "the end of a day that was like the other days," is later echoed in *Endgame*; "passibly" (with sense, with feeling) offers a curious intonation.

215.5 [214]: of Mr Knott he could not speak: the casual phrasing conceals an "unspeakable" agony (**85.4**). Here, if anywhere in *Watt*, the oft-cited conclusion to Wittgenstein's *Tractatus* seems most applicable: "Was man nicht sprechen kann, darüber muss man schweigen" ["Of what one cannot speak one must be silent"].

215.6 [214]: in suitable weather: not that of part III (153), a high wind and bright sun. NB6 (3) has: "his mind semi-conscious as always"; and reads "divine" for "celestial."

216.1 [214]: Arthur: the late draft (NB6, 3) retains "Phelps."

216.2 [215]: gloaming: if Beckett is echoing Harry Lauder's "Roaming in the Gloaming" (**40.7**), then "softly come and go" may be implied (Pat McCarthy to CA).

216.3 [215]: He felt it was his duty to do this: the late draft (NB6, 5) differed in tone: "'Oh!' said Watt, taken by surprise, 'who are you, and how did you get in?'"

216.4 [215]: One moment I was out, and the next I was in: a change Arsene might describe as hymeneal (*Watt* 42).

216.5 [215]: So the moment was come: the late draft (NB6, 5) elaborates this simple sentiment, at the cost of Watt's final passivity: "So the moment was come, so long consented, so ? . Watt felt nothing, a slight irritation perhaps, that he was no longer alone, but so faint that it was nothing." The details about the milk turning and inferior cigar are absent at this point, but the *passé composé* structure with "to be" is present.

216.6 [215]: cloistered fornication: the late draft (NB6, 5) reads "cohabitation."

216.7 [215]: The fricatives: consonants such as [f], [v], [s], [z], and [n], characterized by the friction of the breath in the almost-closed sound passage; in the late writing (NB6, 7), Watt's pleasure derived from the labials, such as [p], [b], [f], [v], [m], and [w], where the sounds are modified by the lips. Compare his appreciation of "explosives" (**208.5**).

217.1 [215]: an encountered nightsong: cryptically alluding to the deletion ("proscript" on the analogy of "prologue"), from the earlier drafts, of Leopardi's "Canto notturno di un pastore errante dell'asia" (TS, 49) (**212.2, 222.6, #22**).

217.2 [215]: he reappeared, to Micks: as Arsene (63): "he appeared again, to Watt."

217.3 [216]: the grousebag: as the name suggests, originally a bag used in hunting small game (the grouse is a small, reddish-brown game bird of the family *Tetraonidae*, hunted particularly in Scotland), with useful pockets ("straps, and buckles"). The French text offers (225) "la gibecière." These bags have not been mentioned, but a "water-tight grousebag," into which Watt vomited on leaving the house (**223.3**), was mentioned (NB4, 166) as hanging from a peg on the wall; the later draft (NB6, 9) reads: "of which mention has been made." The other, and similar grousebag of the next paragraph is "introduced for the first time" (NB6, 9). The point of this byplay is uncertain.

217.4 [216]: a greatcoat: the outer garb of many a Beckett protagonist. Beckett owned such a coat, inherited from his father who had bought it in the early days of motoring (as intimated below, where "Watt's father" and Beckett's father are identified). Murphy (72) wears a like coat, non-porous and of an aeruginous green, within which he is hermetically enclosed, like a monad. Watt is likened (**16.7**) to a roll of tarpaulin. In *First Love* (29), "this" coat is part of the narrator's "travelling custom"; in "The Expelled" (59) it impedes his efforts to leave by the window; in "The Calmative" (65) it is green, with a velvet collar, "such as motorists wore about 1900, my father's"; in "The End" (78) it is burned with other clothes. Mercier and Camier share the one greatcoat, and the handkerchief in its pocket; in the *Three Novels* the coat, with its collar of velvet or shag, a hat fastened to its buttonhole, suggests the shared identity of the protagonists. A similar coat features in "Cascando," "Heard in the Dark I," *Film*, *That Time*, *From an Abandoned Work* (his father's), *All Strange Away*, *Stirrings Still*, "Ghost Trio," and " . . . But the Clouds . . ."; asserting "identity" even as character and memory fade (*Grove Companion* 235-36).

217.5 [216]: or a little more than a stone: in avoirdupois measurement of weight, then used in the British Isles and Ireland, a stone is fourteen pounds. Preparing his Calder text for the French translation Beckett marked this appositional phrase for deletion; the translation reads (225): "entre quinze et seize livres, poids commerce."

217.6 [216]: a small sum: in the late writing (NB6, 11), a "derisive" sum; the widow there was "deserving" rather than "meritorious."

218.1 [216]: motoring in its infancy: for William Beckett's motoring, and his ownership of a De Dion Bouton, see O'Brien, *The Beckett Country* (9). The phrase, "some seventy years before," reads in the late draft (NB6, 11): "fifty or sixty years before"; the difference perhaps representing the delay in publication.

218.2 [216]: and of course occasional fleeting immersion in canal water: added as a late insert (NB6, 10), without the, er, bathetic "of course."

218.3 [217]: scored and contunded: superficially scarred and cut, and (an archaic term) pounded or bruised. Compare, with respect to thickness, strength, and impermeability, Murphy's coat (107), which, too, is subject to change in time.

218.4 [217]: a factitious murrey chrysanthemum: an artificial, mulberry-colored autumnal flower ("murrey" an heraldic term). In "vive morte ma seule saison" (1947), life is a long autumn, a natural opposition that of lilies (**136.1**) and chrysanthemums.

218.5 [217]: a block hat: a stiff felt hat that takes its name and shape from the wooden block on which it was made. In French (226): "un feutre rigid." Malone's strange visitor (*Malone Dies* 269) wears a block hat; the narrator of *Company* (16) recalls a "once buff block hat"; its like is mentioned in *Ill Seen Ill Said* (60).

218.6 [217]: The one green! The other yellow!: the familiar pattern of green and yellow, indicative of decay in the natural world (**9.7**).

218.7 [217]: For so it is with time: in the late draft (NB6, 15), this repeated phrase was followed by a variation: "that lightens what is light, that darkens what is dark." There seems no good reason for its omission. Compare the Third Collect in the Anglican service, for aid against all perils: "Lighten our darkness, we beseech thee, O Lord."

219.1 [217]: for eight pence: the late draft (NB6, 15) crosses out "~~four and six~~" and replaces it with "half a crown." The final change completes the pattern of absurdity invoked in the opening section, whereby Watt, who had borrowed 5/-, now possesses 4/4 (**17.3**). The Calder "eightpence" conforms more tightly to British usage.

219.2 [217]: a fortiori: as an inevitable consequence. The effect of the commas is to slow the progression and to emphasize banality, as the possible pun on "foot" and "fort." A similar collocation is made in *Malone Dies* (248).

219.3 [218]: shipshape: the late draft first read (NB6, 15), "~~in excellent repair~~." Unable to cope with the pun, the French translation (227) offers: "en état de marche." The Calder "seashore" neglects the littoral emphasis of the Grove "sea-shore."

219.4 [218]: a twelve . . . a ten: earlier (NB6, 17), an eight and a ten, Watt's foot a nine. Watt might take comfort from Belacqua's problem with his right boot (*Dream* 130), and the radiant explanation offered (132), when the shopkeeper says that the rare client whose feet are of equal size must pay for the asymmetry of an article for the average person.

219.5 [218]: in preference to the other three: that is, Watt has four choices with respect to how he wears his socks: {left, left}; {right, right}; {left, right}; {right, left}. The real curiosity of this small but apparently exhaustive paradigm is that the text nowhere explains on which foot he wears the boot and on which the shoe, and so, *a footiori,* the precise foot on which he wears two socks remains unknown. Compare *Molloy* (55), and *Malone Dies* (249), where similar confusions ensue.

219.6 [218]: from more than one point of view: the late draft (NB6, 18) reads "from every point of view" and "from the eye"; the changes, apparently insignificant, suggest that Watt's trousers, like his father's, are fistular (**74.5**).

219.7 [218]: a collar: the detachable kind, to be affixed to the shirt by studs.

220.1 [219]: raising in amaze an astonished hand to a thunderstruck mouth: an obscure fossil (added only in the final rewriting) from the early drafts (TS, 157), where the narrator, "we," about to part, is standing with Arsene in the passage of Quin's house, and expresses the timid sense of an "other" who might possibly understand:

> 'What other?' said Arsene.
> 'Oh!' we cried, starting back in surprise and raising in amaze an astonished hand to a thunderstruck mouth, 'well now just fancy that.'

Robinson (113) invokes the image of Dostoevsky, which entered *The Idiot*, as he viewed Holbein's *Descent from the Cross*, a picture depicting God in the state of human decay; the agitated effect upon his face, and the frightened expression that often anticipated an epileptic fit. This is the more appropriate in the light of a comment recorded in Beckett's earlier notes on Psychology (TCD 10971/8, 34), from Otto Rank's *The Trauma of Birth*: "The aura preceding the great epileptic attack, with its feeling of blessedness so wonderfully described by Dostoevsky, corresponds to the prenatal libido gratification, while the subsequent convulsions recapitulate the act of birth." See **233.5** and **241.2**.

220.2 [219]: lymphatic: disposed to sluggishness or fattiness, from a presumed excess of water in the tissues.

220.3 [219]: vain entelechies: unlike "we" in the early draft (**220.1**), or Arsene, Watt has nothing to say as he leaves; but all that is unspoken, including earlier drafts deleted, leave "traces" on the air, in a manner that uncannily anticipates the finale of *Texts for Nothing*.

221.1 [219]: he felt the draught: a prelude to the Cartesian dream (**223.3**, **225.2**).

221.2 [220]: to shut the door . . . set down his bags . . . sit down: a final paradigm, lacking the complexity of those in part III, yet a source of consternation for Watt. It appears as a late insert (NB6, 22). A simple truth table of the three considerations and their negations outlines the eight alternatives in the order that Beckett presents them:

1. {A B C}   2. {A B -C}
3. {A -B C}   4. {-A B C}
5. {A -B -C}   6. {-A B -C}
7. {-A -B C}   8. {-A -B -C}

Kenner is not correct, then, to suggest that Watt, having rehearsed every combination of these actions, undertakes none (101); rather, Watt takes the eighth permitted alternative.

221.3 [220]: a rider: an extra clause added, not necessarily (as here) related to the main point at issue. Watt's failure to make a decision between his various choices means he remains, for longer than is conducive to his comfort, in a "semi-upright station" (**222.4**).

222.1 [221]: arms on the table: a posture adopted by the protagonist or narrator in Beckett's later works, notably the poem, "Mort de A. D." (1949) and the short prose piece closely related to it, "Stirrings Still" (1983).

222.2 [221]: dives from dreadful heights into rocky waters: an "obsessional image," based on Beckett's childhood memory of the Victorian seawater baths near the "Forty Foot" hole, Dún Laoghaire, where the father urges the son to plunge from a high board into the water full of large rocks. Beckett noted the obvious Freudian implications (TCD 10971/8, 34): "Dreams of plunging into water telescopes the birth trauma (plunge) & the regressive tendency." The image appears in an early poem, "For Future Reference," then resurfaces in *Dream* (34), *Eleuthéria* (125), and *Company* (18). Anne Atik says that Beckett often mentioned it (33), and shortly before his death he asked Herbert Blau about recurring dreams of this kind (*Grove Companion* 145).

222.3 [221]: a numerous public: John Fletcher (92) notes the Gallic flavor, a direct rendering of the French "public numereux"; "remarked" in the next sentence has a similar intonation, as does "force" (see **10.1**) in the sentence following that. In the French translation (230), however, Beckett preferred: "devant une nombreuse assistance."

222.4 [221]: semi-upright station: again (**32.8**) intimating the stations of the cross, a *via dolorosa* leading to a slow crucifixion. Watt's position is between one bowed beneath the cross he carries and one seeking to return to the womb (see **140.1**, for Otto Rank's sense of crucifixion as "prevention of the embryonal position").

222.5 [221]: he only realised it much later: one might inquire, how? If Watt's accounts, as reported to Sam, are based on memory, then already implicit is the paradox of memory as fabrication, or creation, essential to *Company* and the genesis of the later short fictions.

222.6 [221]: unusual splendour: Leopardi's *Canto notturno* (**212.2**, **217.**1) invokes both the beauty of the moon, and its nothingness. The deliberately bland phrase, "by some writers," replaces the too-obvious irony of the late draft (NB6, 31): "by acute observers."

223.1 [222]: hortulan beauties: prosaically, the beauties of the garden; added to the late draft (NB6, 31). Insofar as Mr. Knott's garden is a *hortus conclusus*, or closed garden, Watt's parting (as Molloy from Lousse) is from a paradise to which he may never return.

223.2 [222]: some pendulous umbel: an inflorescence of pedicels, or flower stalks, of equal length, radiating from a common center to form a rounded, clustered flower head; here, hanging downwards. A "horn," in this setting, is a yoke-elm, or hornbeam, a tree of the birch family with catkins that may reach four inches in length (see *Dream* 162). The French translation offers "peut-être d'une charme" (231), that phrase absent from the typescript (Ohio TS, 166) but added to the galleys by hand (Ohio G222).

223.3 [222]: there was no wind: on the occasion of his parting, Arsene drew attention to "a little wind" (**62.2**), traditionally a sign of the presence of God, as in *Molloy* (60), at a similar parting. More pertinent is the denial of the experience of Descartes in his three dreams of late 1619, when he saw clearly the road he would follow. Baillet comments (38): "Il crut appercevoir à travers de leurs ombres les vestiges du chemin que Dieu lui traçait pour suivre sa volonté dans son choix de vie" ["He believed he saw across their shadows the outlines of the road that God was tracing for him that he might follow His will in the choice of his own life"]. But at this moment of truth there is no wind, Watt feels nothing, and he has nothing to say.

223.4 [222]: the passing weakness: as the late draft makes clear (NB4, 166), the reference was originally to Watt's tearful departure as he reaches the public road (208); that version included details about his mighty vomit. In the final text, the weakness is more evidently that "already mentioned" in part I (**33.1**), when Watt en route to Mr. Knott's house was detained in the ditch. Parallels between Watt's coming and his going are marked (the long grass, the moonlight, the passing weakness). This has encouraged Heath Lees to suggest (9) that the descant mentioned at the end is in all likelihood sung (**#34**), but that Watt, now so out of tune with his environment, does not hear it.

223.5 [222]: freestone: limestone or sandstone grit, with an obvious irony.

223.6 [222]: A strayed ass, or goat: emblems of Christ's entry into Jerusalem, and those passed over. In the late draft (NB6, 33), there is only the ass, which looked at Watt with eyes "so indifferent, so indifferent," before it laid back its head "among the shadows" (NB6, 35). Watt, on his way to Mr. Knott's house, had lain among the "pretty nettles" (33). The goat anticipates "Riley's puckaun," dragging its pale and chain, at the end of the novel (245-46), and that in the Potter's Field in part IV of *Mercier and Camier* (56).

224.1 [223]: the stone steps: added as an insert to the late draft (NB6, 36v, 38v), and echoing the final image of *Whoroscope*, the starless, inscrutable hour at which the Seigneur du Perron mounts the bitter steps, the pun on *perron*, "stone steps."

224.2 [223]: umbers: soils with iron and manganese oxides used to make pigments and dyes; here, the dusky brown foothills. Watt's lifting his eyes unto the hills (Psalm 121) anticipates the fall from sky to hills to plain in the last sentence of the novel (**246.4**).

224.3 [223]: the eyes: a variation of a familiar motif, the sudden apparition, in the clouds or sky or ashes, or against the blooming buzzing confusion, of a face; see "Enueg II," *Murphy* (4), "Old Earth," "Still 3," and "Words and Music." But here it is Watt who is blurrily perceived. The sky as "the waters" invokes the spirit of God moving upon "the face of the waters" (Genesis 1:2). The paragraph is rhetorically balanced, moving from the wicket and the permanent way (the railway), to as far as the eye might see, then the recession of the stars (the Milky Way?), and back to the wicket.

224.4 [223]: the wicket: a small gate within a larger one. With reference to Bunyan's *Pilgrim's Progress* (1678), it is used in *Molloy*, in both the Molloy and Moran sections, as the threshold of an Eden to which, having once passed through, the protagonist can never return. Having climbed the wicket, Watt's "prospects" are better described as retrospects.

224.5 [223]: coalsacks: in the Milky Way, clouds of galactic dust and dark nebulae that obscure the stars beyond and reveal a blurred and dirty aspect to the eye. Beckett recorded the word (DN #1052) from Sir James Jeans's *The*

Universe Around Us (29), then deployed it in *Dream* (16), *Murphy* (188), and (more literally) in *How It Is*.

224.6 [223]: focussed: not noted in the galleys (G76), nor in Beckett's corrections of the Olympia text; but in marking his Grove text for Calder Beckett requested "focused." An unusual emphasis; one might have expected "focused upon" or "brought into focus."

224.7 [223]: the many touching prospects . . . highway: literally, that which lies before. The phrasing echoes, for no obvious reason, Dr. Johnson's comment to Boswell, that the noblest prospect a Scotchman sees is the high-road to England (*Life*, 6 July 1763, 145).

225.1 [224]: the chimneys of Mr Knott's house: O'Brien offers a photograph (*The Beckett Country* 6). Compare **36.3**; Watt has learnt this matter during his service, which suggests either that his duties have taken him outside the house (but when?), or that Beckett's memory has intruded without regard to narrative consistency. The galleys (G76) and Olympia text have "chimmeys," the error not then noted by Beckett, who marked it in his Olympia copy for correction by Grove.

225.2 [224]: a figure: noting the explicit parallels with Watt (the dress, the hat, the gait), Doherty (47) sums up the enigma: "Watt sees himself approaching himself." For the experience of alterity, seeing oneself as other, compare the central experience of "Arènes de Lutèce" and the encounter that Molloy and Moran each has in the Dark Wood with his Shadow. Noting the intimations of Christ, Doherty suggests that through this experience Watt becomes the parodic Christ figure foresuffered earlier. To be sure, Watt's sufferings are like a slow crucifixion, and there may be an intimation of the providential figure that mysteriously appears in part V of Eliot's *The Waste Land*, or the "unsubstantial image" that Stephen Dedalus seeks to encounter, or that will encounter him (*Portrait* 65); but the import of the experience remains enigmatic. Although impatient, and momentarily falling into the old error (227), Watt is not really lacerated by curiosity as he might once have been; and he seems to have no intimation that the figure might be, in some way, himself and/or Christ. Unlike Descartes, he has no revelation, and though he professes to regard the "hallucination" as "possessing exceptional interest" (228), after it fades and disappears he expresses no further interest in the phenomenon.

225.3 [224]: man . . . woman . . . priest . . . nun: in Irish jest, the appropriate paradigm; complicated by Watt's inevitable awareness (227) that any one of these four figures might be any of the other three dressed as man, woman, priest or nun respectively. References to priest or nun, and the consequent permutations, were late additions to the manuscripts. Watt's inability to distinguish the sex of this figure recalls Tetty Nixon's uncertainty as to whether the figure of Watt is that of a man or a woman (**16.6**).

225.4 [224]: night-wanderer: the word may invoke Goethe's "Wanderers Nachtlied," or Leopardi's wandering shepherd (**217.1, #22**).

226.1 [225]: a single garment: the "uninterrupted surfaces" suggest the seamless garment of Christ, and "asexual" invokes something of the "creedless, colourless, sexless Christ" defined by Belacqua in *Dream* (35) in the context of mystical transelementation.

226.2 [225]: yellow with age: compare the description of Watt's block hat (218), once mustard but now pepper.

226.3 [225]: the gait: markedly anthropoid (note the extended arms), or possibly ursine (**31.5**), yet reminiscent of Watt's funambulistic stagger (**31.3**). The error, "a kind or shackled smartness," is present in the Olympia and Grove editions; although not noted by Beckett, it was corrected in the Calder edition.

226.4 [225]: *The only cure is diet*: identified by John Pilling ("Long Shadows," 65), who calls it "unusually recondite even for Beckett"), as a tag, "sola diaeta curari," from the *Tardes passiones* II.xii of the fifth-century physician, Caelius Aurelianus. Beckett's immediate source (as Pilling implies) is the entry for *diaeta* in Lewis and Short's Latin dictionary. The French text offers (235): *"Seul remède le régime."*

226.5 [225]: or for this woman: the galleys (G76) have "of for," the mistake overlooked by Beckett and so reproduced in the Olympia text; Beckett on his Olympia copy noted it for correction by Grove, where the change was made.

226.6 [225]: company: not as the later prose-poem (1980), yet with something of that work's sense of images "devised" by one alone in the dark; also, perhaps, an intimation of Psalms 55:14: "We took sweet counsel together, and walked unto the house of God in company." But Watt remains alone.

226.7 [225]: whether this was a good thing: the Calder text offers an unfortunate *plopf*: "whether shit was a good thing." This was changed without comment by Beckett when he prepared that text for the French translation.

227.1 [226]: how should he know: a last exhausted permutation, four terms in the simplest possible order: {A B C D}, {B A C D}, {C A B D}, {D A B C}.

227.2 [226]: this old error: the rational prurit, or itch to know (**141.4**). The phrase "substance shadowy" intimates Kant's phenomenal world, the noumena unknowable; while "lacerated" echoes the "lacero" of Leopardi's "Canto notturno" (line 32), rather than Swift's savage indignation. Watt's mistake, even now, is to concern himself with the phenomenological aspects of the figure (its size, its sex, its clothing), in the expectation that these will give some insight into its noumenal essence.

227.3 [226]: his nails pricked his palms: intimating the stigmata, yet also suggesting that Watt's sufferings are largely self-induced; hence the agitated wish to know.

227.4 [226]: staffage: in painting, human or animal figures added to a landscape; as Molloy notes (63): "Homo mensura cannot do without staffage."

227.5 [227]: a millstone: compare (to little effect) Matthew 18:6: "it were better for him that a millstone were hanged about his neck."

228.1 [227]: Watt was puzzling over this: the late draft (NB6, 51) reads: "Watt was shutting his eyes, and at the same time seething his brains." His sense of the figure as possessing "exceptional interest" (in NB6 [51], "even beauty") echoes Mr. Hackett's interest in the apparition of Watt himself; but his choice of "hallucination" precludes any serious consideration of its relevance. Damian Love comments: "[Beckett's] satire is directed at the Cartesian method of systematic inquiry. The Cartesian conception of a mind that has direct and privileged access to its own contents underlies the urge to reify and objectively examine the subjective 'self' and its experiences. If this urge is taken to extremes, it becomes apparent that the mind is not so designed and will tend to short-circuit. The Cartesian epistemological project is erected upon a model of the human mind more akin to pathology than normality. When Watt rounds off his disintegration with a reference to the schizophrenic poet Hölderlin (239), the inference is clear. But [Beckett's] concern goes beyond satire to the ultimate experiential consequences of a crisis such as Watt's. The *cogito* buckles under the strain: 'I think, therefore I am' is not after all a clear and distinct idea. A normal healthy mind takes the 'I' for granted and puts no pressure on it, but for schizophrenics identity can become distorted. They may experience a bizarre conjunction of virtual solipsism and a terrifying loss of self; thoughts may seem to emanate from some external source; or the world seem appallingly dependent on one's mental concentration. As Watt, having left Mr. Knott's house, gazes entranced at a spectral figure with a gait strangely like his own (225-28), he is moving into territory where 'self' is an uncertain quantity" (*Grove Companion* 505).

228.2 [227]: the name of Case: remotely suggesting the celebrated opening of Wittgenstein's *Tractatus*: "The world is all that is the case." The "exception" of the Sunday (to Monday) night was not present in the late draft (NB6, 53).

228.3 [227]: *Songs by the Way*: a collection of inspirational verse, alternatively entitled "Homeward" (1894), by George Russell (1867-1935), Irish poet and Theosophist commonly known as "AE" (*aeon*, a mystical eternity), but dismissed in Beckett's scathing review, "Recent Irish Poetry" (1934), as one who "enters his heart's desire with such precipitation as to positively intrude into the void" (*Disjecta* 71). What Mr. Case reads remains a mystery, but the late draft (NB6, 53) leaves a gap and spells out: "(Quotation)"; Beckett intending something suitable but later preferring the lacuna (*Grove Companion* 492-93). The sentiment, "and at the same time improve his mind," does not appear in that final draft. The French translation (237) offers "*Chants d'un chemineau.*"

228.4 [227]: as it espoused, now pouting, now revulsed: a transferred epithet, perhaps indicative of the feelings of his lonely wife.

228.5 [228]: through the windows, of his box a glimpse: thus in the galleys (G77), without comment, but Beckett in marking his Olympia text for Grove first deleted the comma after "windows," then requested that one be added after "box." Perhaps because of a marginal "STET," intended to refer to the former, the latter was not introduced; Beckett marked it again on his Grove copy for Calder, where the changes were made.

228.6 [228]: what time it was: narrative nonsense that arises as a consequence of direct speech being reported indirectly; presumably the fault of Sam. Similar pedantry informs the next request, Watt using "could" when he should have used "might" (because, indeed, he could, but whether he might is quite another matter); and "a waiting room" when he might more accurately have said, as in the late draft (NB6, 55), "the waiting room."

229.1 [228]: a teaser: a knotty point (see **147.5**).

229.2 [228]: the waiting room . . . the booking office . . . the stationmaster's sanctum: in the late draft (NB6, 56), Beckett sketched the floor-plan of the three rooms, on graph paper, to illustrate the restricted access of each within the other, and in the proportions of the Golden Rectangle (a potentially infinite series of rectangles inset within one another, like Russian dolls, the longer side of the one generating the shorter side of the outer and greater, while its shorter side in turn forms the longer side of the inner and lesser). This schema was finally ignored, for the booking office is exterior to (and larger than) the waiting room and access to the inner sanctum is no longer by means of the middle rectangle, but rather directly from the booking office. The change was consequent on the need for Watt (1) to be locked in the waiting room, but (2) that waiting room be within the booking room so that the accident with the door (237) may happen.

229.3 [228]: Mr Gorman . . . Mr Nolan: in the late draft (NB6, 59), respectively "Mr Farrell" and "Mr Tully," names from Beckett's Foxrock world. "Mr Farrell" was modeled on Thomas Farrell, stationmaster at Foxrock, whose station was adjudged best kept of the network (O'Brien 32); in *All That Fall*, where this praise is echoed (26), he is "Mr Barrell." The change makes him, perhaps, the husband and cuckold of the fishwoman, Mrs. Gorman, who has had admirers before and after and even during him (see **139.1**, but also **238.1**). "Mr Tully" takes his name a small dairy near Cooldrinagh (O'Brien 19) (**149.2**); there seems no obvious reason for the change to "Mr Nolan."

230.1 [229]: the fulness of time: Galatians 4:4: "But when the fulness of time was come, God sent forth his Son, made of a woman, made under the law."

230.2 [229]: lest: the galleys (G78) and Olympia text read "less." The error was at first overlooked by Beckett, who then marked it on his copy of the Olympia text for correction by Grove, where the change was made.

230.3 [229]: trouser's . . . trousers': a subtle distinction, confused by Calder (who repeats "trouser's"); however, in the late draft (NB6, 60), the second apostrophe is as the first. Compare, above, "gentlemens' lavatories" (Calder "corrects" this to "gentlemen's"), and the obscene crescendo of *Murphy* (77): "chandlers . . . chandler's . . . chandlers.'"

231.1 [230]: pain . . . pleasure: in the Epicurean sense (*Murphy* 6) of pleasure as at best a relative good, a reaction from pain—a doctrine that underlies the pessimistic doctrine of suffering in Schopenhauer, to which the following images make mute testimony.

231.2 [231]: enlarged: set free, or at large, but with reference to the Chinese boxes of the station giving access to the larger ones of the Big World.

232.1 [231]: Watt lay on the seat: having said he will walk up and down, or sit on a seat (in NB6 [67], "the seat"), Watt lies down, unwittingly exemplifying Chamfort's Maxim #155: "Quand on soutient que les gens les moins sensibles sont à tout prendre, les plus heureux, je me rappelle le proverbe indien: 'Il vaut mieux être assis que debout, être couché qu'assis; mort que tout cela.'" This is summarized in the Whoroscope Notebook (66), and invoked in *Murphy* (79). Beckett offered a free translation (*Poems* 181): "Better on your arse than on your feet, / Flat on your back than either, dead than the lot" (**186.2**).

232.2 [231]: without thought or sensation: Watt's experience is not that of Murphy, retreating into the inner darkness of the third part of his mind, but it can be defined in terms of *coenaesthesis*, a word Beckett recorded in the Dream Notebook (96) from Max Nordau's *Degeneration* (249): the general feeling of experience arising from the sum of bodily feelings rather than the definite sensations of specific senses, an experience that occurs beneath the threshold of consciousness, a state Schopenhauer called will-lessness (compare *Murphy* 113). Estragon has a similar sense (*Waiting for Godot* 40.b) of all the dead voices. To Mary Manning (30 August 1937), Beckett described: "an end to the temptation of light, its polite scorching & considerations. It is food for children and insects. There is an end of making up one's mind, like a pound of tea. An end of putting the butter of consciousness into opinions. The real consciousness is the chaos, a grey commotion of the mind" (*Grove Companion* 100-01). Here, there is a "flurry of little grey paws" as the mice flutter in his mind, and the noise of the passing express is described as a "commotion."

232.3 [231]: a flurry of mice: time has passed, like the express, without any conscious recording by Watt's mind. Watt earlier welcomed being abandoned by his last rats, left to face the silence without "the gnawing, the scurrying, the little cries" (**72.1**, **84.1**).

232.4 [231]: likely a sensation: partly, but not entirely undermining the experience of *coenaesthesis* (**232.2**) by noting its origin, despite Watt's failure to register the effect, in the passing express; an oblique reflection of the scholastic axiom, *nihil in intellectu quod non prius in sensu*, there is "nothing in the mind that is not first in the senses."

232.5 [232]: commotion: from L. *commovere*, "to move or disturb"; used here with both the sense of recurrent motion and that of mental perturbation, as in *Murphy* (112).

232.6 [232]: the screen: what linguists have termed the *Zwischenwelt* (the "between world"), or the screen that language imposes between consciousness and the world. Rabinovitz notes (149) the word's suggestions of Schopenhauer's sense of the veil of Mâyâ.

232.7 [232]: biannual equinoctial nocturnal emission in vacuo: Watt masturbates twice-yearly, on the nights of the equinox.

233.1 [232]: then forward on his face: thus in all English texts, but corrected by Beckett to "its" when preparing his Calder text for the French translation (the difference does not register in French). In the galleys (G79), the next phrase reads: "or backward on its ~~sinciput~~"; Beckett writing in the margin: "back."

233.2 [232]: closing like a groom: that is, the doors of the bridal chamber, a prelude to intimacy, as in Watt's experience of his mind.

233.3 [233]: a little wale: a narrow raised surface, or a small streak; compare the "Pale wales in the east" ("Yellow" 165).

233.4 [233]: like a ? 's: thus in the late draft (NB6, 95).

233.5 [233]: sigmoidal: intimating the embryonic position, and so anticipating the grotesque images of birth to come (**234.2**, **241.2**). Consider Otto Rank's *The Trauma of Birth*, as recorded in Beckett's notes on Psychology (TCD 10971/8, 34): "Anxiety of child left alone in dark room due to his unconscious being reminded (er-innert) of intrauterine situation." Watt's experience at the station iterates Tetty's account of Larry's birth, for the child. Noting this image of the womb, Büttner (136ff) underlines the further significance of the fixed chair (the placenta), the unpleasant smell [Augustine's *inter faeces et urinas nascimur*—CA], and the post-partum slops.

234.1 [233]: accommodate: the galleys (G79) and the Olympia text read "accomodate," the error at first overlooked by Beckett, who marked it on his Olympia copy for correction by Grove, where the change was made. Given the rain and sleet, the word has intimations of Lear's "unaccommodated man" (**41.3**), the station as womb offering refuge from the vicissitudes of Nature without.

234.2 [233]: Price: unknown, but her "extreme spareness" links her to Miss Carriage of *Murphy*, who derives from Beckett's childhood neighbor, Mrs. Coote, the "small thin sour woman" identified in *Company* (28) and in O'Brien, *The Beckett Country* (15). The mysterious whispering voice, and the thin lips sticking and unsticking, intimate both the lips and vagina (**234.3**) and imply the umbilical mother-fetus relation (**333.5**). Beer notes (67) the curious anticipation of *Not I*. This paragraph caused some difficulty in the late draft (NB6, 79, 81), a short passage deleted when it was accommodated here.

234.3 [233]: the narrows of the menopause: the Whoroscope Notebook records (18): "shooting the rapids of the menopause" (colors flying, indeed). No source is indicated. The "pale bows of mucus" neatly bring together her voice and vagina (the lips), and the metaphor (a canoe).

234.4 [234]: was not intrinsic to its limits: that is, does not constitute ceiling, floor, or walls. The phrasing is pseudo-scholastic, hinting at the pre-Socratic doctrine of the limit, and the debate as to how the limit gave form to the boundless (*Grove Companion* 145).

234.5 [234]: contabulated: in Johnson's *Dictionary*: "a joining of boards together"; so small smelly objects, or tiny dead creatures, might be lodged within the cracks. Alternatively, Watt may have Othered his farts (Damian Love to CA).

235.1 [234]: digital emunction: using the fingers to blow the nose, as Molloy also does (25). See **#12**: "Watt snites."

235.2 [235]: little by little: by insensible degrees (**44.6**), infinitesimal stages; a recurrent motif (**64.3, 182.4, 194.4**).

235.3 [235]: curetting the nails: scraping a bodily cavity (here, the toe-nails) with a *curette* (a small scoop), to get a sample for diagnostic purposes.

235. 4 [235]: scouring the webholes: scraping the thin tissue between the toes; a detail not present in the late draft (NB6, 88).

236.1 [235]: a beautiful grey colour: without the earlier hint of red (*Watt* 37), and lacking the "unsoiled light" of the new day that ends part I (64).

236.2 [236]: the horse Joss: identified by O'Brien (33) as a print of "Boss" Croker's Derby-winning Orby, "whose name Beckett confused with Joss"; O'Brien is confused, as this sad nag is nothing of the kind. Rather, it could be from the series of horse paintings by Edwin Cooper, one of which ("Eleanor") still hangs [2004] in Foxe's pub, Glencullen. The French translation offers (246) "un grand chromo," and calls Joss "l'illustre cheval."

236.3 [236]: an inscription of great ⸮ ,: a teaser: NB6 (91) spells out: "unusual height, width and distinctiveness"; but the replacement of these with "great" and a gap leads one to assume that the missing word is *clarity*. Joss is pidgin English for "God"; compare *Murphy* (27): "a fake jossy."

236.4 [236]: The horse seemed hardly able to stand: an image of exhaustion in a world where grace and pity are denied; the horse for Beckett was often an emblem of mute, silent suffering (*Grove Companion* 258-59).

236.5 [236]: would perhaps not be always here: relating the fate of this picture to that of others in the establishment of Mr. Knott, as a term in a series (**131.1**).

236.6 [236]: the flies: compare the "puny, sluggish, torpid" flies of *Molloy* (166): "That is a strange race of flies"; or like images in "La Mouche," "Serena I," and *Texts for Nothing* 6, of flies pressed against the window pane, seeking warmth. Like the butterflies of Yeats's "Blood and the Moon," these flies suggest life reduced to its fundamental sound, any hope of transcendence denied (*Grove Companion* 199).

237.1 [236]: in the morning .: the extra spacing appeared in the galleys (G80), but was overlooked and persisted into the Olympia text; marking his Olympia copy for Grove Beckett noted the error, but it persisted into Grove, before being adjusted in Calder.

237.2 [236]: than a lark sing: thus in the galleys (G80), and in the Olympia and first Grove printings, but in marking his Grove for Calder Beckett requested the change from "sing" to "from singing." In the late draft (NB6, 95), the lark "drops" rather than "rises."

237.3 [237]: Few pennyworths gave more joy: the "penny papers" (1d. being the usual price), but equally, "to spend a penny," or visit the necessary "house of office."

237.4 [237]: innumerable semicircles: those described by the outer edge of a flying door, before it hits with a bang the wall. Watt's obstinate physicality interrupts the flying arc in much the way that the circle in the picture (**128.6**) is interrupted by the breach; the perfection of infinity is lost, and the center drains away through the breach (**130.2**; *nadir* an anagram of "drain"?), as the fetus falls from perfection in birth (Marcel Fernandes to CA) when the intrauterine state is ruptured.

238.1 [237]: taking leave of his mother: the late draft (NB6, 98) reads "wife" (but see **229.3**). Rabinovitz surmises (123) that Mr. Gorman is not the husband but the son of the fishwoman, so that were Watt to pursue his assiduities the sullen silent sot might become his stepson. A narrative blackout occurs here, the text not recording Mr. Nolan's discovery of Watt's unconscious body, his presumed solicitude or fear, nor his decision to seek help from Mr. Gorman.

238.2 [237]: a whiteness that he would not have believed possible: the galleys (G81) and Olympia text omitted "not," an error at first overlooked by Beckett, who marked it on his copy of the Olympia text for correction by Grove, where the change was made. Rabinovitz notes (138-39), that Watt's vision of the ceiling intimates Dante's looking up into the light at the end of the *Paradiso*, something he finds difficult to describe, for "it is not to be believed that any creature should penetrate with so clear an eye." Watt could not have believed it possible, "if it had been reported to him"; the late draft (NB6, 98) reads: "if he had not seen it with his own eyes."

238.3 [238]: a bone broke: a deliberate gaelicism; in the late draft (NB6, 99), "broken."

238.4 [238]: (Hiatus in MS): in the late draft (NB6, 100) the Latin phrase is added: "(nonnulla desunt)," identified by Smith (183) as an echo of Swift's *Battle of the Books*. Beckett in the galleys (G80) instructed the printers to leave more space: "Espace 2 l." He also corrected the "Ms" (G81), insisting that the "S" (as on page 241) also be capitalized.

239.1 [238]: There is not a moment to lose: the exact words of Mr. Spiro (28), as his train approaches the station. The incessant coming and going (but never staying) of trains is a constant counterpoint to the frenetic action of this scene.

239.2 [238]: the glans (Mr Gorman had a very long arm) penis: the French translation (248-49) offers a similar parenthesis: Mr. Gorman lowers the hand that holds the watch "jusqu'au niveau du membre (il avait le bras très long) viril." Beckett reconsidered the problem of the watch, presumably on a fob, and added a footnote: "(1) Et la chaîne?"

239.3 [238]: it was as he feared, later than he hoped: complementing Watt's earlier sentiment (228): "It was as he feared, earlier than he hoped."

239.4 [239]: Bloody well you know what bucket . . . pocket handkerchief: preparing his Calder text for the French translation Beckett marked this long passage for deletion; but in the event it was retained. The "water" evokes the fragment of Hölderlin, being the operative missing word in the poem (Rabinovitz 172).

239.5 [239]: Saturday: since it is not Sunday, the blasphemy (*bloody*, "by our lady") is acceptable. Like *Waiting for Godot*, or part V of Eliot's *The Waste Land*, the action may take place on Easter Saturday (Arthur arrived [**149.1**] as the paschal bells were sounding), where only the certainty is the crucifixion as the possibility of salvation is unknown.

239.6 [239]: *von Klippe zu Klippe geworfen*: a broken fragment from "Hyperions Schicksalslied" (1789) of Johann Christian Friedrich Hölderlin (1770-1843), a Schwabian poet admired by Beckett. Hölderlin suffered from schizophrenia and spent his last years in madness, Beckett later visiting the tower in Tübingen where he had been confined. The lines (not accurately cited, "Endlos" intensifying "Jahrlang") foreshadow Watt's breakdown: "Doch uns ist gegeben / Auf keine Stätte zu ruhn / Es schwinden, es fallen / Die leidenden Menschen / Blindings von einer / Stunde zur andern, / Wie Wasser von Klippe / Zu Klippe geworfen / Jahrlang ins Ungewisse hinab" ["But it is not given us to rest in any place; suffering humanity perishes and falls blindly from one hour to another, like water dashed from crag to crag year after year, down into the unknown"]. This is cited in Beckett's notes from German literature (TCD 10971/1, 31V). In the galleys (G81) he insisted that "hinab" be brought "à la ligne" (right-hand justified); Calder failed to do so. As Damian Love notes, the image of mankind doomed to restless motion and the abyss prefigures the fate of Hölderlin, soon to lapse into silence; but equally that of Watt who "feels himself going the same way" ("Art of Madness" 153). See Büttner (70).

239.7 [239]: *a sullen silent sot*: from George Farquhar's *The Beaux Stratagem* (Act II.i), the experience of Mrs. Sullen, as in the Whoroscope Notebook (71): "O Sister, Sister! if ever you marry, / beware of a sullen, silent sot, one / that's always musing but never thinks."

239.8 [239]: Is that the gob?: Watt's mouth, as opposed to a hole in his trousers (Büttner unwittingly asks [138] if it is a breech-birth). Mr. Gorman's "holt" reads in the later draft (NB6, 101) "hold."

240.1 [240]: Lady McCann: true to her traditions, catholic and military, Lady McCann arrives at the first sign of blood. She goes, she returns; "Her reasons for doing this were not known" does not appear in the late draft (NB6, 103), but for an explanation see **31.6**. One would not wish to destroy the fine ambiguity of "other meals and visitors" with a critical annunciation, but the French translation (250) is not so subtle: "où elle recevait, entre autres norritures et visites, le saint sacrement."

240.2 [240]: Arsy Cox: not identified by O'Brien; presumably a figure from Foxrock. The French translation (250) offers an interesting array: Cox les Miches; Waller l'Eventré; Miller Cacaguele; and Madame Quat'Sous le Coup Pim" ("Cette vieille pute").

240.3 [240]: Herring-gut Waller: not identified by O'Brien; "herring-gutted" defines a horse, the abdomen narrowing sharply toward the flanks.

240.4 [243]: Cack-faced Miller: identified by O'Brien (53, 350) as Ivan ("Shit-faced") Miller, of Miller & Co. Wine Merchants, Thomas Street; regarded in his youth (recalled O'Brien's informant, Mrs. Brazil) as one of the "bucks who was up to all sorts of pranks."

240.5 [244]: Mrs Penny-a-hoist Pim: a surname anticipating *How It Is*. Mr. Nolan calls her an old "put," from Fr. *putain*, "a whore." In the late draft (NB6, 103), she was Mrs. "Connemarra" (exploiting the "con").

240.6 [240]: my private burreau: a deliberate mis-spelling (*bureau* suggesting *burrow*).

241.1 [240]: still plenty of spring in my: the legible manuscript (despite the "locus illegibilitis" of NB6 [105]), reveals the missing word as "mattress" (NB6, 103). In the galleys (G82) Beckett again insisted that "MS" be capitalized. The French translation (251) transposes the jest: "Monsieur Gorman, dit-elle, qu'importe la cime chenue [the snowy top] si la verdeur demeure dans la vallée et dans—mais vous m'avez compris."

241.2 [241]: Blood now perfused the slime: an obscene birth. Watt is about to exit, if not from "the great cunt of existence" (*Malone Dies* 283), at least from the novel. His "birth," like that of Malone, is a dying into another state; for Malone, the Unnamable; for Watt, the strange figure of part III, the asylum an antechamber of death. In the late draft (NB6, 109), Mr. Farrell [Gorman] made a foolish comment, soon deleted: "'Nothing like a nice bit of blood, the first thing in the morning' said Mr Farrell, 'after a heavy night.'"

241.3 [241]: an unrefreshing night: in the manner of Chaucer's Wife of Bath; Mrs. Case was earlier (233) said to be a strange woman.

242.1 [242]: a fair glimpse: the prospect of a fair behind.

242.2 [242]: Mr Nolan murmured something: in the late draft (NB6, 109), this is spelled out: "'Tell him that one about spring and winter' he said." Mr. Gorman's "Grossly exaggerated" was not then present.

243.1 [242]: Mr Cole: not named in the late draft (NB6, 109), a gap left; thus "coal" (to make the trains come and go); in the nursery rhyme ("Old King Cole"), he calls for a light. Büttner (138) sees him as a Knott figure.

243.2 [243]: Return, my little man: Calder introduced an erroneous "McCan."

243.3 [243]: Lady McCann was less amused: in the late draft (NB6, 111), she was "less affected"; the change suggests Victorian censure.

244.1 [243]: Who is he?: the late draft reads (NB6, 115): "Who are you? said Mr Cox. / And what do you want? said Mr Waller. / Speak, said Lady McCann." Lady McCann's "Really?" (NB6, 115) finally became "Is it a white man?"

244.2 [244]: The round end or the square end?: respectively, the turntable at Harcourt Street Station and the siding at Bray, the "ends" of the Southern and Eastern Railway (the "Slow and Easy") serving Foxrock. Watt is almost at "the end of the line."

244.3 [244]: The nearer end. / The nearest end: Watt was once a university man (23); the pedantry is lost in the French translation (254-55). With the possible exception of "obscure locks" (124) and "Ruse a by" (128), this is the only time Watt has said anything.

245.1 [244]: Three and one: three shillings and one penny, there being twelve pennies to a shilling. There are vague Trinitarian overtones (Pat McCarthy to CA); but consider the Catholic accountant, who couldn't tell the difference between 3/1 and 1/3. In the "Lestrygonians" chapter of *Ulysses* Leopold Bloom pays Mr. Sweeney, the chemist, 3/1 for Molly's perfume and a cake of scented soap.

245.2 [245]: Mrs Pim: Mrs. Penny-a-hoist Pim (240). As the train did not take up a single passenger, the text insists, Watt's going is as uncertain as his coming.

245.3 [245]: a bicycle for a Miss Walker: presumably, a Swift.

245.4 [245]: a bad old bugger: as Doherty concludes (20), the comedy of *Murphy* has given way to "a metaphysical farce of cruelty" in an unconcerned and self-satisfied Irish world which can smugly proclaim that "Life isn't such a bad old bugger."

246.1 [245]: Riley's puckaun: a "puckoon," or billy-goat. Somewhere in the annals of folklore one Pat Murphy swallowed a billy-goat, to find the horns sticking out of his arse.

246.2 [246]: the long wet dream: the consequence of a biannual equinoctial nocturnal emission in vacuo, no doubt (**232.7**). Compare the Unnamable's envy (379): "some people are lucky, born of a wet dream and dead before morning."

246.3 [246]: Mr Nolan looked at Mr Case: a gesture toward a final paradigm, each looking at the others, a total of six apparently random looks {AB}, {BA}, {CB}, {CA}, {AC}, {BC} (a triangle, with Mr. Gorman at its apex), with a repeat of {CB} and {CA}.

246.4 [246]: the sky falling to the hills . . . to the plain: reversing Watt's earlier perspective (**224.2**). Rabinovitz notes (135) that the ending is underscored with Schopenhauer's sense that the beauty of the world, however beautiful it may be in the sunshine, is not enough to compensate for the misery of existence ("On the Vanity and Suffering of Life," *WWI* III.392). NB6 signs off with "Dec. 28th 1944." The "hills" were then "mountains" (NB6, 119), "rising to the sky," the vista "as pretty a picture" as "a man" might "wish to see." The sentence as finally phrased is cluttered with clichés, and the novel ends, "in the early morning light," upon the heights of bathos.

Addenda

The thirty-seven Addenda to *Watt* represent, according to Beckett, precious and illuminating material, and only fatigue and disgust prevented their incorporation (this note was added to the galleys [G86], with the instruction: "Mettre au bas de la première page des Addenda"). The order of the addenda differs in the galleys, which constitute their first record; the heading "Addenda (1)" occurs partway through (G84). The galleys, frankly, aborted the Addenda. Beckett ("When he had recovered his calm" [*Watt* 252]) corrected the mess, starting with a note before the [then] first item, and insisting that they be placed in "l'ordre indiqué: 1-2-3-4-5-6." The final ordering probably represents his intentions. Most of the fragments were considered during the genesis of the novel, but their partial presence is a problem. Like the notes to Eliot's *The Waste Land* (or Beckett's *Whoroscope*), they can neither be taken seriously nor yet be quite denied. As Ruby Cohn says (*Canon* 113), erratic and macaronic as they are, they emphasize Watt's vulnerability and failure. As enigmatic fossil records they bear witness to earlier states of creation; some, finally extinct, were too beautiful (**#22**) not to be acknowledged; but, like all records of the rocks, they pose problems for creationists. Most come from the HRHRC Notebooks; some from the Whoroscope Notebook; a few from other identified sources; and one from places unknown. See also my "Fatigue and Disgust," and the entry for "*Watt*, Addenda" in the *Grove Companion* (632-37). For convenience, citations are given by entry, rather than page.

#1: her married life one long drawsheet: "Leda, née Swan, demi-mondaine, of Enniskillen"; mother of James Quin (the original of Mr. Knott), and wife to Alexander; a faded and dejected woman who passes away after the death of her fourth Willy, her last-born, "half-heartedly pressing a crucifix of bog-oak to what was left of her bosom, in the bed in which etc., etc., her married life appearing to her in retrospect as one longdrawnout drawsheet, to the great regret of all who had known her" (NB1, 51; TS, 41). A *drawsheet*, on the natal bed, is a sheet that can be drawn without disturbing the patient (compare *Footfalls*). Of her eleven children (Willy, Willy, little Leda, Willy [Anthony in NB1], Agnes [Deirdre in NB1], Lawrence, Prisca, Zoe, Perpetua, Willy), James, an orphan from the age of thirteen, is the sole survivor. The second Willy, like the family of Mahood (*The Unnamable* 318), died of sausage-poisoning.

#2: Art Conn O'Connery: the Elder; forbear of Art and Con, and painter of the second picture in Erskine's room, that of Alexander Quin (in early drafts, in Quin's dining room). His untimely death at 81 from heart-failure brought on by (some say) a surfeit of corned beef and cabbage (NB2, 7), or a rush of blood to the head provoked by the unmasking of Parnell (TS, 91), was a loss to Rathgar. "Black velvet" (TS, 91) denotes a backdrop to a portrait, but is also a mixture of stout and champagne; in "Echo's Bones" (11), Lord Gall of Wormwood mixes himself "a stiff black velvet." George Chinnery (1774-1852), born in England, resided in Dublin from 1797 until 1802, when he sailed for India never to returned; he painted landscapes and portraits, the Dublin National Gallery owning since 1918 his *A Portrait of a Mandarin* (the

"Mandarin" in *Dream*). John Joseph Slattery was a portraitist active in Dublin between 1846 and 1858. Their names, with those of John Hallberg and the Hon. Will Pickersgall, R.A., are noted by Beckett on a working verso (NB1, 110v), where the portrait of Quin's father is by a pupil of Hallberg and that of his mother by a disciple of Chinnery (the one hung over the fireplace, the other above the sideboard). O'Brien suggests (148-50) that the portrait may include the landscape painter James Arthur O'Connor (1792-1841) and Jan "Velvet" Brueghel (1568-1625), both in the National Gallery. Beckett notes in his German Diaries (III, 21, 30/12/36; VI, 3, 17/3/37) having seen several paintings by Velvet Breughel ("primarily a painter of animals & vegetation"). In preparing his Calder text for the translation, Beckett cut Addenda #2 and #3, which are omitted from the French and German texts.

#3: the Master of the Leopardstown Halflengths: portrait painter of Mrs. Alexander Quin (TS, 93; but see **#2** for a different attribution). Leopardstown (from *Baile-na-Lobhar*, or "leperstowne," the site of a fourteenth-century lazary) is a racecourse visible from the Foxrock railway station (**29.14**). Behind this fragment lies the tale of the *Mus eventratus mcgilligani*, and the dissertation of Matthew David McGilligan, then a priest, who earns an unorthodox passage to the Holy City when he is sent away for asking after the Sacred Body when a rat has eaten it (**28.9**). In Rome he pursues his priestly vocation until one day, in the Doria Gallery, his eyes fall upon an object that opens them, "the celebrated painting by Gerald of the Nights [Gherardo delle notti, or Gerrit van Honthorst (1590-1656)] of a girl in her nightdress catching a flea by candlelight" (NB2, 7; TS, 105). No less than Stephen Dedalus (for this is an outrageous parody of the wading girl scene in *Portrait*), he becomes an Artist, and Master of Leopardstown (its gates passed daily on the way from his house at Sandyford Cross to the off-license), and of half-lengths (the upper portions of the body), though at the time of his unfortunate demise (this suggests being killed by the train, as in Joyce's "A Painful Case") he was extending his mastery of longer forms (TS, 107). The painting that initiates his epiphany, *Donna che si spulcia*, is in the Galleria Doria Pamphilj, where Beckett presumably saw it (it is no longer attributed directly to Hornthorst), but his response is shaped by Wilenski's *Dutch Art*, which introduced him to the effects of "spotlight" painting. O'Brien (364) senses a hint of the mildly erotic 16th century Flemish "Master of Female Half-Lengths."

#4: who may tell the tale: words attributed to the author's sole executrix, Madame Pompedur de Videlay-Chémoy ("Pompette"), 69ter Rue de Vieux Port, Cette [a Spanish enclave in North Africa]; a form formerly divine, recalling, in old age and in solitude, the tale of an old has-been that might have been (NB2, 37-41; TS, 115-19). The echo of Madame de Pompedur is distinct, while "Sucky Molly" of *Malone Dies* (262) is "Pompette" in *Malone meurt* (147). Beckett noted on the manuscript (NB2, 40) "Isaiah 40:12," to which the poem responds: "Who hath measured the waters in the hollow of his hand, and meted out heaven with a span, and comprehended the dust of the earth in a measure, and weighed the mountains in scales, and the hills in a balance?" The last lines reflect *Isaiah* 40:17: "All nations before him are as nothing, and they are counted to him less than nothing, and vanity." The final line in the galleys (G84) and Olympia text (at first overlooked by Beckett, then noted for correction by Grove) reads, "in worlds enclose," an inadvertent echo of "I do not like that other world" from *Ulysses*. The French version of the poem (259) ends (Ohio NB5): "dans les mots / néant enfermera?," accentuating the "Nothing" that is the theme of the early addenda. Near the end of his life (5 December 1988), Beckett wrote to Jocelyn Herbert about being "re-educated in the art of semi-upright ambulation" and going ga-ga, citing the line: "Who can tell the tale / Of the old man?" (Sean Lawlor to CA; see also **#8**).

#5: judicious Hooker's heat-pimples: in an early draft (NB2, 65; TS, 135ff), "we" (the narrator) meets Arsene and Eamon (the duck) at the foot of the stairs, in a dark passage (**#37**); they remain some time in mutual affection and content. Arsene comments: "You said that what warmed you to Hooker was his heat-pimples and his habit of never looking a person straight in the face, and that for these endearing traits you were willing to forgive him the rest" (NB2, 65; TS, 137). The Whoroscope Notebook records (81): "Hooker's heatspots (I. W.)"; preparing his Calder text for the French translation Beckett noted "Walton." This is Izaak Walton's *The Life of Mr. Richard Hooker, the Author of those Learned Books of the Laws of Ecclesiastical Polity* (London, 1675). Walton, having sung the praises of "Judicious Hooker," suggests that visitors to the Parsonage of Bourne might find: "an obscure, harmless man, a man in poor Cloaths, his Loyns usually girt in a course Gown, or Canonical Coat; of a mean stature, and stooping, and yet more lowly in the thoughts of his Soul; his Body being worn out, not with Age, but Study, and Holy Mortification; and his Face full of Heat-pimples, begot by his unactivity and sedentary life" (Rabinovitz 164). The phrase, "judicious Hooker," derives from the poem preceding the *Life*, "Hail, Sacred Mother, British Church, all hail," stanza 3: "Of Reverend and Judicious Hooker sing" (Walton 157); this echoes the Epitaph "long since presented to the World, in memory of Mr. Hooker, by Sir *William Cooper*, who also built him a fair Monument in *Borne Church*, and acknowledges him to have been his Spiritual Father" (227):

> Though nothing can be spoke worthy of his fame,
> Or the remembrance of that precious name,
> Judicious Hooker, though this cost be spent
> On him, that hath a lasting Monument
> In his own Books, yet ought we to express,
> If not his Worth, yet our Respectfulness.

#6: limits to part's equality with whole: the conversation in Quin's hallway takes a pseudo-mathematical turn, the point being that the relationship between the lamentable tale of error, folly, waste and ruin (Ltefwr), on the one hand, and life (L) and experience (E), on the other, challenges the Euclidean axiom that the whole is greater than any of its parts. "Ltefwr" is alternatively "X" (compare *Texts for Nothing* 7 [129], "that paradigm of human kind"). "We" offers Arsene (NB2, 72-73) several equations to demonstrate that X (or Otefwr) "equals life equals life plus experience equals life plus twice experience equals life plus thrice experience equals life plus ninetynine times experience equals (if we face the facts squarely in the face) any number of lives less one times experience equals any number of lives less nothing times the sum total of two lives and any old number of lives less one times experience all divided by two" (TS, 145). The equation is repeated, with squares and cubes in place of "two" and "three," only to conclude that experience raised to the power of any number of lives comes to much the same, particularly when the values are one (unity) or nothing. In other words, experience adds nothing to life, a conclusion that appalls "we":

> Arsene said nothing.
> "Surely you dont [sic] mean to suggest that" we said. "That would be too appalling to contemplate."
> "No" said Arsene, raising his head and hanging it, "no, I wouldn't go as far as that."
> "There are limits to the part's equality with the whole" we said. "Overstep them and chaos is bound to ensue."

#7: dead calm . . . to naught gone: as in the early drafts (NB2, 81; TS, 153), but there with a capital "D" for "dead" and a final comment: "Highly remarkable." The talk between Arsene and "we" had turned to "the unconscious mind! What a subject for a short story" (NB2, 79), and the attempt to go "deep down in those palaeozoic profounds, midst mammoth Old Red Sandstone phalli and Carboniferous pudenda . . . The upper Silurian! The lower Silurian! The truth! The truth! [insert on NB2, 78] . . . the Cambrian! the uterine! the pre-uterine"; until emerging in "the agar-agar [the universal jelly] . . . close eyes, all close, great improvement, pronounced improvement" (TS, 149-53). The details are taken directly from a "Table of Geological Eras" in the Whoroscope Notebook (62v). Earlier (NB1, 18), Quin had a feeling of unaccustomed change, as when in the stillness a murmur ceases: "My God" said Quin "I must have been meditating." This is the geology of consciousness, or, in French, *conscience*, suggesting the strata of guilt and repression. Compare Murphy's experience of non-Newtonian motion; or Malone's experience of tumult followed by calm, from naught come, to naught gone; or Clov's sense, not unlike Arsene's, on a day no more or less remarkable than any other, that something has changed.

#8: Bid us sigh: from the early drafts (NB2, 63; TS, 135), "we" making a brisk remark about it being time for us to be getting on, then standing irresolutely at the foot of the stairs, "hearkening to far-off iterant words, now faint, now clear, as though borne by a fitful wind, and watching with helpless eye their shadowy gyre." As Harvey notes (391), these lines are from James Thomson's "To Fortune." They are preceded by: "For ever, Fortune, wilt thou prove / An unrelenting foe to Love, / And, when we meet a mutual heart / Come in between, and bid us part." This is the complaint of an unhappy lover, but anticipates Arsene's paean to "The Seasons" (*Watt* 47). By dropping Thomson's question mark Beckett turns the quatrain into an imperative ("You do not reply, I see," said Arsene). The period ending the third line was inadvertent, but has not been corrected in any current text. Writing to Barney

Rosset (21 November 1957), Beckett noted: "I suggested to him [Alan Schneider, about to produce *Endgame*] we might replace Clov's song by the Thomson quatrain in the *Watt* Addenda. This would require another music. If he agrees I could ask John [his musician cousin, John Beckett] to do a setting." Nothing came of the suggestion, but the verse was part of his being. In his outline of "Human Wishes" (NB III, n.p.; 1938), Beckett cited the first two lines; and 49 years later (17 January 1987) to Mary Manning he echoed them thus: "Bid us sigh on from day to day / And will [*sic*] & wish the soul away."

#9: Watt learned to accept: on the final page of NB5 (182), Beckett jotted down details ("Notes") to be included, though in practice none was, directly. Instead, several **(#9-#13)** became part of the Addenda, precisely as recorded. Preparing his Calder text for the French translation Beckett noted in the margin "voir p 77"; this refers to the passage (page 80 in the Grove text): "Watt learned towards the end of this stay in Mr Knott's house to accept that nothing had happened, that a nothing had happened, learned to bear it and even, in a shy way, to like it. But then it was too late" (**80.2**). "Watt learned" and "to accept" are underlined in Beckett's Jupiter text (77).

#10: Note that Arsene's declaration gradually came back to Watt: Beckett's reminder to himself, as recorded at the end of NB5 (182): "Part 2 (p. 15 - typescript). Insert that Arsene's declaration came back little by little to Watt." This marks the decision to tell the tale erratically through Watt (later by Sam), a perspective not originally present.

#11: One night Watt goes on roof: this he does not do in the novel, but in the drafts Quin's house is described: "There was a ground floor, a first floor and a second floor. And access to the roof was provided by a sky-light in its midst, for those who wished to go on the roof" (TS, 81). At the end of NB5 (182): "Part III. One night Watt goes out on the roof." Compare *Dream* (26-27), where Belacqua looks up to the night sky stretched like a skin, and dreams of his head tearing a great rip in the taut sky, of climbing out above the deluge, into a quiet zone above the nightmare.

#12: Watt snites: from the Anglo-Saxon *snȳtan*, to blow the nose. Beckett wrote in the manuscript (NB5, 182): "Part IV. Watt snites in his toilet paper." Compare *Watt*, 117: "But Watt never used a handkerchief." The word (from Johnson's *Dictionary*) is in the Whoroscope Notebook (83v), but was eliminated from the description of Watt's nasal masturbation (234-35).

#13: Meals: the drafts comment: "~~Out of sheer *Schadenfreude* simply~~ In order to annoy the table, Quin changed his seat at each repast. He even carried this disposition so far, on days of ill-humour, as to change his seat between courses" (TS, 23; rewriting NB1, 35). Quin's activity with the chalk may reflect Horace's "Creta, an carbone notandi?" ["Are they to be marked with chalk or charcoal?"], i.e., are the days happy or not? (*Satires* 2.3.246). Quin's erratic ways anticipate the equally mysterious moves of Mr. Knott.

#14: the maddened prizeman: Arsene, who, but for the boil on his bottom might have been the recipient of the Madden Prize (**46.7**). Quin had two true and faithful servants, Erskine and Arsene, a butler-valet and cook-general: "The butler's name was Erskine, pleasantly corrupted into Foreskin by his closer companions, and he was the Madden— or, as some would have it, the Maddened-Prizeman" (NB1, 85; TS, 67). Arsene's name is "affectionately corrupted" into "But-Not-Heard." Neither had taken part in the Great War, nor Ireland's fight for freedom. Other drafts had Arthur, then valet, as a Madden prizeman (NB1, 27; TS, 15). Mercier and Camier (chapter 3) meet in the train a ravaged old man whose name is Madden and whose theme is fornication. In preparing his Calder text of *Watt* for the French translation Beckett noted "Madden P"; but the note was deleted from the published text.

#15: the sheet of dark water: in the early drafts, a silence ensues in the midst of a conversation between Quin and his valet, Arthur, concerning Quin's difficulties in finding his way about the house, in particular the location of the lavatories (**203.3**). Quin, about to descend the stairs and meet a strange man (Hackett), listens to the empty echo of his words and the nothingness behind them (NB1, 31; TS, 19).

#16: never been properly born: testifying to an early impulse behind the novel, Quin's sense of the nothingness of his own being. Beckett noted on an early verso (NB1, 76): "Quin never properly born"; he expanded this in later drafts (NB1, 83, 85; TS, 65): "The plain fact of the matter seems to be, that Quin had never been properly born. / The five dead little brothers support this view, as do the five dead little sisters. / His relatively great age, and comparative freedom from grave bodily disease, confirm this conception. / For all the good that frequent departures out of Ireland had done him, he might as well have stayed there." The sentiment was one of Beckett's favorites. It echoes his sense of the embryonic self, that *être manqué*, and his fascination with the comment made by Jung after a Tavistock lecture (1935), about a little girl whose dreams of death revealed that: "She had never been born entirely" (see *Footfalls*, "Rough for Radio II," and *Not I*).

#17: the foetal soul is full grown: the themes of the unborn soul and nothingness continue in the drafts (NB1, 71; TS, 55). An unnumbered chapter is sub-headed "The Nothingness" and records: "The feeling of nothingness, born in Quin with the first beat of his heart, if not before, died in him with the last, and not before. And between these acts it waned not, neither did it wax, but its strength at its beginning was as its strength at its end, and its strength at its middle as its strength at its beginning. The foetal soul is full-grown (Cp. Cangiamila's Sacred Embryology and the De Synodo Diocesana, Bk. 7, Chap. 4, Section 6, of Pope Benedict XIV)." Francesco Emanuele Cangiamila (1702-63) was a Sicilian theologian whose celebrated work, *L'Embriologia sacra* (1745) concerns such matters as Caesarian birth and the problems of salvation in difficult circumstances, teachings noted approvingly by Benedict. "Embryology" is spelled correctly on the galleys (G86), but the mistake entered the Olympia text and persisted into Grove, despite Beckett marking it for correction; in marking his Grove text for Calder Beckett again requested the change. It is unlikely that Beckett had read the *Embriologia sacra*, or Benedict's *De Synodo Diocesana libri tredecim* (1748), a summa of ecclesiastical traditions from the Synod of 1725, for his learned reference is wrong: Cangiamila and the problem of uterine baptism is discussed at XL.vii.xiii in Benedict, then at VII.v.iv, in a tone not unlike that of the Messrs. de la Sorbonne in *Tristram Shandy* I.xx. This pedantry is excessive, but illustrates the danger of apparently exact details leading into blind alleys—precisely Watt's experience.

#18: sempiternal penumbra: darkness with a beginning but no end, as the "rosa sempiterna" of Dante's *Paradiso* XXX.124, the light of Paradise (I.76). Compare Quin's coal-hole: "In the coal-hole, high and dry, lay the coal, the slag, the coke, the anthracite, the logs and the kindling, and there dangled also there, in the sempiternal penumbra, suspended from stout ~~nails~~ pegs inserted in the wall for no other purpose, the coal-hammer, the coal-chisel, the coal-shovel, the hatchet and the wedge" (NB1, 107; TS 85).

#19: for all the good that frequent departures out of Ireland had done him, he might just as well have stayed there: except for the later "just," as recorded in NB1 (85); see **#16**, above. Compare Descartes's retreat to the *poêle* (1619) in book I of the *Méthode*, where he reflects that this succeeded much better than if he had "never departed from his country or his books" (Rabinovitz, *Development* 125).

#20: a round wooden table: this mahogany table, described in the drafts (TS, 89), is like Quin's round bed, which survives into the novel (207). First in the bed and later, under the table, "Quin began the fatal journey towards the light of day" (NB1, 35; TS, 25). In NB2 (3) the table "~~occupied the centre of the room~~"; this was crossed out and replaced by: "filled the middle ground." The change reflects a move toward an artistic perspective. A "frustrum" is a disappointed cone, a truncated conical solid.

#21: zitto! zitto! das nur das Publikum nichts merke!: It. & Ger. "Hush, hush, so that the public may notice nothing." Not in the drafts of *Watt*, but quoted in the Whoroscope Notebook (83) with the "conspiracy of silence against Schop__er__." In his Calder copy, annotated for translation into French, Beckett added: "Dies ist vergleicht ihre ganze Politik," noting at the bottom of the page (249) its source in Schopenhauer's *Über die 4fache* [vierfache] *Wurzel des Satzes vom zureichenden Grunde*, Chap. 4 ["Concerning the four-fold root of the Principle of Sufficient Reason"]; adding "against the 'Philosophie Professoren' who ignored his prizewinning essay on the freedom of the Will."

#22: on the waste, beneath the sky: a haunting passage that goes back to the sense of Nothingness (the sky above, the waste below) of Quin's first awareness and of which his life partook. This is the primal scene of the novel (NB1, 69-79; TS, 61). The sentiment arises partly from Leopardi, the typescript noting explicitly (49) his "Night Song of the Wandering Shepherd of

Asia" and "Desert Flower," both of which invoke the littleness of the human spirit against the immensity of the desert and waste. Quin lacks awareness of "something else" that was neither "suprajacent sky nor subjacent waste," for the "sense of adjacence" was wanting in him. That lack of differentiation between sky, waste, and Quin is accentuated, but the passage from "[T]he dark colour was so dark" to "as to defy identification as such" was added later to the typescript (60v). That scene was "to say the least lurid" (61). The "further peculiarities" assumed minor changes, the most important being the evolution from a "landscape" (NB1, 79) to a "soul-landscape"; the elimination of "pleasantly" from "The temperature was pleasantly warm"; the change of (the waste, the sky) "heaved up and down" (NB1) to "fell and rose" (TS, 69); and the simplification of "Complete silence reigned" (NB1) and "Silence reigned supreme" (TS) to "All was silent" (final text). The identification of Quin with the consciousness that was to become Watt (rather than Knott) is marked.

#23: Watt will not / abate one jot: the poem exists in draft form (NB3, 26), and in the typescript (205), in a form virtually identical save for initial capitalization, the substitution of "Johnny" for "Watt," the phrase "Naught's habitat" in line 7 ("Knott" had not yet materialized), and the final curiosity (*Watt* 250), "abate one tot" (this appeared in the drafts and typescript, then into galleys (G85) and the Olympia and Grove editions; but Beckett when marking his Grove text for Calder requested the correction). The narrator was then a small man called Johnny, who visits Quin's establishment and converses with Arsene in the hall. The subject of the poem was the meeting in the evening at Quin's house, the record of which was to be published in a book called *A Clean Old Man* ("'A little gritty, perhaps' we said" [anticipating the joke about a policeman in *Waiting for Godot*]). Destined to become Book of the Week in 2080, its praises are sung in the leap-year song, "Fifty two point two eight five seven one four two," in the novel transferred to the indifferent mixed choir (**34.1**). The sentiment derives from Milton's sonnet (XXII) to Cyriack Skinner:

> Cyriak, this three years' day these eyes, though clear
>   To outward view of blemish or of spot,
>   Bereft of light thir seeing have forgot;
>   Nor to thir idle orbs doth sight appear
> Of Sun or Moon or Star throughout the near,
>   Or man or woman. Yet I argue not
>   Against Heaven's hand or will, nor bate a jot
>   Of heart and hope; but still bear up and steer
> Right onward. What supports me, dost thou ask?
>   The conscience, Friend, to have lost them overplied
>   In liberty's defense, my noble task,
> Of which all Europe talks from side to side.
>   This thought might lead me through the world's vain mask
>   Content though blind, had I no better guide.

#24: die Merde hat mich wieder: a parody of Goethe's "die Erde hat mich wieder!" ["the earth has me again!"], from *Faust* (Part 1, "Nacht" 784), after

Faust, about to take poison, hears the Easter bells and listens to the heavenly choirs; he obeys their summons to return to life. Beckett recorded the original line in his "Black Notebook" (BIF 5003, 59). The macaronic "Merde" appears in the Whoroscope Notebook (36), and might be dated a little after "2/10/36" (as on the verso of 33). The detail is not mentioned in the *Watt* drafts, but its link to both ditches and heavenly choirs is manifest.

#25: pereant qui ante nos nostra dixerunt: L. "let those who used our words before us perish," a dictum attributed to St. Jerome (his commentary on *Ecclesiastes* against the ancients who stole his best thoughts), who took it from Aelius Donatus (a 4th century grammarian), who based it on a line from Terence. Beckett found it in Bartlett's *Familiar Quotations,* attributed to an anonymous author, and he copied it into the Whoroscope Notebook (19): "Jerome relates that his preceptor Donatus, explaining Terence's Nihil est dictum quod non sit dictuur prius railed at ancients for pinching his best thoughts: Pereant qui ante nos nostra dixerunt." It does not appear in the drafts of *Watt*, but in a marginal note in his Calder text, prepared for the French translation, Beckett retraced the trail from Jerome to Donatus to Terence.

#26: Second picture in Erskine's room: an extract taken almost verbatim from NB2 (9-13) and the typescript (93-97). The portrait is that of Mr. Alexander Quin, father of James (see **#2**); Master of Arts (Galway) and Bachelor of Music (Kentucky) (NB1, 51; TS, 41). The unlikely phrase, "which Watt has no difficuly [sic] in identifying," earlier read: "which expert inspection through a firstrate magnifying-glass had identified" (TS, 93); "prolongs pavilion of left ear" there read, "prolonged the pavilion of his left ear" (a "pavilion" is also the bell of a wind instrument). Heath Lees (23) shows how the manuscript change from the first inversion of C major to the second is what creates the effect of "faint cacophony of remote harmonics stealing over dying accord." "Jesuit tactility" implies the art of Murillo, or the Spanish school; "Heem" is identified in NB2 (9) as "Heem the Younger," not Jan Davidszoon de Heem (1606-84), but his lesser-known brother, David Davidszoon (1610-69); for "O'Connor," see **#2**. "Cacophony" (Fr. *caca,* "shit") picks up, perhaps, the "hard stool." "Pectoral" denotes muscles of chest, responsible for movement of the arms; "subaxillary" those of the lower arm; and "hypogastrial" those of the lower stomach. The galleys (G85) introduced an extra, surrealist line after "scattered in ears": "with every filthy, and seeds might have been scattered in ears"; there overlooked by Beckett, but the garbled line was struck out when he marked his Olympia text for Grove. The "Latin quote" was never specified, but the typescript noted: "Traces of similar ablution invaded the hairless occiput" (TS, 93). The fragment crucially suggests that Quin/Knott, like all around him, may equally be serial (**#29**). This painting moves from Quin's drawing-room to Erskine's bedroom, contradicting the observation (*Watt* 128) that the only object of note therein is the enigmatic picture of the circle and dot.

#27: like a thicket flower unrecorded: in the drafts (NB3, 155; TS, 298) this is part of an elaborate discussion about the mating possibilities between Irish Setters and Palestine Retrievers (**111.1**), to produce the right kind of famished dog; leading to an enormous spectacle mounted (as it were) by the Lynch family, charging spectators for admission; and speculating as to where such customs may have originated (Eire? Pelasgia? the Hardy country?); only to conclude: "Nothing is known, as far as can be ascertained. Did it, as age succeeded age, and misery changed name, die only to revive, revive only to die, perhaps several, perhaps many, perhaps very many times? Or in unbroken sequence never cease, but in its being steadfastly stand fast, with greater vigour now and now with less, somewhere eternally and never nowhere, from its inception to the present time, and like a thicket flower unrecorded?" Despite the apparent echo of Gray's *Elegy*, "Full many a flower is born to blush unseen," the more immediate image is Leopardi's "La ginesta, o il fiore del desierto" ["The Broom, or Desert Flower"] (**#22**).

#28: Watt's Davus complex (morbid dread of sphinxes): in the Whoroscope Notebook (24), but not in the drafts of *Watt*. In Terence's *Andria* (194), a slave quips: "Dáuos sum, non Oédipus" ["I am Davus, not Oedipus"], as he feigns ignorance of matters amorous. In his review of the poetry of Denis Devlin (*transition* 27 [April-May 1938]: 289-90), Beckett in defence of the enigmatic in art condemned "the gogetters, the gerrymanders, Davus and the morbid fear of sphinxes, solution clapped on problem like a snuffer on a candle, the great crossword public on all its planes." The allusion is to the questions put to the Sphinx by Oedipus, used by Schopenhauer as an emblem of "the riddle of the world" (*WWI* II.384). The spelling of "sphinxes" appeared without comment in the galleys (G85) and Olympia text; but when marking his Olympia text for Grove Beckett requested "sphinges" (the pedantic plural). This change was not made by Grove, but Beckett again requested it, and Calder obliged. Hence the French translation (265): "complexe de Davus de Watt (crainte morbide des sphynges)."

#29: One night Arthur came to Watt's room: with **#22**, the most important of the Addenda, as it encapsulates many early details from the Notebooks and touches lightly on the novel's central themes. The episode, with variations to reflect the change of protagonist, is present in all the early drafts: an encounter between Quin and an old man in Quin's garden; the implication of the published addendum is that Arthur has been mistaken for Quin (Knott). Quin takes pleasure ("Thank you, Boss") in reflecting that the "dewy sward" is his (NB1, 21; NB3, 1; TS, 11); "not" (compare Mr. Hackett's sentiments about "his" bench) was a later negation. Some of the dialogue (working for Quin's father as a lad, cleaning the boots) was earlier given to Mr. Hackett (NB1, 43; TS, 30). The passage anticipates Watt's encounter with Knott in the garden (*Watt* 145), and permits the joke about the passing shrub, or bush, which proves to be a hardy laurel; the earliest draft (NB1, 21) had quoted Virgil's *Georgics* II.132-33: "Et si non alium late iacterat odorem, laurus erat" ["most like a laurel to view, and were a laurel but for the difference of wide-wafted fragrance"]; compare *How It Is* (35): "distant perfume of laurel felicity." The bush, or shrub, was said to be "not a monkey-puzzle" (NB1, 23).

In NB5 (93ff.), Arthur is called "Martin," and the late revision (otherwise similar to the published text) adds the crucial final reference to the Knott family and its serial nature, a surprisingly late development. An error, "that is was not a rush" (line 16), introduced in the galleys (G84) but overlooked by Beckett and so present in the Olympia text, persisted into the Grove despite Beckett's marking it for correction ("that it was not a rush"); Beckett marked it again on his Grove text for Calder. This pattern of error is reflected in "when I was a boy" (line 25), introduced into galleys (G84) and thence into the Olympia text, marked by Beckett for correction but no change made by Grove, again requested and finally corrected in Calder to "when you was a boy." The French translation (266-66) calls the rush "un genêt d'Espagne," and has the *vieillard* describe himself and Arthur as each "un petit merdeur"; but retains the "laurier hardi" byplay and is otherwise faithful to the original. This finale offers a further arabesque on the theme of relative immortality, expressed in *Proust* (21) in terms of the whisky's grudge against the decanter, and in "Draff" (175) as the words of the rose to the rose: "No gardener has died, comma, within rosaceous memory" (**57.6**). Watt might once have been pleased to think that Mr. Knott, too, was serial, "in a vermicular series"; but he is an old rose now, and indifferent to the gardener. See **131.7**, for this as an argument against Spinoza's immanent God.

#30: Watt looking as though nearing end of course of injections of sterile pus: this cheerful vision appears nowhere in the drafts; compare the inoculation of anthropoid apes in *Murphy* (50). In the Calder text, and hence the French and German translations, this inexplicably follows the descant (**#34**).

#31: das fruchtbare Bathos der Erfahrung: Ger. "the fruitful bathos of experience." From Kant's *Prolegomena zu einer jeden künfigen Metaphysik die als Wissenschaft wird auftreten können* ["Prolegomena to Any Future Metaphysics That Will Be Able to Present Itself as a Science"], where Kant attacks a reviewer who had misunderstood his *Critique of Pure Reason*, and had referred to it as an example of the higher idealism. In reply, Kant uses "Bathos" in its Greek sense of a deep place, in contrast with "High towers, and metaphysically tall men like them, round both of which there is commonly a lot of wind." The citation can be misread (as Beckett perhaps intended) as "Pathos," or suffering (Rabinovitz 166, 173). It appears in the Whoroscope Notebook (51v), between two extracts from Mauthner's *Beiträge der Sprache*, an accidental juxtaposition. In preparing his Calder text for the French translation Beckett noted in the margin: "Kant."

#32: faede hunc mundum intravi, anxius vixi, perturbatus egredior, causa causarum miserere mei: L. "in filth I entered this world, anxious I lived, troubled I go out of it, on account of these causes have mercy on me." Cited in the Whoroscope Notebook (38) as the "Last words of Aristotle." From Lemprière's *Dictionary* (the entry for "Aristotle"), but the mis-transcription ("faede" for "fœde") is Beckett's own.

#33: change all the names: in NB3 (62), Beckett instructs himself: "Walterise selon P. 81," i.e., change all the names, e.g., from "Arsene" or "Erskine" to

"Walter," and from "Walter" to "Vincent," in accordance with his later practice. In the passage that follows he does so (**59.2**). The note encapsulates a moment of textual metamorphosis.

#34: descant heard by Watt on way to station (IV): no such mention of a "descant" is made in the published novel; but Beckett was too fond of the piece to let it die away. Originally included in the drafts, it was attributed to a "Distant Mixed Fifth-rate Choir," heard by those in Quin's passage-way waiting for anything "of note." The full rendition of the descant appears in NB2 (34-36), with a condensed, final version in the typescript (115), in such a way as to suggest the intricacy of the verbal composition. No music is provided, but the bass's attempts to keep up ("phew!") anticipate his strain with the Mixed Choir that largely supplanted it (**33.8**). Heath Lees suggests (9) that the numeral "(IV)" is added to prevent the reader confusing it with the threne of chapter One; he argues that although the descant does not in fact appear in chapter IV there is a strong implication that the song is sung, but Watt, by now so much out of his tune with his world, does not hear it (**223.4**). Beckett plays with a version in French (NB2, 35): "De tout notre coeur / Respire tête un peu / Souprenand à l'écart / L'air tenu / des joies finies / de tristesse finissantes / sombrement un peu / l'air tenu."

#35: parole non ci appulcro: It. "I will add no words to embellish it." Susan Senneff notes (144) that this derives from Dante's *Inferno* VII.60, the irony being that Virgil, by describing the corruption of avaricious cardinals, is unable to remain silent. Beckett cites it in the Whoroscope Notebook (69). Preparing his Calder text for the French translation Beckett noted in the margin: "Dante." In the drafts (NB3, 84), the phrase appeared near a duet to be sung or chanted by Erskine and Watt (or Johnny, as he then was) after they have prepared the poss of Mr. Quin. The words that might have embellished the hiatus are the celebrated ones from Voltaire's *Candide*: "O che sciagura d'essere senza [coglioni]!" (**8.4**, **85.7**).

#36: Threne heard by Watt: one of the few Addenda directly related to the final text, by the footnote (33): "(1) What, it may be enquired, was the music of this threne? What at least, it may be demanded, did the soprano sing?" Answer: the song beginning "Fifty two point two" (**34.1**, **35.1**), the part for the soprano given here. No reference to this threne (neither verbal phrase nor musical note) appears in the galleys, but the Olympia text introduced it with an erroneous "on way for station," which Beckett on his copy marked for correction by Grove, where the change was made. When Beckett returned the corrected proofs, he pleaded to John Calder (12 February 1963) to set the threne in the proper place, but despite this it was overlooked (a large blank space was left). Beckett elected to delete this addendum when preparing his Jupiter text for the French translation; but he earlier told John Fletcher (21 November 1964) that the omission was "Unintentional on my part. No alterations in reprints, except spelling mistakes." As Heath Lees notes (7), the music in the "Addenda" is tortuous. Some editions (Olympia, Grove, Italian) give the complete sentence with the music; others (Calder, Swedish, Spanish) retain the introductory sentence but omit the music; yet others (Minuit, German) omit both; while the Norwegian translation retains both but "corrects" the "mistakes" of key and time-signature. Lees contends (21) that Watt hears the music in D-flat minor; but the Addendum is in the key of B-minor (as the great mass by Bach), a tone lower, which corresponds (Lees suggests) to how Murphy (who hears a tone too low) and Watt (who shares that infirmity) would have pitched it. The last phrase, he notes (22), is an implied inversion of the main phrase which then "careers off into the leading note of the key, setting up a contradictory effect of expectancy on what should be the final cadence, and so . . . destroying the validity of the notional governing pitch." Susan Senneff, more simply but with less precision, analyses the "annoying monotony" of the threne in terms of its musical nonsense and in relation to Watt's movement from naught to silence, his severance from the world of meaningful sounds.

#37: no symbols where none intended: on page 80 of the Grove Press edition Watt thinks about Arsene, and wonders what has become of the duck (**80.6**), the only final mention of this bird (see **45.6**). This is a truly magnificent fossil, in a state of perfect preservation, but one that finally disappeared (at Beckett's instigation) from the Calder edition. It can be reassembled only with reference to the manuscripts (NB2, 55ff; TS, 127ff), the encounter between the narrator (Johnny Watt, who refers to himself as "we") and two bipeds: one featherless, a maddened prize-man named Arsene; the other feathered, an India Runner Duck named Eamon. A long conversation ensues in the darkened hallway of Mr. Quin's house, of which this is the conclusion: on the uttering of the sentiment, "Each in his different way, all are in the dark," a match is struck, and burns bravely, until its fire reaches the fingers and it is dropped; whereupon "it continued for a little while bravely to burn, till it could burn no longer, bravely or otherwise. Then it went out" (NB3, 11; TS, 183). In that brief light, much is revealed: "the dark in which we were, each in his or her own way, and Eamon and Arsene and the passage and the stairs and the bells and the newell—and we." It is too easy: a little light in the big dark; a feathered and featherless biped; a dark passage; purgatorial stairs (a "newell" is the still point of a turning staircase); hints of the Eucharist in distant bells. But "we" remains in the dark. In a context so insistently demanding symbolic interpretation, in the presence of details so often used to translate consciousness into meaning (**73.5**), all Watt can say is: "no symbols where none intended" (in the French translation, 268, "honni soit qui symboles y voit"). That phrase, present from the earliest revisions (NB3, 11; TS, 185), by a strange synecdoche stands for the entire novel.

Addendum 1:

Textual Changes and Errata in the Major Editions of *Watt*

The list on the following pages assumes that:

(1) "marked on O for G" indicates a change made on Beckett's personal copy of the Olympia Press edition for the Grove Press first edition; and will assume, unless otherwise stated, that the error or peculiarity was present in the galleys

(2) "marked on G for C" indicates a change on Beckett's personal copy of the Grove first edition; and assumes, unless otherwise stated, that the changes indicated were made in the Calder (Jupiter) edition

(3) basic errors "marked on G for C" that make no reference to O assume that the mistake was overlooked by Beckett in his somewhat casual proofing of the Olympia galleys, unless there is some indication to the contrary; "changed in C" (or words to that effect) indicate that the change first appeared in the Calder edition, with or without Beckett's sanction, but without any specific change noted in Beckett's Grove text

(4) any changes made are assumed to affect all editions subsequent to that change; exceptions are noted specifically

(5) figures in bold indicate that the details are discussed further in the designated note; bolded figures in [square] brackets are not thus discussed

(6) oddities from the galleys, the French translation, or other sources are noted only when representing a significant change of textual emphasis

(7) despite differences of pagination, the Olympia Traveller's Series text ("OT") is subsumed beneath the Olympia; citations of the Grove (including the Evergreen) are to the first edition, but the many "silent" corrections (apparently added to the second reprinting) are noted

(8) changes introduced in Calder are invariably reproduced in Picador (P) and (with obvious errors sometimes corrected) in most translations

(9) pagination is given by page and line to the Grove and Calder editions, the Olympia matching the Grove (except between 45-64, where, after a major deletion, the difference is one extra page in the Olympia [square brackets])

(10) pp. 137-38 and 161-92 of Beckett's personal Grove Press copy, which he marked up for the Calder edition, are missing

(11) consistent stylistic changes, such as Calder's use of "Mr." rather than "Mr" (note the curiosity of British usage in the American text, and vice versa) and repeated patterns of hyphenation, are noted only with respect to significant details or as a first instance of a tendency

(12) "in" in my comments means in the text; "on" means added to the text.

Page	Olympia Press	Grove Press first edition		Calder (Jupiter)		Cross-reference & Comment
Part I	1	I		I		
7:8	He knew were not [OT, 7: He knew they were not]	He knew were not [He knew they were not]	5:7	He knew were not	7.1	O (but not OT) has Arabic 1
					7.4	"they" added silently in G reprints; not noted for C; and omitted in C
8:21	said (1) Mr Hackett	said (1) Mr Hackett	6:11	said[1] Mr. Hackett	8.3	different citation in C & P
8:28	three quarters	three quarters	6:17	three-quarters	[8]	hyphen added in C
9:22	past, oh not the last [OT, 9: pass, oh not the last]	pass, oh not the last	7:12	pass, oh not the last	9.5	O corrected in G but new error made; marked on G for change in C
14:25	carpetrods	carpetrods	12:17	carpet-rods	[14]	hyphen added in C
18:37	It is true—	It is true—	16:29	It is true. . . .	[18]	C prefers the ellipsis to the dash
19:12	[Line omitted]	That depends where he got on, said Mr Nixon.	17:8	That depends where he got on, said Mr. Nixon	19.3	line restored in G; added by hand on SB's copy of O
21:7	[OT, 20: omitted] the accoutrement	the accoutrement	19:8	his accoutrement	21.1	"accowtrement" in galleys; "his" introduced in C
23:17, 19	boot	boot	21:15, 17	boot	23.2	galleys change "shoe" to "boot"
26:13	Was it possible that this was his hat.	Was it possible that this was his hat.	24:14	Was it possible that this was his hat?	26.1	question mark introduced in C
27:31	tonsure	tonsure	25:32	tonsure	27.7	galleys change "ringworm" to "tonsure"
28:26	Lourdes [at the left]	Lourdes [at the left]	26:28	Lourdes [at left, not indented]	28.8	address at right in OT (30)
29:21	mur-mured	mur-mured	27:23	mur-murmured	29.13	error introduced in C
31:17	gentlemen [OT, 33: gentleman]	gentlemen	29:21	gentleman	31.4	marked in O for G but not changed; marked on G for C
32:33	on his bum	on his bum	31:4	on his bum	32.9	galleys change "head" to "bum"
33:31	the high pouting hemlock	the high pouting hemlock	32:3	the high pouting hemlock	33.6	error introduced in C
33:35	a mixed choir (1)	a mixed choir (1)	31:7	a mixed choir[1]	33.8	different citation in C & P
34	[Mixed choir]			marked on C for deletion	34.1	deleted in Fr. translation

35:1	Fifty-one point one	Fifty-one point one	33:24	Fifty-one point one	35.1	error introduced in galleys but not corrected in any current text; C leaves no spacing about the verse
39:8	to-night	tonight	37:21		[39]	C deletes hyphen
39:14	short statement:	short statement.	37:25	short statement.	39,2	period substituted in C
45:25	But what is this [OT, 49: retains poem]	[text deleted; gap remains]	44:5	[text deleted; no gap]	45.6	major deletion after O for G; O & G differ until page 67
46:15 [47:15] nor a trust [OT, 51: not a trust]	nor a trust	not a trust	44:30		46.6	marked on O for G but not changed; marked on G for C
47:2 [48:2] mothers, fathers, fathers' [OT, 51: mothers', fathers, fathers']	mothers' fathers' fathers'	mothers' fathers' fathers'	45:19		46.11	marked on O for G
47:18 [48:18] oillamp	oillamp	oil-lamp	45:34		[47]	silently changed in C
47:25 [48:25] a third time	a third time	a third time	46:6		47.14	Fr: translation has "2nd"
48:5 [49:5] Like Tyler?	Like Tyler?	Like Tyler?	46:24		48.2	Fr: "Comme la machine à vapeur?"
48:10 [49:10] successives	successives	successive	46:28		48.3	marked on O for G
49:20 [50:24] scatch their names [OT, 54: scratch]	scatch their names	scratch their names	48:8		48.4	marked on O for G
52:12 [53:12] vitamens [OT, 55: vitamins]	vitamens	vitamins	50:33		52.1	marked on O for G but not changed; marked on G for C
52:25 [53:25] coprophile	coprophile	coprophile	51:12		52.3	Fr: has "coprophage"
53:5 [53:55] from behind	from behind	from behind	51:28		[53]	OT (58) adds a comma
53:17 [54:17] chyme, or chile	chyme, or chile	chyme, or chyle	52:6		53.3	marked on O for G but not changed; marked on G for C
54:24 [55:24] vegetables,nuts	vegetables,nuts	vegetables, nuts	53:14		54.1	changed in C & OT
57:1 [58:1] Now the day is over [retained in OT, 63]	Now the day is over	[song deleted, text adjusted]	[55]		57.1	marked on O for deletion; no change in G; marked "Cut" on G for C; deleted in C
57:16 [58:16] Hallow's E'en	Hallow's E'en	Hallow-e'en	56:7		57.2	marked on O for G, but not changed; marked on G for C; Fr: "Toussaint"
57:16 [58:16] Guy Fawkes	Guy Fawkes	Guy Fawkes	56:7		57.3	Fr: "des Trépasses"
58:26 [59:26] knockkneed	knockkneed	knock-kneed	57:17		[58]	hyphens throughout C & P
58:35 [59:35] Knott	Knott	Mr. Knott	57:25		58.5	not marked by SB

Page	Olympia Press	Grove Press first edition	Calder (Jupiter)		Cross-reference & Comment
61:15 [62:15]	never knew	never knew never knew	never knew knew	60:10	61.2	marked on galleys for O, but not added; marked on O for G
61:30 [62:30]	as is now the case [OT, 68: as was the case]	as is now the case	as is now the case	60:25	[61]	error introduced into OT
63:28 [64:28]	Goodnight	Goodnight	Good night	62:25	[63]	silently changed in C
64:18 [65:18]	nine a.m.	nine a.m.	9 a.m.	63:16	[64]	numeral introduced in C
Part II						
67:1	Mr Knott	Mr Knott	MR. KNOTT	64:1	[67]	small capitals introduced in C
67:6	first floor	first floor	first-floor	64:6	[67]	hyphenation preferred in C & P; thus all similar instances
69:24	the outer world,	the outer world,	the outer world	66:12	[67]	comma omitted by Calder
70:3	without it's coming [OT, 76: without its coming]	without it's coming	without its coming	66:29	70.1	marked on O for G, but not changed; marked on G for C
71:16	to music-room	to the music-room	to the music-room	68:6	71.1	"the" added on O for G
72:26	subtraction [OT, 79: substraction]	subtraction	subtraction	69:17	[72]	error introduced in OT
74:16	he had seen a great quantity, both of legs and of trousers,	[correct sequence of lines]	[correct sequence of lines]	71:8	74.6	correct in galleys, but line misplaced at line 21 in O; marked on O for G
74:18	ceased so rapidly	ceased so rapidly	ceased so rapidly	71:9	[74]	four lines omitted in OT (81)
77:5	or the door become a door	or the door become a door	on the door become a door	77:5	77.2	galleys changed "became" to "become"; change to "on" marked on G for C
79:24	penomena [OT, 86: phenomena]	phenomena	phenomena	76:23	79.2	marked on O for G
79:29	throught [OT, 87: thought]	thought	thought	76:28	79.2	corrected without comment
80:27	He wondered what had become of the duck... He also wondered... [OT retains this passage]	He wondered what had become of the duck... He also wondered...	He wondered what Arsene had meant	77:24	80.6	duck marked for deletion on O but not changed in G; marked "Cut" on G for C; "also" deleted in C
80:37	realised	realised	realized	77:28	[80]	change made in C
81:21	that is was	that is was	that it was	78:15	81.4	marked in O for G but not changed; marked on G for C

81:38	alway hope	78:30	always hope	81.4	marked on O for G
82:11	take again (1)	79:7	take again[1]	[82]	different citation in C & P
83:8	It it a raven [It is a raven]	80:4	It is a raven	83.2	marked on O for G; silently corrected in reprints of G; marked on G for C
83:37	tumulus [OT, 91: cumulus]	80:31	tumulus	83.7	silently corrected in reprints of G & OT; error remains in C, but corrected in Fr.
86:82	realised	83:28	realized	[80]	change made in C
87:8	meat cheese [OT, 95: meat, cheese]	84:6	meat, cheese	87.2	comma added on O for G but unchanged; marked on G for C
87:15	camomille [OT, 95: camomile]	84:13	camomile	87.13	marked on O for G but unchanged; marked on G for C
89:3	coal was also	86:6	coal also was	89.2	marked on O for G but unchanged; marked on G for C
93:2	his arrival [OT, 90: its arrival]	90:2	its arrival	93.1	marked on O for G (other "its" changed) but not changed; marked on G for C
95:25	strange most strange [OT, 104: strange, most strange,]	92:28	strange most strange	[95]	commas added in OT
96:11	ten o'cluck strock [OT, 105: ten o'clock struck]	93:16	ten o'cluck strock	[96]	"corrected" in OT
96:23	a fortiori	93:27	a fortiori	[96]	italics added in OT (105)
98:8	dogowner	95:15	dog-owner	[98]	hyphen added in C
98:37	second local's man [OT, 108: second local man's]	96:10	second local man's	98.3	marked on O for G but unchanged; marked on G for C
100:20	to see, and admire;	97:30	to see, and admire,	[100]	semi-colon changed to comma in C
100:22	sixpence [OT, 110: sixpence]	97:32	sixpence	100.1	marked on O for G
100:37	Mr Knott's service,	97:30	Mr. Knott's service	[100]	comma omitted in C
101:35	as least as	99:13	at least as	101.8	marked on G for C
102:13	aged [OT, 111: aged]	99:28	aged	102.1	italicised "e" noted in O for G, but unchanged; not noted in G for C

Page	Olympia Press	Grove Press first edition	Calder (Jupiter)	Cross-reference & Comment
102:18	?	?	?	[102] extraneous comma in O deleted
102:29	but a bleeder (1)	but a bleeder (1)	but a bleeder[1]	[102] different citation in C & P
102:31	Frank's daughter Bridie	Frank's daughter Bridie	Frank's daughter Bridie	102.6 error unchanged in any current text; "Jack" noted for the Fr. translation
102:37	enlargment	enlargment	enlargement	102.7 marked on O for G but unchanged; marked on G for C
103:9	excema [OT, 113: excema]	excema	eczema	103.1 marked on O for G but unchanged; marked on G for C
104:1	Mr Knott's service (1)	Mr Knott's service (1)	Mr. Knott's service[1]	[104] different citation in C & P
104:31	exsanguious [OT, 114: exsanguinous]	exsanguious	exsanguine	104.6 marked on O for G but unchanged; marked on G for C
105:6-7	anyth-ing	anyth-ing	anything	105.2 marked on O for G but unchanged; marked in C & OT
105:38	or Liz	or Liz	of Liz	105.4 marked on O for G but unchanged; marked on G for C; adjusted in C & OT
106:32	daugter [OT, 117: daughter]	daughter	daughter	106.4 marked on O for G
107:25	an eye on [OT, 118: and eye on]	an eye on	an eye on	[107] error introduced in OT
109:22	Art and Con [OT, 120: Art Con]	Art and Con	Art and Con	[109] "and" omitted in OT
111:33	backdoor	backdoor	back door	[111] silently changed in C
112:4	backdoorstep	backdoorstep	back doorstep	[112] silently changed in C
112:15	Add to his [OT, 123: Add to this]	Add to his [Add to this]	Add to this	112.2 marked on O for G; silently corrected in reprints of G; marked on G for C
115:35	As is was	As is was	As it was	115.3 marked on O for G but unchanged; marked on G for C
117:2	mecanism [OT, 128: mechanism]	mecanism	mechanism	117.1 marked on O for G but unchanged; marked on G for C
119:26	than nobody [OT, 131: that nobody]	than nobody [that nobody]	that nobody	119.1 silently corrected in reprints of G; marked on G for C
121:1	his big white chamber pot	his big white chamber pot	his big chamber pot	121.1 "white" dropped in C & P
122:23	on the qui vive	on the qui vive	on the *qui vive*	122.2 italicised in C & P

125:38	Watt told me,	124:4	Watt told me,	[125]	period in C
126:25	or rather weres [OT, 139: or rather were]	124:26	or rather were	126.2	marked on O for G
127:11	a trouser's pocket	125:14	a trouser's pocket	127.2	marked on O for G but unchanged; marked on G for C
130:10	for even in vain	128:13	for ever in vain	130.1	marked on O for G
131:1	to-day ... to-morrow	129:7	today ... tomorrow	[131]	changes made in C
132:4	tenth rate xenium	130:7	tenth-rate xenium	132.2	"xenium?" marked on O for C, but unchanged; also marked on G for C
132:15	Yes what	130:22	Yet what	132.3	marked on O for G
132:37	reread	131:17	re-read	[132]	hyphen introduced in C
[137]	[pp. 137-38 of SB's copy of G missing]				
140:1	Saturday, But	138:24	Saturday, But	[140]	error in all editions
140:11	greypink	138:34	grey-pink	[140]	hyphen introduced in C
141:8	But if was not Mrs Gorman [OT, 154: But if it was not Mrs Gorman]	139:33	But if it was not Mrs. Gorman	141.1	galleys error not noted on O for G; silently corrected in G reprints with new error ("it was"), this amended in C
141:28	to do so more	140:18	to do so on more	141.3	marked on O for G
142:36	than a dying perfume.	141:26	than a dying perfume,	142.4	not noted by SB; but amended in C
142:37	three times a day [four times a day]	141:27:	four times a day	142.6	"three" silently changed in G reprints to "four"; yet marked on G for C
143:4	he bottle [OT, 156: the bottle]	141:31	the bottle	143.1	marked on O for G
146:34	others sorrows [OT, 159: other sorrows]	145:27	other sorrows	146.5	marked on O for G
148:30	yellowist [OT, 163: yellowest]	147:27	yellowist	148.5	"corrected" only in OT
148:31	half ender, ended	147:27	half ended, ended	148.5	marked on O for G
148:33	on arising, on arising	147:30	on arising	148.6	galleys correct; marked on O for G

Page	Olympia Press	Grove Press first edition	Calder (Jupiter)	Cross-reference & Comment
Part III				
152:14	windowlesness [OT, 166: windowlessness]	windowlessness	windowlessness	[152.1] *marked on O for G*
152:16	could some [OT, 166: could come]	could come	could come	152.1 *marked in O for G*
153:16	a bright sun mixed (1)	a bright sun mixed (1)	a bright sun mixed[1]	[153] *different citation in C & P*
153:37	Nothing in known	Nothing is known	Nothing is known	153.2 *marked in O for G*
153:37	volte-face	volte-face	volte-face	[153] *italicised in OT*
154:1	as so little [OT, 168: was so little]	was so little	was so little	154.1 *marked in O for G*
155:7	hardly to otherwise [OT, 169: hardly do otherwise]	hardly do otherwise	hardly do otherwise	155.1 *marked in O for G*
155:33	morcels	morcels	morsels	[155] *silently corrected in C*
156:22	manner . [OT, 171: manner.]	manner .	manner.	156.2 *marked on O for G but not changed; marked on G for C*
158:16	palissades	palissades	palissades	[156] *Fr. spelling in all texts*
158:21	if possible what follows	if possible what follows	if possible, what follows	158.2 *marked on O for G but unchanged; marked on G for C*
158:22	that it would	that it would	that it would	[158] *error ("than") in all texts*
158:33	croaking	croaking	croaking	158.3 *galleys read "singing"*
[161]		[pp. 161-92 of SB's copy of G missing]		
162:1	sow [OT, 175: retains "sow"]	sow [cow]	cow	162.1 *marked on O for G; silently corrected on reprints of G*
164:4, 6	occured	occured	occurred	[164] *silently corrected in C*
164:33	to every man.	to every man.	to every man,	[164] *silently corrected in C*
166:15	Thus I missed I presume	Thus I missed I presume	Thus I missed I presume	166.2 *error in all texts save Fr. translation; the galleys correctly read "suspect"*
166:35	of great interest touching	of great interest touching	of great interest touching	166.4 *"I suppose" missing in galleys and all texts; restored in Fr.*
167:30	ton yag	ton yag	don yag	167.1 *error introduced in C*
168:27	ho no	ho no	ho no	[168] *comma added after "ho" in OT (184)*
169:16	called of	called of	called of ?	[169] *awkward placing of "?" in C*
170:33	hasardous	hasardous	hazardous	170.7 *Fr. spelling anglicised in C*

171:6	(from which he emerged...	169:25	(from which he emerged...	171.1	text deleted in C & P
171:22	six months		six months	171.4	Fr. translation: "six semaines"
172:6	accomodation	170:10	accommodation	[172]	silently corrected in C
173:3	medullars	171:10	medullas	173.2	marked on O for G but unchanged
	[OT, 189: medullars]				
173:21	his MS, which, qua MS,	171:28	his MS., which, qua MS.,	[173]	periods introduced in C; italicised in OT
	[OT, 189: qua MS,]				
175:15	Mr Fitzwein looked	173:26	Mr. Fitzwein looks	175.2	present tense used in C & P
178:31	this it not all	177:12	this is not all	[178]	silently changed in C
179:11	no number of the committee	177:28	no member of the committee	179.2	correction first appears in C
179:36	numbr two	178:18	number two	179.3	marked on O for G but unchanged
180:26	to x squared	179:9	to say x squared	180.2	insert added on O for G; "x" and "y" italicised in OT (198)
181:2	singlehanded	179:23	single-handed	[181]	hyphen introduced in C
181:14	colloborators	179:34	colloborators	181.4	marked on O for G but unchanged
183:5	Ego autem! (1)	181:29:	Ego autem!¹	183.1	different citation in C & P
184:10	M. de Baker	182:33	Mr. de Baker	184.3	not noted by SB; corrected in C
184:13	His very what?,	185:3	His very what?,	[184]	error in all texts
184:22	M. Fitzwein	183:11	Mr. Fitzwein	184.3	marked on O for G but unchanged
184:28	(the French extraction)	183:16	(the French extraction)	184.6	deleted from the Fr. translation
186:32	sweet seventeen	185:24	sweet seventeen	186.2	Fr. translation has "soixante-seize"
186:37	to-day	185:29	today	[186]	hyphen deleted from C
187:20	M. de Baker	186:14	Mr. de Baker	[187]	silently corrected in C
188:33	Not horsey, fishy	187:28	Not horsey, fishy	188.2	deleted from the Fr. translation
188:36	M. Fitzwein	187:31	Mr. Fitzwein	[188]	silently corrected in C
189:19	good-evening	188:17	good evening	[189]	hyphen removed in C
190:13	Five hundred and nineteen thousand three hundred and thirteen.	189:12	Five hundred and nineteen thousand three hundred and thirteen.	190.1	underlined (by SB) in O, with "?" then "STET"; changed on Fr. galleys to 659,413
190:17	three quarters	189:16	three-quarters	[190]	silently corrected in C
190:29	Silence, Mr Louit	189:27	Silence, Mr. Louit	[190]	comma deleted in OT (209)
190:34	of five	189:32	or five	[190]	silently corrected in C
191:29	belive	190:29	believe	191.3	error entered O; marked on O for G
	[OT, 210: believe]				

Page	Olympia Press	Grove Press first edition		Calder (Jupiter)	Cross-reference & Comment	
191:32	eastern windows	western windows	190:31	western windows	191.4	marked on O for G
191:37	It was question time	It was question time.	191:2	It was question time.	191.5	large section marked on C for deletion in Fr. text
192:23	vanqu-ished [OT, 211: vanquished]	vanqu-ished	191:25	vanquished	[192]	incorrect hyphenation noted on O for G but unchanged
193:16	said Louit	said Louit	192:18	said Louit,	193.1	erroneous comma in C silently corrected in C
195:14	M. Fitzwein	M. Fitzwein	194:21	Mr. Fitzwein	195.1	marked on O for G
195:23	found	round	194:29	round	195.3	
200:4	this ambience	this ambience	199:22	this ambience	200.1	"ambiance" on OT (219)
204:6	from the window [OT, 224: from the window]	from the window	203:28	from the window	204.1	marked on O for G but unchanged; marked on G for C
205:6	night-stool [OT, 225: nightstool]	night-stool	204:26	night-stool	[205]	anomalous in O & G which prefer "nightstool"; hyphenated in C
205:7	washhand-stand	washhand-stand	204:27	wash-hand-stand	[205]	change of hyphenation in C
206:38	nineteen days	nineteen days	206:28	nineteen days	206.1	error ("twenty") not noted in English texts; marked on C for Fr: translation
207:14	almost one minute	almost one minute	207:7	almost one minute	207.3	error ("degree") not noted in English texts; marked on C for Fr: translation
208:2	vegetable-garden	vegetable-garden	207:31	vegetable garden	208.2	hyphen omitted in C
208:12	he reckoned	he reckoned	208:6	be reckoned	208.2	error introduced in C
209:17	middlesized	middlesized	209:11	middle-sized	209.7	hyphen introduced in C
209:31, 38	yellow, and	yellow, and	209:25, 31	yellow, and	209.7	comma in all texts
211:8	For daily changed	For daily changed	211:7	For daily changed	[211]	error ("changes") in OT (232)
211:24	thay they	thay they	211:23	that they	211.2	marked on O for G but unchanged; marked on G for C
211:26	into his night-dress (1)	into his night-dress (1)	211:25	into his nightdress1	[211]	no hyphen; different citation in C & P
211:31	For Watt did not	For Watt did not [For Mr Knott did not]	211:30	For Mr. Knott did not	211.3	Mr Knott marked on O for G; silently corrected in reprints of G; marked on G for C
212:8	organised	organised	212:8	organized	[212]	change made in C
212:14	dying in London	dying in London	212:14	dying in London	212.1	changed in the galleys, "living"

Part IV

217:27	little more than a stone	216:18	little more than a stone	**217.5**	*marked on C, deleted in Fr.*
218:17	flowerhole	217:10	flower-hole	**[218]**	*hyphen introduced in C*
219:1	eight pence	217:10	eightpence	**219.1**	*change made in C*
219:2	a fortiori	217:32	a fortiori	**[219]**	*italicised in OT (241)*
219:7	sea-shore	218:2	seashore	**219.3**	*hyphen deleted in C*
221:9	set down his bags.	220:7	set down his bags,	**[221]**	*silently corrected in C*
224:24	focussed	223:25	focused	**224.4**	*marked on O for G but unchanged; marked on G for C*
225:3	chimneys	224:6	chimneys	**225.1**	*marked on O for G*
226:18	or shackled smartness	225:21	of shackled smartness	**226.3**	*not noted by SB, but corrected in C*
226:22	of for this woman [OT, 249: or for this woman]	225:25	or for this woman	**226.5**	*marked on O for G*
226:30	whether this was a good thing	225:33	whether shit was a good thing	**226.7**	*error introduced in C*
227:32	half-an-hour	227:2	half an hour	**[227]**	*hyphens omitted in C*
228:18	*Songs by the Way*	227:24	*Songs by the Way*	**[228]**	*"Songs be the Way" in OT (251)*
228:33	windows, of his box	228:6	windows, of his box,	**228.4**	*marked on O for G but unchanged; marked on G for C*
230:3	gentlemens'	228:14	gentlemen's	**230.3**	*"error" introduced in C*
230:9	the fulness of time	229:20	the fullness of time	**[230]**	*"fullness" in OT (253)*
230:15	less his trouser's	229:25	lest his trouser's	**230.2**	*marked on O for G*
230:16	as trousers' pockets	229:26	as trouser's pockets	**230.3**	*distinction confused in C*
230:18	less his watch-chain	229:28	lest his watch-chain	**230.2**	*marked on O for G*
230:21	station-keys	229:30	station keys	**[230]**	*hyphen omitted in C; thus for "station-till" and "-doors"*
231:7	realised	230:20	realized	**[231]**	*change made in C*
233:8	on his face	232:24	on his face	**233.1**	*"his" changed to "its" on C for Fr. translation*
234:3	accomodate	233:20	accommodate	**234.1**	*marked on O for G*
237:6	morning . [OT, 261: morning.]	236:23	morning.	**237.1**	*marked on O for G but unchanged; marked on G for C*
237:10	than a lark sing	236:27	than a lark from singing	**237.2**	*marked on G for C*
238:7	he would have	237:27	he would not have	**238.2**	*marked on O for G*
238:36	(Hiatus in MS)	238:20	(Hiatus in MS.)	**[238]**	*period added in C*

Page	Olympia Press	Grove Press first edition	Calder (Jupiter)	Cross-reference & Comment
239:2	five fifty-five	five fifty-five	five-fifty-five	[239] hyphen added in C; thus for all subsequent references to train times
239:3	and .. (Hiatus in MS)	and .. (Hiatus in MS)	and ... (Hiatus in MS.)	[239] full ellipsis and period in C
239:10	a very long arm	a very long arm	a very long arm	239.3 Fr. translation adds a footnote
239:24	bloody—	bloody—	bloody....	[239] ellipsis preferred in C
239:28-29	geworfen ... hinab	geworfen ... hinab	geworfen ... hinab	239.7 C & P fail to justify at right
239:33-34	[6 periods, thrice]	[six periods, thrice]	[6 periods, then 8, then 6]	239.8 periods erratic in C & P
242:13	recognise	recognise	recognize	[242] changed in C
243:16	Lady McCann	Lady McCann	Lady McCan	243.2 error introduced in C
243:19-21	[6 periods, 6 times]	[6 periods, 6 times]	[3 periods, 6 times]	[243] periods reduced in C & P

Addenda

	Addenda (1)	Addenda (1)	ADDENDA[1]	[247] capitals: different citation in C & P
			Marked on C to be deleted in Fr.	deleted in the Fr. translation
#2, #3				
#4	in worlds enclose	in words enclose	in words enclose	#2, #3 marked on O for G
#8	years are flown.	years are flown.	years are flown.	#4 period in all texts
#17	Embriology	Embriology	Embryology	#8 correct in galleys; error introduced in O; marked on O for G and on G for C
#23	abate one tot	abate one tot	abate one jot	#17 perhaps intentional in O & G; marked on G for C
#26	with every filthy ... ears	[confused line deleted]	[confused line deleted]	#23 marked on O for G
#26	latin	latin	Latin	#26 capitalized in C
#28	sphinxes	sphinxes	sphinges	#26 marked on O for G
#29	that is was not a rush	that is was not a rush	that it was not a rush	#28 unchanged; marked on G for C
#29	when I was a boy	when I was a boy	when you was a boy	#29 unchanged; marked on G for C
#29	Good-day	Good-day	Good day	#29 unchanged; marked on G for C
#30	Watt ... sterile pus	Watt ... sterile pus	Watt ... sterile pus	#29 hyphen omitted in C & P
#32	faede hunc mundum	faede hunc mundum	faede hunc mundum	#30 placed after #34 in C & Fr
#36	on way for station	on way from station	on way from station	#32 error ("hune") in OT
				#36 marked on O for G; blank space but no music in C & P;

The author took this photo during the Sydney Beckett Symposium, January 2003.

Addendum 2

The Evolution of *Watt*

I trace the evolution of *Watt* through the nine "levels" identified in my Introduction, my annotations related to these. References to the drafts ("level 1" to "level 3") and early typescript ("level 2") follow the HRHRC numbering, rather than Beckett's, to allow for interfoliations and additions on the versos, typically used not for primary drafts but for changes and inserts. A reference such as "NB3, 69; TS, 245" implies that the notebook detail equally constitutes part of the later recension. I use square brackets for editorial comments and later textual developments. Minor retouches are ignored, and evolutionary dead-ends, often extensive, are mentioned only briefly with reference to their legacy.

My "level 4" is the [missing] final typescript, a hypothetical construct from the late drafts before it and the "level 5" galley proofs set from it. As this is my implied point of reference (the "*avant-texte*"), I pay considerable attention to it. My four other "levels" are the published texts. The evolutionary pattern has largely settled, but differences complicate any so-called "text" of *Watt*; for the Olympia ("level 6"), Grove ("level 7"), and Calder ("level 8") versions each make significant changes, with new errors entering even as others are corrected. Calder is not obviously an improvement on Grove (neither more accurate nor definitive), despite the many changes made. A ninth level, the French translation, reflects an evolutionary drift beyond its English template (the Olympia Traveller's text also drifted from this original, but that was not Beckett's doing). A final consideration (as noted in my Introduction) is the need for a further recension ("level 10"), an "ideal" (or at least better) edition of *Watt*, derived from an awareness of its evolutionary history. This composition constitutes the substrate of such an edition.

Level 1: the "early" drafts (NB1 through NB4; parts of the early typescript).

NB1: "I / Paris"; a soft-cover, stapled "Lutèce" exercise book, bound in semi-stiff mustard-colored paper; white ruled paper 19.5 x 30 cm., 50 leaves, preceded by seven loose leaves of plain paper, 21 x 27 cm. (the first drafts); total leaves 56 (Coetzee 252) [in fact 57, but the HRHRC numbering is to 112]. Beckett's later outside cover note (signed, "Watt I") states that *Watt* was written in France during the war 1940-45 and published in 1953 by the Olympia Press. The first (loose) page records: "Begun evening of Tuesday 11/2/41." Extensively revised, with "multiple deletions and amendations" and "lavish doodles and drawings" (Admussen 90), NB1 reveals the novel's first intent: it depicts Quin, the ancestor of both Knott and Watt; describes his house; and testifies to the sense of Nothing at the heart of his experience.

• (NB1, 3): "who, what, where, by what means, why, in what way, when": the first words of an Ur-*Watt*, the scholastic *memoria technica* [*quis, quid, ubi, quibis auxiliis, cur, quomodo, quando* (*qualis*)], by which any subject can be divided into parts for analysis, or patterns extended infinitely (Watt does both). Hence Quin [*qui ne*, or negative intentionality], as a reductio of the categories.

Not finally manifest thus, but the influence pervasive (**title**, **23.1**). Beckett's Philosophy Notebook (Aristotle) records the categories (TCD 16967, 99ff).

• (NB1, 3): the image of an old man: "Socrates is a man [substance, who], 70 years old [quantity, what], wise [quality, how (mental)], teacher of Plato [relation, what to whom], at evening [time, when], in prison [place, where], sitting on his bed [position, how (physical)], having fetters on his legs [possession, whose], teaching his disciples [active, by what means], being questioned by them [passive, by what means]." The categories generate the later Watt (NB1, 7ff) and the Beckett protagonist of the next forty years: "X is a man, 70 years old, ignorant, alone, at evening, in his room, in bed, having pains, listening, remembering" (NB1, 3) (**82.2**).

• (NB1, 5, 17; TS, 1): "To endeavour to formulate a modest demand as to of whom it is question. And as to of what. To essay a tentative outline or rough-sketch of mind of same. And of body of same. To hazard a manner of inquiry or search after possible relations with other persons. And with other things. To throw out a cautious feeler with regard to the situation in time. And with respect to the situation in space. To propose with gentlemanly diffidence: the vexed question of the possession; the knotty problem of the act; the well-known teaser of the suffering." Cited in Cohn (*Canon* 111): "The purpose of the novel is, then, inordinately and ironically ambitious."

• (NB1, 11ff): gradual fixing on the name of Quin, variants being: John James MacSimon; John James MacRoe ("an old cod"); John James Macevoy (McEvoy); John James Molloy; James Molloy: "Jack or Jim, twas all the same to him" (NB1, 11; TS, 1). In NB1 (19), "Molloy" is crossed out and "Quin" [much later?] penciled in. James soon established as the son of Alexander Quin, whose portrait is in the drawing-room, with another of his mother (NB1, 35, 110v; TS, 91-93) (**130.3**, **#2**, **#3**). "Leda, née Swan, mother of James Quin and wife to Alexander" almost survives into the Addenda (**#1**); her ten dead children (NB1, 51; TS, 41) do not.

• (NB1, 13-21; TS, 3, 9): the piano-tuner, first ~~Hicks~~, then Green (**70.3**); essential details (hammers, dampers) featured [the episode later moved to part II] (**72.1**).

• (NB1, 14, 16; TS, 7): early drafts of "To Nelly" ("sweet Nymph") written by Grehan, or Green, "to Anthea" [minor changes later made] (**11.2** to **12.9**).

• (NB1, 21-25; TS, 11): Quin meets an old man in his garden; (TS, 30): Arthur [later] meets a mendicant there (**143.4**) [in the late drafts, the old man was once employed by the Knott family (**#29**)]. The theme of relative immortality (the gardener to the rose) thus present from the outset. The "hardy laurel" (NB1, 21) and "passing bush or shrub" [*sic*] (23) persisted; the gardener was retained; and "cleaning the boots" was added late to part II (**95.1**).

• (NB1, 27; TS, 15): Quin's valet, Arthur, a Madden[ed] Prizeman; then (NB1, 85; TS, 67) Quin's butler, Erskine ("Foreskin"), likewise [the detail later dropped] (**46.7**, **#14**).

• Quin's house: (NB1, 31; TS, 19): Quin, at night, cannot find the lavatories [Knott is finally "unfamiliar with the premises" (**203.3**)]. (NB1, 35; TS, 23): Quin changes his seat at every meal (**#13**); (NB1, 35; TS, 25): under his round table, he began "the fatal journey towards the light of day" (**207.3**, **#20**); (NB1, 107; TS, 85): the "sempiternal penumbra" of his coal-hole (**#18**). Pilling notes

(*BBG*, 172) that NB1 renders Quin enigmatic ("vaguening") yet substantiates him in the "reality" of his household (**18.2**).

• (NB1, 35ff; TS, 25ff): the dinner party, given by Mr. and Mrs. Quin; the birth of James; "Berry" first "~~Gibbs~~" then "Sparrow" and the duck a goose (**13.4**).

• (NB1, 27, 39ff; TS, 19, 233ff): Quin encounters a "strange man" ("Hunchy" before "Hackett") who arrives in the middle of the night (**7.2**), and tells of falling off the ladder (15.8); he once "cleaned the boots" for Quin's father (**95.1**, **#29**).

• (NB1, 51ff; TS, 41ff): the Quin family history outlined in considerable detail (**#1**) [most subsequently deleted]; (NB1, 69): Quin hears the echo of his words, and the nothingness behind them (**#15**).

• (NB1, 69; TS, 55): a chapter called "The ~~Isolation~~ Nothingness"; a "pensation" [later a "soul-scape"]; Nothing born in Quin and with him until he dies; Cangiamila and Pope Benedict XIV (**#17**); (NB1, 69-79; TS, 61ff): the sky above, the waste below the Nothingness of Quin's first awareness as the primal scene of the novel to be; the growing identification of Quin with a consciousness [finally] more Watt than Knott (**#22**); (NB1, 76, 83, 85; TS, 65): Quin's conviction that he had never been properly born (the embryonic self, the être manqué) (**#16, #19**).

• incidentals: (NB1, 60, 62-65): drafts of the unhappy accountant's song (**28.10**); (NB1, 87; TS, 67): Quin's preference for one type (short, fat) of servant (**61.1**); (NB1, 87, 101): Erskine and Arsene ("we had nearly written Eustace!") here named; (NB1, 89): space not wanting, nor time lacking, later attributed to Arsene, then Louit (**62.1**); (NB1, 91, 97ff; TS, 73ff): a long chapter on "The Eyes" ("windows of the soul") once present; (NB1, 95; TS, 75): prize of a "self-propelling wheel-chair" from Lourdes (**27.8, 106.3**) [but no Mr. Spiro]; (NB1, 103-11; TS 81ff): Quin's house, its floors, its kitchen, its furnishings [in detail], its coalhole (**#13**), its doors.

NB2: headed and signed "WATT II" on the outer cover; dated on the first page "31/12/41" (Lake's "3/12/41" is incorrect). Written in Paris. A soft-covered "Lutèce" exercise book, with a deep green cover; 50 ruled pages; many versos filled, extensively revised, doodles and drawings, but "written with greater ease than A1" (Admussen 90). NB2 rehearses NB1's description of Quin's "household" before moving into a discussion in Quin's hallway between the narrator and Arsene, the notebook ending just before Arsene's evocation of spring, which continues into NB3.

• Quin's house: the skylight (**#11**); the Berber carpet, the "Hicks" sideboard, a dumb-waiter [all later deleted]; the grate (**37.4**); the plate; the staircase and newell (**40.2**). (NB2, 3; TS, 25): the table "~~occupied the centre of the room~~" crossed out and "filled the middle ground" written in (**#20**).

• the painting: (NB2, 7): the Chinnery-Slattery connection (**#2**); (NB2, 7; TS, 91-93): the portrait of James Quin [later Alexander] by Art Conn O'Connery, dead of a surfeit of corned beef and cabbage (**130.3, #2**); (NB2, 9-13; TS, 93-97): the "second picture in Erskine's room" [so-called only in the Addenda] in Quin's drawing room; "Heem" identified as the Younger (**#26**); (NB2, 12): the bust of Buxtehude added to Quin's drawing [later, music] room (**71.3**).

• (NB2, 15ff; TS, 105ff): the *Mus eventratus mcgilligani*, with the Master of the Leopardstown Halflengths (**28.9**, **#3**); (NB2, 19): a short list of ecclesiastical authorities (**29.2**); (NB2, 25): "eels of the lake of Genoa" [*sic*] as part of McGilligan's meditation (**28.1**).

• versification: (NB2, 28ff; TS, 111): a poem to "Jerry of the Nights" (**#3**); (NB2, 34-36; TS, 115): a descant ("With all our heart") in full, as the intended song of the Mixed Choir (**#34**); (NB2, 40-41; TS, 119): "Who may tell the tale" (**#4**); (NB2, 61-63; TS, 135): "Bid us sigh" (**#8**); (NB2, 70-71; TS, 143): "Not a grief" set as verse (46.5) [twenty lines; the first four items added later, four others deleted]; (NB2, 83-84; TS, 155): "*We shall be here all night*" (**47.14**); (NB2, 86-87; TS, 159): "The whacks, the moans" set out as a Shakespearean sonnet (**46.9**).

• surviving fossils: (NB2, 37-42; TS, 115-19): an old has-been who might have been (**#4**); (NB2, 51; TS, 125): "little by little" (**64.3**); "things of note" (**128.4**); and "The tutelary newel" (**#37**); (NB2, 72-73; TS, 143): "And if I could begin it all over again" (**47.13**, **#6**); (NB2, 72-73; TS, 145): "that would be too appalling [horrible] to contemplate" [finally in part II] (**134.6**, **#6**); (NB2, 81; TS, 157): "raising in amaze an astonished hand to a thunderstruck mouth" [moved from Quin's hallway to part IV] (**220.1**).

• fossils that did not survive: (NB2, 42-49; TS, 109ff: a long passage on various doors, door-knobs, steps, and bells; (NB2, 51-53; TS, 125-27): the box, or casket.

• (NB2, 53ff; TS, 127ff): a long, meandering conversation in Quin's hallway, between "Johnny" Watt ("we") and two bipeds (one feathered), Arsene and Eamon (his India[n] Runner Duck, a bottle-shaped bird) (**45.6**, **#37**); (NB2, 60v; TS, 133): composition of the Runner Duck poem and commentary (**45.6**); (NB2, 65; TS, 135ff): Hooker's heat-pimples (**#5**, **#37**); (NB2, 67; TS, 141): a "nodding acquaintance" on Westminster Bridge (**45.8**); (NB2, 71, 72ff): "All error, folly, waste & ruin" (**#6**); (NB2, 79ff; TS, 149-53): Arsene's talk of "the unconscious mind" (**#7**); (NB2, 91; TS, 161): an exchange of ties and trousers [later dropped].

• (NB2, 98; TS, 169): the "fathers' mothers'" paradigm, with Christ and Mary, Adam and Eve (**46.11**), with reference to Bishop Ussher's 6,000 years.

NB3: a hard-cover exercise book with dark marbled board wrappers, 96 sheets of white squared paper (HRHRC 1 to 192), 19.5 x 31 cm., rear flyleaf and cover with "extraneous material" (Coetzee 252): notes on George III & IV, Shelley's wives, and the Avignon popes. "Watt III" signed on the inner fly, with "3 Paris / Roussillon" scrawled in blue pencil; the first page dated "5.5.42" and "7.5.42"; the third "8.7.42"; a later entry "4 Sept. 42" (Vanves, a suburb of Paris). Roussillon mentioned: "Nov. 18" [1942]; then "March 1st" [1943]. Extensively revised with many versos filled: "Doodles, calculations, anagrams, musical notations, and the Lynch family tree" (Admussen 91). NB3 continues Arsene's monologue (from NB2), moving into the future part II of the novel; earlier material is rewritten, more recognizably the final version; "Johnny" Watt (earlier, "we") testifies to a more complex narrative perspective, but "Quin" still present.

- (NB3, inner fly): paradigm of: "1 The Coming / 2 Downstairs / 3 Upstairs [2 and 3 bracketed as "The Being"] / 4 The Going (**133.2**). [Probably added much later].
- (NB3, 1): speculations, crossed out, not later evident, about the creative consciousness, "double and obscure"; God and Paul de Kock; consciousness and acts, and seeing that it is good; "witness in the reading"; and odd comments: "Knott is at rest. I am not" (a first mention of "Knott," curious since "Quin" is still present; indeed, on this page); and "prefer one's Pilate to one's high priests" (NB3, 2).
- narrative voice initially "we": (NB3, 19; TS, 197): "our name was Johnny."
- Arsene's statement continued (much detail later completely cut): (NB3, 5): "uneaten" added to "sheep's placentas" (**47.2**); (NB3, 11; TS, 183): "all are in the dark" and "no symbols where none intended" (**#37**); (NB3, 17; TS, 193): Arsene's "prophetic ejaculation" (**39.3**); (NB3, 22; TS, 201): "DENOS IOPSI" introduced (**33.6**) [a ditch, but no journey]; (NB3, 29; TS, 211): the "Clean Old Man" book and a "gritty" jest about policemen [later deleted] (**56.3**); (NB3, 31): "stages" become TS [213]: "unwindings" [finally "excoriations"] (**48.3**); (NB3, 31; TS, 215): the story of the rabbi's trousers (**48.3**).
- (NB3, 26; TS, 205): first draft of "Watt will not / abate one jot"; but with "Johnny" and "Naught's habitat" [neither Watt nor Knott] (**#23**). ["Abate one tot" present from the first drafts to the first editions; finally "corrected" in Calder] (**34.1, #23**).
- (NB3, 32, 35; TS, 219): "The Tuesday scowls" (**46.8**), associated with the Mixed Choir.
- (NB3, 34-37; TS, 223): "Fifty two point two" song set out in detail (**34.1**); the second verse reading [correctly]: "Fifty-two point one" (**35.1**). [No hint of Watt in the ditch].
- (NB3, 40v; TS, 228): the cromlech [insert] before Arsene's farewell (**49.4**); (NB3, 41-43; TS, 227-29): [Johnny's] "sorrow" replaces "wisdom," after hearing the angelic choir (**50.3**); the collection "egg or shell" (**50.3**); (NB3, 41; TS, 227): "a little wind" as a sign to leave Quin's hallway (**62.2**).
- Mary: (NB3, 45; TS, 230): the "third person" argument (**50.9**); (NB3, 46v): "vitamines" [*sic*] as insert (**52.1**); (NB3, 48v): coarse feeder sequence inserts boa-constrictor and Aran Islander (**52.3**); (NB3, 49): "upward direction" added (**53.1**); (NB3, 49): "chyme, or chile" [causing a later error] (**53.4**).
- (NB3, 55): "Winter and summer": indicating the arrival in Roussillon, "Nov. 18" then "March 1st" (**55.2**) [a long break before "Continuing"]; (NB3, 59; TS, 237): Arsene's hymn "a little high" (**57.1**); (NB3, 59; TS, 238): "neither comes nor goes," a small ditty (**57.4**); (NB3, 63; TS, 243-44): an early hint of the Anglican confession (**63.6**).
- (NB3, 62-65): final name changes of the servants: "Walterise selon P. 81"; "Walter" written into the sequence (NB3, 62v, insert) (**59.2, #33**). [No sense in NB3 of the final ending of part I, as the arrival of Watt chez Knott is not yet contemplated; that is, coming and going was present as a theme before Watt came and went].
- Quin as master: (NB3, 69; TS, 245): Watt's indeterminate service (**67.2**); (NB3, 69; TS, 245): Quin an [implied] sun-god, rising immediately after the [comma unqualified] statement that he was a good master (**86.2**).

• Quin's poss: (NB3, 69; TS, 245): described in terms of John Earle (**87.1**); (NB3, 71; TS, 246): ingredients of his "invariable Eintopf" multiplied by seven (**87.2**); (NB3, 78): "POINCARÉ" noted (**87.6**); precise measurement (**88.1**); (NB3, 80; TS, 251): Quin's "ñum ñum" as he drinks it [soon deleted] (**88.2**); (NB3, 84v; TS, 254): Erskine's song, with music and words from "che sciagura" (**85.7**); "parole non ci appulcro" (**#35**); (NB3, 85; TS, 254): Quin eats with a soup spoon (**89.1**).

• (NB3, 72v, 73; TS, 247): "Quin was responsible" paradigm, first a verso insert (**89.2**).

• the famished dog: (NB3, 86-89; TS, 255-56): attempt to calculate the odds by echoing the mixed choir [later repressed] (**92.1**); (NB3, 89; TS, 258): a first (faint) intimation of the serial theme (**93.4**); (NB3, 93; TS, 260): "This messenger" [*sic*] in a brief parenthesis (**95.1**); (NB3, 93; TS, 260): "ten o'cluck strock from the old church clock" (**96.1**); (NB3, 98; TS, 261): "lurcher" replaces "dog" (**97.3**); (NB3, 96-99; TS, 262): calculations (one error) and formula for the number of solutions (**98.1**).

• the Lynch millennium: (NB3, 104v, 108v): the Lynch family charts, some differences from the final text (**101.1**); (NB3, 104, 108; TS, 266): "Jack" named "Frank" (**101.6, 102.6, 105.1, 108.2**); (NB3, 104): mathematics of the Lynch millennium (**101.1**); (NB3, 108): "Doyly" becomes "Simon" (**102.2**); "17 months" become "nineteen"; (NB3, 111) (**105.3**); (NB3, 109): Liz "delivered of" a child (**104.5**).

• (NB3, 119ff; TS, 275ff): the famished dog breeding sequence, with "bitch" changed (NB3, 130) to "female dog"; (NB3, 155; TS, 298): [Leopardi's] thicket flower (**#27**) saved, when virtually all of this sequence is [later] cut (**111.1**); (NB3, 143; TS, 291): "Frith" comes [and goes] (**143.2**).

• (NB3, 157): "Watt" named as one of Quin's servants (the earlier typescript of NB3 does not reflect this); the narrative perspective begins crucially to change (**125.1**).

• the picture in Erskine's room: (NB3, 173; TS, 317ff): a "coloured reproduction" (**128.4**); speculation re its origin (NB3, 177; TS, 323) (**130.3**); (NB3, 173; TS, 317): the point "Far behind" (**128.6**); "blue" deleted and "almost black" proposed (**128.7**); attached to the wall by tin-tacks (**129.1**); (NB3, 177; TS, 318v-19): dot and circle paradigm (**129.4**); (NB3, 177; TS, 319, 321): excessive mathematical detail (**129.4**); (NB3, 177): "left" and "right," "above" and "below" crossed out and compass points written in; four diagrams (NB3, 176) (**129.7**).

• Quin's servants: (NB3, 183): picking up the Coming, Being, and Going paradigm on the inside front cover (**133.2**); (NB3, 183; TS, 333): the "preestablished arbitrary" predating the serial theme (**134.2**); the acetylene blowlamp (NB3, 191; TS, 345) (**136.3**); (NB3, 184v): "[Quin] was haven" added (**135.1**); (NB3, 189, 191): "the Tomness of Tom," his thereness, his thenness (**136.2**). NB3 (191) ends with the Tom, Dick, and Harry passage [no frog song]. Quin's seriality is latent, not yet explicit.

NB4: a soft-bound exercise book, marbled wrappers of mottled red, the front cover noting (a large black scrawl): "Poor Johnny / Watt / 4 Rousillon"; the inside front cover: "*Samuel Beckett* Watt IV"; the first page: "Rousillon, October 4th, 1943." Interleaved squared white [yellowed] paper and onionskin

(HRHRC 1 to 176); 18.5 x 26.5 cm. Extensively revised, with several pages deleted, and others full of "Schematic diagrams, doodles, calculations" (Admussen 91); both rectos and versos [paper] used, with the onionskin for corrections; Beckett's notes often in French. NB4 continues where NB3 stopped: the garden, the fishwoman, and Louit's story; Knott is still "Quin." The asylum scenes, since recognizably the final text and not depicted in the early typescript, are better considered [in my evaluation] "late" than "early" ("level 3"). Also 50 sheets of squared white [grey] paper, plus three cream [tan] sheets, 177 to 282 in the HRHRC enumeration, rewriting chapter 1, into Arsene's speech, and outlining many of the later paradigms. Coetzee (253) calls these "Beginning of C" (my "level 3"); I concur, but include in this category the asylum scenes and discuss them after the early typescript.

• NB4 begins with details (TS, 347ff), much of it later deleted, relating to the series of servants and pictures.
• details worked into various scenes: (NB4, 2; TS, 351): Watt speculates about the picture(s) (**131.1**); (NB4, 6; TS, 357): Quin's ringing a bell so that Watt may clear his meals (**145.1**); (NB4, 9; TS, 461): the "PLOPF" sequence more explicit, less extended (**147.4**) [transferred to the end of the typescript, and finally to part III]; "assuming that the ground was level" added (**146.2**); (NB4, 10): Quin's telephone call (12:15 p.m.) from "Mr Keith Jones" (**148.1**) [also transferred].
• (NB4, 5; TS, 355): the Frog Song meticulously laid out (**136.5**) [121 intervals, but not 11 x 11]; "the time and the place and the loved one" added as a verso insert (NB4, 4).
• (NB4, 10ff): the gardener Mr. Kevin Gomez (**142.5**), his ancestry (the Spanish Armada) extensively outlined (13ff); (NB4, 25; TS, 361): Watt consoles him (**169.9**); (NB4, 25): "Bandavita" becomes "Bandavagita" (**170.1**).
• (NB4, 26ff; TS, 369): Louit's story as part of that consolation (**171.2**); (NB4, 29; TS, 371): "Coloured Beads" added (**171.4**); (NB4, 28; TS, 373): "hay" and "straw" added (**172.1, 172.2**).
• the examination: (NB4, 33, 47): "Conan" becomes "Nacibal" (**174.1**); (NB4, 36ff): the committee's roles as in the final text; at first not named, then (NB4, 76, 79): "Stern, Mr O'Wein, Mac Meldon, Baker"; a diagram of their [twenty] head movements (no errors) (**174.7**); (NB4, 45; TS, 391): numbers allocated in two inverted hats or mortar-boards (**179.1**); (NB4, 46): "walk [of life]" replaced by "crawl" (**181.3**); (NB4, 46): "If I tell you this": change of topic signaled by change of ink (**181.6**); (NB4, 49): Mr. Gomez falls asleep (**182.4**); (NB4, 52): Beckett errs in multiplying 74 by 74 [the mistake entering all English texts] (**183.4**); (NB4, 53): "A goat, an old goat!" (**184.1**); (NB4, 52-53): the Recording Secretary says "Eine" ("or Fuck") (**184.2**); (NB4, 53; TS, 405): passing of wind more audible (**184.5**); (NB4, 65): the treasurer swivels his head "like a bear" (**31.5, 191.2**); (NB4, 67, 73): errors in cubing introduced (**195.1**); (NB4, 77): the names of the examination committee as: Kelly, O'Wein, Mac Meldon, Stern, Baker (**174.7**); (NB4, 77 [diagram, 73]): the exitus in inverted alphabetical order (**195.4**); (NB4, 78): "small [porter]" replaced by "stout" ["Power" there from the outset] (**197.3**); (NB4, 81): Watt does not as readily tire of telling Louit's tale [the rest later deleted].

- the fishwoman: (NB4, 82-89; TS, 445-59): placed after Louit's story; "Mrs Watt" (the "Mrs Watson" of part II?); "Mrs Piscoe" has lovers before and after [not yet during] her husband (**138.1**); (NB4, 84): the "man's man" paradigm as "M" and "W" (**139.2**); (NB4, 88): "probably tractable ? " (**142.1**).
- the finale of part II: (NB4, 89-90; TS, 461): "So sad, so alone" and "Sadder, aloner" (**148.3**); (NB4, 90): "yellowest" (**148.5**); "But the night was not over" marked for deletion; Watt's months of service noted; (NB4, 91): Easter bells ring at intervals to match the frogs (**136.4**); (NB4, 93): the arrival of a "strange man" (Quin's sense of Mr. Hackett), named "Phelps" (**149.3**).

Level 2: the [early] typescript.

Described by Admussen (92) as 222 sheets of typing paper (blue and black ribbon, black carbon); the first 111 onionskin [octavo; HRHRC numbering, 1 to 226]; the next 38 pink [folio; HRHRC 227 to 302], untypically typed both recto and verso; the remaining 73 gray [octavo; HRHRC 303 to 462, the final two pages mis-numbered]: "Incomplete typescript differing considerably from published text." Admussen's numbering does not match that of the HRHRC (some pages seem not to have been considered). Like Carlton Lake before him, he appreciates that the typescript is "composite," yet does not indicate clearly the distinct periods of composition. Beckett contributed to the confusion, as his signed note on the first page ("Original typescript of *Watt*. Incomplete") implies a unity. As Coetzee has shown, this is not so, despite the one typewriter used throughout; in all likelihood, Beckett typed up his drafts as he went, rather than as a distinct act of re-creation. The first set of pages (HRHRC 1-226) is obviously much earlier than the rest; but some pages within that earlier still. A few pages (HRHRC 183/184 and 459-62) are mis-numbered. The "outline" Cohn notes (111) is a more compact (and legible) rendition of earlier material; but most "shaping" (112) was done before NB5 and NB6 (perhaps part of NB4), not after.

Yet at some point Beckett took stock, gathering the retyped material together. This point seems to be (conceptually) in the middle of the fourth notebook. Most of NB4 is pre-typescript (my "early" or "level 1"), but the latter part, a rewriting of part 1, is in my judgment post-typescript (my "late" or "level 3"). The typescript ends with the close of Watt's first period of service, Easter bells, and the coming of Phelps (see **149.1**); there is a similar closure in NB4 (93), which continues with what is recognizably part III, *Watt* transferred to another pavilion. For my purposes, this hiatus separates the "early" from the "late" materials.

The typescript, then, offers various condensates of earlier material. The first pages are a little murky as the revisions are clearly "early" (Coetzee's level A), even as they were retained into this typescript (his level B). Here, and here alone, I use Coetzee's "A" and "B" [in square brackets] to suggest the primary provenance of detail. Other points noted at "level 2" are either new details, or revisions of earlier materials. Many details from the first three [four] notebooks carry over into the typescript, unchanged; these I double code with "NB" and "TS," as [above] at "level 1."

The thrust of these notes is not to record all aspects of the typescript but rather to note critical moments of change. The typescript, since "incomplete," makes no reference to part IV nor to much of part III, saving materials later transposed from part II (Louit, the garden scene). NB4's rewriting of the opening of part I constitutes virtually a new text. There is thus a leap after the typescript, where the novel is still at a primitive stage, to "level 3," where the text is recognizably *Watt*. Like all punctuated evolution, this "lepp" is more ideal than real, for Beckett's writing and revising apparently overlapped, as indicated [below] by the "cromlech" detail, rewritten in NB5 (1) ["late"] yet present in the typescript (228) ["early"]. Even so, the broad differences are sufficiently marked as to constitute distinct levels.

• much of the first pages a final version of matters discussed in NB1 [above].
• the piano [not yet in part II]: (TS, 3) [A]: "Green" replaced "Hicks" as the piano-tuner; (TS, 9) [A, B]: the hammers and dampers dialogue between Quin and Green extended (**72.1**); (TS, 125) [B]: "things of note" (**72.2**, **128.4**).
• (TS, 11-13) [A, B]: Quin meets an old man in the garden: as in NB1 (21), but "Et si non alium" deleted; "Boss" added; the "monkey-puzzle" becomes a "rush"; "We was boys together" added; "If it hadn't been you" and the wetting of trousers taken from Quin's talk with Hunchy Hackett (NB1, 31), as that was cut; (TS, 13): Quin's journal entry about the hardy laurel (NB1, 25) on a piece of paper that disappears without trace (a penciled insertion) (**#29**).
• (TS, 25) [B]: Quin beneath the round table first conceives the round bed (**207.3**).
• the dinner-party: (TS, 25ff): "geese" becomes "duck" (**13.4**); the "piteous crying" of James first noted.
• (TS, 31) [A, B]: the "Rathcullen" Hacketts become the "Glencullen"; "Hunchy" Hackett still Quin's night visitor; his accident and God's forgiveness refined (**15.7**).
• (TS, 37) [A]: deletion of a comparison with Descartes in Quin's retiring to his bed.
• (TS, 45) [A, B]: Alexander Quin neglects James for the ravanastron (71.4); (TS, 47) [A]: James learns how many wells make a river and how many millet grains a heap (**43.3**); (TS, 49) [A, B]: Quin's love for Leopardi [the "luna candida" and "nightsong" as Watt finally departs] (**217.1**) explicit (**#27**).
• (TS, 53ff) [A, B]: Quin's "soul-landscape" re-worked, a poetic sense of Nothing (the waste, the sky) (**#22**).
• Quin's household [consolidating details of NB1 and NB2]: (TS, 67, 85): Arthur gone; Erskine the "butler-valet" and Arsene a "cook-general" (**56.5**), faithful because their pay is high; (TS, 81) [A]: the house of granite (**16.1**), with three floors and a skylight (**#11**); (TS, 89): the round table on a massive conical frustum (**#20**), four Cornelscourt imitation-walnut chairs; (TS, 125): the "extraordinary newell lamp" (**83.5**).
• the painting[s]: (TS, 93) [A]: the portrait of "James" now that of "Alexander" Quin, by "Black Velvet" O'Connery, whose death was provoked by Parnell's fall (**#2**); the full description of Alexander seated at his piano (**#26**). [The separation of Alexander from James Quin is a crucial step toward the Watt/Knott dichotomy].
• (TS, 51) [A, B]: a final rendition of "The Chartered Accountant's Saturday Night" (**28.10**); (TS, 73, 115) [A, B]: the Lourdes sequence extended (**28.8**);

(TS, 97-103) [A, B]: the *Mus eventratus mcgilligani* in hilarious detail (**28.9**) [later deleted but an echo remains as the committee admonishes Louit: "Not another word . . . not a word more"] (**184.2**); (TS, 101) [B]: more ecclesiastical authorities (**29.2**); (TS, 105) [B]: "eels of Como" extended as part of McGilligan's meditation (**28.1**); (NB2, 25): the painting by "Gerald of the Nights"; (TS, 116v) [A, B]: anagrams of the Holy Family (**27.8**).

• (TS, 115) [A, B]: anticipation of a "Distant Mixed Fifth-rate Choir," to sing the threne (descant) (**33.8**, **#34**).

• small changes (from NB2) in part I: (TS, 133): the Runner Duck poem emended (**45.6**); (TS, 143): the Maddened jest (**46.7**); (TS, 159): "[The] whacks, [the] moans" a sonnet [not yet part of Arsene's statement] (**46.9**); (TS, 145): part's equality with the whole (NB2, 72-73) much reduced (**#6**); (TS, 175): "The roses are blooming" added by hand (**47.8**); (TS, 193): "Prophetic ejaculation!"; (TS, 197ff): "we" becomes "Johnny" [repeating rather than developing NB2]; (TS, 205): "Johnny will not / Abate one tot" improved (**#23**); (TS, 211): "unwindings" of the understanding and the dianoetic laugh, leading to the tale untold [later deleted] of the rabbi's trousers (**48.3**).

• (TS, 211, 215ff): a clearer record of "our" meeting with Arsene in Quin's hall, to be published in *A Good Clean Man*, Book of the Week in 2080, the praises of which (a leap year) to be sung by a mixed choir (**34.1**, **#23**); (TS, 219): "The Tuesday scowls" near the choir, but marked for relocation (**46.8**).

• (TS, 221): the song of the Mixed Choir appears in full [in the text thereafter, but some details deleted] (**34.1**, **#36**); (TS, 223): "currant bun" a "yellow" one (**35.1**).

• (TS, 227, 229): following the mixed choir: "we" crossed out, and "Watt" first inserted; "he" replaces "we" (**50.3**). Pink folio paper indicative of a somewhat later [but still "early"] provenance (NB3). Watt rises [not yet from the ditch].

• small details [pink folio paper, 227ff]: (TS, 227): wisdom like a stamp collection; (TS, 227): "a little wind" signals dawn [finally placed much later]; (TS, 229): sorrow like an egg or shell collection (**50.3**); (TS, 231): "Ann" replaced by "Jane" (**51.1**, **52.4**); (TS, 232): "vitamens" by "vitamines" (NB3, 46) (**52.1**); (TS, 232): "boa-constrictor" and "Aran Islander" deleted, but "naturist" added; Beckett's preference [not adopted until the French translation] for "coprophage" (**52.3**); (TS, 235ff): the sense of imminent departure accentuated (**55.2**); (TS, 237) "Quin" crossed out and "Knott" written in [apparently the first instance, but probably a much later change]; (TS, 239-42): servants in their final order (**59.2**); (TS, 244): a crude ending of part I added by hand (**64.3**) [the date of this uncertain, but a crucial moment of transition for it signals the change of focus from the pointless passageway dialogue to Watt's experience, this in turn an index of "early" text becoming "late"].

• Mr. Quin as master: (TS, 245): Watt's entering Quin's service on June 26 crossed out (**67.2**, **104.1**); (TS, 245): Quin's rising and meals directly follow the "good master" statement; his days include Thursday (**86.3**) [no existential concerns about the pot].

• the poss: (TS, 245): John Earle *Microcosmography* reference retained (from NB1, 3), the emphasis less the "Clean Old Man" character than the preparation of Quin's poss [Earle echoes later deleted] (**87.1**); (TS, 247): introduction to part II leads directly to preparation of Quin's food (**68.4**); (TS, 247-

48): revisions to Quin's responsibility paradigm (**89.2**); (TS, 246): the ingredients of Quin's poss refined; (TS, 249): the quantities multiplied by fourteen (**87.2**), this change made on the typescript; (TS, 246): Quin eats at noon and 6 p.m. (**88.2**); (TS, 252): "And is it not strange" reflection at this point (**95.2**); (TS, 254): a gap left for the copying of Erskine's ("che sciagura") song from NB3 (84) may have led to the final hiatus (**85.7**).

• small changes in part II (the famished dog sequence as in NB3): (TS, 254): a "pigeon" defecates on a "parish priest" (**91.4**); (TS, 262): the formula for the solutions (one erroneous) given (**98.1**); (TS, 269): the date of Watt's entering Quin's service cut (**67.2**) ["Watt" now clearly established, but "Quin" still present].

• the Lynch millennium (minor changes only from NB3): (TS, 267): Simon's effeminacy, with no hiatus or question mark (**102.3**); (TS, 269): further millennial calculations (**104.4**); (TS, 269): "was delivered of" [a child] (NB3, 109) changed to "expelled" (**104.5**); (TS, 272): "taking off her clothes" (NB3, 112) to "dressing up for the night" (**107.1**); (TS, 275ff): the breeding of famished dogs still extended, despite many cuts; (TS, 280): Watt's mother, wife, and/or little girl, crates and copulation (**111.1**); (TS, 290ff): "Frank" still present (**102.6**); (TS, 299): Quin likened to Christ.

• post-millennium changes: (TS, 300-01): Erskine's duties cut; (TS, 204v): the bell sequence rewritten as an insert; (TS, 307): "a little deranged" now "a little demented" [later "off the hooks"] (**122.1**); (TS, 313): "put in" replaced by "foisted" (**126.1**); "dripping" (NB3, 171) by "putty, or in [*sic*] butter" (**127.1**); (TS, 315): "chance" (NB3, 170) by "Lachesis" (**127.3**); "fly-[buttons]" by "flap-."

• (TS, 311-13): narrative "we" crossed out and "n" entered [not yet "Sam"] (**125.1**). These changes are not *in* the typescript, but *on* it (revisions or inserts); (TS, 312v): the "This does not mean" paragraph added on a verso (upside down); additions of "I" and "my little notebook" (**126.1**).

• (TS, 319): ["by a ruse" (NB3, 173) not yet inverted] (**128.2**).

• the picture (TS, 317): "almost black" crossed out and "blue" returned (**128.7**); (TS, 317): the "coloured reproduction or original" now a "painting" by "the Dutch painter X" [Bram van Velde?] (**129.1**) ["picture" is finally preferred] (**208.4**); (TS, 318v): truth-table of circle and center (**129.4**); what the painter "intended" to "portray" (**129.3**); (TS, 319-21): the earlier mathematics cut (**129.4**); (TS, 323): "left" to "right" as the perspective changes; two diagrams (**129.7**); (TS, 325): why Walter must have brought the painting (**130.3**); (TS, 329): Watt can date the painting (**129.3**) [he does not yet take it down (no "hook") nor does its significance erode] (**129.7**).

• the serial theme: (TS, 333): variations to the servant "out/up/in" sequence (NB3, 183); "depending on" changed to "conforming to," then "consisting with" (**133.3**); (TS, 339-43): "the Tomness of Tom" (several pages) cut (**136.2**); (TS, 351): pictures by Kaspar David Friedrich, Hercules Segher, and Adam Elsheimer removed as Watt's impotence grows (**131.1**); (TS, 358v): "Add to this" (complexion, hair) as an insert, anticipating Knott's features (**147.3**); the Frog Song orchestrated (TS, 355), 11 rows of 11 (**136.5**) [possibly a later insert, as the typescript text is discontinuous (353-59)].

• the garden: (TS, 361ff): Mr. Gomez's long ancestry excised, but otherwise as NB4; the "Mr Graves" written in (TS, 398) may post-date NB5 (**142.5**).

• Louit's story [here part of "part II"] expanded: (TS, 367): "~~Bandavagita~~" replaced by "Bando" (**170.1**); (TS, 369): "~~Primitives~~" (NB4, 26) become "Visicelts" (**171.3**); (NB4, 30; TS, 373, 375): "Handcross" and "Ennis" written into the hiatuses (**172.3, 173.3**); Louit's trip dated "December the 3rd" (**173.3**); (TS, 377, 395ff): "Nacibal" [Caliban] becomes "Nakibal" [not yet "Nackybal"] (**174.1**); (TS, 377): "manure" (NB4, 34) becomes "everyman his own fertiliser" (**174.4**).

• the examination committee referred to by name, not function; NB4 names consistently crossed out and others entered: "Mr Kelly" now Magershon, "O'Wein" Fitzwein, "Mac Meldon" O'Meldon, "Stern" MacStern; "Baker" de Baker;

• (TS, 380v): a new diagram of their head movements (**174.7**); (TS, 391): hats and mortar boards removed (**179.1**); (TS, 401): roof, cupola, spire, dome, treetop, and tower ordered alphabetically (**183.3**); (TS, 403): the ~~Recording Secretary~~ Mr de Baker says, "Not another word" (**184.2**); (TS, 405): a "post hoc" footnote comes and goes; (TS, 415): "~~Victorian epoch~~" becomes "Kulchurkampf" (**188.2**); (TS, 421): "~~like a bear~~" crossed out (**191.2**); (TS, 423): "~~extraction~~" now "extirpation" (**192.1**); (TS, 429): "Little by little" proverb completed (**194.4**); (TS, 441): "the stout porter Power" (**197.3**); (TS, 443; NB4, 81): Louit's duplicity elaborated (**198.2**), then curtailed since space lacking, time wanting (**62.1**); (TS, 441ff): much detail (NB4, 83) crossed out.

• the fishwoman: (TS, 445ff): still placed after the Louit story, but "~~Mrs Piscoe~~" changed (TS, 449) to "Mrs Gorman" (**139.1**); (TS, 449): a comparison of men and women to long-horned bulls and short-horned cows (NB4, 82) crossed out; (TS, 455): "[tractable] disturbance" written in (**142.1**).

• finale of part II [HRHRC pages 459-62 mis-numbered]: (TS, 461): PLOPF "break wind" (NB4, 9) becomes "make a strange noise" (**147.4**); (TS, 461): "yellowest" (NB4, 90) reads "yellowist," as in all editions (**148.5**); (TS, 459): a lyrical passage of the Easter bells (**149.1**); (TS, 461) the months of service (NB4, 90) deleted; "And not the night, not yet" [later, "A little before morning"]; the final, reduced version added [later?] to the last verso (TS, 462), the newcomer renamed Martin (**149.3**) [but Quin remains Quin, the most compelling index of "early" as opposed to "late"].

Level 3: the "late" drafts (part of NB4; NB5, and NB6).

NB4 (93-282): since these drafts (the rewritten parts I and II) post-date the typescript, I consider them "late" rather than "early"; however [as noted above], the asylum scenes cannot be so assigned unambiguously, and the genesis of some charts and diagrams, especially those on the loose sheets, is uncertain. Nor is there (NB4, 93) an emphatic manuscript gap between the arrival of Phelps and Watt's transference; but the new material (Watt and Sam, Watt's inversions, Knott's paradigms, the finale of part III), essentially as published, are better [at least, in this study] considered "late." Pages 141 to 152 (HRHRC numbering) are separated from the notebook; there are no pages ripped out of NB4 at this point (they may have been torn from the end), so the implied sequence of composition is doubtful [more probably, the paradigms came after the aphasia].

The asylum scenes to the end of part III:
• narrative perspective: (NB4, 139): Beckett noted, "Watt tells 4 before 3" (**215.3**); at the end of NB4 (175): "Present dogs, food, picture, etc. as told by W. as Committee told" [this obscurely indicates a change]. NB4 (97): "~~me~~" crossed out and "Sam" written in [part II presumably revised at this time to bring him in incrementally] (**125.1**, **151.4**); "Sam" not immediately the narrative voice, but replaces the nameless "we" (he is integral; not a later revision). With minor exceptions, these late drafts are very close to the final text. Quin initially present (NB4, 92v), in a checked list of details; but Knott soon takes over (see **166.3** for the possible turning point).
• (NB4, 92): preliminary note: "Quin in need of witness" (**203.2**).
• (NB4, 95): "No truck" paragraph added as insert (**153.1**); (NB4, 99) the asylum garden: "overarching boughs" added (**155.2**); gap (?) after "Cork" (**156.1**); (NB4, 101): "~~animals~~" replaced by "quadrupeds."
• (NB4, 102ff): infuriated bull paradigm introduced (**161.2**) [virtually final]; (NB4, 105): periods, rather than semi-colons (**158.1**); (NB4, 106): the Christ, "supposedly by Bosch"; hanging "in the National Gallery" (**159.3**); (NB4, 106): "handkerchief" (**159.5**) [but first inversions present]; "with a pole" [not a perch] (**160.1**).
• Watt's aphasia: (NB4, 114ff): detailed manuscript notes (**164.2** to **168.4**), much crossed out and redone; (NB4, 121): intended patterns of inversions (**164.3**), each illustrated by a "Pardon beg" variation; (NB4, 119-22): "translations" of the inversions (**164.2**, **165.4**, **166.3**, **167.1**, **167.4**, **168.2**, **168.4**); (NB4, 122-23): shaving items ordered alphabetically (**167.1**); (NB4, 129): "suppose, suspect, presume" variations rehearsed, perhaps with an error in the sixth (**165.1**); (NB4, 129): "all went well" variations rehearsed (**164.3**); (NB4, 137): "so much balls" added (**167.2**); (NB4, 136): "Watt began" became "a tendency appeared" (**165.3**); Watt's final mode in vain (**168.4**); (NB4, 136): "o no" lacks aspiration (**168.5**).
• (NB4, 119, 121): a radical speculation: that "Quin" crystallized as "Knott" in Watt's inversion, "Tonk" (**166.3**).
• the garden scene now in part III: NB4 offers an immediate transition from the aphasia to the paradigms, the latter probably composed as the natural consequence of the former.
• the monstrous paradigms in final and almost error-free form; some in NB4 (122ff); many on loose leafs: (NB4, 154-55, 160): Knott's footwear (**200.3**); (NB4, 124, 125, 127): his movements (**203.4**); (NB4, 160ff): his furniture (**204.2**); (NB4, 143-49 [loose leaves separated from the notebook], 164-65): his physical features (**209.7**); (NB4, 150): his night-dress (**211.3**).
• (NB4, 157): introduction of the "when one is no longer young" prose-poem (**201.1**); (NB4, 151 [loose leaf]): the stars [but not London] (**212.1**); a "strip [?] of white light" becomes a "fascia" (**212.2**).
• (NB4, 166): Watt's vomiting on leaving (**208.1**); the water-tight grouse-bag mentioned (**223.4**) [details later deleted].
• (NB4, 169): "~~dry earth~~" crossed out and "bamboos" written in (**209.1**); (NB4, 168); "land against the waves" revises "~~waves against the shore land~~" (NB4, 168); Knott's dactyls include: "[~~illegible~~]," "kakaka," and "quaquaqua."
• (NB4, 170): the ending of part III assumes its final form (**213.4**).

The rewriting of part I [on loose leaves included with NB4].

Substantially the final text; with a few minor changes and new details:

• minor changes to the opening: (NB4, 177): "they" present (**7.4**); (NB4, 181): the policeman's gritty words (**9.2**); (NB4, 191ff): the lady and gentleman gradually "Goff" and "Tetty" (**9.8**); (NB4, 189): "Arthur" becomes "Larry" (**12.11**); (NB4, 189): "Berry" with "Cream" (**13.4**); (NB4, 191): "womb" (NB1, 37; TS, 27) becomes "woom"; then "womb"; and finally (NB4, 191) "wom" (**13.5**); (NB4, 191) "osé" becomes "osy" (**14.1**); (NB4, 196v): "the goat" added (**16.2**); (NB4, 204): the stop "merely facultative" (**19.5**).

• (NB4, 223ff): Mr. Spiro first appears (**27.2**); (NB4, 224): J. Jurms finds his po (**27.8**); (NB4, 227ff): *Mus eventratus mcgilligani* and Chartered Accountant sequences cut (**28.9**, **28.10**, **#3**); MacKenzie's address no longer "Poste restante, Lourdes" (**28.8**).

• (NB4, 229): the "sang cried stated murmured" paradigm in its final form (**29.13**).

• (NB4, 241): the second verse begins "*Fifty-two point one*" (**35.1**) [this the final writing before the galleys, where "*Fifty-one*" is recorded]; (NB4, 240) Watt hears the choir (a note flat) in C sharp major (**33.8**)

• (NB4, 243-49): Arsene's statement substantially as in the final text, but the order of the material (Watt 37-42) differs; (NB4, 251): he begins with "Haw!" (**39.3**).

• changes to Arsene's speech: (NB4, 265): Lisbon's great day in 1759 (**43.5**); (NB4, 267): "Agincourt" becomes "Crécy" (**44.5**); (NB4, 261): the ladder joke is "The Welshman's dream" (**44.8**); (NB4, 275): the inquiry about the name, "Big Ben" (**46.2**); (NB4, 275): Mr. Ash (newly appearing) dies of pneumonia (**46.4**).

• new details (often verso inserts): (NB4, 181): abrupt narrative break (**8.4**); (NB4, 212v): Mr. Nixon's "For example" and Mr. Hackett's reply inserted (*Watt* 22); (NB4, 222v): "anagram of mud" added (**27.2**); (NB4, 228): "so (Indian artist)ish when empty": lacuna not intended (**29.15**); (NB4, 234): "deficient in   ?   ": lacuna intended (**32.4**); (NB4, 245): "bugger these buttons" (*Lear*) enters the text (**63.7**); (NB4, 239): "leaves that are never still" raked from Arsene's speech (**33.4**).

NB5: bound in hard red covers, 90 leaves (180 pp.) of squared white paper, 19.5 x 30 cm., plus front and back fly-leaves. The outer front cover notes: "Samuel Beckett Watt V / Suite et fin / 18.2.45 / 5 Paris / Et debut de L'ABSENT / Malone meurt / Novembre-Janvier 47/48." Beckett noted (100): "Beginning of Malone meurt originally entitled "L'ABSENT"; and on page 180: "End of 1st part of Malone meurt concluded in separate notebook (SB)." Coetzee records (253): "First 50 leaves given to Watt, the next 39 to Malone meurt, leaf 90 to notes on Watt" [the HRHRC numbering doubles these]; Admussen says (91): "Moderate to extensive revision and reorganization but less than in preceding notebooks." The opening pages are ripped out, but NB5 begins with the cromlech passage rewritten (*Watt* 49), then revisits the end of part I. It follows part II to the painting, servants, and frogs (as the final text); then jumps to part III (a note to that effect), restructuring the garden scene and rewriting Louit's examination. Knott has taken over from Quin, but Sam is not yet a presence (in these parts). Several verso and final passages are labeled "A, B, C . . . P" for later insertion. The *Watt* material of NB5 ends (99) with Beckett's (later?) note: "End of continuation of Watt concluded in Notebook VI."

• (NB5, 1): a rewrite of the cromlech passage (**49.4**), introducing new motifs: "blinding my eyes . . . stamp or an egg (**50.3**) . . . place of another man" (**50.9**) [Arsene's earlier prophetic "Haw!" (NB3, 17; TS, 193) not yet interwoven] (**39.3**). [These details are in the pink folio typescript (227ff), which complicates the otherwise useful distinction between "early" and "late" drafts; that is, the typing up of some "early" material must have taken place after the "late" writing was under way].

• (NB5, 2): a rewrite of the end of part I, in virtually final form (**63.9** to **64.4**).

• (NB5, 5ff): opening of part II rewritten; minor changes include: (NB5, 7): the consumptive postman named "Shannon" (**47.7**); "Mr Gomez" no longer "the gardener" [but not yet "Mr. Graves"] (**142.5**); the earlier telephone call now "The telephone seldom rang." A devastating use of the comma prevails.

• (NB5, 8v): a fishwoman reference considered (not added) as an insert (**69.6**).

• (NB5, 13): "various incidents" now "incidents of note" (**72.2**); the piano incident in virtually its final form.

• the "pot" sequences expanded: (NB5, 15ff): "fragility of outer meaning" added (**73.4**); (NB3, 16v): Watt's trousers fistular (**74.5**); (NB5, 17): "Mrs Watson" unnamed here but soon mentioned (NB5, 29) (**74.2**, **80.4**); (NB5, 23): "as though he were a man" includes "in part" [later deleted] (**77.6**); (NB5, 28v): "He had realised" sentence (*Watt* 80-81) a late insert; (NB5, 30v): footnote a late insert (**82.3**); (NB5, 31): "something," then "Grail" replaced by "raven" (**83.2**).

• (NB5, 33): the "extraordinary newell lamp" (TS, 125) brought from Quin's hall (**83.5**).

• (NB5, 37): "the dog" [not yet "Kate"] (**85.5**, **112.3**).

• (NB5, 37): Knott's rising (TS, 245) placed after the piano and pot sequences (**86.2**); his Sunday inactivity added (**86.3**), at the expense of Thursday.

• the poss: (NB5, 37): Erskine's song changed (**85.7**); (NB5, 39): the poss prepared on Sunday (**87.2**); simplified, but new elements added (**87.4**); (NB5, 40v): Knott eats at noon (sharp) and 7 p.m. exactly (a verso insert) (**88.2**).

• (NB5, 42v, 43): the paradigm, "Mr Knott was responsible," in its final form (**89.3**, **90.1**).

• (NB5, 45): the first manifestation of "a voice" (**91.1**) [not yet "little"].

• (NB5, 45): "canon" replaces a "man of parts" (TS, 254); his "privates" now his "crotch"; he is defecated on, by a pigeon (**91.2**).

• (NB5, 53): the parenthesis about cleaning the boots created [later extended]; the gardener not named but a gap left for his name (**95.1**).

• (NB5, 57): a simple contrast of green and red, but a fuller paradigm {red, green, violet, none} on the opposite verso (**96.3**).

• (NB5, 57): final objection added to the number of solutions (**98.1**).

• (NB5, 59ff): embedded instructions to skip the Lynch episode, i.e., to work from the earlier typescript; that section not rewritten save the paragraph, "This set back . . ." (*Watt* 109). NB5 jumps from "without delay" (*Watt* 98) to "This little matter" (111), lacking the long intervening paragraph (**110.2**).

- (NB5, 59): Art and Con appear (**101.7**).
- (NB5, 66v, 67): "grace" added later to "transgression" (**116.2**).
- (NB5, 67): "This refusal" is Watt's alone (**115.3**).
- (NB5, 71-75): fragmented text, with Beckett's instructions to add several passages at various points (**118.2**).
- the picture: (NB5, 77): "object of note" replaces "other thing" (TS, 317) (**128.4**); "reproduction" now a "picture" (**129.1**); "western" crossed out, "eastern" written in (perspective of the object, not the subject) (**128.6**); the point "blue, but blue!" (**128.7**); Watt's knowledge of painting eroded (**129.3**); "endless time" erodes "limitless time" (TS, 319); (NB5, 76v): a truth-table added (**129.4**); (**129.5**); (NB5, 79): co-ordinates in their final form (**129.7**); (NB5, 78v): "by the nadir" a later insert (**130.2**).
- the series of servants, pictures, and (now) frogs: three verso inserts (NB5, 80v): "like Knott's bed, for example" (**130.4**); "There were times" paragraph, with Mr. Nackybal (**131.3**); "This supposition" paragraph (**138.1**). (NB5, 81): "explanation" replaced by "xenia" (**132.2**); (NB5, 83): "this monstrous assumption" added (**132.5**); the servants' coming and going (NB3, 182ff; Watt 133-36) not re-presented here (**133.2**), but to be added from previous drafts; (NB5, 84v): three brief paragraphs ("ancient labour") inserted before the Frog Song (**136.3**).
- (NB5, 93): a major decision noted here to reallocate part of the garden material (NB4, 138ff) in part II to the end of part III; Arthur named "Martin" and the gardener (no longer "Gomez") is briefly "Gorman" (**169.6**); but the decision recorded (NB5, 87) to call him "Mr Graves" (**69.3**, **142.5**).
- (NB5, 94ff): a revised encounter in the garden (**#29**): as the final text, save that "Martin" is taken for Mr. Knott; "Knott" has replaced "Quin" (TS, 11-13); "bush or shrub" becomes "shrub, or bush" [changed order, comma]; and three final paragraphs are added, placing him in a vermicular series with Diderot's rose and gardener.
- (NB5, 182): Beckett added on the inside back cover extra "Notes," four constituting **#9** to **#12** of the Addenda: "Watt learned to accept" (**#19**); Arsene's declaration coming back to Watt (**#10**); "One night Watt goes out on roof" (**#11**); "Watt snites" (**#12**). Other decisions were: to "call the choir a descant" (**33.8**); "Gall incident. Not a ring but a knock" (**77.2**; NB2, 20v); Knott to eat "with a little silver trowel" (**89.1**); and (crucially) to move the story of Louit and "Nacibal" [*sic*], as told by Phelps to Mr. Gomez and overheard by Watt, from part II and to relocate it in part III (**169.6**).

NB6: a soft-covered exercise book with an orange-brown cover ("Jehanne au bucher" ["Joan of Arc at the stake"], 48 leaves of squared paper [HRHRC numbering, 1 to 96], 17.5 x 22 cm.; with a further two sheets of folded notepaper, 13.5 x 17.5 cm, and ten leaves of squared white [gray] paper, 19.5 x 30 cm [HRHRC, 97-120]. Undated; but the last loose sheet (119) is marked "Dec 28, 1944 / END." A later cover note states: "Watt VI concluded [*Samuel Beckett*]" with "6 / Paris" scrawled in crayon. This, the shortest notebook, treats part IV, the text virtually that of the published novel. Admussen notes (92) that the text is "moderately revised," with doodles and a diagram of the waiting room; I consider most of the revisions under my "level 4."

Features include:
- (NB6, 3): Phelps [not yet Arthur] (**216.1**).
- (NB6, 5): Watt is taken by surprise (**216.3**); his feelings of nothingness [later deleted]; the moment come, with a hiatus and question-mark (**216.5**); the milk simply drunk, the cigar lit (**216.5**); (NB6, 7): Watt appreciates Micks's labials (**216.7**).
- Watt's departure, small additions: (NB6, 9): the grousebag, "of which mention has been made" (**217.3**); (NB6, 10v): "immersion in canal water" as insert [no "of course"] (**218.2**); (NB6, 15): "four and six" replaced by "half a crown" [not yet "eight pence"] (**219.1**); "so reasonably" by "for such a sum"; "in excellent repair" by "shipshape" (**219.3**); (NB6, 19): Micks "raising his hand to his mouth" (**220.1**); (NB6, 22v): the bags paradigm as insert (**221.2**); (NB6, 29): Watt regrets not taking leave of Phelps [not Micks]; (NB6, 31): "hortulan beauties" (**223.1**); (NB6, 33): Watt's sense of worry explicit (*Watt* 223); the ass present [but not yet the goat] (**223.6**); (NB6, 36v, 38v): the "stone steps" paragraph added as insert (**224.1**).
- (NB6, 51): the mysterious figure in final form (**225.2**); "would be quite sufficient" replaced by "was not necessary" (*Watt* 227); the figure possesses not only interest but "even beauty"; Watt "straining his eyes and seething his brains" (**228.1**).
- at the station: (NB6, 53): the hiatus marked "(Quotation)" (**228.3**); (NB6, 56, 59): diagram of (C within B within A) nested rooms as the Golden Rectangle (**229.2**); (NB6, 59): "Mr Farrell" and "Mr Tully" (**229.3**).
- (NB6, 91): the inscription of "unusual height, width and distinctiveness" spelled out; no hiatus (**236.3**); (NB6, 95): the lark "drops" (**237.2**); (NB6, 98): Mr. Gorman takes leave of his wife, not his mother; the narrative blackout is less clear (**238.1**).
- Watt's monstrous birthing: (NB6, 100): "(nonnulla desunt)" added to the hiatus (**238.4**); (NB6, 103): Lady McCann's "reasons" not mentioned (**240.1**); (NB6, 103): Mrs "Pim" here "Connemarra"; the "mattress" jest explained (**241.1**), as is Mr. Nolan's murmur (**242.2**); (NB6, 105): parenthesis embraces "(Locus illegibilitis)" (**241.1**); (NB6, 109): gap in the text ["Mr Cole" not yet named] (**243.1**); Mr. Farrell appreciates "a nice bit of blood" (**241.2**); (NB6, 111): Lady McCann is "less affected" (**243.3**); (NB6, 115): Beckett counts the coins to get 3/1 and 1/3.
- final scene: (NB6, 117) "[Riley's] goat" becomes "puckaun" (**246.1**); (NB6, 119): "mountains" (not "hills"); signed off "*Dec 28th 1944 / END*" (**246.4**).

Level 4: the final typescript.

Beckett may not have kept a final typescript, but after the war he gave "another copy" (Knowlson 311) to Denis Devlin to take to America. The quoted words are tricky: precisely how many copies were there? A fair copy was variously in the hands of agents and/or publishers (how long did George Reavey retain his?); read by the Merlin Juveniles; and set by the Olympia Press. These "copies" would have circulated, but there was certainly more than one, as Beckett invariably typed a carbon; none, however, has survived.

This is annoying rather than critical, but my comments must here be presumptive rather than assured. I assume that nothing substantial is missing, as the final typescript could not have been hugely different from the galleys, subject to the qualifications below that new errors entered the galleys and revisions were made on the actual proofs. I note under this "level" details that are in the galleys but not in the "late" drafts, or which represent significant reworking of earlier detail. Some items noted at "level 4" could have been listed under "level 5," and vice versa; I try to distinguish between details likely to have been in the printer's copy as opposed to features of the galleys *per se*, but without a final typescript this is a judgment call. Knowlson believes (303) that *Watt* was completed in Roussillon and that Beckett merely "tinkered" with it after his post-war return to Paris and Dublin. Yet the tinkering was extensive (especially if the final typescript was made in Paris), with much detail added (Beckett now had access to his notebooks and reference materials) and several realignments of the text. This I discuss in some 70 quasi-independent strata (*Watt* resembles *Murphy*, in that the final text reflects a process of block composition). The last words of *Watt* are not, incidentally, "no symbols where none intended" but "Paris 1945."

- 1. the opening (NB4, 177ff): minor changes: "seemed to be" for "was"; "of course" (**7.3**); "he supposed" (8); God a witness that cannot be sworn (**9.1**); the policeman's brief reply (**9.2**); "recent encounter" to "loving" (**9.3**); "oh not the last, but almost" added (**9.5**).
- 2. Goff and Tetty (NB4, 183ff): "strength" changed to "force" (**10.1**); the lady wishes to stroke Mr. Hackett's hunch (**10.2**); "Exceptions are occasionally made" becomes "He is a solicitor" (10); "primeur" (**11.1**) and "knowing your love of literature" (11) added.
- 3. "To Nelly" (NB4, 185ff): poem as in late drafts (**11.2**); "More than enough" finally "Ample"; "The spirit is exhausted" presumably present (**12.10**).
- 4. the night that Larry was born (NB4, 189ff): "God always permits" changed to "D.V."; "Dee always vees" follows (**13.2**); "Goff" and "Tetty" more subtle (**9.8**); Larry "leaped" rather than "bound" (**13.5**); "unspeakable anguish" to "dollar" (**13.7**); "osé" to "osy" (**14.1**); "~~Lyster~~ White" to "Cooper" (**15.2**); "found under a cabbage" added (**15.1**); "cue" becomes "queue" (**15.4**).
- 5. existence off the ladder (NB4, 195ff): as in the late drafts.
- 6. Watt's arrival (NB4, 199ff): "[behind] him" changed to "it" (**16.6**); Mr. Hackett's curiosity ("A male one or a female one?") curbed (**17.2**); Mrs. Nixon's fright added (21); "native of the ~~island~~ place" (NB4, 211) now "rocks" (**21.3**); "grudgingly" added (22); "a common condition I must say" added (22); "I suppose" added (23).
- 7. at the station (NB4, 217ff): Mr. Lowry (**25.2**) and Mr. Evans (**26.4**) named; "Was it . . . his hat" loses its question mark (**26.1**).
- 8. the encounter with Mr. Spiro (NB4, 223ff), as in the late draft: "Anglicans" converted to "freethinkers" (**28.6**); "for he was a man of leisure" added (**29.2**); the textual lacuna less laconic (**29.15**).
- 9. Watt's walking (NB4, 230ff): "gentleman" (**31.4**); "ischium" replaces "the right section of his bosom" (**32.5**); "sudarium" added (**32.8**); "head" [not yet "bum"] (**32.9**); "parts of the body" added (**33.3**); "sounds" changed to "nightsounds" and "bear" to "sustain" (33); "pretty" defines the nettles (33).

- 10. the mixed choir (NB4, 241ff): minor changes only from the early typescript (221); but the crucial error "*Fifty-one point one*" may have entered at this point (**34.1**, **35.1**).
- 11. Watt's arrival at Knott's house: narrative confusion in NB4 (243-49) sorted out.
- 12. Arsene's short statement (*Watt* 39-45): addition of "Haw!" (**39.3**); "a hiding place" now a "refuge" (39); the "banister" a "rail" (40); Watt's "nose" his "snout" (40); Arsene's epiphany brought forward, with day and month given (**42.4**); "warm bright wall" added for the Proustian echo (**42.11**); "one hundred metres high" added (**43.2**); "Lisbon's great day" corrected (**43.5**); "The Welshman's dream" deleted (**44.8**).
- 13. the Runner Duck episode presumably present, as in the galleys (**45.6**); Mr. Ash dies of "premature exhaustion" (**46.4**).
- 14. Arsene's springtime (reference to the early typescript rather than any later draft, but some details appear in NB5): "Not a word" (**46.5**) and "Tuesday scowls" (**46.8**) in their final place; "An ordure," "An excrement," "A turd" and "A cat's flux" added (**46.6**); "cursed [business]" becomes "bloody" (**47.12**).
- 15. *We shall be here all night*, the *risus purus*, and sorrow: "I think" added (48); "from the outer to the inner" added (48); "unwindings" become "excoriations" (**48.3**); the hours "neither happy nor unhappy" added (49); the cromlech relocated (**49.4**); "Yes" added as a link (**48, 50.1**); wiser and sadder reflections assume their final form (**50.3**); "bar parlour or canal" added (**50.7**); when one man takes the place of another: "figments of the id" replace "a nightmare vision" (**51.3**); "vitamens" [*sic*] (**52.1**); "strings" become "cello" (**53.5**). Otherwise much as the early typescript.
- 16. "Winter and summer" (begun at Roussillon): as in earlier drafts, but Arsene's hymn, then high, is now "a little low" (**57.1**).
- 17. servants who come and go (TS, 238ff): the long passage assumes its final form (**57.6ff**); the English confused with the Irish (**58.4**); "space" and "time" find home after long wandering (**62.1**); "bugger these buttons" recurrent; Arsene's final indifference to forgiveness added (**63.7**).
- 18. the ending of part I as in the insert added later to NB5 (2) (**64.3**).
- 19. Mr. Knott as master: the qualification [comma], "in a way" (**67.2**); Watt's indenture less precise (**67.2**); (NB5, 5): "strawberries" now "sea-kale" (**68.1**); "scrap heap" becomes "dunghill" (**68.2**); Watt's "mind" replaced by his "understanding"; "a shame" is remarkable" (**68.3**); "please God" added (**69.1**); the postman, "Shannon," renamed "Severn" (**69.2**); "Mr Graves" replaces "the gardener" (**69.3, 142.5**); the fishwoman insert (NB5, 8v) not finally placed here, but her presence anticipated (**69.6**); "his mouthpiece" now vocal (**69.5**); "it's" (NB5, 9) perpetuated (**70.1**).
- 20. the Galls in their final position (**68.4**): "choon" replaces "temper" (**70.3**); a question mark dropped; "disposition" (NB5, 11) now "command" (**71.1**); details of the music room (Buxtehude) from the earliest drafts (**71.3**), but the ravanastron now compared to a plover (**71.4**); the syntax more knotty (**72.3**).
- 21. fragility of outer meaning; as NB5 (15ff), expanded, with minor changes: "flowering currant" for "violets" (**74.1, 80.3**); Watt's assiduities change (**74.2**); "oh" added to "not into what they really meant" (**75.3**); "intellec-

tually" (NB5, 19) replaced by "at will" (**75.5**); "add to this" a sign of late insertion (**75.7**, **112.2**, **147.3**); deletion of "in part" (NB3, 23) (**77.6**); "hypostasized" (NB5, 24v) now "interpreted" (**78.2**); "to me" added, intimating Sam (**79.1**); "return to the incident of the Galls" added (**79.2**).

• 22. the pot sequence in its final position (**68.4**); "He had realised..." and "It was in vain..." inserts (NB5, 28, 30) now in place (**81.5**).

• 23. Mr. Knott's rising: placed after Erskine's song, breaking the poss sequence (**86.3**).

• 24. the poss: Erskine's "song" (NB5, 37) now without words (**8.4, 85.7, #37**); the poss prepared on Saturday (**87.2**); the dog's dish and details of cleaning up added (**88.3**); Mr. Knott's little plated trowel (**89.1**).

• 25. Mr. Knott was responsible: as in NB5, minor changes only: an inadvertent "Quin" corrected to "Knott" (**89.2**); Knott scrapes his bowl till it shines (89).

• 26. the famished dog (I): the priest defecated on, by a dove (**91.4**); Watt's not knowing the little voice added (**91.1**); comma after "wonderful days" added; "comparatively [rare]" (NB5, 47) finally "very" (92); the famished dog neutered (**93.1**); one "his" missed; "that [purpose]" (NB5, 53) now "no other" (95); "And is it not strange . . ." moved from the poss (TS, 252) to a new parenthesis (**95.2**); "Mr Graves" named (**95.1**); "church" strock from "old church clock" (NB5, 55) (**96.1**); green and red changed to red, green, and violet (**96.3**). Minor solutions no longer "had" (NB5, 59) but "seemed to have" prevailed (98); the "mensuality" of £4.3.4 (TS, 263) now an "annuity" of fifty pounds (**98.3**); (TS, 263): "crumb" to "atom" (**113.4**); (TS, 275; NB5, 59ff): the famished dog breeding program cut (**111.1**); narrative complexity in NB5 simplified (98-109; **110.1, 111.1**).

• 27. the Lynch millennium (the early typescript as a template for the final writing): "stomach" (TS, 266; NB5, 59) becomes "caecum" (**101.2, 109.4**); "Flo" becomes "May" (**101.4**); "Frank" (mostly) "Jack" (**101.6, 102.6**); the hiatus and question mark about Simon introduced (**102.3**); Bridie receives in the outhouse (**102.7**); haemophilia footnote added (**102.8**); "rising generation" added (Watt, 103); "erroneous" footnote added (**104.7**); "of course" and "in the meantime" added (105); the {Bill, Jim, Joe} error enters (**110.2, 110.5**).

• 28. the famished dog (II): "bitch" (NB5) consistently "dog"; the "raging, dying summer" (115) added; the apology enters the refusal (**115.3**); "disobey" (NB5, 67) becomes "transgress" (**116.4**); "appearances" (NB5, 69) give way to "forms" (**117.2**).

• 29. Erskine running up the stairs: as in NB5 (71ff).

• 30. the bell: as in NB5 (73ff), with minor changes: "perplexed" and "dissembled" (**121.2**); "off the hooks" (**122.1**); the narrator clearly Sam (**125.1, 151.4**); small details "foisted" in: "Mention has already been made . . . all the time"; "apart from this"; "for a man like Watt"; "And that does not mean . . . my little notebook"; "never never told at all" (**126.1**); "By a ruse" (NB3, 173; TS, 317) now "Ruse a by" (**128.2, 164.1**).

• 31. the picture: "object of note" replaces "only other thing" (TS, 317) (**128.4**); "It gave" (NB5, 77) changed to "Watt had" [that impression], to adjust perception (**128.5**); left and right (western, eastern) orientation affirmed (**128.6**); Watt knows nothing about art or physics (**129.3, 129.6**); deletion of "circle did not reassure" (NB5, 78v) (**130.2**).

• 32. a term in a series: as Watt's knowledge of art erodes, the wall pictures are removed (**131.1**); "There were times" and "This supposition" paragraphs (NB5, 80v) included (**130.4**, **131.3**); a [second] picture placed (Addenda only) in Erskine's room intimates Knott as serial (**130.3**, **#2**).

• 33. the period of service: as NB5 (85ff), with the earlier coming and going passage (NB3, 182ff; TS, 333ff) integrated (**133.2**); "(tired of underlining . . .)" added (**134.6**); "that would be too [horrible] to contemplate" moved into part II (**134.6**, **#6**); length of service clarified (**134.4**); "Bah" and "Pah" (TS, 335) now "Haw!" (**135.2**); the three new brief paragraphs (NB5, 84v) in final form (**136.3**).

• 34. the frog song: perhaps retaining the 11 by 11 layout (NB4, 8; TS, 355) (**136.5**).

• 35. the fishwoman: finally placed after the frog song (**138.1**); "hold a candle" added (**138.2**); Mrs. Gorman (no longer "Mrs Piscoe") has lovers during her husband (**139.1**); "Mrs Watt" (NB4, 82) gone (**139.1**); the "endocrinal Bandusia" jest (**142.1**, **170.1**).

• 36. the garden scene, as NB5 (87ff): the gardener finally "Mr Graves" (**142.5**); "prostituting himself to some purpose" (**143.3**); "Here then was another series" added; "tavern companions" introduced (**143.4**); Mr. Graves's accent more Irish (**143.3**).

• 37. Watt's encounter with Knott in the garden, as NB4 (6ff) and TS (357-61), with minor changes: "positively [from behind]" (NB4, 9) to "even" (**146.4**); "Add to this" paragraph (TS, 358) included (**147.3**); "plopf" typography improved (**147.4**).

• 38. finale of part II, as NB4 (10ff) and TS (459ff): Watt now "sicker, aloner" (**148.3**); "yellowist" retained (**148.5**); the cut version of Easter bells passage carried over (TS, 462v); the stranger (Phelps, Martin) finally named Arthur (**149.1**).

• 39. introduction to part III, as NB4 (93ff): "No truck" insert (NB4, 99) included, with "[back as] we came" now "we went" (**153.1**); "volte-face" footnote added (**153.4**).

• 40. the asylum garden, as NB4 (98ff), with minor changes: (G51): "dandelion" (NB4, 98) to "pissabed" (**154.3**); (NB4, 98): "ridge" to "crown" (**154.4**); "suggestion" to "vestige" (**155.4**); hiatus (NB4, 101) filled with "Gomorrha" (**156.1**); "speaking to dictation" added (156); "obese [wet-nurse]" (NB4, 102) now "fat" (157); addition of the definite article to "the scissors, the brandy, the iodine" (**157.2**); the "shared [garden]" the "same" (157).

• 41. the meeting of Watt and Sam: "How hideous is the semi-colon" added, with new semi-colons (compare NB4, 105); (**158.1**); "the paling" added (158); commas about "or straits" (NB4, 105) perhaps omitted (158); the Christ now "believed by Bosch" (**159.3**); "National gallery" changed to "Trafalgar Square" (**159.3**); "at the same instant" added (159); "For if anyone" sentence added (**159.3**); (NB4, 106): "fleshy part of the posterior" (NB4, 106) later "the ravine" (**159.5**); "my handkerchief" (NB4, 106) now "panky-hanky" (**159.5**).

• 42. the infuriated boar, or bull, almost as NB4 (109ff): "or a perch" added (**160.1**); "trying to understand" added (162); "heat" (hate, love) changed to "fury" (**162.2**).

• 43. the parting of Watt and Sam, as NB4 (113ff).

• 44. Watt's inversions, as NB4 (114ff, then 133ff): in the list of things suspected, the "thats" (NB4, 114) no longer capitalized (**164.3**); "repetition" (NB4,

133) changed to "battology" (**165.2**); "a tendency appeared" simplified to "began" (**165.3**); "palp" now "niks"; a footnote perhaps present (**165.4**); "empty sounds" now "so much wind" (**166.4**); "I suppose" (NB4, 134) error perhaps made (**166.5**); "stomach to stomach" (NB4, 135) became "pubis to pubis" (**167.2**); "So all went well" perhaps present in the fourth paradigm (**167.3**); "This meant nothing to me" and similar transitions introduced (**167.5, 168.3**); "sentence" and "period" (NB4, 131) twice reversed (**168.1**); "I would hear him say" (NB4, 119) became "said Watt" (168); "together" (NB4, 136) now "simultaneously"; "ho no" aspirated (**168.5**); "course" (NB4, 136) a "brief course" (168); "I recall no instance of this manner" replaces earlier attempts to render it (**168.4**); "ear" (NB4, 138) replaced by "tympan" (**169.2**); the explicit reference to "LOCKE" (NB4, 138) omitted (**169.4**).

• 45. the garden scene of part III, as in TS (367ff), NB4 (12ff), and (NB5, 93ff); brought over from part II (**169.6**), interrupting the flow of "the following information" (*Watt* 169; **166.5**) until "Watt had little to say" (*Watt* 169; **199.2**). "Arthur" and "Mr Graves" replace "Martin and Mr Gorman" (**169.6**); "Bando" present and "3 weeks" (NB4, 12) now "five or six years" (**170.1**).

• 46. the misadventures of Louit, as NB4 (28ff) and TS (369ff); "Nackybal" finally spelled thus (**174.1**).

• 47. the committee, as NB5 (92ff), minor changes: mortar-boards doffed (**179.1**); the cupola sequence (TS, 401) alphabetical (**183.3**); "puckaun" (TS, 413) now "quinch" (**184.1**); the angelus (TS, 405) more subtle (**184.5**); "long turkey cucumber" added (**187.3**); "I can well believe that" added (**191.3**); "eastern windows" error introduced (**191.4**); "question time" (TS, 425) extended (**192.3**); "[What I] hae [said]" perhaps "have" (**194.3**); the committee leaves in random order (**195.4**); "like something out of Poe" added (**196.1**); the "bitter stout porter Power" in its final concatenation (**197.3**).

• 48. Arthur tires of his story, as NB5 (94ff): "particularly" now "truly" (*Watt* 197); "Martin" and "Mr Gorman" now "Arthur" and "Mr Graves" (197); "deciding he would like" (NB5, 97) now "thinking"; "made for" [the house] "turned towards"; "pleasant experience he had had" becomes "afternoon he had spent"; "most" now "very nice" (*Watt* 198); "no other place" simply "no place" (199); "now" and "well" added (199).

• 49. the closing period of Watt's stay; as NB4 (138), minor changes: "on that subject" added (199); "Mr" twice added to "Knott" (199, 200).

• 50. Knott's footwear, as NB4 (153ff), but his outfit is "showy" (**200.2**).

• 51. "when one is no longer young" as NB4 (157); but semi-colon added after "consider" and "cicadas" replace "grasshoppers" (201).

• 52. Knott's needs, as NB4 (158ff): "[ate] heartily" becomes "well" (*Watt* 202); "Mr" twice added to "Knott" (202).

• 53. Knott's movements, as NB4 (122ff).

• 54. Knott's furniture, as NB4 (160ff): "nineteen days" presumably present (**206.1**); "not at all rare" added (**207.2**); "ground" now "floor" (*Watt* 207); "changed regularly on Saint Patrick's Day" added (**207.6**); "Arthur" replaces "Phelps" (208); Watt's vomiting omitted (**223.4**); "considerable [bodily cleanliness]" becomes "some" (208); "or coloured reproduction" added (**208.4**). Knott's voice, as NB4 (169): "excellent [linguist]" now "very fair" (**208.5**); "ailing" added before "ears" (*Watt* 209).

• 55. Knott's physical appearance, as NB4 (143, 149) (**209.7**); "or so it seemed to Watt" added (**211.1**).
• 56. Knott's [un]dressing, as NB4 (169ff): "when living in London" added (**212.1**).
• 57. Sam's farewell to Watt, as NB4 (171).
• 58. part IV, Mick's arrival, as NB6 (1ff), minor changes: (NB6, 1): "warm" now "not quite cold" (**215.4**); "divine" (NB6, 3) becomes "celestial" (**215.6**); "Phelps" becomes "Arthur" (**216.1**); (NB6, 5): Watt no longer surprised (**216.3**); the "moment was come" cut to a simple statement (**216.5**); "to [his rest]" becomes "towards" (216); "was brief" moved to the end of the sentence; "twelve" becomes "midnight, or thereabouts"; Watt asks the man who he is/was (**216.3**); the turning milk and inferior cigar added (**216.5**); "Micks" now "Mr Micks"; "cohabitation" becomes "cloistered fornication" (**216.6**); "Fortunately" now "Happily" (NB6, 7): "labials" now "fricatives" (**216.7**).
• 59. Watt's outfit, as NB6 (7ff): "when he travelled" becomes "when travelling"; the grousebag (NB6, 9) now "already perhaps mentioned"; "introduced for the first time" is cut (**217.3**); "derisive" (NB6, 11) becomes "small," the widow no longer "deserving" but "meritorious" (**217.6**); "fifty or sixty [years]" become "seventy" (**218.1**); "of course" added to the canal water (**218.2**); "buttoned, once buttoned" (NB6, 13) now "once buttoned, buttoned" (218); "a [grandfather]" now "his"; (NB6, 15): "that lightens" repetition deleted (**218.7**); "half a crown" now "eight pence" (**219.1**); "marketable" and "He little suspected that" added (219); "veiled" fills the hiatus of NB6 (17); shoe sizes of ten, eight, and nine become twelve, ten, and eleven (**219.4**); "every [point of view]" becomes "more than one"; "beneath the greatcoat" becomes "from the eye" (**219.6**).
• 60. Micks now "raising in amaze an astonished hand to a thunderstruck mouth" (**220.1**).
• 61. Watt's departure, as NB6 (29ff); "though cold" (NB6, 31) deleted; "[by] acute observers" becomes "some writers" (**222.6**); the goat added; "until [he passed]" becomes "while"; the ass, or goat, lays its head not among the shadows (NB6, 35) but the nettles (**223.6**).
• 62. toward the station, as NB6 (35ff): the "stone steps" (NB6, 36) added (**224.1**).
• 63. the figure, as NB6 (41ff): Watt's "straining his eyes and seething his brains" (NB5, 51) becomes "puzzling over this" (**228.1**).
• 64. at the station, as NB6 (53ff): with the "strange" exception of Sunday night (**228.2**); "Quotation" deleted (**228.3**); "the [waiting-room]" (NB6, 55) becomes "a" (**228.6**); the Golden Rectangle ignored (**229.2**); Messrs. "Farrell" and "Tulley" become "Gorman" and "Nolan" (**229.3**); "trouser's" (NB6, 60) corrected to "trousers'" (**230.3**); "mislaid" (NB6, 61) becomes "lost" (*Watt* 230); "anxious [wife]" becomes "unquiet"; "a [seat]" becomes "the" (**232.1**).
• 65. in the waiting-room, as NB6 (73ff): "his [face]" (NB6, 73) becomes "its"; followed by "or backwards on its sinciput" (**233.1**); "impress" (NB6, 95) becomes "strike" (233); the "Whispering it told" paragraph repositioned (**234.2**).
• 66. daybreak, as NB6 (87ff): "and scouring the webholes" added (**235.4**); a hiatus in the inscription of Joss (**236.3**); the lark now "rises" (**237.2**); "under dictation" added (237).

• 67. Watt's monstrous birthing, as NB6 (98ff): Mr. Gorman now taking leave of his mother (**238.1**); the "walls" become "friezes" (238); "if he had not seen it with his own eyes" (NB6, 98) becomes "if it had been reported to him" (**238.2**); "broke" (NB6, 99) becomes "broken" (**238.3**); "did not" becomes "expected nothing" (238); "it was impossible" (twice) becomes "he could not" (238); "(nonulla desunt)" deleted (**238.4**); "penis" added (239); "hold" (NB6, 101) becomes "holt" (**239.8**); "Her reasons for doing this were not known" added (**240.1**); "Mrs Penny-a-hoist Pim" now so-called (**240.5**); "Locus illegibilitis" (NB6, 105) becomes "(MS illegible)" (**241.1**); Mr. Farrell's "a nice bit of blood" (NB6, 109) deleted (**241.2**); "as an afterthought" added (242); the mattress joke (NB6, 109) obscured (**242.2**).

• 68. Watt's departure, as NB6 (111ff): Lady McCann now "less amused" (**243.3**); "the devil" and "the hell" inflame Mr. Gorman (243); "Who are you?" (NB6, 115) and "what do you want?" become "Who is he?" and "what does he want?"; "Really?" becomes "Is it a white man?" (**244.1**); "reply" becomes "answer immediately"; "there and back" becomes "return"; "The reasons for this are not known" and "in the absence of Mrs Pim" added (244).

• 69. the finale, as NB6 (117-19): "mountains" (NB6, 119) become "hills"; "wish to see" becomes "hope to meet with in a day's march" (**246.4**).

• 70. the Addenda: included with the later typescript, probably (despite the fiasco on the galleys) in the order finally published; but since they are mostly fragments of earlier drafts and not a recension as such, discussion of these potsherds is either (a) covered in the notes above, or (b) left to the annotations.

Level 5: the galleys.

The galley proofs of Watt are at Washington University, Saint Louis, with a photocopy at the BIF, Reading. I follow the Washington numbering (visible on most BIF pages); the Reading numeration doubles my figure. The galleys differ significantly from the early typescript and in considerable if minor detail from the late drafts, but they are mostly identical to the final text and, presumably, to the hypothetical final typescript. Many songs and footnotes were omitted; these Beckett restored, or pointed out in marginal reminders. He was careful with the proofs, especially the Frog Song and Addenda, but by no means "meticulous" (Cohn, *Canon* 113), as many errors snuck through. Obvious slips were corrected on the proofs (see, for example, **42.3**); but others remained. These I note in my Addendum 2 and their textual history is discussed in the individual annotations, but one pattern was recurrent: errors overlooked on the galleys entered the Olympia text; some were corrected in the Grove first edition or silently on reprinting; others, ignored by Grove, were corrected in Calder; yet others persisted. These I note under "level 7" (Grove) or "level 8" (Calder) respectively, that is, at the point of correction rather than where (usually the galleys) the error was introduced.

Curiosities from the galleys include (among hundreds of minor corrections):
• (G2): "~~The spirit is exhausted, said the gentleman~~" deleted (**12.10**).
• (G5): "accoutrement" spelled (deliberately?) as "accowtrement" (as in the *Envoy* extract); [normalized without comment in Olympia] (**21.1**).

- minor changes made on the proofs: "shoe" to "boot" (**23.2**); (G8): "ringworm" to "tonsure" (**27.7**); (G10): "head" to "bum" (**32.9**); (G22): "disposition" to "command" (**71.1**); (G23): "young" [lady] becomes "old" (**74.2**); (G30): "defecated" to "shat" (**91.4**); (G35): "disposition" to "disposal" (*Watt*, 107); (G51): "we were attached" parentheses removed (**155.3**); (G53): "singing" (NB4, 105) to "croaking" (**158.3**); (G54): "sow" to cow" (**162.1**); (G57): "MacStern" to "de Baker" (*Watt*, 186); (G65): "O'Meldon" to "MacStern" (*Watt*, 192; to retain the sequence); (G67): "showy" to "gaudy" (for the rhyme) (**200.2**); (G72): "living [in London]" to "dying" (**212.1**); (G79): "sinciput" to "back" (**233.1**).
- resetting: (G8): re-ordering of the "eels of Como" sequence (**28.1**); (G27): Erskine's "song" [hiatus] (**85.7**); (G81): capitals for "MS" (**238.4**, **241.1**).
- (G10): "Fifty two point two" song omitted, Beckett penning a reminder to leave a full page (**34.1**); the "Fifty-one point one" error [earlier correct] not detected nor corrected (**35.1**).
- omitted details later restored: (G26): last refuge footnote (**82.3**); (G33): hiatus and question mark (**102.3**); (G34): haemophilia footnote (**102.8**); (G34): erroneous figures footnote (**104.7**); (G51): "volte-face" footnote (**153.3**); (G57): Mr. Fitzwein's head (**175.3**); (G61): "Ego autem" footnote (**183.1**); (G66): exitus scrambled, a line dropped (**196.4**); (G72): footnote omitted, causing confusion of Watt and Knott (**211.3**).
- Lynch family adjusted: (G35): "Frank" changed to "Jack" [one missed] (**108.2**); (G36): "Jim" corrected to "Joe" (**110.2**).
- additions/deletions: (G49): worm and flower extended (**146.1**); (G50): "one morning" deleted (**148.6**); (G72): "or put it in his mouth" added (**213.1**).
- (G46): frog song aborted by the printer; detailed instructions about resetting (**136.5**).
- (G55): a mysterious citation suppressed (**165.4**).
- (G66): considerable adjustment of the patterns of exitus (**195.4** to **196.5**).
- (G74, 75): preference for "realized" over "realised" (*Watt*, 219, 222; galleys invariably have "s"; Olympia and Grove [but also Beckett] inconsistent about changing it to "z").
- (G84ff): the Addenda in total disarray, Beckett insisting that they be placed in "l'ordre indiqué" [subsequently re-set].
- (G84ff [or the final typescript]): inclusion within the Addenda from the Whoroscope Notebook of details not strictly *Watt* materials [**#21**, **#24**, **#25**, **#28**, **#31**, **#32**; the source of **#30** is unknown]; these presumably added after Beckett's return to Paris (early 1945).
- (G85): a garbled line ("scattered in ears") entered Olympia (**#26**).
- [G86] threne omitted (**#36**).

Level 6: the Olympia text.

On publication, *Watt* assumed its definitive form, structural changes hereafter being few in terms of evolutionary development, however numerous and important they might be from the perspective of signifying readers. Galley errors, unless corrected on the proofs (as hundreds were), found their way into the Olympia text, which added a few more for good measure (and yet others in its Traveller's Series reprint). The much-maligned Olympia printers did well to follow Beckett's marginal instructions (not always lucid), to make the corrections noted, to restore footnotes and songs, and to make hiatuses as indicated. Some misprints and errors have been considered under the galleys [above]; those continuing into the Grove and/or Calder texts are noted later. The handful of details listed here does not imply an accurate text, but as the matrix of the 1959 Grove text the Olympia edition, however inaccurate, is the summation of what went before and point of origin for what follows. I note only the errors and changes (surprisingly few) introduced at this stage (for the Traveller's Series changes, see my Addendum 1):

• lines, correct in proof, omitted: (G5): "That depends where he got on" (**19.3**); (G24): a line misplaced (**74.7**).

• new errors (correct in the galleys): "accowtrement" reverts to "accoutrement" (**21.1**); "never knew" omitted (**61.2**); an extra "on arising" (**148.6**); "presume" repeated in the third paradigm (**166.2**); "suppose" omitted in the fourth paradigm (**166.5**); "sai" corrected to "said" (G64), as "believe" turned into "belive" (**191.3**); "embriology" (**#17**).

• deletion of type creating odd spacing in the Olympia and Grove editions: (G42): "~~were not~~", with a new error: "or rather weres" (**126.2**); (G48): line omitted ("man's man") (**142.3**); (G50): "~~one morning~~" deleted (**148.6**); (G70): "~~rather~~" deleted (**208.4**).

• Frog Song sorted out (**136.5**).

• in the final footnote, "Mr Knott" appears as "Watt" (**211.3**).

• Addenda in their final order [many small errors later corrected].

• the threne (omitted in the galleys) restored, but an erroneous "on way for station" (**#36**).

Level 7: the Grove Press edition.

The Grove text, offset from the Olympia plates, follows its matrix in pagination and other respects, yet some changes were made, a process continuing silently into the early reprints (I suspect, the first only). A remarkable number of Olympia errors (mostly from the proofs) persisted into the Grove despite Beckett's awareness of them; he had marked up his Olympia text with the (presumed) intention of making the corrections available.

Errors corrected in the first Grove edition include:
• "mothers, fathers' fathers'" (**46.11**); "successives" (**48.3**); "scatch their names" (**48.4**); "never knew" (**61.2**); "to music room" (**71.1**); "throught" (**79.2**); "alway hope" (81); "sixpense" (**100.1**); "daghter" (**106.4**); "than nobody is coming" (**119.1**); "or rather weres" (**126.2**); "for even in vain" (**130.1**); "Yes what" (**132.3**); "[on] more than one occasion" (**141.3**); "than a dying perfume[.]" (142); "to do so [on] more" (**141.3**); "he bottle" (**143.1**); "others sorrows" (**146.5**); "half ender, ended" (**148.5**); "on arising, on arising" (**148.6**); "windowlesness" (**152.1**); "could some" (**152.1**); "Nothing in known" (**153.3**); "as so little" (**154.1**); "hardly to otherwise" (**155.1**); "numbr" (**179.2**); "belive" (**191.3**); "eastern windows" (**191.4**); "vanqu-ished" (192); "turned them found" (**195.3**); "chimmeys" (**225.1**); "of for this woman" (**226.5**); "less" [lest] (**230.2**); "accomodate" (**234.1**); "he would [not] have" (**238.2**); "in worlds enclose" (**#4**).

Errors silently corrected by Grove: these changes were probably made on the first reprinting; but when Beckett marked up his copy for Calder some already changed were still noted. Grove nowhere indicates that any changes were made; the current text is still the first edition in its umpteenth printing. They include:
• "they" restored to "He knew were not his" (**7.4**); "It it a raven" (**83.2**); "tumulus" (**83.7**); "Add to his" (**112.2**); "than nobody is coming" (**119.1**); "three [four] times a day" (**142.6**); "infuriated sow" (**162.1**); "colloborators" (**181.4**); "for Watt [Mr Knott] did not" (**211.3**).

Other changes include:
• restoration of the line omitted from Olympia (**19.3**); another misplaced line corrected (**74.7**); a confused galley line, present in Olympia, deleted from the Addenda (**#26**).
• new errors introduced: correction of "past, oh not the last" (**9.5**); "if was not" changed on reprinting to "it was not" (**141.1**).
• the Runner Duck episode cut; hence the curious indentation (page 45) and a discrepancy between the Grove and Olympia pagination until page 67 (**45.6**); "what had become of the duck" marked for deletion, but retained in Grove (**80.6**).
• "*Now the day is over*" marked for deletion, but retained in Grove (**57.1**).
• "say" added "to [say] x squared" (as in G60 and Olympia) (**180.2**). [Not trivial, as Beckett on his Olympia copy had marked the change—one Grove would not have made without his approval—so, why were other marked changes not made?]
• wording for the threne corrected to "on way from station" (**#36**).

Level 8: the Calder (Jupiter) text.

A resetting of the text, and thus a different pagination; incorporating the changes Beckett had marked on his copy of the Grove first printing. Calder made minor changes of spelling and style: hyphenation, ellipsis for the dash, footnotes in superscript, question marks where previously none, a more frequent use of italics and small capitals. Not all of these were authorized, or justified. Curiously, the British text uses American punctuation in words like "Mr." whereas the American follows Beckett's British practice ("Mr"); likewise, words like "realised" and "organised" (British spelling in the American text) became "realized" and "organized" in the British text. There is no evidence that these changes had Beckett's approval, and Calder's impulse to anglicize French tonalities (**170.7**) is unfortunate. The Calder text smoothes many rough edges, but it introduces so many new errors that overall it is no improvement on the Grove.

Many errors originating from (or before) the galleys but not corrected by Olympia or Grove were finally corrected in Calder. These include:
• "pass. oh not the last" [error in Grove] (**9.5**); "gentlemen" (**31.4**); "nor a trust" (**46.5**); "vitamens" (**52.1**); "chile" (**53.4**); "vegetables,nuts" (**54.1**); "without it's coming" (**70.1**); "or the door" (**77.2**); "that is was" (**81.4**); "camomille" (**87.13**); "his arrival" (**93.1**). "second local's man" (**98.3**); "as least as" (**101.8**); italicized "e" (**102.1**); "enlargment" (**102.8**); "excema" (**103.1**); "anyth-ing"

(**105.2**); "the death or Liz" (**105.4**); "as is was" (**115.5**); "mecanism" (**117.1**); "a trouser's pocket" (**127.2**); "manner." (**156.2**); comma after "if possible" (**158.2**); "medullars" (**173.2**); "M. de Baker" and "M. Fitzwein" (**184.3**); "trom the window" (**204.1**); "thay they" (**211.2**); "focussed" (**224.6**); "a kind or shackled smartness" (**226.3**); "the windows, of his box" [commas] (**228.5**); "in the morning." (**237.1**); *"Embriology"* (**#17**); "abate one tot" [jot] (**#23**); "that is [it] was not a rush" (**#29**); "when you [I] was a boy" (**#29**).

Other changes made (or not made):
• *further corrections*: (44): adjustment of the irregular indentation following the deletion of the Runner Duck (**45.6**); (57): "Knott" dignified as "Mr. Knott" (**58.5**); (102): "exsanguine" finally preferred to "exsanguious" (**104.6**); (139): "if/it was not" to "if it was not" (**141.1**); (178): "No number" to "No member" (**179.2**).
• *changes of expression*: (19): "the [accoutrement]" to "his" (**21.1**); (81): new paragraph proposed after "his last rats, at last" (**84.1**); (86): "[coal] was also" to "also was" (**89.1**); (237): "[than a lark] sing" to "from singing" (**237.2**).
• *new errors*: (27): "mur-murmured" (**29.13**); (32): "high pounting hemlock" (**33.6**); (44): continuous text [paragraph break preferable] (**45.6**); (83): "tumulus" [despite the Grove correction] (**83.7**); (118): chamber pot loses "white" (**121.1**); (165): "don yag" for "ton yag" (**167.4**); (207): "be [he] reckoned" (**208.2**); (226): "whether shit was a good thing" (**226.7**); (229): "trouser's's" apostrophe confused (**230.3**); (239): failure to right-justify the Hölderlin fragment (**239.6**); (243): "Lady McCan" (**243.2**); (255): "sterile pus" addendum re-located (**#30**); (255): "on way from station" corrected, but the threne omitted and a blank space left (**#36**).
• *deletions*: [55]: "Now the day is over" (**57.1**); [77]: "what had become of the duck" tidied (**80.6**); [169]: parenthesis concerning the research prize (**171.2**).
• *preferences*: (130): "xenia" to "xenium" (**132.2**); (132ff): hyphenated compounds such as "ground-floor" (**134.4**); "sphinxes" to "sphinges" (**#28**).
• *questionable decisions*: (169): "hasardous" to "hazardous" [forfeiting the French echo] (**170.7**); (173): tense changed from "looked" to "looks" (**175.2**); (209): hyphenating of "middle-sized" (**209.7**); (219): removal of [littoral] hyphen from "sea-shore" (**219.3**).

Level 9: the French translation.

Less a distinct stage of textual evolution than a by-blow of the Calder template; hence no "Runner Duck" interlude nor any other Calder deletions. Some changes are the consequence of English intransigency in translation; others indicate a different thinking about the text and/or the chance to improve on the Calder edition. If the French text is a minor development of Watt's textual history, it is not irrelevant to Beckett's thinking about what the novel should be, nor how that thinking changed over twenty years.

• *changes consequent on English*: (11-12): bird songs deleted (**11.3**); (11-12): "Byrne" and "Hyde" to "Dunn" and "Denìs" (**11.5**, **11.6**); (46-47): sonnet form ("The whacks, the moans") changed (**46.9**); (48): Wat Tyler replaced by James Watt's "machine à vapeur" (**48.2**); (58): "Hallow's E'en" and "Guy

Fawkes" to "la Toussaint" and "des Trépassés" (**57.3**). Many minor changes of nuance and expression.

• *other changes*: (20): "driver" to "wattman" (**20.1**); (47): "a third time" to "2nd" (**47.14**); (115): Kate and Cis each a "chien," not "chienne" (**112.3**); (177): "six months" to "six semaines" (**171.2**); (194): "sweet seventeen" to "soixante-seize printemps" (**186.3**).

• *corrected errors*: (53): "coprophile" to "coprophage" (**52.3**); (78): "cumulus" (**83.7**); (171-73): "imagine, presume, suppose" sequences corrected, but a different order used (**165.1**); "nineteen [days]" marked on Beckett's Calder text to be changed to "vingt" (**206.1**); (217): "minute" (wrong in all English texts) changed to "degré" (**207.4**); "forward on his face" (in all English texts) corrected to "its" (Calder 232), although French does not mark this distinction (**233.1**).

• *errors (new and old)*: (105): [old error compounded] "la fille de Frank (?) Bridie": "Frank" for "Jack," thus remains in all texts (**102.6**); (113): {Bill, Jim, Joe} corrected in the Ohio draft, but the error remains in the text (**110.2**).

• *footnotes changed to a new pattern*: (28): "anagram of mud" (**27.2**); (35): "Mixed Choir" footnote augmented (**34.1**); (190): "à peu près" added (**183.1**).

• *further cuts (actual and suggested)*: "Fifty two point two" song cut (**34.1**); co-ordinates of the picture reversed (Calder 128), but the changes not made (**129.7**); [148]: "turd" and "fart" passage omitted (**143.2**); [190]: text deleted: "the right old hairy mottled hand . . . old bony knee" (**183.2**); (191-92): arithmetical errors corrected, 762 replacing 742 (**183.4**); however (197), the French drafts offered 873 when an error is required [this caught at the last] (**190.1**); [193]: "the French extraction" (Calder 183) omitted (**184.7**); also, Mr. Magershon's "Is that all?" (Calder 184); and Mr. de Baker's "Not horsey, fishy" (Calder 187) (**186.1**); [196]: Mr. O'Meldon's reciprocated thanks to Louit deleted (**189.2**); [199]: byplay over square roots cut (**191.5**); [206]: the Nackybal con unexplained (**198.1**); (225): "little more than a stone" omitted (**217.5**); [248]: "Bloody well you know what bucket" passage marked (Calder 239) for deletion, but retained; Addenda **#2** and **#3** omitted; words and music of the threne omitted (**#36**).

• "Watt learned to accept" (**#9**) cross-referenced on the marked Jupiter text to page 77 [Calder] to assert (at the end, as in the beginning) that "nothing" was Watt's lot.

Bibliography

This bibliography is in three sections: texts and manuscripts by Beckett used in this study; critical studies relating to *Watt*; background works and sources. Where possible, citations are from Beckett's copies or editions that he is known to have used. Casual quotations are drawn from standard editions, or from background works included here; Biblical references are normally to the King James Version. "BIF" designates the Beckett International Foundation, University of Reading; "HRHRC" the Harry Ransom Center, University of Texas at Austin; and "*JOBS*" the Journal of Beckett Studies. Texts are cited in the annotations by author or short title, as seems most appropriate.

A. Works by Beckett:

Black Notebook [1931-32?]. BIF [5004].

"Che Sciagura." *TCD: A College Miscellany* XXXVI (Nov. 14 1929): 42.

Collected Shorter Plays. New York; Grove Press, 1984.

Disjecta: Miscellaneous Writings and a Dramatic Fragment by Samuel Beckett, ed. Ruby Cohn. New York: Grove Press, 1983.

Dream of Fair to middling Women, ed. Eoin O'Brien and Edith Fournier. Dublin: Black Cat, 1992.

Dream Notebook [1930-32?]. BIF [5000]. Published as *Beckett's Dream Notebook*, ed. John Pilling. Reading: Beckett International Foundation, 1999.

"Echo's Bones" [unpublished typescript, 1934]. Baker Library, Dartmouth College. [Photocopy at the BIF].

En attendant Godot. Paris: Éditions de Minuit, 1952.

Endgame: A Play in One Act Followed by Act Without Words: A Mime for One Player. New York: Grove Press, 1958.

"Extract from *Watt*" [1]. *Envoy* 1.2 (January 1950): 11-19. [Watt's arrival by tram, part I].

"Extract from *Watt*" [2]. *Irish Writing* 17 (December 1951): 11-16. [The beginning and the final paragraph of part III].

"Extract from *Watt*" [3]. *Merlin* 3.1 (Winter 1952-53): 118-26. [The close of Watt's stay with Mr. Knott, part III].

"Extract from *Watt*" [4]. *Irish Writing* 22 (March 1953): 16-24. [The Galls father and son, part II].

Film. New York: Grove Press, 1969.

"German Diaries" [6 Notebooks, 1936-37]. BIF [no acquisition number listed].

Happy Days. New York: Grove Press, 1961.

How It Is. 1961; New York: Grove Press, 1964.

"Human Wishes" [3 Notebooks, 1936-38]. BIF [3461/1-3].

Letters to Mary Manning [Mary Manning Howe]. HRHRC [TXRCOO-A1, 8:10-11].

Letters to Thomas McGreevy. Trinity College, Dublin. TCD [10402].

"L'Histoire de Watt," traduit par Ludovic et Agnès Janvier en collaboration avec l'auteur. *Les Lettres nouvelles* (septembre-octobre 1968): 11-16. [The opening of part IV].

L'Innommable. Paris: Éditions de Minuit, 1952.

Malone meurt. Paris: Éditions de Minuit, 1951.

Mercier and Camier. 1970; New York: Grove Press, 1974.

Mercier et Camier. Paris: Éditions de Minuit, 1970.

Molloy. Paris: Éditions de Minuit, 1951.

More Pricks Than Kicks. 1934; rpt. London: Grove Press, 1970.

Murphy. 1938; rpt. New York: Grove Press, 1957.

Murphy, trans. Samuel Beckett et Alfred Péron. Paris: Bordas, 1947.

Notes on Dutch Art [1934?]. BIF [5001].

Notes on Fritz Mauthner [1938?]. TCD [10971/5/1-4].

Notes on Geulincx [1936]. TCD [10971/6/1-36].

Notes on Philosophy [1931-32?]. TCD [10967].

Notes on Psychology [1934-35]. TCD [10971/7/1-17; 10971/8/1-36].

Nowhow On: Company: Ill Seen Ill Said: Worstward Ho. 1980, 1981, 1983; rpt. New York: Grove Press, 1996.

Proust & 3 Dialogues with Georges Duthuit. 1931 and 1949; rpt. New York: Grove Press, 1970.

Samuel Beckett: The Complete Short Prose, 1929-1989, ed. S. E. Gontarski. New York: Grove Press, 1995.

Sottisier Notebook [1976-82]. BIF [2901].

Three Novels by Samuel Beckett: Molloy; Malone Dies: The Unnamable. 1955, 1956, 1958; rpt. New York: Grove Weidenfeld, 1991.

Waiting for Godot. 1952; New York: Grove Press, 1954.

Watt. Paris: Olympia Press [Collective Merlin], 1953. [Beckett's personal copy, BIF, marked for corrections by Grove].

Watt. 1953; rpt. Paris: Olympia [Traveller's Companion], 1958.

Watt. 1953; rpt. New York: Grove Press, 1959. [Beckett's personal copy, BIF, marked for correction by Calder, pp. 137-38 and 161-92 missing].

Watt. 1953; rpt. New York: Grove Press, 1959. [10th printing, with minor silent corrections].

Watt. 1953; rpt. London: John Calder [Jupiter Edition], 1963. [Beckett's personal copy, BIF, annotated for translation into French, Special Collections, Ohio State University].

Watt, trans. Ludovic and Agnès Janvier, in collaboration with the author. Paris: Éditions de Minuit, 1968.

Watt, Deutsch von Elmar Tophoven. Frankfurt a. m.: Suhrkamp, 1970.

"Watt," traduit par Ludovic et Agnès Janvier en collaboration avec l'auteur. *L'Ephémère* 6 (été 1968): 81-89. [From part II: "Watt pensait quelquefois à Arsene . . . à sa perte d'espèce." Illustrated by Bram van Velde's "Desins inédits, 1968"].

Whoroscope Notebook [1934-38]. BIF [3000/1].

The following manuscripts collections have been consulted:

Beckett International Foundation, University of Reading: for Beckett's personal copies of *Watt*; for some of the early "extracts" from *Watt*; for Beckett's notes on philosophy, literature, and psychology; for the "Human Wishes" notebooks; and for many miscellaneous details.

Harry Ransom Center, University of Texas at Austin; for the six notebooks (945 pages) of autograph manuscript (Boxes 6: 5-7, and 7: 1-4), and the early typescript of *Watt* (Box 7: 5-6); for some of the early "extracts" from *Watt*; for the manuscript notebooks of the *Three Novels*; for correspondence between Beckett and John Fletcher, Mary Manning, Mania Péron, and George Reavey; and for various items in the Samuel Beckett (TXRCOO-A1) and Carlton Lake (TXRCOO-A2) Collections.

Ohio State University: the Samuel Beckett Special Collection (Spe. Ms. Eng. 27), for the manuscripts and notebooks of Beckett's translation of *Watt* into French); and for his personal copy of the Calder [Jupiter] *Watt* marked up for that purpose.

Trinity College, Dublin: for Beckett's correspondence with Thomas MacGreevy (TCD 10402). Beckett's notes on Philosophy, Psychology, and Arnold Geulincx (TCD 10967 to 10971) were consulted, in photocopy or on microfilm, at the BIF.

Washington University, St. Louis: for the galley proofs of Watt; a photocopy of these was also used at the BIF (1524/1).

Useful information concerning the various manuscripts may be found in:

Admussen, Richard. *The Samuel Beckett Manuscripts: A Study.* Boston: G. K. Hall, 1979.

Bryden, Mary, Julian Garforth, and Peter Mills. *Beckett at Reading: Catalogue of the Beckett Manuscript Collection at the University of Reading.* Reading: Whiteknights Press and the Beckett International Foundation, 1998.

Coetzee, J. M. "The English Fiction of Samuel Beckett: An Essay in Stylistic Analysis." Ph.D. diss., University of Texas at Austin, 1969. [Also listed in B, Critical Studies].

Cohn, Ruby. *A Beckett Canon.* Ann Arbor: U of Michigan P, 2001. [Also listed in B, Critical Studies].

Federman, Raymond, and John Fletcher. *Samuel Beckett: His Works and His Critics: An Essay in Bibliography.* Berkeley and Los Angeles: U of California P, 1970.

Lake, Carlton, ed. *No Symbols Where None Intended: A Catalogue of Books, Manuscripts, and Other Materials Relating to Samuel Beckett in the Collections of the Humanities Research Center.* Austin: Harry Ransom Humanities Research Center, 1984.

B. Critical Studies Relevant to *Watt*:

Acheson, James. "A Note on the Ladder Joke in *Watt*." *JOBS* 2.1 (1992): 115-16.

Ackerley, C. J. "Fatigue and Disgust: The Addenda to Watt," in *Samuel Beckett Today / Aujourd'hui* 2 (1993): 175-88.

---. "The Rat which Ate of the Consecrated Wafer: A Theological Crux in Samuel Beckett's *Watt*." In *Word and Stage: Essays for Colin Gibson*. Otago Studies in English 6. Dunedin: University of Otago, 1998. 233-41.

---. *Demented Particulars: The Annotated Murphy.* 1998; 2nd ed., rev., Tallahassee, FL: Journal of Beckett Studies Books, 2004.

---. "Samuel Beckett and Mathematics." *Cuadernos de literatura Inglesa y Norteamericana* (Buenos Aires) 3.1-2 (mayo-noviembre 1998): 77-102.

---. "Samuel Beckett and the Bible: A Guide." *JOBS* 9.1 (autumn 1999): 53-125.

---. "An 'Other Object of Note': Circle and Point in Samuel Beckett's Watt." Forthcoming in *Beckett Today / Aujourd'hui*.

---. "The Geology of the Imagination." *JOBS* 13.2 (spring 2004): 150-63; and in *Beckett the European*, ed. Dirk van Hulle, Tallahassee, FL: Journal of Beckett Studies Books, 2005. 150-63.

---, and S. E. Gontarski. *The Grove Companion to Samuel Beckett.* New York: Grove Press, 2004; rpt., with corrections, London: Faber and Faber (forthcoming 2006).

Atik, Ann. *How It Was: A Memoir of Samuel Beckett.* London: Faber and Faber, 2001.

Bair, Deirdre. *Samuel Beckett: A Biography*. London: Jonathan Cape, 1978.

Baker, Phil. *Beckett and the Mythology of Psychoanalysis*. Basingstoke: Macmillan, 1997.

Beer, Ann. "*Watt*, Knott and Beckett's Bilingualism." *JOBS* 10 (1985): 37-75.

Ben-Zvi, Linda. "Samuel Beckett, Fritz Mauthner, and the Limits of Language." *PMLA* 95.2 (March 1980): 183-200.

---. "Fritz Mauthner for Company." *JOBS* 9 (1984): 65-88.

Bryden, Mary. *Beckett and the Idea of God*. Basingstoke: Macmillan, 1998.

Büttner, Gottfried. *Samuel Beckett's Novel* Watt, trans. Joseph P. Dolan. Philadelphia: U of Pennsylvania P, 1984.

Calder, John, ed. *Beckett at 60: A Festscrift*. London: Calder and Boyars, 1967.

---, ed. *A Samuel Beckett Reader*. London: Calder and Boyars, 1967. [Containing an extract from *Watt* (the meeting with Mr. Spiro)]

---, ed. *A Samuel Beckett Reader*. London: Picador, 1983. [Despite the identical title, this "Reader" offers a different episode from *Watt* (the Galls father and son)]

Chalker, John. "The Satiric Shape of Watt." In *Beckett the Shape Changer*, ed. Katherine Worth. London: Routledge & Kegan Paul, 1975. 21-37.

Coe, Richard N. *Samuel Beckett*. New York: Grove Press, 1967.

Coetzee, J. M. "The English Fiction of Samuel Beckett: An Essay in Stylistic Analysis." Ph.D. diss., University of Texas at Austin, 1969.

---. "The Manuscript Revisions of Beckett's *Watt*." *Journal of Modern Literature* 2 (1972): 472-80.

Cohn, Ruby. "Philosophical Fragments in Works of Samuel Beckett." *Criticism* 6.1 (Winter 1964): 33-43. Rpt. in Martin Esslin, ed., *Samuel Beckett: A Collection of Critical Essays*. Englewood Cliffs, N. J.: Prentice-Hall, 1965, 169-77.

---. "Watt in the Light of *The Castle*." *Comparative Literature* 13 (spring 1961): 154-66.

---. *Samuel Beckett: The Comic Gamut*. New Brunswick, N. J.: Rutgers UP, 1962.

---. *A Beckett Canon*. Ann Arbor: U of Michigan P, 2001.

Cousineau, Thomas J. "Watt: Language as Interdiction and Consolation." *JOBS* 4 (1979): 1-13.

Culik, Hugh. "Mindful of the Body: Medical Allusions in Beckett's Murphy." *Eire-Ireland* 14.1 (spring 1979): 84-91.

---. "Entropic Order. Beckett's Mercier and Camier." *Eire-Ireland* 17.1 (spring 1982): 91-106.

Davis, R. J., J. R. Bryer, M. J. Friedman & P. C. Hoy, eds. *Samuel Beckett: calepins de bibliographie*, 2. Paris: Lettres modernes Minard, 1972.

Di Pierro, John C. *Structures in Beckett's* Watt. York, S.C.: French Literature Publications, 1981.

Doherty, Francis. *Samuel Beckett*. London: Hutchinson, 1971.

Federman, Raymond. *Journey to Chaos: Samuel Beckett's Early Fiction*. Berkeley and Los Angeles: U of California P, 1965.

Fletcher, John. *The Novels of Samuel Beckett*. London: Chatto & Windus, 1967.

Gontarski, S. E. *The Intent of Undoing in Samuel Beckett's Dramatic Texts*. Bloomington: Indiana UP, 1985.

---, ed. *The Beckett Studies Reader*. Gainesville, FL: UP of Florida, 1993.

Graver, Lawrence, and Raymond Federman. *Samuel Beckett: The Critical Heritage*. London: Routledge & Kegan Paul, 1979.

Harvey, Lawrence. *Samuel Beckett, Poet and Critic*. Princeton: Princeton UP, 1970.

Henning, Sylvie Debevic. *Beckett's Critical Complicity: Carnival, Contestation, and Tradition*. Lexington, Ky.: U of Kentucky P, 1988.

Hesla, David. *The Shape of Chaos: An Interpretation of the Art of Samuel Beckett*. Minneapolis: U of Minnesota P, 1971. [Including a revised edition (chapter 3, "The Defeat of the Proto-Zetetic: Watt") of his "The Shape of Chaos: A Reading of Samuel Beckett's *Watt*" (*Critique* 6 [1963]: 85-105)].

Hill, Leslie. *Beckett's Fiction: In Different Words*. Cambridge: Cambridge UP, 1990.

Hoefer, Jacqueline. "Watt." *Perspective* 11.3 (autumn 1959): 166-82. Rpt. in *Samuel Beckett: A Collection of Critical Essays*, ed. Martin Esslin. Englewood Cliffs, N.J.: Prentice Hall, 1965. 62-76.

Howard, J. Alane. "The Roots of Beckett's Aesthetic: Mathematical Allusions in Watt." *Papers on Language and Literature* 30.4 (1994): 346-51.

Janvier, Ludovic, and Agnès Vaquin-Janvier. "Traduire *Watt* avec Beckett." *Revue d'esthétique* numéro hors-série "Samuel Beckett" (1986): 57-64.

Jouffroy, Alain. "Hommage à Samuel Beckett." *Les Lettres françaises* 1267 (22-28 janvier, 1969): 1, 3-9. [Includes a translation from the recently published French translation of *Watt*, "Arsene parle" (5-9)].

Keller, John Robert. *Samuel Beckett and the Primacy of Love*. Manchester and New York: Manchester UP, 2002.

Kennedy, Sighle. "'The Simple Games that Time Plays with Space': An Introduction to Samuel Beckett's Manuscripts of *Watt*." *Centerpoint* 2.3 (Fall 1977): 55-60.

Kenner, Hugh. *Samuel Beckett: A Critical Study*. New York: Grove Press, 1961.

Knowlson, James. *Damned to Fame: The Life of Samuel Beckett*. New York: Simon and Schuster, 1996.

---, with John Haynes. *Images of Beckett*. Cambridge; Cambridge UP, 2003.

Lees, Heath. "Watt: Music, Tuning and Tonality." *JOBS* 9 (1984): 5-24; rpt. in *The Beckett Studies Reader*, ed. S. E. Gontarski. 167-185.

Love, Damian. "Samuel Beckett and the Art of Madness." D. Phil. diss, St. Anne's College, University of Oxford, 2004.

Low, Richard. "Mock Evangelism in Beckett's *Watt*." *Modern Language Studies* 2 (1972): 74-75.

Mayoux, Jean-Jacques. "'Molloy': un événement littéraire une oeuvre." In Samuel Beckett, *Molloy*. Paris: Éditions de Minuit, 1951. 241-74.

McMillan, Dougald. "Samuel Beckett and the Visual Arts: The Embarrassment of Allegory." In *On Beckett: Essays and Criticism*, ed. S. E. Gontarski. New York: Grove Press, 1986. 29-45.

Mercier, Vivien. *Beckett/Beckett*. New York: Oxford UP, 1977.

Mintz, Samuel. "Beckett's *Murphy*: A Cartesian Novel." *Perspective* 11.3 (autumn 1959): 156-65.

Mood, John J. "'The Personal System': Samuel Beckett's *Watt*." *PMLA* 86 (1971): 255-65.

Moorjani, Angela. *Abysmal Games in the Novels of Samuel Beckett*. Chapel Hill: U of North Carolina P, 1982.

O'Brien, Eoin. *The Beckett Country: Samuel Beckett's Ireland*. Dublin: Black Cat, 1986.

Park, Eric. "Fundamental Sounds: Music in Samuel Beckett's *Murphy* and *Watt*." *Modern Fiction Studies* 21 (summer 1975): 157-71.

Perloff, Marjorie. *Wittgenstein's Ladder*. Chicago: U of Chicago P, 1996.

Piette, Adam. *Remembering and the Sound of Words: Mallarmé, Proust, Joyce, Beckett*. Oxford: Clarendon, 1996.

Pilling, John. *Samuel Beckett*. London: Routledge & Kegan Paul, 1979.

---, ed. *The Cambridge Companion to Beckett*. Cambridge: Cambridge UP, 1994.

---. "A Short Statement with Long Shadows: *Watt*'s Arsene and his Kind(s)." In *Beckett On and On . . .*, ed. Lois Oppenheim and Marius Buning. London: Associated University Presses, 1996. 61-68.

---. *Beckett before* Godot. Cambridge: Cambridge UP, 1998.

---. *A Companion to Dream of Fair to middling Women*. Tallahassee, FL: Journal of Beckett Studies Books, 2004.

Rabaté, Jean-Michel. *The Ghosts of Modernity*. Gainesville, FL: UP of Florida, 1996.

Rabinovitz, Rubin. *The Development of Samuel Beckett's Fiction*. Urbana: U of Illinois P, 1984. [Includes "The Addenda to *Watt*," 151-75].

Robinson, Fred Miller. "Watt." In *Samuel Beckett*, ed. Harold Bloom. New York: Chelsea House [Modern Critical Views], 1985. 147-92.

Robinson, Michael. *The Long Sonata of the Dead: A Study of Samuel Beckett*. London: Rupert Hart-Davis, 1969.

Seaver, Richard W. "Samuel Beckett: An Introduction." *Merlin* 1 (autumn, 1952): 73-79; rpt. in Graver and Federman, 79-87.

---, ed. *I Can't Go On, I'll Go On: A Samuel Beckett Reader*. New York: Grove Weidenfeld, 1976.

---. "Beckett vient à l'Olympia Press." Paris: *L'Herne* (1976): 97-100.

---. "Beckett and *Merlin*." In *On Beckett: Essays and Criticism*, ed. S. E. Gontarski. New York: Grove Press, 1986. 19-28.

Senneff, Susan. "Song and Music in Beckett's *Watt*." *Modern Fiction Studies* 10 (1964): 137-49.

Skerl, Jennie. "Fritz Mauthner's 'Critique of Language' in Samuel Beckett's *Watt*." *Contemporary Literature* 15 (1974): 474-87.

Smith, Frederik N. "The Epistemology of Fictional Failure: Swift's *Tale of a Tub* and Beckett's *Watt*." *Texas Studies in Literature* XV.4 (winter 1974): 649-72.

---. "*Godot* and the Manuscripts of *Watt*." *JOBS* 11.1 (spring 2001): 38-53.

---. *Beckett's Eighteenth Century*. New York: St. Martin's, 2002.

Solomon, Philip Howard. "A Ladder Image in *Watt*." *Papers on Language and Literature* 7 (1971): 422-27.

Swanson, Eleanor. "Samuel Beckett's *Watt*: A Coming and a Going." *Modern Fiction Studies* 17 (1971): 264-68.

Trivisonno, Ann M. "Meaning and Function of the Quest in Beckett's *Watt*." *Critique* 12 (1969): 28-38.

Wahrhaft, Sidney. "Threne and Theme in *Watt*." *Wisconsin Studies in Contemporary Literature* 4 (1963): 261-78.

Webb, Eugene. *Samuel Beckett: A Study of His Novels*. Seattle and London: U of Washington P, 1971.

Winston, Matthew. "Watt's First Footnote." *Journal of Modern Literature* 6 (1971): 69-82.

C. General studies used in this work

Alexander, Arch. B. D. *A Short History of Philosophy*. Glasgow: James Maclehose & Sons, 1907.

Augustine, Saint. *Confessions*, trans. William Watts [Loeb Classical Library]. 2 vols; London: Heinemann, 1922.

---. *Confessions*, trans. E.B. Pusey. London: Dent [Everyman], 1907.

Baillet, Adrien. *La Vie de Monsieur Des-cartes*. 2 tomes; Paris: Daniel Horthemels, 1691.

Bergson, Henri. *Creative Evolution*, trans. Arthur Mitchell. London: Macmillan, 1911.

Bickersteth, Geoffrey L. (editor and translator). *The Poems of Leopardi*. New York: Russell & Russell, 1923.

Bleuler, Eugene. *Textbook of Psychiatry*, trans. A. A. Brill. New York: Macmillan. 1924.

Boswell, James. *Life of Johnson, Including Their Tour to the Hebrides*, ed. J. W. Croker. London: John Murray, 1847.

---, *Boswell's Life of Johnson*, ed. George Birkbeck Hill (1887); 6 vols., rev. L. F. Powell, Oxford: Clarendon, 1934-1950.

Brett, George S. *History of Psychology*. 3 vols; London: Allen & Unwin, 1912-21.

Burnet, John. *Early Greek Philosophy*. 1892; 3rd ed., rev., London: A. & C. Black, 1920.

---. *Greek Philosophy: Thales to Plato*. 1914; rpt. London: Macmillan, 1950.

Burton, Robert. *The Anatomy of Melancholy, what it is, with all the kinds, course, symptoms, prognostics, and several cures of it. In three partitions; with their several sections, members and subsections, philosophically, medically, historically opened and cut up. By Democritus Junior [Robert Burton], with a satyrical preface, conducing to the following discourse* [1562]. A new edition. London: Chatto & Windus, 1881.

Cary, Henry Francis. *The Vision: or, Hell, Purgatory, and Paradise, of Dante Alighieri*. Translated by the Rev. Henry Francis Cary, M.A. London: Bell and Daldy, 1869. [Beckett's personal copy at the BIF, with the invaluable annotations omitted from the popular Everyman edition].

Cooper, the Rev. William M. [pseud. of James Glass Bertram]. *Flagellation and the Flagellants: A History of the Rod in all Countries from the Earliest Period to the Present Time*. London: John Camden Hotten, 1869.

Dante Alighieri. *La Divina commedia*. II edizione, commento di C. T. Dragone. Alba: Edizione Paoline, 1959. [Beckett's personal copy, BIF].

---. *The Divine Comedy*, trans., with a commentary, by Charles S. Singleton [Bollingen Series LXXX]. 6 vols, 1970; rpt. Princeton: Princeton UP, 1977.

Darwin, Charles. *On the Origin of Species*. London: John Murray, 1859.

Descartes, René. *Oeuvres choisis de Descartes*. Nouvelle édition, Paris: Garnier Frères [n.d.]

---. *A Discourse on Method, Meditations and Principles*, trans. John Veitch and intr. A. D. Lindsay. London: Dent [Everyman], 1912.

Diderot, Denis. "Entretien entre d'Alembert et Diderot: Le Rêve de d'Alembert: Suite de l'entretien." In *Oeuvres philosophiques de Diderot*, édition de Paul Vernière. Paris: Garnier Frères, 1964. 247-385.

---. *Jacques le fataliste*. In *Ouvres romanesques*, édition de Henri Bénac. Paris: Garnier Frères [n.d.]. 493-780.

---. *Le Neveu de Rameau*. In *Ouvres romanesques*, édition de Henri Bénac. Paris: Garnier Frères [n.d.]. 395-492.

Ellmann, Richard. *James Joyce*. London: Oxford UP, 1959; 2nd ed., rev., New York, Oxford, Toronto: Oxford UP, 1982. [The first edition usually preferred].

Evans, E. P. *The Criminal Prosecution and Capital Punishment of Animals*. London: Heinemann, 1906.

Farquhar, George. *The Beaux' Stratagem*. In *George Farquhar* [Mermaid Series], ed. William Archer. New York: A. A. Wyn, Inc., 1949. 353-455.

Flaubert, Gustave. *Bouvard et Pécuchet*. 1881; rpt. Paris: L'Aventurine [Classiques universales], 2003.

Freud, Sigmund. *The Standard Edition of the Complete Psychological Works of Sigmund Freud*, ed. James Strachey, in collaboration with Anna Freud. 24 vols; London: Hogarth Press and the Institute of Psychoanalysis, 1953-74.

Garnier, Pierre. *Onanisme seul et à deux*. Paris: Garnier Frères, [1885].

Geulincx, Arnoldus. *Opera Philosophica*, recongnivit J. P. N. Land. 3 vols; Hague Comitum: Martinum Nijhoff, 1891-93.

Guggenheim, Marguerite. *Out of This Century: The Informal Memoirs of Peggy Guggenheim*. New York: Dial, 1946.

---. *Confessions of an Art Addict*. New York: Macmillan, 1960.

Hölderlin, Friedrich. *Sämtliche Werke*. Leipzig: Im Insel-Verlag, n.d. [Beckett's personal copy, BIF, dated on front inner cover: "SB 24/12/37"].

Houston, Stewart Chamberlain. *Immanuel Kant*. London: John Lane, the Bodley Head, 1914.

Inge, William Ralph. *Christian Mysticism*. 1899; 2nd ed., London: Methuen, 1912.

Johnson, Samuel. *A Dictionary of the English Language, in which words are deduced from their originals and illustrated in their different significations by examples from the best writers*. 10th ed., 2 vols; London, 1810.

---. *Johnsonian Miscellanies*, ed. George Birkbeck Hill. 2 vols; London: Constable, 1897.

Joyce, James. *A Portrait of the Artist as a Young Man*. 1916; rpt. Harmondsworth: Penguin, 1960.

---. *Ulysses*. 1922; rpt. ed. Jeri Johnson, Oxford: Oxford UP [World's Classics], 1992.

---. *Finnegans Wake*. New York: Viking, 1939.

Koffka, Kurt. *The Growth of the Mind*, trans. R. M. Ogden. 1924; 2nd ed., rev., London: Kegan Paul, Trench, Trubner & Co., 1931.

---. *Principles of Gestalt Psychology*. New York: Harcourt, Brace and World, 1935.

Köhler, Wolfgang. *The Mentality of Apes,* trans. Ella Winter. 1917; 2nd ed., rev., London: Kegan Paul, Trench, Trubner & Co., 1925.

Kretschmer, Ernst. *Physique and Character*, tr. W. J. H. Sprott (2nd edition). London: Routledge & Kegan Paul, 1936.

Leibnitz, Gottfried. *The Monadology and Other Philosophical Writings*, trans. and ed. Robert Latta. London: Oxford UP, 1898.

Lemprière's Classical Dictionary. 1865; rpt. London: Bracken Books, 1984.

Mahaffy, J. P. *Descartes*. Edinburgh and London: William Blackwood, 1880.

Mauthner, Fritz. *Beiträge zu einer Kritik der Sprache*. 3 Bände; Leipzig: F. Meiner, 1923.

Maxwell, Constantine. *A History of Trinity College*, Dublin, 1591-1892. Dublin: The University Press, 1946.

Nordau, Max. *Degeneration*. 1895; rpt. London: Heinemann, 1913.

Praz, Mario. *The Romantic Agony* [1930], trans. Angus Davidson. 1933; 2nd ed., London, New York, Toronto: Oxford UP, 1951.

Proust, Marcel. *A la recherche du temps perdu* [Édition de la *Nouvelle revue française*]. 16 vols; Paris: Gallimard, 1919-27. [SB's copy, lightly annotated, BIF]. Individual texts cited by short title: *Swann*; *Jeunes filles*; *Guermantes*; *Sodome et Gomorrhe*; *La Prisonnière*; *Albertine disparue*; *Le Temps retrouvé*.

---. *Remembrance of Things Past*, trans. C. K. Scott Moncrieff [Bks 1-6] & Frederick A. Blossom [Bk.7]. 2 vols; 1924 & 1927; rpt. New York: Random, 1934.

Roa Bastos, Augustos. *Yo, el Supremo*. 1974; rpt. Mexico, D. F.: Editorial Diana, 1990.

Rudrum, Alan, and Jennifer Drake-Brockman, eds. *The Works of Thomas Vaughan*. Oxford: Clarendon, 1984.

Rushdie, Salman. *The Wizard of Oz*. London: British Film Institute, 1992.

Sartre, Jean-Paul. *La Nausée*. Paris: Gallimard, 1957. Translated by Robert Baldick as *Nausea*. London: Penguin, 2000.

Schopenhauer, Arthur. *On the Fourfold Root of the Principle of Sufficient Reason and On the Will in Nature*, trans. Mme Karl Hillebrand. 1887; rev. ed., London: George Bell, 1915.

---. *Parega and Paralipomena: Short Philosophical Essays*, trans. E. F. J. Payne. 2 vols; Oxford: Clarendon, 1974.

---. *The World as Will and Idea*, trans. R. B. Haldane and J. Kemp. 1883; 3 vols; rpt. London: Kegan Paul, Trench, Trübner & Co, 1896.

Spinoza, Baruch. *Ethica*. In *The Chief Works of Benedict de Spinoza*, vol.2; trans. and ed. R. H. M. Elwes. London: George Bell, 1909.

Swift, Jonathan. *A Tale of a Tub, to which is added The Battle of the Books and The Mechanical Operation of the Spirit* [1704], ed. A. C. Guthketch and D. Nicol Smith. Oxford: Clarendon, 1920.

Taylor, Jeremy. *Holy Living and Dying, together with Prayers Containing the Whole Duty of a Christian and the Parts of Devotion Fitted to All Occasions, and Furnished for All Necessities*. New edition, carefully revised; London: Henry G. Bohn, 1851.

Walpole, Hugh. *Judith Paris*. London: Macmillan, 1931.

Walton, Izaak. *The Life of Mr. Richard Hooker, the Author of those Learned Books of the Laws of Ecclesiastical Polity*. London, 1675; rpt. London: Oxford UP [World's Classics], 1927.

Weisenburg, T. H., and K. R. McBride. *Aphasia: A Clinical and Psychological Study*. New York: Commonwealth Fund, 1935.

Welch, Robert, ed. *The Oxford Companion to Irish Literature*. Oxford: Clarendon, 1996.

Whitla, Sir William. *Dictionary of Treatment*. London: Renshaw, 1920.

Wilenski, R. H. *An Introduction to Dutch Art*. London: Faber and Gwyer, 1929.

Windelband, Dr. Wilhelm. *A History of Philosophy, with special reference to the formation and development of its problems and conceptions*, trans. James H. Tufts. 2nd ed., rev. and enlarged, London: Macmillan, 1914.

Wittgenstein, Ludwig. *Tractatus Logico-Philosophicus*. London: Kegan Paul, Trench, Trubner & Co., 1933.

Index

As this is a thematic listing, rather than one determined by key words, many references are virtual rather than actual. The Index is keyed to the annotations, which use the Grove Press pagination; important entries are italicized. "T" signifies "Title"; numbers preceded by # refer to the Addenda. Details are included if (a) the reference is primary (that is, explicitly cited in *Watt* or in the commentary), or (b) secondary but thematically significant, either in this novel or in Beckett's wider works. Minor details are cited if they contribute to an intertextual pattern of motifs or borrowings.

Abraham's bosom: 12.11; 20.3.
"Act without Words I": 104.5.
Adler, Alfred: 83.3; 139.2.
"ainsi a-t-on beau": 43.5.
"Alba" [the Alba]: 136.4; 209.1.
"All Strange Away": 83.4; 217.4.
All That Fall: 83.6; 101.7; 197.1; 229.3.
d'Alembert, Jean: 57.6; *93.4*; 101.7; 131.7; #29.
Alexander, Arch. B. D.: 50.9; 77.5; 82.2.
Alexander of Hales: 28.9; 29.2; 29.3; 29.5.
All That Fall: 16.7; 29.14;
anthropomorphism: *77.5*; 77.6; 77.7; 78.1; 85.2; 91.3; 91.5; *129.7*; 155.6; 174.6; *202.1*; 212.3; 225.3; 226.3.
"Antipepsis": 170.7.
aphasia: 73.2; 74.4; 85.4; 128.2; 164.1; 164.2; 164.3; 165.3; 165.4; 166.1; 166.3; 166.6; 167.1; 167.3; 167.4; 167.5; 168.1; 168.2; 168.3; 168.4.
apperception: 43.3; *48.3*.
Aquinas, Saint Thomas: 28.3; 28.9; 29.2; 29.8.
"Arènes de Lutèce: 225.2.
Aristophanes: 209.2.
Aristotle: 29.5; 82.2; #31.
Arsene: T; 15.8; 18.3; 27.5; 33.4; 34.1; 37.4; 38.2; 39.2; 39.3; 39.5; 39.6; 40.1; 40.5; 41.1; 41.2; 43.1; 43.3; 43.4; 43.5; 44.3; 44.7; 44.12; 45.1; 45.2; 45.3; 45.5; 45.6; 46.7; 47.11; 47.15; 48.3; 48.4; 49.2; 49.3; 50.6; 52.4; 55.2; 56.3; *56.5*; 57.1; 57.4; 57.6; 59.2; 61.1; 62.2; 62.5; 63.3; 63.6; 63.7; 63.8; 63.9; 67.3; 68.5; 80.5; *80.6*; 82.3; 135.2; 136.5; 190.2; 216.4; 217.2; 220.1; 220.3; 223.3; #5; #6; #7; #8; #10; #14; #23; #32.
art [visual]: 28.9; *42.5*; *44.12*; 48.1; 71.3; 73.2; 75.1; *93.4*; 101.7; 128.4; 128.6; *129.1*; *129.3*; *129.4*; 129.5; 129.6; *129.7*; 130.2; 130.3; 130.4; 131.1; 151.2; 151.3; 159.3; 208.4; 227.4; 236.2; 236.5; #2; #3; #26; #28.
Art and Con [O'Connor, Art Con]: 71.3; 91.5; *101.7*; 174.1; 198.1; #2.
Arthur: 12.11; 46.7; 55.2; 59.2; 149.3; 151.2; 169.6; 182.3; 216.1; 239.5; #14; #15; #29.
Ash, Mr: 45.6; 46.4.
"Assumption": 146.1.
astronomy [stars]: 129.7; *212.1*; 224.1; 222.4; 224.3; 224.5; #11.

asylum: 17.4; 33.5; 39.6; 75.5; 82.3; 83.1; 118.1; 129.1; 151.2; 151.3; 151.4; *151.5*; 152.1; 160.3; 166.1; 171.1; 234.1; 239.6; 241.2.
Atik, Anne: 222.2.
"Avant *Fin de partie*": 149.3.
Augustine, Saint: 29.1; 44.7; 70.5; 77.5; 91.1; 147.3; 209.7; 233.5.

Baillet, Adrien: 26.1; 26.6; 27.4; 29.13; 209.4; 223.3.
Bair, Deirdre: 13.5.
Bando [Bandusia]: *142.1*; *170.1*; *170.1*; 198.2.
Bartlett [*Familiar Quotations*]: #25.
Baudelaire, Charles: 41.5.
Beckett International Foundation (BIF): 43.5; 48.1; 129.3; 132.2; 151.5; 159.3; #24.
Beckett, John: #8.
Beckett, Samuel [biographical]: T; 9.1; 11.5; 13.1; 13.5; 16.5; 19.3; 19.5; 19.6; 21.1; 26.3; 26.7; 27.8; 28.1; 28.2; 28.8; 31.5; 36.3; 45.2; 47.9; 55.2; 57.1; 61.1; 73.2; 74.8; 77.5; 77.7; 80.2; 83.2; 91.1; 98.1; 100.3; 101.3; 101.5; 102.6; 104.7; 113.1; 115.3; 149.1; 149.2; 158.1; 162.1; 170.6; 190.1; 212.1; 217.4; 218.1; 222.2; 232.2; 234.2; "Addenda"; #3; #4; #8.
Beer, Ann: 13.7; 27.2; 82.1; 83.3; 99.2; 154.5; 201.1; 234.2.
Belacqua: 15.3; 27.5; 29.1; 39.6; 44.9; 45.3; 47.1; 47.3; 57.4; 175.1; 192.4; 219.4; 226.1; #11.
Benedict XIV, Pope: *#17*.
Bergson, Henri: *74.10*.
Berkeley, Bishop: 42.1; 87.4; *203.2*.
Bible: 9.1; 12.7; 12.11; 13.5; 20.2; 23.3; 27.2; 33.6; 37.3; 40.1; 44.13; 44.14; 46.3; 49.1; 49.5; 51.5; 55.3; 57.4; 57.5; 58.2; 58.3; 59.1; 60.1; 62.2; 62.6; 63.8; 68.2; 81.1; 81.3; 82.2; 85.3; 86.3; 89.3; 101.1; 103.2; 104.2; 108.3; 110.4; 116.2; 130.2; 134.2; 135.1; 135.5; 146.3; 146.4; 147.2; 151.5; 155.6; 165.2; 166.3; 169.8; 169.10; 181.5; 181.8; 182.1; 182.5; 196.2; 209.5; 224.2; 224.3; 226.6; 227.5; 230.1; #4; #25.
bicycle: 26.2; 57.4; 245.3.
Big Ben [Sir Benjamin Hall]: 46.2.
big house: 30.3; *36.3*; 39.2; 40.2; 54.2; 54.3; 57.6; 71.3; 83.4; 118.2; #11; #15; #37.
billiards [snooker]: 14.5; 15.3; 15.4.
Bion, Wilfred: 161.1.
birds: 11.3; 12.1; 12.2; 12.7; 29.1; 33.4; 37.4; 39.5; 42.8; *43.2*; 43.4; 44.4; 47.3; 64.3; 71.4; 82.2; 83.2; 91.3; 91.4; 144.3; 144.4; *155.6*; 158.3; 194.4; 217.3; 237.2.
birth: 12.11; *13.1*; 13.5; 13.6; 15.1; 15.2; 16.3; *17.5*; 26.7; 26.8; 27.1; *33.2*; 75.4; 104.4; 104.5; 105.3; 109.3; 130.2; 140.1; 170.6; 220.1; 222.2; 222.4; 233.5; 234.2; 239.8; *241.2*; 246.2; *#16*; *#17*.
Blau, Herbert: 222.2.
blue and white: 64.4; 128.7.
body: 8.1; 25.1; 27.5; 28.3; 28.5; *28.9*; 30.4; 32.2; 32.4; 32.5; *33.3*; 39.4; 40.8; 44.3; 62.5; 74.5; 74.6; 101.2; 101.5; 102.4; 114.1; 133.2; 157.1; 164.4; 167.2; 167.4; 169.2; 173.2; 174.8; 176.1; 176.2; 177.3; 182.2; 183.2; 184.5;

200.3; 207.3; *209.7*; 220.2; 227.3; 234.2; 234.3; 235.1; 235.3; 235.4; 237.3; 237.4; 238.3; 239.2; 241.2; #1; #2; #3; #5; #12; *#26*.
Bonaventura, Saint: 28.9; 29.2; 29.3; 29.5.
The Bookman: 27.3.
Book of Common Prayer: 46.11; 58.2; 59.1; 63.5; 63.6; 63.8; 110.1; 125.1; 131.6; 182.2; 218.7.
boot: *17.3*; 23.2; 95.1; 219.1; 219.2; 219.3; 219.4; 219.5.
Bosch, Hieronymus: 151.2; *159.3*.
Boswell, James: 15.6; 26.4; 151.5; 224.7.
"Breath": 58.1.
Brett, George S.: 48.3.
Browning, Robert: 136.4.
Brueghel, Jan "Velvet": #2.
Bryden, Mary: 9.8; 28.1; 32.7.
bull [boar, cow, sow]: *160.2*; 161.1; *161.2*; 162.1.
Bunyan, John: 224.4.
Buridan's ass: 7.6.
Burnet, John: 43.3; 148.2.
Burton, Robert: 23.4; 27.2; 102.1; 169.9.
"...But the Clouds...": 217.4.
Büttner, Gottfried: 7.2; 148.2; 169.7; 233.5; 239.6; 239.8; 243.1.
buttocks: 28.4; 28.5; 28.7; 28.9; 32.9; 40.6; 146.4; 159.5; 181.1; 211.3; 242.1.
Buxtehude, Dietrich: *71.3*.
Byrne, J. J.: *11.5*; 101.4.

Caelius Aurelianus: 226.4.
Calder [Jupiter *Watt*]: 7.4; 9.5; 21.1; 26.1; 29.13; 31.4; 33.6; *34.1*; 39.2; 45.6; 46.5; 47.14; 52.1; 53.4; 54.1; 57.1; 57.2; 58.5; 61.2; 63.5; 67.2; 70.1; 77.2; 80.5; 81.4; 83.2; 83.7; 84.1; 87.3; 87.4; 89.2; 93.1; 101.8; 102.1; 102.6; 102.8; 103.1; 104.4; 104.6; 104.7; 105.4; 112.2; 115.5; 117.1; 119.1; 121.1; 127.2; 129.7; 132.2; 134.4; 141.1; 142.4; 142.6; 143.2; 148.5; 153.4; 156.2; 158.1; 158.2; 164.1; 167.4; 170.7; 171.2; 175.2; 179.2; 183.2; 184.3; 184.7; 186.1; 188.3; 189.2; 191.5; 193.1; 198.1; 203.4; 204.1; 206.1; 207.4; 208.2; 209.7; 211.2; 211.3; 217.5; 219.3; 224.6; 226.3; 226.7; 228.4; 230.3; 233.1; 237.1; 239.4; 239.6; 243.2; #2; #5; #9; #14; #21; #23; #25; #28; #29; #30; #31; #35; #36; #37.
"The Calmative": 217.4.
"Calvary by Night": 146.1.
Carroll, Lewis: 83.2; 159.2.
canal [Grand Canal]: 9.6; 18.1; 174.1; 198.1; 218.2.
Cangiamila, Emanuele: *#17*.
"Cascando": 217.4.
Case, Mr: 228.2; 228.3; 228.4; 228.5; 241.3; 246.3.
"Catastrophe": 31.5.
Cavendish, Sir Charles: 209.4.
Celtic twilight: 11.6; 40.4.
Chamfort: 186.2; *232.1*.
Charlemont Street Bridge: 18.1.

Chaucer, Geoffrey: 47.11; 241.3.
"Che Sciagura": 8.4; 85.6; 170.5; *170.6*; #35.
chess: 26.3.
Chinnery, George: #2.
Christ: 9.1; 12.11; 16.2; 20.2; 22.2; 26.7; 27.8; 32.8; 33.6; 39.4; 40.6; 42.8; 44.4; 46.11; 48.3; 50.6; 50.8; 78.1; 120.2; 151.2; 159.3; 182.1; 213.3; 223.6; 225.2; 226.1; 227.3.
cliché [received idea]: 7.4; 8.3; 8.4; 9.1; 9.2; 10.1; 13.2; 13.5; 13.6; 13.7; 14.1; 15.1; 17.2; 17.5; 20.2; 21.3; 40.1; 41.2; 41.8; 42.2; 50.4; 64.3; 68.5; 69.1; 83.1; 97.3; 98.2; 106.1; 112.1; 117.3; 122.1; *132.2*; 139.2; 142.3; 153.1; 154.1; 159.3; 171.1; 172.2; 177.1; 178.1; 181.2; 181.4; 208.3; 213.1; 215.5; 217.6; 218.1; 237.3; 245.4; *246.4*.
Coe, Richard: 39.2; 131.1; 131.5; 134.3; 215.3.
coenaesthesia: 37.4; 39.6; 72.1; *232.2*; 232.3; 232.4.
Coetzee, J. M.: 28.8; 31.6; 45.4; 120.2; 129.5; 129.6; 130.4; 131.3; 133.2; 159.2.
Cohn, Ruby: 8.3; 14.5; 16.5; 24.1; 26.6; 36.5; 45.6; 63.4; 74.8; 164.1; 203.2; 209.6; "Addenda."
Cole, Mr: 243.1.
Coleridge, S. T.: 45.9.
come and go: 16.6; 18.3; 26.4; 31.6; 38.1; 39.6; 39.7; *40.6*; 44.10; *57.4*; 57.5; 50.6; *57.4*; 57.5; *57.6*; *58.1*; *58.2*; 61.1; 63.10; 105.3; 130.3; 132.1; *133.2*; 153.1; 169.7; 216.2; 218.5; 220.3; 223.4; 239.1; 241.2; 243.1; 245.2.
comma [punctuation]: 7.3; 9.5; 16.4; 26.1; 39.1; 39.2; *46.11*; 50.4; 57.6; 63.5; 63.9; *67.2*; 69.1; *70.3*; 85.7; 125.1; 127.2; 142.4; 149.1; 151.2; 158.1; 158.2; 213.2; 219.2; 230.3; #8.
Company: 47.2; 63.4; 91.1; 195.1; 222.2; 222.5; 226.6; 234.2.
Concina, Daniello: 28.9; 29.2; 29.11.
Conrad, Joseph: 134.1.
consciousness [mind]: 8.3; 10.3; 40.2; 43.3; 44.11; 51.3; 73.2; 84.1; 84.2; 237.4; 122.2; 151.5; 163.3; 175.1; 212.3; 215.6; 220.1; 232.2; 232.3; 232.4; 232.5; 232.6; 233.1; #7; #22; #37.
Cooldrinagh: 36.3; 47.1; 47.5; 54.3; 149.1; 149.2; 229.3.
Cooper, William M.: 15.2.
Cork: *156.1*.
corncrake: 47.3.
Cox, Arsy: 240.2; 244.1.
Crane, Ralph: 80.6.
Cream and Berry: *13.4*; 15.4.
Crécy: 44.5.
Croce, Benedetto: 32.3.
Croker's Gallops [Boss Croker]: 47.1; 54.3; 236.2.
crucifixion [*Crux*]: 27.6; 39.4; 42.1; 45.10; 140.1; 154.2; 213.3; 220.1; 222.4; 225.2; 239.5; #1.
Culik, Hugh: 70.3.

Dalton, John: 51.6; 96.3.
Daniels, Samuel: 12.9.

Dante: 21.2; 26.8; 27.5; 37.4; 54.2; 61.3; 63.3; 70.2; 115.2; 146.6; 195.2; 201.1; 238.4; #18; #35.
"Dante and the Lobster": 13.6; 27.5; 33.4; 44.9; 134.2; 143.5.
"Dante ... Bruno .. Vico . Joyce": 32.3; 73.5.
Daphne: 44.9.
Darwin, Charles: 39.2; 85.6; *194.1*.
Davus complex: *#28*.
death: 9.7; 16.5; 17.5; 27.5; 29.14; 33.4; 37.4; 39.6; 42.1; 42.5; 45.2; 47.3; 47.4; 55.3; 57.3; 57.4; 57.5; *57.6*; 58.1; 58.2; 63.4; 69.2; 72.1; 74.10; 84.2; 93.4; 98.2; 101.5; 102.1; 104.2; *104.4*; 105.3; 105.4; 106.1; 106.2; 109.3; 111.2; 122.3; 127.3; 130.2; 131.7; 134.1; 135.5; 142.2; 142.5; 144.2; 154.2; 155.6; 186.2; 212.1; 218.4; 222.2; 222.4; 232.1; 234.5; 241.2; 246.2; #7; #16; #17; #27; #32.
de Baker, Mr: *174.7*; 184.3; 184.7; 185.1; 188.2; 191.3; 195.2; 196.5.
Demented Particulars: 79.2; 102.5.
Democritus: 48.3; 76.2.
Denison, Sir Edmund Beckett: 46.2.
Dens, Peter: 28.9; 29.2; 29.12.
Descartes: 26.1; 26.2; 26.6; 27.4; 29.13; 37.4; 43.3; 44.7; 45.3; 64.2; 68.3; 70.5; 74.9; 75.2; 85.8; 117.3; 129.4; 131.4; 148.3; 159.1; 209.4; 221.1; *223.3*; 224.1; 225.3; 228.1; #19.
desire: 11.2; 11.3; 11.4; 11.5; *44.11*; *44.13*; 55.1; 55.3; 56.2; 57.5; 129.4; 133.2; 166.1.
"Les Deux besoins": 131.4; 203.2.
Devlin, Denis: #28.
Diana, Antonino: 28.9; 29.2; 29.10.
Diderot, Denis: 43.5; 51.5; 93.4; 101.7; 131.7; 134.2.
"Dieppe": 7.6; *40.5*.
"Ding-Dong": 9.7; 40.6; 57.4; 61.3.
Di Pierro, John: T.
Disjecta: 39.5; 73.5; 98.2; 131.4; 146.1; 228.3.
dog [famished dog]: 11.2; 11.1; 37.1; 44.14; 47.1; 57.4; 69.2; 73.2; 78.1; 85.3; *88.3*; 91.5; 92.2; *92.3*; 93.2; 93.4; 96.2; 96.3; 97.3; 100.4; 101.7; *111.1*; *112.3*; 113.1; 113.2; 120.2; 131.5; 136.5; 143.2; 172.4; #27.
Doherty, Francis: 37.1; 40.3; 44.7; 44.9; 63.7; 63.8; 115.5; 116.2; 132.4; 225.2; 245.4.
"Dortmunder": 209.1; 209.5.
Dostoevsky, Fyodor: 44.3; 220.1.
"Draff": 47.1; 50.9; 57.6; 93.4; 143.5; 212.1; #29.
Dream Notebook: 23.4; 27.2; 29.1; 40.6; 40.8; 41.8; 45.3; 96.3; 182.6; 209.1; 224.5; 232.2.
Dream of Fair to middling Women: 13.6; 15.2; 22.1; 28.7; 29.3; 33.4; 40.6; 41.5; 42.8; 45.3; 46.10; 47.4; 47.7; 47.8; 52.6; 57.1; 57.4; 71.4; 74.1; 131.4; 136.4; 146.1; 154.4; 170.4; 181.2; 182.6; 183.5; 219.4; 222.2; 223.2; 224.5; 226.1; #2; #11.
Dublin: 7.2; 9.6; 13.4; 13.6; 16.1; 16.4; *18.1*; 19.4; 19.6; 20.3; 45.7; 48.1; 50.7; 70.3; 151.5; 170.5; 170.6; 174.1; 196.3; 222.2; 244.2; #2.
duck [Runner Duck]: 13.4; 44.4; *45.6*; *80.6*; 209.5; #5; *#37*.

Dún Laoghaire: 46.7; 222.2.
Duthuit, Georges: 115.2; 129.1.

Earle, John: *87.1*.
Easter: *33.8*; 64.4; *239.5*; #24.
"Echo's Bones": 20.3; 29.1; 70.3; 93.4; *192.4*; 197.3; #2.
Eden: 47.1; 118.1; 141.4; *154.1*; 155.6; 169.6; 224.4.
Eleuthéria: 115.2; 222.2.
Eliot, T. S.: 11.3; 16.6; 40.3; 41.8; 43.4; 57.2; 191.1; 225.2; 239.5; "Addenda."
Elsheimer, Adam: 48.1; 131.1.
"Embers": 173.2.
embryo [womb]: *13.5*; 13.6; 25.3; 26.1; 26.8; 27.1; 33.2; 140.1; 175.1; 222.4; 233.5; 234.1; 237.4; #16.
Empedocles [strife of opposites]: 162.2.
"The End": 118.1; 209.3; 217.4.
Endgame: 32.8; 43.1; *43.3*; 44.7; 46.10; 52.4; 57.4; 63.9; 83.4; 102.4; 135.5; 149.3; 215.4; #7; #8.
"Enough": 135.5.
"Enueg I": 9.6; 47.8.
"Enueg II": 9.7; 22.1; 32.8; 224.3.
Epicurus: *208.1*; 209.1; 231.1.
equilibrium: 31.1; 75.1; 88.1; 95.2; 131.5; 147.1; 191.1; 233.1; #17.
errors: T; 7.4; 8.3; 9.1; 9.5; 19.3; 21.1; 26.1; *29.13*; 31.4; 32.4; 33.6; *35.1*; 42.3; 45.3; 46.1; 46.5; 46.11; 48.3; 51.1; 52.1; 52.3; 53.4; 54.1; 57.1; 59.2; 61.1; 67.1; 70.1; *70.3*; 73.4; 74.7; 77.2; 79.2; 81.4; 82.2; 83.2; 83.7; 87.3; 87.4; *89.2*; 89.3; 92.3; 93.1; 96.1; 98.1; 98.3; 100.1; 101.6; 101.8; 101.1; 102.6; 103.1; 103.3; 104.6; 104.7; 105.1; 105.2; *105.3*; 105.4; 106.2; 106.4; 108.2; 109.1; 109.2; 109.3; 110.2; 110.3; 110.5; 112.2; 115.3; 115.5; 117.1; 119.1; 126.2; 126.3; 127.2; 128.6; 130.1; 132.2; 132.3; 134.4; 141.1; 141.2; 141.3; 141.4; 142.4; 142.6; 143.1; 144.2; 146.1; 146.5; 147.4; 148.3; *148.5*; 148.6; 149.1; 149.3; 151.1; 152.1; 153.4; 156.2; 157.1; 158.1; 159.1; 162.1; 163.3; 164.1; 165.1; 166.2; 166.5; 167.4; 169.7; 170.7; 171.4; 173.2; 175.2; 179.2; 181.4; *183.4*; 184.3; 185.1; 187.2; 188.3; 190.2; 191.1; 191.3; 191.4; 193.1; 194.3; *195.1*; 195.3; 196.4; 196.5; 203.4; 204.1; 204.2; 206.1; *207.4*; 208.2; 208.5; 209.7; 211.2; *211.3*; 215.1; 218.1; 218.7; 221.2; 224.6; 225.1; *225.2*; 226.3; 226.5; 226.7; *227.2*; 228.4; 230.2; 233.1; 234.1; 236.2; 237.1; 238.2; 239.6; 243.2; #8; #17; #23; #26; #28; #29; #30; #31; #32; #34; #36.
Erskine: 8.4; 46.7; 56.5; 59.2; 61.1; 67.3; 68.3; 74.2; 85.7; 87.2; 118.2; 120.3; 121.2; 128.3; 130.3; 136.5; 151.2; 159.3; #2; *#14*; #26; #32; #35.
Eubulides of Miletus: *43.3*.
Evans, E. P. [Evans]: 26.4; *28.1*; 28.9; 91.4.
Everyman: 63.4.
Exelmans, Marshal: 209.3.
"The Expelled": 47.9; 74.1; 83.6; *104.5*; 134.2; 217.4.
"Extract from *Watt*" [*Envoy, Irish Writing, Merlin*]: *16.4*; 18.2; 20.1; 21.1. 70.3; 82.3; 85.8; 151.2; 157.1; 199.2; 213.2.

facultative: 10.3; 19.5; 32.7.
failure:T; 8.4; 9.7; 10.1; 15.6; 16.6; 19.5; 23.1; 27.3; 27.8; 28.8; 29.13; 32.4; 33.1; 33.2; 33.7; 37.2; 37.4; 39.5; *40.1*; 40.2; 40.6; 41.5; 41.6; *43.1*; *43.3*; 43.4; 44.5; 44.7; 44.8; 44.9; 44.10; 44.11; 44.12; *44.13*; 45.1; 45.4; 45.5; 46.1; 46.5; 46.6; 46.7; 46.8; 46.9; 46.10; 47.2; 47.4; 47.10; 47.12; 47.13; *48.3*; 49.1; 49.5; 50.3; 51.5; 57.3; 58.3; *60.1*; 61.2; 62.4; 62.5; 63.6; 63.7; 64.3; 67.2; 67.3; 69.4; 70.2; 70.3; 70.5; *73.2*; 73.4; 73.5; 73.6; 74.6; *74.8*; 74.9; 75.4; 75.5; 75.6; 76.1; 77.4; 77.5; 78.1; 79.2; 80.2; 81.3; *82.1*; 82.3; 83.1; 83.6; 85.4; 85.6; 90.1; 93.4; 94.1; 97.1; 101.1; 103.3; 104.7; 105.3; 109.3; 110.3; 113.2; 115.2; 115.6; 121.2; 124.1; 125.1; 129.3; 130.1; 130.3; 134.6; *136.3*; 140.1; 141.2; 143.3; 144.2; 146.1; 146.3; 146.6; 147.2; 147.4; *148.2*; *148.3*; 148.4; 164.2; 164.3; 164.4; *166.1*; 166.2; 167.5; 170.6; 172.4; 192.2; 194.1; 197.4; *198.2*; 208.1; *208.4*; 219.4; 219.5; 220.3; 222.2; 223.6; 224.3; 224.4; 225.2; "Addenda"; #1; #4; #6; #8; #9; #14; *#16*; *#17*; #19; #28; #30; #32; #34; #35; #36; *#37*.
Farquhar, George: 239.7.
father: 13.5; 26.3; 27.5; 46.11; *73.6*; 74.5; 74.6; 74.10; 91.1; 93.4; 130.3; 143.4; *217.4*; 219.6; 222.2.
Feldman, Matthew: 26.8; 74.8.
Fernandes, Marcel: 32.4; 37.4; 44.4; 153.3; 237.4.
figure [at end of novel]: 16.6; 77.5; *225.2*; *228.1*.
Film [film]: 74.1; 74.10; 159.4; 197.1; 217.4.
"**Fingal**": 82.3; 134.2; 153.1.
First Love: 13.6; 16.1; 217.4.
Fitzwein, Mr: *174.7*; 175.2; 175.3; 177.3; 180.4; 184.3; 187.1; 191.5; 195.4; 196.2.
Fizzles: 46.10; 56.2; 200.2.
Flaubert, Gustave: 10.1.
Fletcher, John: 28.8; 44.8; 74.8; 120.1; 222.3; #36.
flies ["La Mouche"]: *236.6*.
flowering currant: *74.1*; 80.2;
Fontenelle, Bernard de: 93.4.
Footfalls: #1; #16.
"**For Future Reference**": 222.2.
Foxrock: 15.6; 19.6; 29.14; 31.2; 36.3; 47.1; 47.8; 48.2; 49.3; 54.3; 69.2; 118.1; 149.1; 151.5; 154.1; 229.3; 240.2; 240.3; 240.4; 244.2; #3.
France: 19.5; 28.2; 28.8; 44.5.
French: 8.3; 8.4; 9.1; 10.1; 10.3; 11.1; 13.7; 14.1; 15.1; 19.1; 19.5; 21.1; 27.2; 30.1; 31.3; 33.3; 40.8; 42.1; 43.1; 50.4; 58.4; 63.3; 67.1; 68.3; 70.4; 73.3; 83.2; 85.7; 92.2; 99.2; 102.8; 104.4; 104.7; 115.4; 120.1; 134.2; 136.5; 142.1; 148.2; 151.1; 151.2; 154.3; 160.4; 165.4; 166.1; 166.3; 167.4; 168.2; *170.1*; 170.4; 170.7; 171.4; 183.1; 183.4; 184.7; 191.2; 197.2; 209.2; 211.3; 215.1; 217.5; 222.3; 232.1; 238.4; 240.5; "Addenda"; #7; #9; #26.
French *Watt*: T; 8.4; 10.1; 11.2; 11.3; 11.5; 11.6; 12.5; 13.5; 13.7; 14.1; 14.5; 17.3; 19.5; 20.1; 21.1; 21.3; 26.1; 27.2; 27.8; 28.3; 28.4; 28.8; 29.13; 29.15; 30.1; 31.3; 32.5; 32.7; *34.1*; 36.2; 39.2; 40.3; 40.5; 41.5; 42.7; 44.8; 45.6; 47.2; 47.14; 48.2; 48.3; 49.3; 50.6; 51.6; 52.3; 53.1; 53.4; 56.1; 56.4; 57.1; 57.2; 57.3; 57.4; 61.1; 63.3; 69.2; 70.3; 74.1; 75.5; 77.1; 80.6; 83.7; 97.3;

101.4; 102.6; 104.4; 110.3; 112.3; 113.1; 113.3; 120.1; 121.1; 128.4; 129.7; 132.2; 138.2; 142.6; 143.2; 143.5; 154.1; 158.1; 159.3; 160.1; 162.1; 163.1; 164.1; 165.1; 166.2; 166.3; 167.4; 168.2; 171.2; 171.4; 174.4; 181.1; 183.1; 183.2; 183.3; 183.4; 184.1; 184.4; 184.7; 186.1; 186.3; 187.2; 187.3; 188.3; 189.2; 190.1; 191.2; 191.5; 193.1; 197.3; 198.1; 203.4; 204.2; 206.1; *207.4*; 209.7; 215.2; 217.3; 217.5; 218.5; 219.3; 222.3; 223.2; 226.4; 226.7; 228.3; 233.1; 236.2; 239.2; 239.2; 239.4; 239.9; 240.2; 241.1; 244.3; #2; #4; #9; #14; #21; #25; #28; #29; #30; #31; #34; #35; #36; #37.
Freud, Sigmund: 38.1; 44.2; 51.3; 80.4; 138.2; 222.2.
Friedrich, Kaspar David: 131.1.
friendship: 44.12; 44.13; 148.1; 191.1.
frogs [Frog Song]: 93.4; 129.4; *136.5*; 149.1.
"From an Abandoned Work": 40.6; 46.10; 135.5; 217.4.
fundamental sounds: T; 7.6; 67.2; 91.5; *136.5*; 236.6.

Galileo: 131.4.
Gall, Lord, of Wormwood: 29.1; 70.3; 197.3; #2.
Galls father and son: 68.4; 70.2; *70.3*; 70.4; 70.5; 73.2; 74.6; 77.2; 78.1; 112.3; 128.4.
Garnier, Pierre: 70.3; 182.6; 209.6.
German Diaries: 26.1; 27.3; 151.3; #2.
"German Letter of 1937": 39.5.
Germany [German]: 9.8; 21.3; 33.8; 36.1; 39.5; 40.4; 74.8; 77.7; 87.2; 102.6; 128.4; 132.2; 159.3; 188.2; 197.2; 215.5; 232.6; *239.6*; #21; #24; #2; #30; #31.
geology: *"Addenda"*; #7; #37.
Gestalt [figure and ground]: 73.2; 77.5; 113.2; 129.4; *208.4*.
Geulincx, Arnold: 57.4; 62.5; 77.7; 83.7; 84.2; 97.2; 102.1; 131.4; *133.2*.
"Ghost Trio": 217.4.
Giles, H. G.: 23.4.
Glencullen: 15.7; 16.1; *149.1*; 236.2.
"Gnome": 132.2.
goat: 16.2; 184.1; 223.6; 246.1.
God [gods]: T; 9.1; 11.4; 12.9; 13.2; 15.8; 26.7; 28.1; 29.1; 32.7; 41.1; 41.3; 41.9; *42.1*; *44.7*; 46.1; 47.1; 47.15; 50.9; 57.4; 57.5; 59.1; 61.3; 62.3; 62.5; 62.5; 67.2; 69.1; 76.1; 77.5; 77.6; 78.1; 82.3; 85.2; 85.4; 91.3; 91.4; 91.5; 113.2; 115.6; 122.3; 129.4; 131.4; 131.7; 133.1; 134.2; 135.1; 135.4; 146.4; 147.3; 148.3; 149.1; *155.6*; 165.2; 169.7; 191.2; *202.1*; *203.2*; 209.5; *209.7*; 211.3; 218.7; 223.3; 224.3; 226.6; 230.1; 236.3; 237.4; #29; #32.
Goethe, Wolfgang von [*Faust*]: *33.8*; 36.1; 132.2; 225.4; *#24*.
Gomez, Mr: 69.3; 142.5; 169.9; 171.2; 182.4.
Gorgias: 45.5; 97.1; *148.2*.
Gorman, Mr.: 13.4; 45.10; 169.6; 229.3; 239.2; 238.1; 239.2; 239.9; 241.1; 241.2; 242.2; 246.3.
Gorman, Mrs [fishwoman, Mrs Piscoe]: T; 10.1; 69.6; 85.5; 136.5; 138.1; *139.1*; 141.1; 142.3; 229.3; 238.1.
grammar [rhetoric]: 8.2; 8.3; 14.6; 24.1; 37.4; *39.2*; 39.3; 50.6; 72.3; 74.7; 80.1; 89.2; *91.5*; 96.2; 97.1; 100.2; 110.3; 112.3; 128.1; 128.2; 129.2; 132.1; 131.1; 133.3; 134.5; 139.1; 141.1; 148.5; 154.4; 154.5; 155.3; 157.2; 159.3;

162.2; 165.1; 165.2; 165.3; 165.4; 166.1; 166.2; 166.3; 166.5; 166.6; 167.1; 167.3; 167.4; 167.5; 168.1; 168.2; 168.3; 168.4; 168.5; 197.2; *197.3*; 207.2; 216.5; 221.3; 224.6; 228.4; 228.6; 230.3; *244.3*; #8.
Graves, Mr [gardener]: 27.5; 39.2; 69.3; 85.2; 85.4; *93.4*; 95.1; 101.7; 131.5; *142.5*; 143.4; 143.5; 160.2; 169.6; 169.10; 223.1; *#29*.
Graves, Robert: 12.7.
Gray, Thomas: #27.
greatcoat: 9.7; 16.7; 63.7; *217.4*; 212.1; 218.3; 218.4.
Greek: 9.8; 42.1; 43.3; 73.1; 160.5; 171.6; 209.2; #31.
green [and yellow]: 9.6; *9.7*; 22.1; 38.2; 47.5; 217.4; 218.6.
Grehan [Green]: 11.2; 12.3; 70.3; 72.1.
Grove Companion: 7.2; 8.1; 9.7; 10.3; 11.5; 15.2; 16.1; 17.5; 26.7; 27.3; 31.5; 32.7; 39.6; 40.6; 42.8; 43.3; 43.5; 47.1; 47.4; 55.1; 56.3; 61.1; 70.3; *73.2*; 73.5; 74.9; 75.4; 77.5; 84.2; 85.6; 85.7; 97.2; 111.2; 114.1; 115.2; 122.2; 131.5; 140.1; 141.1; 149.3; 151.2; 174.1; 174.7; 188.2; 194.1; 209.3; 209.5; 217.4; 222.2; 228.1; 228.3; 232.2; 234.4; 236.4; 236.6; "Addenda."
Grove Press: 71; 7.4; 9.5; 19.3; 21.1; 31.4; 31.4; 45.5; 46.5; 46.11; 48.3; 49.3; 52.1; 53.4; 54.1; 57.1; 57.2; 57.4; 58.5; 61.2; 63.5; 67.1; 70.1; 74.7; 77.2; 79.2; 80.6; 81.4; 83.2; 83.7; 84.1; 87.3; 87.4; 89.2; 93.1; 98.3; 100.1; 101.8; 102.1; 102.6; 102.8; 103.1; 105.4; 106.4; 112.2; 115.5; 117.1; 119.1; 126.2; 127.2; 128.6; 130.1; 132.2; 132.3; 141.3; 142.3; 142.4; 142.6; 143.1; 146.5; 148.5; 152.1; 153.4; 154.1; 155.1; 156.2; 158.2; 162.1; 164.1; 165.1; 170.7; 171.2; 175.2; 179.2; 180.2; 181.4; 184.3; 193.1; 191.4; 195.3; 204.1; 207.4; 211.2; 211.3; 219.3; 224.6; 225.1; 226.3; 226.5; 228.4; 230.2; 233.1; 234.1; 237.1; 237.2; 238.2; #4; #9; #23; #26; #28; #29; #36; *#37*.
Guggenheim, Peggy: 13.5.
Guy Fawkes [Hallow-e'en]: 57.2; 57.3.
Gwynne, Nell: 11.2.

habit: 44.14; 74.4; 194.1.
Habbakuk: 45.6; 209.5.
Hackett, Frances: 7.2.
Hackett, Hunchy: *7.2*; 9.4; 10.2; 10.3; 13.2; 15.1; 15.6; 15.7; 15.8; 16.1; 16.3; 17.1; 17.2; 17.3; 18.1; 18.2; 19.2; 21.3; 24.1; 24.3; 44.7; 49.3; 75.1; 82.1; 95.1; 114.1; 158.4; 187.1; 203.3; 228.1; #15; *#29*.
Hallberg, John: #2.
Happy Days: 42.1; 46.10; 57.4;102.7.
Harcourt Street Station: 18.1; 19.6; 25.3.
hard words: 21.1; 28.4; 30.5; 31.1; 31.3; 41.7; 50.5; 61.3; 62.5; 70.2; 74.3; 74.5; 75.7; 85.3; 140.2; 141.2; 142.4; 144.1; 154.3; 165.2; 169.9; 171.5; 181.1; 182.6; 199.3; 212.3; 218.3; 218.4; 234.5; 235.1; #11.
hardy laurel: 49.2; 61.1; 155.5; *#29*.
Hardy, Thomas: 129.2; #27.
Harry Ransom Center: 28.8; 45.6; 59.2; 77.5; 149.1; 164.2; 165.4; 166.3; 167.4; 168.2; "Addenda."
Harvey, Lawrence: 16.5; 25.3; 59.1; 84.2; 201.1; 209.1; 212.1; #8.
hat: 9.7; *26.1*; 38.1; 56.2; 82.1; 179.1; 200.2; 218.5; 226.2.
Hayman, David: 45.7; 129.1.

"Heard in the Dark I": 47.2; 217.4.
Heem, David Davidszoon: #26.
Henno, Francisco: 28.9; 29.2; 29.8.
Heraclitus: 43.4; 81.2; 132.1.
Herbert, Jocelyn: #4.
Hesla, David: 8.3; 26.8; 32.7; 48.3; 56.5; 77.5; 134.2; 168.2; 212.3.
Higgins, Aidan: 19.3.
"L'Histoire de Watt": 215.2.
Hoefer, Jacqueline: 44.8; 45.4; 75.3.
Hooker, Richard: #5.
Hölderlin, Johann: 40.4; 228.1; 239.4; *239.6*.
Homer [*Odyssey*]: 207.3; 240.5.
Honthorst, Gerrit van: #3.
Horace: 43.3; *142.1*; 170.1; #13.
horse: 188.1; 188.2; 236.2; 236.4; 240.5.
Houston, S. C.: 45.8.
"The Housewife's Lament": 47.4.
How It Is: 29.14; 30.4; 33.7; 33.8; 42.1; 46.10; 61.2; 74.1; 77.5; 85.6; 91.1; 117.3; 134.2; 181.3; 224.5; 240.5; #29.
"Human Wishes": 48.3; 98.2; 100.4; 151.4; 151.5; 165.2; #8.
hurebers of Beaune [and other pests]: 28.1.
Huysmanns, J-K.: 53.1.
Hyde, Douglas: *11.6*.
Hymen: 12.9; 42.9; 216.4.
Hymns Ancient and Modern: 47.15; 57.1; 91.4.

Ill Seen Ill Said: 74.8; 207.4; 218.5.
incident of note: *72.2*; 73.2; *128.4*; #26; #34.
indifference: 10.3; 20.2; *32.7*; 32.9; 39.6; 39.7; 44.13; 45.4; 51.1; 58.3; 63.6; 67.3; 73.2; 73.4; 74.2; 74.8; 74.9; 80.2; 104.7; 110.3; 120.2; 152.2; *208.1*; *208.4*; 211.1; 213.1; 216.5; *225.2*; 232.1; 232.2; 232.3; 236.6; #9; #19.
Inge, Dean Ralph: 28.7; 41.8; 44.7; 45.3; 77.5.
Ireland: 11.5; 11.6; 12.11; 18.1; 32.1; 57.2; 100.3; 111.1; 142.5; 156.1; 160.1; 170.6; 171.3; 171.5; 172.3; 173.3; *174.1*; 174.6; 187.3; 217.5; 225.3; 228.3; 245.4; #14; *#16*; *#19*; #27.
Irish [Gaelic]: 11.6; 38.1; 58.4; 68.5; 70.3; 169.1; 173.3; 184.1; 238.3; 246.1.
irrationality [absurdity, madness]: 7.4; 7.6; 17.3; 23.2; 27.3; *34.1*; 35.1; 37.1; 37.2; 37.4; 40.4; 43.4; 45.4; 45.5; 50.9; *70.3*; 70.5; 71.3; *73.2*; 73.5; 85.8; 88.3; 90.1; *91.5*; 92.1; 93.2; 94.1; *95.1*; 98.1; 100.2; 100.4; 117.3; 120.3; 122.1; 123.1; *129.4*; 130.4; 131.1; 131.5; 132.4; 132.4; 134.5; *136.3*; 141.1; *148.3*; 151.2; 151.5; 155.4; 155.6; 159.1; 160.2; 161.2; *166.1*; 166.6; 175.1; 179.1; *204.2*; 219.1; 219.4; 221.3; 228.1; 239.6; #21; #23.
Italian: 8.4; 33.3; 44.10; 44.13; 131.4; 136.4; 212.2; 217.1; #3; #21; #35.

Janvier, Ludovic and Agnès: 13.5; 47.2; 215.2.
Jeans, Sir James: 224.5.
Jeffreys, Judge: 144.2.
Jerome, Saint [Donatus]: #25.

Jerusalem Artichoke: 45.6; 187.3.
"je suis ce cours de sable qui glisse": 43.1.
Job: 12.7; 41.6; 62.6.
John of the Cross: 28.7; 45.1; 166.1.
Johnny Fox's pub: 16.3; 236.2.
Johnny Watt: T; 59.2; 87.2; 220.1; #23; #35; #37.
Johnson, Samuel: 9.8; 13.3; 15.6; 21.1; *21.3*; 26.4; 27.5; 28.4; 30.4; 30.5; 31.1; 41.7; 60.1; 74.3; 85.3; 98.2; 100.4; 141.2; 142.4; 151.4; 169.9; 199.3; 212.3; 224.7; 234.5; #8; #12.
Joss: 27.8; *236.2*; 236.3.
Jouffroy, Alain ["Arsene Parle"]: 39.2; 53.5.
Joyce, James: 43.1; 83.2; 136.5; #3.
　　Portrait: 7.2; 14.6; 21.2; 29.2; 29.7; 31.2; 35.2; 38.1; 43.2; 50.7; 63.3; 81.2; 117.2; 172.1; 225.2; *#3*.
　　Ulysses: 8.1; 11.5; 12.11; 24.3; 29.2; 39.2; 50.1; 50.8; 70.2; 70.3; 114.1; 129.2; 146.1; 155.2; 165.4; 168.2; 170.1; 173.3; 174.4; 178.1; 183.2; 213.4; 245.1; #4, #20.
　　Finnegans Wake: *45.7*; 46.11.
Juliana of Norwich: 41.8.
Jung, Carl: *91.1*; 225.2; #16.
Juvenal: 60.1.

Kafka, Franz: 74.8.
Kandinsky, Wassily: 128.4; 174.4.
Kant, Immanuel: 40.9; 45.7; *45.8*; 58.3; 75.3; 86.1; 91.5; 136.2; 227.2; #31.
Keaton, Buster: 136.3.
Keats, John: 11.3; 33.4; 39.6; 44.7; 69.2; 184.4.
Keller, John Robert: 83.3.
Kenner, Hugh: 8.3; 26.2; 30.4; 75.3; 83.7; 117.3; 133.2; 136.5; 221.2.
Kleist, Heinrich von: *163.3*.
Knott, Mr: T; 7.2; 8.3; 13.4; 17.4; 18.3; 19.5; 27.4; 30.3; 33.2; 38.2; 40.1; 40.2; 41.1; 41.6; *42.1*; 42.7; 44.13; 45.7; 49.2; 54.2; *57.4*; *57.5*; *57.6*; 58.2; 58.5; 61.1; 61.3; *67.2*; 67.3; 68.3; 68.4; 72.2; 72.3; 82.1; 82.2; 83.1; 84.1; *86.2*; 87.1; 87.4; 88.3; 89.1; *89.3*; *93.4*; 101.1; 101.7; 104.1; 118.1; 121.2; 128.3; 129.4; 130.3; 130.4; 131.5; 131.7; 132.4; 134.2; 135.1; 143.4; 146.2; 147.3; 147.4; *148.2*; 164.2; *166.1*; 166.3; 167.4; 168.2; 169.7; 199.2; 200.1; 200.2; *200.3*; 202.1; *203.2*; *203.4*; 207.4; 207.5; 208.5; *209.7*; 211.3; 212.1; 215.5; 223.1; 223.4; 223.6; 225.1; 228.1; 236.5; 243.1; *#1*; #13; #22; #26; *#29*; #35.
knowledge [epistemology, ignorance]: T; 7.2; 31.5; 40.9; 44.2; 44.7; 44.9; 45.3; 45.4; 45.5; 45.8; 47.6; 50.3; 50.9; 51.1; 61.2; 62.5; 63.4; 64.2; 67.2; 67.3; 68.5; 70.5; *73.5*; 73.6; 74.8; 74.9; 74.10; 75.3; 75.4; *77.5*; 77.7; *78.1*; 78.2; 79.2; 80.2; 80.4; 85.1; 86.1; *89.3*; 90.1; 91.1; *97.1*; 117.3; *125.1*; 129.3; 129.4; 129.5; 129.6; 130.3; 131.1; 132.4; 135.4; *136.5*; 141.4; 146.2; *148.2*; *148.3*; 148.4; 152.1; 159.1; 165.1; 165.3; 165.4; *166.1*; 166.2; 166.6; 167.3; 167.4; 167.5; 168.1; 168.2; 168.3; 168.4; 169.1; 169.4; 169.5; 198.1; 199.2; 200.3; 201.1; *208.1*; 212.3; 215.5; 222.5; 225.1; 227.1; *227.2*; 227.3; 228.1; 228.3; 232.2; 232.3; 232.4; 240.1; #26; #27; *#28*; *#31*.

Knowlson, James: 13.4; 31.2; 31.5; 81.2; 83.3; 162.1.
Kostka, Saint Stanislaus: 29.2.
Krapp [*Krapp's Last Tape*]: 38.1; 40.2; 43.5; 47.6; 57.1; 74.1; 131.4; 172.5.
Külpe, Oswald: T.
Kulturkampf: 188.2.
Kundera, Milan: 39.8.

Lachesis: *127.3*.
lacunae: 29.15; 32.1; 32.4.
ladder: *15.8*; 39.5; 40.3; 44.6; *44.7*; *44.8*; 45.1; 83.4.
Laloy [*La Musique chinoise*]: 209.1.
language (problems of): T; 8.3; 13.7; 14.1; 14.5; 14.6; 15.1; 17.2; 18.2; 21.1; 22.2; 23.1; 27.2; 27.3; 27.8; 28.4; 35.2; 37.4; 39.5; 43.3; 44.8; 48.3; 62.5; 73.1; *73.2*; *73.4*; *73.5*; 74.3; 74.4; 74.6; *74.8*; 74.9; 81.1; *81.2*; 83.1; 83.2; 85.4; *89.3*; 93.2; 117.3; 128.4; 131.2; 138.2; 141.2; 142.4; 143.5; 144.1; 154.2; 154.3; 154.5; 155.4; 155.7; 164.1; 164.2; 164.3; 165.1; 165.2; 165.3; 165.4; 166.2; 166.3; 166.4; 166.6; 167.1; 167.3; 167.4; 167.5; 168.1; 168.2; 168.3; 168.4; 168.5; 169.1; 171.5; 180.4; 208.5; 209.2; 209.3; 209.4; 209.5; 215.5; 216.7; 239.4; 239.8; #37.
Laplace, Marquis de: 135.4.
larches: 47.1; 47.5.
Larry [Lazarus]: *12.11*; 12.12; 163.2; 233.5.
Latimer and Ridley: 62.3.
Latin: 13.2; 15.8; 17.5; 27.2; 28.5; 37.2; 40.6; 40.9; 41.7; 44.9; 48.3; 57.4; 62.5; 63.8; 102.1; 129.2; 133.2; 171.5; 183.1; 187.2; 219.2; 226.4; 227.4; 232.4; 232.5; 233.5; 238.4; #24; #26; #31.
Lauder, Harry: 40.7; 216.2.
Lawlor, Sean: 104.7; #4.
leap year: *34.1*; 47.10.
Lees, Heath: 70.3; 71.3; 71.4; 73.2; 136.5; *149.1*; 223.4; #26; #34; #36.
left and right: 18.1; 19.4; 28.5; 28.6; *29.7*; 30.4; 142.5; 169.8; 172.1; 174.7; 182.5; 183.2; 192.2; *200.3*; 213.1; 219.5.
Leibniz, Gottfried: 40.9; 41.9; 43.3; *43.5*; *134.2*; 152.1.
Lemprière: #32.
Leopardi, Giacomo: 9.4; 44.13; 57.5; 60.1; 212.2; 217.1; 222.6; 225.4; 227.2; #22; #27.
Leopardstown: 28.9; 29.14; 29.15; 130.3; #3.
"Lightning Calculation": 74.10.
Lisbon: *43.4*; 134.2.
little by little: 43.2; *43.3*; 44.6; 64.3; 182.4; 194.4; 235.2; #10.
Locke, John: 169.4; 169.5; 199.2.
logical paradigms: 7.6; 27.4; 27.8; *29.13*; 30.4; 32.7; 34.1; 35.1; 37.2; *46.11*; 47.15; 51.2; 52.2; 57.6; 59.2; 60.2; 61.1; 82.2; 86.3; *89.3*; 90.1; *92.3*; 94.1; 98.1; 108.1; 109.1; 110.2; 110.3; 110.5; 121.2; *129.4*; 131.1; 133.1; 133.2; 135.3; *136.5*; 139.2; 142.3; 147.3; 147.4; 155.6; 157.1; 160.2; 161.2; 164.1; 164.3; 164.4; *165.1*; 165.3; 165.4; 166.2; 166.3; 166.5; 167.1; 167.3; 167.4; 168.1; 168.2; 168.3; *168.4*; *174.7*; 177.2; 180.2; 183.1; 195.4; 196.2; 196.4; 199.2; *200.3*; *203.4*; *204.2*; 206.1; 207.1; *209.7*; 211.1; 219.5; 220.3;

221.3; 225.3; 227.2; 229.2; 231.2; 246.3.
Lombard, Peter: 28.9; 29.2; 29.4.
London: 45.8; 151.5; 159.3; 172.3; *212.1*.
"The Lost Ones": 44.7; 129.7.
Louit: 62.1; 138.1; 169.5; *171.2*; 171.3; 172.4; 173.2; 173.3; 174.7; 180.3; 181.5; 185.1; 189.2; 190.2; 191.5; 192.2; 193.1; 194.4; 197.3; 198.1; 198.2.
love [sex]: 8.4; 9.3; 10.1; 11.2; 11.3; 11.4; 11.5; 11.7; 12.2; 12.3; 12.4; 12.5; 12.8; 12.9; 13.3; 14.2; 14.5; 21.3; 28.3; 30.1; 42.9; *44.11*; 49.3; 49.6; 50.7; 61.3; 74.2; 74.3; 76.1; 85.7; 91.2; 102.6; 107.1; 139.2; 140.1; 140.2; 141.1; 141.4; 142.1; 142.2; 142.3; 142.4; 143.2; 154.4; 162.2; 170.3; 170.4; 170.5; 170.6; 174.7; 182.6; 183.5; 216.6; 226.1; 228.4; 229.3; 238.1; 233.2; 239.2; 239.7; 240.5; 241.1; 241.3; *#8*; #14.
Love, Damian: 40.4; *73.2*; 74.10; 82.1; 228.1; 234.5; 239.6.
Lourdes: 27.8; *28.8*: 106.3.
Lovelace, Richard: 11.2; 11.4.
Lowry, Mr: 25.2.
Lucky: 16.5; 24.2; 32.6; 39.2; 67.3; 174.1.
Lyly, John: 11.3.
Lynch family: *91.5*; 100.4; *101.1*; 101.7; 101.9; 102.1; 102.2; 102.4; 102.6; 103.3; 104.4; 104.5; 105.1; *105.3*; 105.4; 106.2; 106.4; 108.2; 109.1; 109.2; 109.3; 110.2; 110.5; 120.2; #27.

MacGreevy, Thomas: 19.5; 40.6.
machine: T; 26.2; 75.1; 75.2.
MacKenzie, Martin Ignatius: 17.3; *28.10*.
Macmillan, Dugald: 159.3.
Macon: 28.1; 28.2.
MacStern, Mr: *174.7*; 196.5.
Madden Prize [Samuel Madden]: 46.7; *#14*; #37.
Magershon, Mr: *174.7*; 177.3; 186.1; 186.3; 191.1; 191.5; 192.4; 194.1; 196.5.
Mahaffy, John: 131.4; 209.4.
"Malacoda": 33.4; 212.1.
Malone Dies **[Malone, Macmann]**: 8.1; 9.3; 10.2; 16.1; 20.3; 21.1; 33.8; 35.1; 39.7; 43.3; 47.8; 55.1; 62.5; 74.10; 110.4; 118.1; 151.5; 175.1; 218.5; 219.2; 219.5; 241.2; #4; #7.
Mangianele, Vito: 174.1.
Manning [Susan, Mary]: 149.1; 232.2; #8.
manuscripts: 20.1; 26.7; 46.6; 46.7; 105.3.
    early drafts: T; 7.2; 9.4; 11.2; 11.3; 11.4; 11.6; 12.10; 13.4; 13.5; 13.7; 14.1; 14.5; 16.3; 18.2; 27.8; 28.9; 28.10; 33.6; 34.1; 39.3; 40.2; 43.3; 45.6; 46.3; 46.5; 46.7; 46.8; 46.9; 46.11; 47.2; 47.15; 48.3; 49.3; 50.3; 50.5; 50.7; 50.9; 51.3; 52.1; 52.3; 52.4; 53.4; 55.2; 56.3; 57.1; 57.4; 59.2; 61.1; 62.1; 62.2; 63.6; 64.3; 67.2; 69.3; 70.3; 71.3; 71.4; 85.7; 86.2; 86.3; 87.1; 87.2; 87.4; 87.6; 88.2; 89.1; 89.3; 92.1; 93.4; 95.1; 96.1; 97.3; 98.1; 99.1; 100.2; 101.1; 101.4; 102.2; 102.6; 103.1; 104.4; 104.5; 105.3; 106.3; 107.1; 111.1; 118.2; 125.1; 127.1; 127.3; 128.1; 128.2; 128.4; 128.6; 128.7; 129.3; 129.4; 129.7; 130.3; 131.1; 132.5; 133.1; 133.2; 133.3; 134.2; 134.6; 135.1;

136.2; 136.3; 138.1; 139.1; 139.2; 142.1; 142.5; 143.2; 145.1; 146.2; 146.4; 147.5; 148.1; 148.3; 148.5; 169.9; 170.1; 171.2; 171.3; 171.5; 172.1; 172.2; 172.3; 173.3; 174.1; 174.4; 174.7; 179.1; 179.4; 181.4; 181.6; 182.4; 183.4; 184.1; 184.2; 184.5; 191.2; 194.1; 195.1; 195.4; 197.3; 198.2; 200.4; 203.3; *204.2;* 207.3; 215.3; #1; #2; #3; #4; #5; #6; #7; #8; #9; #10; #11; #12; #13; #14; #15; #16; #17; #18; #19; #20; *#22; #23; #26; #27; #29;* #34; #35; #37.

typescript: 7.2; 11.2; 12.10; 13.4; 13.5; 13.7; 16.1; 16.3; 27.8; 28.1; 28.8; 28.9; 28.10; 33.6; 33.8; 34.1; 35.1; 39.3; 45.6; 46.3; 46.5; 46.8; 46.9; 46.11; 47.8; 47.13; 47.15; 48.3; 49.3; 50.3; 50.5; 50.9; 51.1; 51.3; 52.1; 52.3; 52.4; 53.4; 56.3; 56.5; 57.4; 58.4; 59.2; 61.1; 62.1; 62.2; 63.6; 63.7; 64.3; 67.2; 68.4; 70.3; 71.4; 72.1; 72.2; 83.5; 85.7; 86.2; 87.1; 87.2; 88.2; 89.1; 89.3; 90.1; 91.2; 91.4; 92.1; 93.4; 96.2; 97.3; 98.1; 98.3; 99.1; 100.2; 101.2; 101.6; 102.3; 102.6; 102.7; 104.4; 104.5; 106.3; 107.1; 111.1; 113.4; 118.2; 121.2; 122.1; 122.3; 125.1; 126.1; 127.1; 127.2; 127.3; 128.1; 128.2; 128.4; 128.6; 128.7; 129.3; 129.4; 129.7; 130.3; 131.1; 133.1; 133.3; 134.2; 134.6; 135.2; 136.2; 136.3; 138.1; 139.1; 142.1; 142.5; 143.2; 145.1; 147.4; 147.5; 148.3; 148.5; 149.1; 149.3; 166.3; 169.9; 170.1; 171.2; 171.3; 172.1; 172.2; 172.3; 174.1; 174.4; 174.7; 177.1; 177.2; 183.3; 184.1; 184.5; 187.3; 188.2; 191.3; 192.1; 192.2; 192.3; 194.3; 194.4; 195.4; 196.1; 197.3; 198.1; 203.3; 208.4; 217.1; 220.1; #1; #2; #3; #4; #5; #6; #7; #8; #11; #13; #14; #15; #16; #17; #18; #20; *#22; #23; #26; #27; #29;* #34; #37.

late drafts: 7.3; 8.3; 8.4; 9.2; 9.3; 9.5; 9.8; 10.1; 10.2; 11.1; 12.10; 13.2; 13.5; 13.6; 13.7; 14.1; 15.1; 15.2; 15.4; 16.2; 16.6; 17.2; 19.5; 21.1; 21.3; 25.2; 26.4; 27.2; 27.8; 32.1; 32.4; 32.5; 32.7; 33.3; 33.8; 42.4; 43.2; 44.8; 46.1; 46.2; 46.4; 47.7; 50.3; 63.7; 64.3; 68.1; 68.2; 68.3; 68.4; 69.1; 69.2; 69.3; 69.5; 69.6; 72.2; 72.3; 73.4; 74.1; 74.2; 75.5; 77.2; 77.6; 79.1; 79.2; 80.4; 81.5; 82.3; 85.7; 86.3; 87.2; 87.4; 88.3; 89.1; 89.3; 90.1; 91.1; 91.4; 95.1; 96.3; 98.1; 98.3; 110.2; 116.2; 117.2; 118.2; 128.4; 128.5; 128.6; 128.7; 129.3; 129.5; 129.7; 130.2; 130.4; 131.3; 131.8; 132.2; 132.5; 133.2; 136.3; 136.5; 142.5; 143.3; 143.4; 148.5; 153.3; 153.4; 154.3; 154.4; 155.2; 155.4; 156.1; 157.2; 158.1; 158.3; 159.3; 159.5; 160.1; 162.2; 164.3; 165.1; 165.2; 165.3; 165.4; *166.3;* 166.5; 167.1; 167.2; 167.4; 167.5; 168.1; 168.3; 168.4; 168.5; 169.4; 169.5; 169.6; 173.2; 174.7; 179.1; 199.2; 201.1; 203.2; 207.2; 207.6; 208.1; 208.4; 208.5; 209.1; 209.2; 209.7; 211.1; 211.2; 213.2; 215.3; 215.4; 215.6; 216.2; 216.5; 216.6; 216.7; 217.3; 217.6; 218.1; 218.2; 218.7; 219.1; 219.3; 219.4; 219.6; 221.2; 222.6 223.1; 223.4; 223.6; 224.1; 228.2; 228.3; 228.6; 229.2; 230.3; 233.4; 236.3; 234.2; 235.4; 237.2; 238.1; 238.2; 238.3; 238.4; 239.8; 240.1; 240.5; 241.1; 241.2; 243.1; 243.3; 244.1; *246.4;* #29.

galleys: 7.1; 7.3; 9.5; 12.10; 19.3; 21.1; 21.3; 23.2; 27.7; 28.1; 28.6; 29.15; 31.4; 32.9; 34.1; *35.1;* 42.3; 42.11; 45.3; 45.6; 46.5; 46.11; 48.3; 49.3; 50.4; 52.1; 53.4; 61.2; 67.1; 70.1; 72.2; 73.4; 74.2; 74.7; 77.2; 77.5; 79.2; 81.2; 81.4; 82.3; 83.2; 83.7; 85.7; 87.2; 87.3; 87.4; 91.4; 93.1; 93.2; 96.2; 98.3; 100.1; 101.8; 102.1; 102.3; 102.6; 103.1; 104.7; 105.4; 106.4; 108.2; 110.2; 110.3; 112.2; 115.5; 117.1; 118.2; 119.1; 126.2; 126.3; 127.2; 128.1; 128.4; 128.5; 129.3; 130.1; 132.2; 132.3; 134.4; *136.5;* 141.1; 141.3; 142.1; 142.3; 142.6; 146.1; 146.5; 148.5; 148.6; 151.1; 152.1; 153.2; 154.1; 154.3; 155.1; 155.3; 156.2; 158.2; 158.3; 162.1; 163.3; 165.4; 166.2; 166.5; 167.5; 168.3; 170.7; 171.4; 173.2; 175.3; 179.3; 180.2; 181.4; 183.1; 184.3; 185.1;

188.3; 190.2; 191.1; 191.3; 191.4; 194.3; 195.3; 196.4; 196.5; 200.2; 200.3; 203.1; 203.4; 204.1; 204.2; 208.4; 211.2; 211.3; 212.1; 213.1; 224.6; 225.1; 226.5; 228.5; 230.2; 233.1; 234.1; 237.1; 237.2; 238.2; 239.6; 241.1; "*Addenda*"; #4; #23; #26; #28; #29; #36.
    French translation: 11.2; 29.13; 29.15; 34.1; 36.2; 102.6; 110.3; 113.3; 129.7; 164.2; 165.1; 165.4; 166.5; 167.4; 183.1; 183.4; 187.2; 190.1; 203.4; 204.2; 223.2; #4.
    miscellaneous [other texts]: 18.2; 20.1; 21.3; 56.5; 102.5.
Marston, John: 55.1.
Martin: 149.1; 149.3; 169.6; #29.
Marx, Groucho: 14.2.
Mary [Ann, Jane]: 46.11; 50.8; 50.9; 51.1; 52.4; 55.1; 64.4; 163.2; 184.5.
mathematics: *17.3*; 29.13; *34.1*; *35.1*; 41.1; 42.7; 47.12; 49.3; 50.9; 61.1; *70.3*; 71.3; 83.6; 86.2; 86.3; 87.6; 88.1; *89.3*; 92.1; 94.1; *98.1*; 101.1; 103.3; *104.4*: *105.3*; 106.2; 108.1; 109.2; 109.3; 110.2; 110.3; 124.1; 128.4; 129.1; *129.4*; 133.1; 133.2; *136.5*; 139.2; 142.3; *148.3*; 149.1; 157.1; 160.5; 161.2; 165.1; 171.1; 171.3; *174.1*; 174.7; 180.2; 182.1; *183.4*; 184.8; 188.1; 190.1; 191.5; 193.1; 194.2; *195.1*; 195.4; 196.2; 196.4; *200.3*; *203.4*; *204.2*; 206.1; 207.4; 209.4; *209.7*; 229.2; 237.4; 246.3; #6; #20; #23; #36.
Mauthner, Fritz: 48.3; 73.5; 74.9; *77.7*; #31.
Mayoux, Jean-Jacques: 42.1.
McCann, Lady: 31.2; 31.6; *32.1*; 32.2; 240.1; 243.2; 243.3; 244.1.
McCarthy, Pat: 24.3; 30.5; 45.7; 46.11; 81.2; 82.1; 151.2; 207.3; 216.2; 245.1.
McGilligan, Matthew David: 28.1; *28.9*; 29.1; 29.14; 184.2; *#3*.
McGovern, Barry: 15.7.
meaning: T; 7.3; 7.4; 7.6; 8.1; 8.3; 19.2; 23.1; 26.6; 27.3; 29.1; 29.13; 29.15; 32.4; 37.2; *39.5*; 39.6; *40.2*; 40.9; 41.3; 41.8; 41.9; 42.6; *43.1*; *43.3*; *44.6*; *44.7*; 44.10; *44.13*; 44.14; 45.3; 45.5; 45.6; 45.7; *48.3*; 50.9; 51.6; 57.4; 57.5; 58.3; 61.2; 62.1; *62.5*; 67.2; 67.3; 68.5; 70.2; 70.5; 71.1; 72.2; 72.3; 73.1; *73.2*; *73.4*; *73.5*; 73.6; 74.6; *74.8*; 74.9; 74.10; *75.3*; 75.4; 75.5; 75.6; 76.1; *76.2*; *77.5*; 77.6; 77.7; *78.1*; 78.2; 80.4; *80.6*; 81.1; *81.2*; *82.1*; 82.2; *83.1*; 83.2; 83.4; 83.6; 85.2; 85.4; 86.1; 89.3; 90.1; *91.1*; *91.5*; 93.4; 94.1; *98.1*; 104.7; 110.3; 112.2; 113.2; 114.1; *117.3*; *121.2*; *125.1*; 126.1; 128.5; *129.3*; *129.4*; 129.6; *130.4*; *131.4*; 131.5; 131.8; *132.2*; *132.4*; 132.5; 133.3; 134.2; 134.3; 135.4; 136.2; *136.3*; 136.5; 141.4; 143.5; 147.4; *147.5*; *148.2*; 148.4; 151.2; 151.4; 154.5; 159.1; 159.3; 164.2; 164.3; 165.1; 165.3; 165.4; 166.1; 166.2; 166.3; 166.4; 167.1; 167.3; 167.4; 167.5; 168.1; 168.2; 168.3; 168.4; 169.1; 169.5; 169.10; 180.2; 191.5; 188.3; 192.1; 192.2; 200.3; 215.2; 215.3; 215.5; 219.2; 220.3; 222.5; *225.3*; 227.1; 227.2; 228.1; 234.4; #17; #22; *#36*; *#37*.
medical misadventures: 13.7; 14.5; 15.2; 15.6; 15.8; 26.4; 27.7; 28.7; 28.8; 28.10; 32.4; 32.5; 33.6; 44.3; 44.13; 46.4; 51.6; 52.3; 52.5; 52.6; 53.1; 53.2; 53.3; 53.4; 53.6; 69.2; 70.3; 73.2; 74.3; 74.5; 85.3; *87.4*; 101.2; 101.5; 101.9; 102.4; 102.5; 102.8; *103.1*; 104.6; 109.4; 141.5; *142.1*; 144.1; 148.3; 154.3; 157.2; 169.2; 169.3; 169.4; 170.1; 170.2; 170.3; 170.4; 177.3; 180.1; 182.6; 184.6; 197.1; 207.3; 208.1; 209.6; 212.2; 220.1; 220.2; 234.3; 235.3; #1; #5; #30.
memory 13.1; 13.5; 23.1; 73.6; *74.1*; 74.6; *74.8*; *74.9*; 75.5; 77.3; 80.2; 80.4; 83.4; 93.4; 110.1; 117.3; 159.2; 217.4; *222.2*; 222.5; 225.1.

Mercier and Camier: 9.6; 9.7; 13.4; 20.3; 24.1; 26.8; 33.8; 39.6; 43.3; 56.2; 61.1; 70.3; 74.5; 142.5; 174.7; 212.1; 217.4; 223.6; #14.
Merlin [Richard Seaver, Alexander Trocchi]: *199.2*.
Micks: 38.2; 57.6; 59.2; 62.4; 208.5; 217.2.
microcosm [little world]: 10.3; *36.3*; 39.6; 62.5; 231.2; #37.
milk: 23.4; 36.2; 216.5.
Miller, Cack-faced: 240.2; 240.4.
Milton, John: 24.1; 27.5; 28.4; #23.
mirlitonnades: 58.1.
mirror [mirror-dance]: 159.4; *163.3*; 167.4.
mixed choir: *33.8*; *34.1*; *35.1*; 46.8; 50.3; 62.1; 92.1; #23; #24; *#34*.
Modernism: *44.6*.
Molloy: 13.4; 21.1; 26.1; 26.7; 28.5; 33.2; 33.8; 36.3; 37.4; 41.3; 42.1; 42.2; 42.5; 44.12; 47.1; 47.4; 48.1; 56.2; 62.2; 64.4; 74.1; 77.4; 77.6; 83.4; 118.1; 129.4; 131.7; 134.2; 141.1; 144.1; 149.1; 169.1; 184.5; 208.1; 208.3; 213.4; 219.5; 223.1; 223.3; 224.4; 225.2; 227.4; 235.1; 236.5; #12.
monad: 40.9; 41.9; 43.3; *134.2*; *152.1*; 217.4.
Mood, John: 29.13; 43.4; 59.2; 83.1; 89.3; 92.3; 102.6; 108.1; 110.3; 110.5; 133.2; 135.3; 136.5; 142.3; 147.4; 157.1; 161.2; 180.2; 195.1; 195.4; 200.3; 204.2; 209.7.
moon: 9.7; 30.3; 33.5; 212.2; 222.6.
Moore, Thomas [*Lallah Rookh*]: 183.5.
Moran: 13.4; 21.1; 25.3; 26.7; 28.5; 36.3; 37.4; 41.3; 62.2; 134.2; 149.1; 208.3; 213.4; 224.4; 225.2.
More Pricks Than Kicks: 169.10.
"Mort de A. D.": 222.1.
mother: 11.2; 13.5; 16.3; 26.8; 38.1; 46.11; 47.4; 48.1; 83.3; 101.9; 131.4; 233.5; 234.2; 238.1.
motion: 8.1; *30.4*; 30.5; 32.6; *57.4*; 114.1; 128.5; *129.5*; *131.4*; 133.2; 159.2; 163.3; 232.2; 232.3; 232.5.
Murillo, Bartolomé: #26.
Murphy: 9.2; 10.3; 13.4; 14.5; 20.2; 26.1; 26.7; 27.1; 27.8; 30.3; 32.7; 33.3; 33.4; 35.2; 39.6; 40.6; 40.9; 41.6; 44.8; 47.3; 48.2; 48.3; 51.3; 52.5; 53.1; 54.3; 57.1; 57.4; 57.7; 61.1; 63.3; 73.2; 73.5; 73.6; 74.5; 74.10; 75.2; 75.4; 76.2; 79.1; 83.3; 84.2; 102.5; 103.1; 113.2; 128.4; 129.4; 129.5; 134.2; 141.5; 143.3; 144.2; 151.5; 152.1; 169.1; 170.5; 174.7; 175.1; 182.6; 192.2; 194.1; 197.1; 197.3; 212.1; 213.4; 217.4; 218.3; 224.3; 224.5; 230.3; 231.1; 232.1; 232.2; 232.5; 234.2; 236.3; 245.4; #7; #30; #36.
music [song]: 7.5; 8.4; 11.2; 11.3; 11.6; *11.7*; 12.4; 12.8; 12.9; 12.11; 16.4; *33.8*; *34.1*; *35.1*; 47.3; *47.4*; *47.8*; 47.15; 53.5; *57.1*; 57.4; *70.3*; 71.3; *72.1*; 72.2; 73.2; 74.9; 82.2; 85.7; 91.2; 92.1; 102.4; 122.3; *136.5*; 147.4; *149.1*; 151.3; *209.1*; 223.4; 239.5; #8; #23; #24; #26; #34; #36.
Musset, Alfred de: 42.8.
mysticism: T; 15.8; 28.7; 29.3; 32.7; 37.2; 39.5; 40.3; 41.2; *43.1*; *43.4*; 44.4; *44.6*; *44.7*; 45.1; 45.3; 45.4; 48.3; 56.5; 77.5; *129.1*; *136.5*; 146.1; *166.1*; 191.1; 202.1; 225.2; 226.1; 228.3; 236.6; 238.4; #3.

Nabokov, Vladimir: 27.1.

"Nacht und Träume": 32.8; 63.9.
Nackybal, Mr: 131.3; *174.1*; 174.7; 180.4; 181.2; 188.3.
Napoleon: 135.4.
narrative [self-awareness]: 7.2; 8.3; 8.4; 10.1; 15.7; 16.2; 17.2; 17.3; 19.2; 19.4; 28.2; 33.5; 39.2; 40.6; *45.6*; 46.5; 46.6; 46.8; 46.9; 47.13; 48.4; 50.3; *55.2*; 59.2; 61.1; 63.9; 67.3; 68.4; 69.6; 74.8; 74.10; 77.1; 79.1; 95.1; 96.1; 102.3; 115.3; *125.1*; 126.1; 131.3; 134.6; 136.3; 138.1; 142.1; 149.3; *151.2*; *151.4*; 153.3; 155.2; 156.1; 163.3; 164.1; 169.4; 169.5; 169.6; 172.3; *180.3*; 181.6; *199.2*; *201.1*; 211.3; 213.4; 215.1; 215.2; 215.3; 215.4; 217.1; 222.6; 223.4; 224.2; 228.3; 228.6; 229.2; 233.4; 236.3; *238.1*; 238.4; 239.1; 241.1; 243.3; 246.4; *"Addenda"*; #7; #10; #20; #33; #34; #37.
nature [physical world]: 15.5; *41.3*; 45.2; *47.1*; 47.2; 47.4; 47.5; 47.11; 53.1; *57.6*; 68.2; 69.5; 74.1; 76.1; 82.1; 83.7; 98.2; 111.2; 117.3; 118.1; 131.2; 135.5; 136.1; 142.5; 146.1; 151.3; 154.1; 154.2; 155.2; 155.6; 161.1; 172.5; 173.1; 174.2; 174.3; 174.4; 174.5; 174.6; 181.8; 182.1; 182.2; 208.1; 208.2; 208.3; 209.1; 213.3; 215.6; 218.4; 218.6; 223.1; 223.2; 224.2; 234.1; 237.2; 246.4; *#22*.
necessity [contingency]: 10.3; 19.5; 32.7; 40.5; *50.9*; 70.3; 97.2; 133.2; 133.3; *203.4*; *209.7*; 223.5.
negative theology: *77.5*; 77.6; 77.7; 209.7.
Nelly: *11.2*; 12.8; 70.3.
Nixon, Goff and Tetty: *9.8*; 12.10; 13.3; 15.6; 17.1; 17.4; 18.1; 18.2; 19.1; 19.3; 23.1; 38.2; 40.3; 225.3; 233.5.
Nohow On: 74.8;
Nolan, Mr: 229.3; 238.1; 240.5; 242.2; 246.3.
Nominalism [Realism]: 27.3; 27.4; 29.1; 29.6; 29.9; 73.5; 77.7; 81.2; *91.5*; 112.3; 117.2; 120.2.
Nordau, Max: 96.3; 128.7; 232.2;
nothing: 9.8; 18.2; 31.5; 36.1; 39.5; 39.8; 41.3; 41.6; 44.11; *48.3*; 58.2; 58.3; 62.5; *73.2*; *76.2*; *77.5*; 77.6; 80.2; 84.2; 92.3; 97.1; 130.2; *148.2*; 148.4; *166.1*; 168.2; 181.5; 192.2; 201.1; 216.5; 222.6; 223.3; #4; #6; #7; *#9*; *#15*; *#16*; *#17*; *#18*; #19; *#22*; *#23*; #25; #27; #36; #37.
"Not I": 47.1; 234.2; #16.
Novalis: *146.1*.
"Now the Day is Over": 16.4; *57.1*.

object [subject]: 8.3; 33.3; 37.4; 41.4; 44.6; 44.11; *81.2*; 128.5; *128.6*; *129.7*; #26.
O'Brien, Eoin [*The Beckett Country*]: 16.1; 19.6; 25.3; 36.3; 47.7; 48.2; 49.3; 54.3; 69.2; 149.1; 149.2; 154.1; 191.4; 218.1; 225.1; 229.3; 234.2; 236.2; 240.2; 240.3; 240.4; #2; #3.
O'Brien, Flann: 9.2; 50.9.
O'Casey, Sean: 27.3.
Occasionalism: 30.4; 57.4; 77.7.
O'Connor [James Arthur]: 172.4; #2; #26.
O'Dea: 28.9; 29.2.
OED: 144.1.
"Old Earth": 224.3.

Olympia Press: 7.1; 7.4; 9.5; 19.3; 21.1; 31.4; *45.6*; 46.5; 46.11; 48.3; 49.3; 52.1; 53.4; 57.1; 58.5; 61.2; 67.1; 70.1; 74.7; 79.2; *80.6*; 81.4; 82.3; 83.2; 83.7; 87.3; 87.4; 89.3; 93.1; 96.1; 98.3; 100.1; 101.8; 102.1; 102.6; 102.8; 103.1; 105.4; 106.4; 112.2; 115.5; 117.1; 119.1; 126.2; 127.2; 130.1; 132.2; 132.3; 136.5; 141.1; 141.3; 142.3; 142.4; 142.6; 143.1; 146.5; 148.5; 148.6; 152.1; 153.4; 154.1; 155.1; 156.2; 158.2; 162.1; 164.1; 166.2; 170.7; 179.2; 180.2; 181.4; 184.3; 190.1; 191.3; 191.4; 195.3; 196.5; 199.2; 204.1; 207.4; 209.5; 211.3; 224.6; 225.1; 226.3; 226.5; 228.4; 230.2; 233.1; 234.1; 237.1; 237.2; 238.2; #4; #23; #26; #28; #29; #36.
O'Meldon, Mr: 174.1; 189.2; 195.1; 196.4; 196.5.
onanism: 44.8; 53.6; 181.2; 209.2; 232.7; 246.2; #12.
Ovid: 44.9.

paradox [teasers]: 7.5; 7.6; 9.8; 17.2; 37.4; 39.5; 42.3; *43.3*; 43.5; 45.4; 51.5; 81.2; 83.6; 85.4; 85.5; 86.3; 87.6; 91.5; 92.2; 96.2; 120.2; 123.1; 128.3; *128.6*; *129.7*; 131.1; 131.5; 131.8; 132.2; 132.4; 134.3; 134.6; 136.2; 136.3; 144.3; *147.5*; 159.2; *160.2*; 165.1; 184.3; 207.1; 215.3; 217.3; 219.5; 221.2; 221.3; 222.5; *225.2*; 225.3; *228.1*; 229.1; 229.2; 236.3; 239.2; 245.2; "Addenda"; #13; *#28*.
Parnell: #2.
particulars [accidents]: 8.2; 23.1; 26.6; 27.3; 39.2; 42.4; 50.9; *73.5*; 76.1; 77.4; *81.2*; 82.2; 85.8; 129.5; 146.2; 147.3; 154.5; 181.6; 181.7; 182.4; #18.
"Peintres de l'Empêchement": *81.2*; 129.1.
"La Peinture des van Velde": 43.5; 100.2; 129.1.
pelican: *42.8*; 43.4; 44.4.
perception: 63.9; 63.10; 73.5; *74.10*; 75.3; *82.1*; 83.7; 85.8; 88.1; 93.4; 113.2; 128.5; *128.6*; 160.5; *203.2*; 211.1; 217.2; 219.6; 224.2; 224.3; 224.4; 225.2; 225.3; 228.4; #23.
Péron, Mania: 151.2.
Petrarch: 136.4.
Phelps: 149.3; 216.1.
physics: T; 8.1; 14.5; 21.2; 55.1; 69.4; 75.1; 95.2; 114.1; *129.5*; 129.6; *131.4*; 131.5; 131.7; 149.1; *160.6*.
piano: 11.2; *70.3*; *72.1*; 82.2.
Pickersgall, Hon. Will: #2.
"A Piece of Monologue": 47.1; 47.9.
Pilling, John: 27.2; 39.2; 226.4.
Pim, Mrs Penny-a-hoist: 240.2; 240.5; 241.1; 245.2.
Pinget, Robert [*The Old Tune*]: 13.4.
pity [sorrow, suffering]: 15.6; *31.5*; 47.2; 49.5; 50.3; 117.4; 147.5; 155.6; *159.3*; 191.5; 192.4; 225.2; 227.3; 236.4; *245.4*; 246.4; #31.
Plato: 50.9; 51.6; 76.1; *81.2*; 72.2; 85.6; 117.2.
"Play": 33.8; 56.5; 83.4.
Poe, Edgar Allan: 83.2; 196.1.
Poincaré, Henri: 87.6.
policeman: 9.2; 9.4; 56.2; 212.1; #23.
Pompedur, Madame de: #4.
poss: 8.4; 42.7; 87.1; *87.2*; 87.5; 88.1; 88.2; 88.3; 87.6; 92.3; 95.2; #35.

pot: 43.4; 68.4; 73.2; *81.2*; *82.1*; 83.4; 87.2; 88.1; 121.1.
Pound, Ezra: 42.5; 44.6.
Pozzo: 49.10.
pre-established harmony [arbitrary]: 40.9; 41.1; 41.9; *43.5*; 68.2; 72.1; *89.3*; 93.2; 93.3; *93.4*; 98.1; 117.1; 131.1; *134.2*; 134.6; 136.3; 180.2; 230.1.
pre-Socratics: 57.4; 76.2; 77.7; 113.4; *129.5*; 162.2; 234.4.
Price [Mrs Coote]: 234.2.
Prince William's Seat: *16.1*.
Prometheus: 116.1.
Protagoras: 77.7; 202.1.
Proust, Marcel: 9.1; 39.6; 42.5; 42.11; 43.1; 44.5; 45.3; 63.3; 73.5; 74.1; 75.5; 79.2; 80.2; 83.4; 136.1; 136.5; 156.1.
Proust: 30.3; 44.11; 44.12; 44.13; 44.14; 50.2; 57.6; 73.5; 75.5; 93.4; 151.5; 204.2; #29.
pseudocouple: *13.4*; 101.2; 101.7; 102.4; 103.2; 159.3; 174.7.
psychology [psychiatry]: T; 33.7; 70.3; 73,2; 74.4; 74.6; 74.10; 79.2; 83.3; 104.5; 108.1; 111.1; 113.2; 139.2; *149.1*; 174.8; 175.1; 220.1; 222.2; 222.4; 233.5.
pun [verbal jest, anagram]: T; 10.2; 12.3; 12.6; 12.10; 13.7; 14.3; 14.4; 15.4; 17.3; 18.2; 20.1; 20.2; 23.4; 26.1; 27.2; *27.8*; 28.4; 37.2; 39.2; 40.3; 41.2; 42.2; 42.10; 43.3; 44.8; 47.10; 47.12; 51.4; 56.3; 56.4; 56.5; 69.4; 70.3; 72.2; 74.5; *76.2*; 77.5; 82.1; 83.2; 91.2; *91.5*; 93.4; 96.2; 97.3; 101.4; 104.3; 115.1; 122.1; 130.2; 136.4; *142.1*; 147.4; 151.2; 155.5; 159.5; *160.1*; 160.3; 166.4; *170.1*; 171.6; *174.1*; 183.4; 188.2; 192.1; *197.3*; 213.1; 219.2; 219.3; 219.6; 224.1; 224.7; 225.3; 232.5; 234.3; 237.4; 240.5; 240.6; 241.1; 242.1; 243.1; 244.2; #1; #2; #24; #26; #29.
puppet: 9.4; 10.2; 163.3.
Pythagoras: 70.3; 71.3; 149.1.

quest [necessary journey]: T; *17.4*; 77.5; 97.2; 129.1; *166.1*.
quietism: 29.7; *32.7*.
Quin [James & Alexander]: T; 7.2; 8.4; 11.2; 12.10: 13.5; 16.1; *20.3*; 40.2; 43.3; 46.7; 50.3; 61.1; 62.2; 67.2; 68.4; 71.3; 71.4; 72.1; 83.4; 86.2; 86.3; 87.1; 87.2; 88.2; 89.1; 89.3; 93.4; 101.7; 130.3; 143.4; 145.1; 148.1; 149.1; 166.3; 203.2; 203.3; 207.3; 220.1; #1; #2; #3; #11; #13; #14; #15; #16; #17; #18; #19; #20; *#21*; #22; #23; *#26*; #29; #34; *#37*.
qui vive: 122.2.

Rabelais: 48.3.
Rabinovitz, Rubin: 37.4; 85.8; 136.2; 232.6; 238.1; 238.4; 239.4; 246.4; #5; #19; #31.
Ramsay, Nicola: 159.4.
Rank, Otto: 26.7; 26.8; 27.1; 140.1; 220.1; 222.4; 233.5.
rats [mice]: 28.1; *28.9*; 39.6; 72.1; 84.1; 184.2; 232.2; *232.3*; #3.
ravanastron: *71.4*.
"Recent Irish Poetry": 228.3.
red and gray: 37.4; 38.1; 236.1.
religion: 9.1; 11.5; 16.3; 17.4; 20.2; 22.2; 27.6; 27.7; *27.8*; 28.1; 28.3; 28.4; 28.5; 28.6; 28.7; 28.8; *28.9*; 28.10; 29.1; 29.2; 29.3; 29.4; 29.5; 29.6; 298.7;

29.8; 29.9; 29.10; 29.11; 29.12; 30.2; 31.6; 32.3; 32.7; 33.6; 33.7; 33.8; 34.1; 36.1; 36.2; 39.3; 39.4; 40.1; 40.3; *40.6*; 41.1; 41.8; 41.9; *42.1*; 42.8; 43.4; 43.5; 44.4; 44.7; 44.8; 45.1; 46.1; 46.3; 46.4; 46.11; 47.8; 47.15; 48.1; 48.3; 49.1; 49.5; 50.8; *50.9*; 51.5; 55.3; 56.5; 57.1; 57.2; 57.3; *57.4*; 57.5; *57.6*; 58.1; *58.2*; 58.3; 58.5; 59.1; 60.1; 61.3; 62.2; 62.3; 62.5; 62.6; 63.1; 63.4; 63.5; 63.6; 63.8; 64.1; 64.4; 67.2; 67.3; 68.2; 77.5; 77.6; 78.1; 81.1; 81.3; 82.3; 83.6; 83.7; 85.1; 85.2; 85.4; 86.2; 86.3; 87.1; 88.3; 89.3; 91.2; 91.3; 91.4; 91.5; 93.4; 101.1; 101.3; 104.2; 106.3; 110.4; 113.3; 113.4; 115.1; 115.2; 115.4; 115.6; 116.2; 120.2; 122.3; 129.4; 131.5; 131.6; 131.7; 132.1; 134.2; 134.3; 135.1; 135.2; 135.5; 140.1; 141.4; 144.3; 144.4; 146.3; 146.4; 146.6; 147.2; 147.3; 148.2; 148.3; *149.1*; *151.5*; 154.1; 155.6; 155.7; 156.1; 159.3; 163.1; 163.2; 165.2; *166.1*; 166.3; 166.4; 169.6; 169.7; 169.8; 169.10; 170.6; 172.3; 177.1; 178.1; 181.5; 181.8; 182.1; 182.2; 182.5; 184.2; 184.5; 188.2; 191.2; 196.2; 199.1; 200.1; 202.1; 203.1; *203.2*; 209.5; 211.3; 213.3; 215.5; 215.6; 218.7; 220.1; 222.4; 223.1; 223.3; 223.6; 224.2; 224.3; 224.4; 225.2; 225.3; 226.1; 226.6; 227.3; 227.5; 230.1; 236.3; 238.2; 239.5; 240.1; 245.1; *246.4*; #1; *#3*; #5; *#17*; #22; #24; #25; *#29*; #32; #37.
Rembrandt: 48.1; 129.3.
Renard, Jules: 40.8.
risus purus [laugh]: 27.5; 39.3; 47.15; *48.3*; 135.2; 143.2.
Roa Bastos, Augusto: 20.3.
Robinson, Michael: 27.3; 39.5; 82.1; 83.2; 93.2; 131.1; 136.3; 151.3; 155.6; 166.1; 220.1.
Romanticism: 30.3; 40.7; 47.1; *146.1*; 216.2.
Rosset, Barney: 151.2; #8.
Roussillon: 31.5; 55.2.
"Rough for Radio II": #16.
"Rough for Theatre I" ["The Gloaming"]: 102.4.
"Rough for Theatre II": 15.5.
Rushdie, Salman: 80.6.
Russell, George (AE): 228.3.
Ryan, John: 16.4; 21.1.

St. John of God: 118.1; 151.5; 154.1.
"Saint-Lô": 40.2.
Sam: 8.3; 17.4; 32.3; 69.5; *74.8*; 75.6; 77.1; *79.1*; 115.3; *125.1*; 126.1; 136.3; *151.2*; *151.4*; 153.1; 154.1; 155.6; 159.1; 159.4; 222.5; 228.6; #10.
A Samuel Beckett Reader [two versions]: 24.2; 67.1; 80.5.
Sanchez, François: 28.9; 29.2; 29.6.
"Sanies I": 40.6; 47.1.
"Sanies II": 15.2.
Sartre, Jean-Paul: 44.9; 82.1; 83.1.
sausage-poisoning: #1.
schizophrenia: 52.5; *73.2*; 74.10; 91.1; 129.4; 228.1; 239.6.
Schneider, Alan: #8.
scholasticism: T; 23.1; 28.9; 29.1; 29.3; 29.4; 29.5; 29.6; 29.7; 29.8; 29.9; 40.9; 45.5; 57.4; 73.5; 75.6; *77.5*; 77.7; *81.2*; 82.2; *91.5*; 174.7; 232.4; 234.4.

Schopenhauer, Arthur: 8.1; 44.13; 67.2; 102.1; 114.1; 129.5; 136.2; 231.1; 232.2; 232.6; 246.4; #21; #28.
Seaver, Richard: 199.2.
Seghers, Hercules: 131.1.
self: 8.1; 8.3; 32.2; 33.3; 37.4; 40.2; 41.4; 43.4; 50.3; 64.1; 64.2; 74.9; 74.10; 83.7; 129.4; 136.2; *151.1*; 178.1; 217.4; 228.1.
Senneff, Susan: 136.4; #35; #36.
"Serena I": 19.5; 56.5; 141.5; 236.6.
"Serena II": 47.1.
"Serena III": 57.4.
series [serial universe]: 27.1: 38.2; *57.6*; 61.1; 72.1; 72.2; *93.4*; 101.9; 129.2; *130.3*; *131.1*; 131.5; 133.2; 133.3; *134.2*; 134.3; 136.3; *136.5*; 143.4; 149.1; 165.1; 171.1; 236.5; *#26*; *#29*.
Shakespeare, William: 9.7; 12.3; 12.4; 12.5; 41.3; 42.10; 46.9; 58.1; *63.7*; 87.6; 155.6; 174.1; 184.4; *213.4*; 234.1.
Shannon, Bill [Severn, Joseph]: 47.7; *69.2*.
sheep: 47.2; 47.12.
Sieyes, Abbé: 148.2.
Sisyphis: *26.7*.
Slattery, John Joseph: #2.
Smith, Frederik: 151.4; 166.3; 238.4.
Socrates: 33.6; 75.4; 78.1; 82.2; 148.3.
solitude: 42.1; 44.12; 63.2; *148.3*; 154.5; 226.6; 232.2; 232.3; #4; #22.
Soto, Dominic: 28.8; 29.2; 29.9.
Sottisier Notebook: 43.5.
space [extension]: 8.1; 21.2; 29.1; 32.2; 42.4; 42.6; 43.2; 57.4; 62.1; 67.2; 75.1; 114.1; 128.4; 129.3; 129.4; *129.5*; 129.6; 129.7; 131.5; 134.3; 144.3; 158.4.
Spenser, Edmund ["Epithalamium"]: 11.7; 12.8.
Spinoza, Baruch: 77.5; 131.7; 168.2; #29.
Spiro, Mr: *27.2*; 28.4; 239.1.
Stations of the Cross [*via dolorosa*]: 32.8; 221.3; 222.4; 234.1; #34.
Staunton, Howard: 26.3.
Stekel, Wilhelm: 161.1.
Stendhal [Henri Beyle]: 53.5; 56.5.
stick [stone]: 8.1; 32.2; 144.3; 158.4; 174.1; 227.5.
Still ["Still 3"]: 39.7; 224.3.
Stirrings Still: 39.7; 217.4; 222.1.
stout porter [Power]: *197.3*.
Suarez, Francisco: 28.9; 29.2; 29.7.
sudarium: *32.8*; 63.9; 117.4; 163.1.
suicide: 13.6.
Swift, Jonathan: T; 166.3; 227.2; 238.4; 245.3.
symbol: 73.3; 73.4; *73.5*; 75.4; 81.2; 146.1; 159.3; *#37*.
Synge, J. M.: 37.4; 40.4.

TCD notes [literature & philosophy]: 11.2; 12.8; 12.9; 26.7; 27.1; 29.3; 29.5; 43.3; *48.3*; 50.9; 51.3; 62.3; 62.5; 70.2; 77.7; 82.2; 87.1; 131.4; 139.2; 152.1; 161.1; 208.1; 220.1; 222.2; 233.5; 239.6.

Terence: #25; #28.
"Text 2": 42.8.
Texts for Nothing: 19.6; 42.1; 48.3; 142.5; 220.3; 236.6; #6.
That Time: 19.6; 196.3; 217.4.
Theseus [Ariadne]: 63.2; 63.3.
Thomas à Kempis: *32.7*; *40.6*; 50.6; 97.2; 178.1.
Thompson, James: #8.
"Three Dialogues": *129.1*; 174.4
time: 10.1; 18.3; 21.2; 33.1; 40.2; 42.4; 42.6; 42.7; 43.2; 44.6; 45.6; 45.7; 45.10; 46.2; 62.1; 67.2; 67.3; 68.2; *73.2*; 74.1; 75.1; 77.7; 82.2; 87.6; 88.2; 96.1; 103.3; 103.4; 128.4; 129.3; 129.4; *129.5*; 129.6; 131.5; 132.4; 132.5; 134.3; 136.3; 136.4; 151.2; 152.2; 165.2; 204.2; 206.1; 207.4; 209.5; 216.5; 218.6; 228.4; 239.2; 239.3; *239.5*; #27.
"To My Daughter": 111.1; 170.4.
tot ["Summo ergo sum"]: 17.3; 28.10; 75.7; 103.3; 105.1; 109.2; 109.3; 245.1; #23.
train: 17.4; 19.6; 25.3; 26.5; 29.14; 31.6; 36.3; 232.2; 232.3; 232.4; 239.1; 244.2; 245.2; #14.
tram: 8.2; 9.5; *16.5*; 19.4; 19.5; 26.2; 26.8; 96.2; 196.2; 196.3.
Trilogy [*Three Novels*]: 39.2; 41.3; 61.1; 85.4; 91.1; 217.4; #1.
Trinity College: 46.7; 87.4; 147.2; 174.7; 191.4; 196.3.
turkey cucumber: 187.3.
Tyler, Wat: T; 48.2.

The Unnamable: 13.4; 26.8; 33.7; 37.4; 57.4; 74.5; 83.4; 85.6; 97.2; 125.1; 131.4; 134.,1; 241.2; 246.2.
Ussher, Arland: 13.5.

Valéry, Paul [Monsieur Teste]: 10.3; 32.7.
van Velde, Geer & Bram: 43.5; 100.2; 129.1; 130.3.
Vaughan, Thomas: 76.1.
verba inania: 73.5.
Vermeer, Jan: 42.5.
Veronica, Saint: 32.8; 117.4.
Vico, Giambattista: 32.3; 77.7.
Vincent: 59.2; 61.1; #32.
Virgil: 21.3; #29; #35.
Visicelts: 171.3.
"vive morte ma seule saison": 44.1; 218.4.
voice[s]: 29.13; 33.7; 33.8; 37.4; *73.2*; 73.7; 74.9; *91.1*; 151.4; *201.1*; 232.2; 234.3.
Voltaire [*Candide*]: 8.4; *41.9*; *43.5*; 85.6; 134.2; #35.

Waiting for Godot: 13.4; 16.5; 28.2; 32.6; 39.2; 42.1; 42.6; 45.10; 61.1; 62.2; 67.3; 152.2; 169.7; 174.1; 232.2; 239.5; #23.
Walker, Miss: 245.3.
"Walking Out": *47.1*; 47.2; 47.3.
Waller, Herring-gut: 240.2; 240.3; 244.1.

Walpole, Hugh [*Judith Paris*]: 31.5; 191.2.
Walter: 57.6; 59.2; 61.1; 130.3; #33.
Walton, Izaak: #5.
Watson, Dr: 159.5.
Watson, Mrs: 74.2; 74.3; *80.4*; 139.1.
Watt [as character]: T; 8.3; 8.4; 10.3; 13.4; 17.1; 17.3; *17.4*; 19.2; 19.5; 23.4; 26.1; 26.8; 27.4; 27.5; 29.13; 30.3; *30.4*; 30.5; 31.1; 31.3; 32.3; 33.4; 32.6; *32.7*; 32.9; 33.1; 33.2; 33.5; 33.7; 36.2; 37.1; 37.2; 37.4; 38.2; 39.1; 39.6; 40.8; 41.1; 42.1; 44.13; 45.5; 48.2; 48.3; 50.5; 60.2; 62.4; 62.5; 63.9; 67.2; 68.3; 70.3; 70.5; 72.2; 73.2; 73.4; *73.6*; 74.8; 74.9; 74.10; 75.1; 76.1; 76.2; 77.1; 77.4; 77.5; 80.2; 80.5; 81.3; *82.2*; 84.2; 85.8; 88.1; 89.3; 90.1; 91.1; 93.2; 95.2; 104.1; 111.1; 113.3; 120.3; 121.1; 121.2; *125.1*; 128.2; 128.5; 129.1; *129.3*; *129.4*; 129.5; *129.6*; 129.7; 130.4; 131.1; 136.3; 139.1; 139.2; 142.3; 142.5; 144.3; 147.4; *164.1*; 165.2; 165.3; *166.1*; 168.2; 169.5; 169.8; *199.2*; 208.1; 215.5; 215.6; 216.3; 216.5; 216.7; 217.2; 217.3; *217.4*; 219.1; 219.4; 219.5; 219.6; 221.1; 221.2; 222.5; 223.3; 223.4; 225.2; 225.3; 226.3; 228.1; 232.2; 232.3; 232.4; 232.7; 233.5; 238.1; 238.2; #9; #10; #11; #12; #28; *#29*.
Watt, Henry J.: T.
Watt, James: T; 48.2.
wattman: T; 16.5; 20.1.
Watts, George Frederic: 20.2.
"The Way": 77.5.
Webster, John [*The Duchess of Malfi*]: 28.3.
Westminster Bridge: *45.8*.
"What a Misfortune": 15.3; 32,8; 44.7; 115.2.
"A Wet Night": 57.4.
Whoroscope: 148.3; "Addenda."
Whoroscope Notebook: 15.6; 17.5; 26.7; 30.5; 32.5; 32.7; 33.3; 45.8; 46.1; 50.3; 52.3; 53.3; 55.1; 57.4; 58.3; 77.5; 78.1; 87.1; 102.1; 102.5; 144.1; 168.5; 187.3; 208.1; 209.2; 224.1; 232.1; 234.3; 239.7; "Addenda"; #5; #7; #12; #21; #24; #28; #31; #32; #35.
wind: 33.4; *62.2*; 153.2; 166.4; 221.1; *223.3*; #31.
Wilenski: 48.1; #3.
Windelband, Wilhelm: 29.6; 43.3; 48.3; 77.5; 85.6; 91.5; 129.3; 152.1.
Winston, Mathew: 8.3.
witness: *9.1*; *42.1*; 46.1; 57.5; 58.5; 113.3; 115.4; 115.6; 192.1; 203.1; *203.2*.
Wittgenstein, Ludwig: *44.8*; 75.3; 215.5; 228.5.
"Words and Music": 224.3.
Wynn's Hotel: 20.3.

Yeats, Jack B.: 40.6.
Yeats, William B.: 44.7; 55.4; 102.4; 236.6.
"Yellow": 233.3.
yellow [and green]: *9.7*; 30.3; *42.5*; 226.2.

Zeno: *43.3*; 64.3; 182.4.

Epigraph

Watt is not
A well-wrought pot
Cracks appear
When he serves Knott

From the coming
To the going
From the to-ing
To the fro-ing

From the stirring
Of the clays
From the turning
To the glaze

Others serve
Then make their tot
But Watt is not
A well-wrought pot.